What's on the CD

*T*he CD included with the *MCSE: SQL 7 Administration Study Guide* contains several valuable tools to help you prepare for your exam.

NOTE: You can access the files on the CD through a user-friendly graphical interface by running the CLICKME.EXE file located in the root directory.

The Sybex MCSE EdgeTest for *SQL Server 7 Administration*

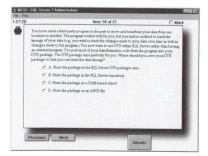

A custom exam prep program that allows you to quiz yourself on all of the review questions found at the end of each chapter in the book. Test yourself chapter by chapter or randomly to ensure that you're ready to take the real exam. Brief explanations of correct answers are provided.

Network Press MCSE Study Guide Sampler

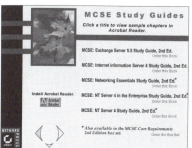

Preview sample chapters from Sybex's best-selling line of MCSE study guides. From the four core requirements to the most popular electives, you'll see why Sybex MCSE Study Guides have become the self-study method of choice for thousands seeking MCSE certification.

Microsoft *Train_Cert Offline* Web Site

Look to Microsoft's *Train_Cert Offline* Web site for a snapshot of Microsoft's Education and Certification Web site. Offline will provide you with all of the information you need to plot your course for MCSE certification. You'll need to run Internet Explorer 5.0 to access all of the features of the Train_Cert Offline Web site.

NOTE: Please consult the README file located in the root directory of the CD for a more detailed description of the CD's contents.

SQL Server 7 Evaluation Edition

SQL Server 7.0 is the leading Microsoft Windows database. It can help improve the quality of decision-making at all levels of your business with scaleable business solutions, powerful data warehousing, and integration with Microsoft Office 2000. An evaluation copy of this software is included on this CD.

MCSE: SQL Server 7
Administration
Study Guide

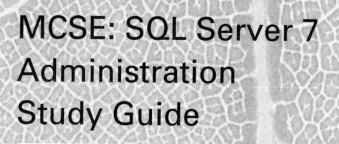

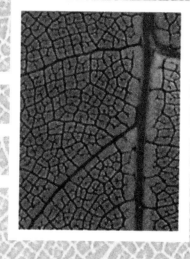

MCSE: SQL Server™ 7 Administration Study Guide

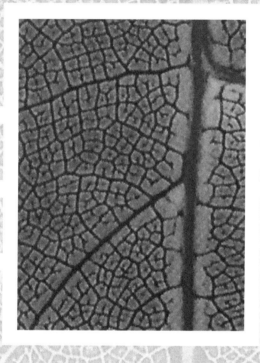

Lance Mortensen
Rick Sawtell

San Francisco • Paris • Düsseldorf • Soest • London

Associate Publisher: Guy Hart-Davis
Contracts and Licensing Manager: Kristine O'Callaghan
Acquisitions & Developmental Editor: Neil Edde
Editor: Muriel Solar
Project Editor: Rebecca Rider
Technical Editors: Jim Cooper, Richard Waymire
Book Designer: Bill Gibson
Graphic Illustrator: Tony Jonick
Electronic Publishing Specialist: Bill Gibson
Project Team Leader: David Zielonka
Proofreaders: Tory McLearn, Theresa Mori
Indexer: Nancy Guenther
Companion CD: Ginger Warner
Cover Designer: Archer Design
Cover Photographer: The Image Bank

SYBEX, Network Press, and the Network Press logo are registered trademarks of SYBEX Inc.

Screen reproductions produced with Collage Complete.
Collage Complete is a trademark of Inner Media Inc.

The CD Interface music is from GIRA Sound AURIA Music Library © GIRA Sound 1996.

Microsoft® Internet Explorer ©1996 Microsoft Corporation. All rights reserved. Microsoft, the Microsoft Internet Explorer logo, Windows, Windows NT, and the Windows logo are either registered trademarks or trademarks of Microsoft Corporation in the United States and/or other countries.

Use of the Microsoft Approved Study Guide Logo on this product signifies that it has been independently reviewed and approved in complying with the following standards:

- acceptable coverage of all content related to Microsoft exam number 70-028, entitled Administering Microsoft® SQL Server™ 7.0.
- sufficient performance-based exercises that relate closely to all required content; and
- technically accurate content, based on sampling of text.

SYBEX is an independent entity from Microsoft Corporation, and not affiliated with Microsoft Corporation in any manner. This publication may be used in assisting students to prepare for a Microsoft Certified Professional Exam. Neither Microsoft Corporation, its designated review company, nor SYBEX warrants that use of this publication will ensure passing the relevant exam. Microsoft is either a registered trademark or trademark of Microsoft Corporation in the United States and/or other countries.

TRADEMARKS: SYBEX has attempted throughout this book to distinguish proprietary trademarks from descriptive terms by following the capitalization style used by the manufacturer.

The author and publisher have made their best efforts to prepare this book, and the content is based upon final release software whenever possible. Portions of the manuscript may be based upon pre-release versions supplied by software manufacturer(s). The author and the publisher make no representation or warranties of any kind with regard to the completeness or accuracy of the contents herein and accept no liability of any kind including but not limited to performance, merchantability, fitness for any particular purpose, or any losses or damages of any kind caused or alleged to be caused directly or indirectly from this book.

Library of Congress Card Number: 99-61298
ISBN: 0-7821-2382-1

Manufactured in the United States of America

10 9 8 7 6 5 4 3 2 1

Approved Study Guide

November 1, 1997

Dear SYBEX Customer:

Microsoft is pleased to inform you that SYBEX is a participant in the Microsoft® Independent Courseware Vendor (ICV) program. Microsoft ICVs design, develop, and market self-paced courseware, books, and other products that support Microsoft software and the Microsoft Certified Professional (MCP) program.

To be accepted into the Microsoft ICV program, an ICV must meet set criteria. In addition, Microsoft reviews and approves each ICV training product before permission is granted to use the Microsoft Certified Professional Approved Study Guide logo on that product. This logo assures the consumer that the product has passed the following Microsoft standards:

- The course contains accurate product information.
- The course includes labs and activities during which the student can apply knowledge and skills learned from the course.
- The course teaches skills that help prepare the student to take corresponding MCP exams.

Microsoft ICVs continually develop and release new MCP Approved Study Guides. To prepare for a particular Microsoft certification exam, a student may choose one or more single, self-paced training courses or a series of training courses.

You will be pleased with the quality and effectiveness of the MCP Approved Study Guides available from SYBEX.

Sincerely,

Holly Heath
ICV Account Manager
Microsoft Training & Certification

MICROSOFT INDEPENDENT COURSEWARE VENDOR PROGRAM

Dedicated to all the new users of Microsoft SQL Server. We hope you will find out just how good a program SQL Server 7 actually is.

Acknowledgments

I would like to thank all of the wonderful people at Sybex who worked on this project. Special thanks to Rebecca and Muriel, whose skill and hard work makes this whole process a lot more enjoyable. I would also like to thank Joe Jorden, whose technical contributions and well written chapters kept this project on time and technically accurate. I really appreciate the hard work you put in. Lance, thanks again for working with me on another job well done! I would also like to thank J. Morgan Smith who is a fantastic Microsoft Certified Trainer and an MCSE. Morgan, of all the chapters in this book, your chapter on linked servers was one of the most difficult to put together. Gathering the hardware and software alone was time consuming; then implementing the linked servers and writing about them was a mountain of work. Thank you so much for a job well done!

I would like to say thanks to one of the most extraordinary people in the world, Melissa. I might not show it enough, or say it enough, but your love and support mean so much to me. I couldn't do this without you. Thanks Mom and Dad for all the guidance, subtle nudges (and not so subtle nudges) that helped me to steer my life into this wonderful world of computing. Finally, no dedication is complete without the mention of my intrepid feline, Keyna.

Rick Sawtell

I'd like to thank the crew at Sybex, especially Muriel for keeping her sanity; Rebecca, for helping us survive the experience; and Neil, for creating and maintaining such a good book series.

I'd also like to thank Rick for doing (as usual) a great job (BTW, my whiplash from the Dodge Stealth is recovering fine), and Joe for helping us to meet deadlines.

As always, thanks and love go to my wife for bravely deciding to build a house even in the midst of all my chaos (sorry about the move while I am out of town), and to my kids—Bryce, Jessany, Devin, and Logan—who love to play Pokemon games with their Dad whenever they can.

Lance Mortensen

Contents at a Glance

Table of Contents

Table of Exercises

Introduction

The Microsoft Certified Systems Engineer (MCSE) certification is *the* hottest ticket to career advancement in the computer industry today. Hundreds of thousands of corporations and organizations worldwide are choosing Microsoft products for their networks. This has created a tremendous need for qualified personnel and consultants to help implement and support these networks. MCSE certification and the recently introduced MCSE+Internet (or MCSE+I) certification are your way to show that you have the professional abilities these corporations and organizations need.

There's an old Army Reserve commercial in which a person can't get employed because he has no experience, and he can't get experience because he can't get employed—a classic "Catch-22" situation. Although certification is best used in conjunction with real-life experience, it can go a long way in making up for lack of experience.

The value of certification is undeniable. Many people get certified just to compete in the job marketplace. For example, if you were an employer and you had two candidates with the same experience— but one was also certified—which one would you hire? The fact is that even though the number of certified professionals has grown tremendously, the demand has grown at least as fast as, if not faster than, the number of certified people.

Whether you are just getting started or are ready to move ahead in the computer industry, the knowledge and skills you have are your most valuable assets. Microsoft, recognizing this, has developed its Microsoft Certified Professional (MCP) program to give you credentials that verify your ability to work with Microsoft products effectively and professionally. The Microsoft Certified Systems Engineer (MCSE) certification is the premier MCP credential, designed for professionals who support Microsoft networks.

Microsoft has recently announced a new certification called the Microsoft Certified Database Administrator (MCDBA). The MCDBA certification will have four core required tests, one of which is SQL Server 7 Administration. Currently the four required tests are SQL Server 7 Administration, SQL Server 7 Implementation, NT Server, and NT Server in the Enterprise. Electives include SQL Datawarehouse, IIS, TCP/IP, and others.

Is This Book for You?

If you want to become certified as a Microsoft Certified Systems Engineer (MCSE), this book is for you. *Microsoft Certified Professional Magazine's* recent surveys reveal the average MCSE is earning more than $65,000 (U.S.) per year, while the average MCSE consultant is earning more than $95,000 per year. If you want to acquire the solid background you need to pass one of Microsoft's required client exams, take a step closer to your MCSE, and boost your career efforts, this book is for you.

If you want to learn the basics of how SQL Server 7 works, and if you want to learn techniques that you can apply in your day-to-day work as a systems engineer or administrator, this book is for you, too. You'll find clear explanations of the concepts you need to grasp and learn about the fundamentals of SQL Server 7 operations, ranging from installation to optimizing and monitoring performance to running on a network. You will also find troubleshooting information for each topic.

MCSE: SQL Server 7 Administration Study Guide provides clear explanations of the fundamental concepts you must grasp both to become certified and to do your job effectively and efficiently. Our intention in writing this book was not merely to help you pass the MCSE tests. We have tried to make the book comprehensive and detailed enough that it will remain a valuable resource for you once you have passed your test and become a certified systems engineering professional.

What Does This Book Cover?

Think of this book as your guide to Microsoft SQL Server administration. It begins by covering the most basic of SQL Server concepts, including an introduction to SQL Server, its platform (Windows NT), and its version of the SQL language (Transaction-SQL, or T-SQL). The chapters that follow cover the topics you need to know for the exam and in your day-to-day work as a database administrator:

- Installing, upgrading, and configuring SQL Server

- Using the SQL Server utilities to administer your system

- Creating and managing databases and users

- Setting up database security

- Backing up and restoring databases

- Automating maintenance tasks

- Managing, copying, and moving data

- Setting up replication

- Tuning SQL Server performance

- Troubleshooting SQL Server

Throughout each chapter, you will find hands-on exercises that take you step-by-step through the various tasks. At the end of each chapter, practice questions test your knowledge of the topics covered in that chapter. You will find the answers to those questions in Appendix A.

We have also provided several appendices with additional information that you may find useful in your work as a SQL Server system administrator. Appendix A contains the answers and explanations for the questions from the back of each chapter. Appendix B contains a glossary of terms related to SQL Server and database administration.

How Do You Become an MCSE, MCSE+I, or MCDBA?

Attaining MCSE, MCSE+I, or MCDBA status is a serious challenge. The exams cover a wide range of topics and require dedicated study and expertise. Many people who have achieved other computer industry credentials have had troubles with the MCSE. This difficulty, however, is why the MCSE certificates are so valuable. If achieving MCSE status were easy, the market would be quickly flooded by MCSEs, and the certification would quickly become meaningless. Microsoft, keenly aware of this fact, has taken steps to ensure that certification means its holder is truly knowledgeable and skilled.

Exam Requirements

Successful candidates have to pass a minimum set of exams that measure technical proficiency and expertise:

- Candidates for the MCSE must pass four core requirements and two electives. SQL Server 7 Administration is one of the electives you can take.

- Candidates for the MCSE+Internet must pass seven core requirements and two electives. One of the electives can be SQL Server 7 Administration.

- Candidates for the MCDBA must pass four core requirements and one elective. SQL Server 7 Administration is one of the four required tests.

Exam #	Title	MCSE	MCSE+ Internet
70-058	Networking Essentials	Required	Required
70-067	Windows NT Server 4.0	Required	Required
70-068	Windows NT Server 4.0 in the Enterprise	Required	Required
70-073 or 70-064	Windows NT Workstation 4.0 or Windows 95	Required	Required
70-059	Internetworking with TCP/IP on Windows NT 4.0	Elective	Required
70-077 or 70-087	Internet Information Server 3.0 and Index Server 1.1 or Internet Information Server 4.0	Elective	Required
70-079	Internet Explorer Administration Kit	Elective	Required
70-076 or 70-081	Exchange Server 5 or Exchange Server 5.5	Elective	Elective
70-026 or 70-028	**System Administration for SQL Server 7** or **Administering Microsoft SQL Server 7**	**Elective**	**Elective**
70-088	Proxy Server 2.0	Elective	Elective
70-085	SNA Server 4.0	Elective	Elective
70-018	Systems Management Server 1.2	Elective	Elective

For a more detailed description of the Microsoft certification programs, go to http://www.microsoft.com/train_cert.

This book is a part of a series of Network Press MCSE Study Guides, published by Sybex, that cover all the core requirements of the MCSE and MCSE+I tracks as well as the electives you need.

Where Do You Take the Exams?

You may take the exams at any of more than 1000 Sylvan Authorized Prometric Testing Centers and VUE Testing Centers around the world. For the location of a testing center near you, call Sylvan Prometric at 800-755-EXAM (755-3926) or VUE at 888-837-8616. Outside the United States and Canada, contact Microsoft or your local Sylvan Prometric or VUE registration center. To register for a Microsoft Certified Professional exam:

1. Determine the number of the exam you want to take.

2. Register with the registration center nearest to you. At this point, you will be asked for advance payment for the exam—as of March 1999, the exams are $100 each. Exams must be taken within one year of payment. You can schedule exams from one working day to six weeks prior to the date of the exam. You can cancel or reschedule your exam with notice of at least two working days prior to the exam. Same-day registration is available in some locations, subject to space availability. Where same-day registration is available, you must register a minimum of two hours before test time.

You can also register for your exams online at http://www .sylvanprometric.com/ or http://www.vue.com/ms/

When you schedule the exam, you'll be provided with instructions regarding appointment and cancellation procedures, ID requirements, and information about the testing center location. In addition, you will receive a registration and payment confirmation letter from Sylvan Prometric or VUE.

Microsoft requires certification candidates to accept the terms of a non-disclosure agreement before taking certification exams.

What Is Adaptive Testing?

At this writing (Spring 1999), Microsoft is in the process of converting all of its exams to a new format, called *adaptive testing*. This format is radically different from the conventional format previously used for Microsoft certification exams. If you have never taken an adaptive test, there are a few things you should know.

When new tests first come out, they are usually the standard format—about 60 questions in 80 minutes. After enough people have taken the test an adaptive version of the test is created. Although the SQL Server 7 test started as the standard version, by the end of 1999 it will probably be adaptive.

Conventional tests and adaptive tests differ in that conventional tests are static, containing a fixed number of questions, while adaptive tests change, depending upon your answers to the questions presented. The number of questions presented in your adaptive test will depend on how long it takes the exam to figure out what your level of ability is (according to the statistical measurements upon which the exam questions are ranked).

To determine a test-taker's level of ability, the exam will present questions in increasing or decreasing orders of difficulty. By presenting sequences of questions with predetermined levels of difficulty, the exam is supposedly able to figure out your level of understanding.

For example, we have three test-takers, Herman, Sally, and Rashad. Herman doesn't know much about the subject, Sally is moderately informed, and Rashad is an expert. Herman answers his first question incorrectly, so the exam gives him a second, easier question. He misses that, so the exam gives him a few more easy questions, all of which he misses. Shortly thereafter, the exam ends, and he receives his failure report. Sally, meanwhile, answers her first question correctly, so the exam gives her a more difficult question, which she answers correctly. She then receives an even more difficult question, which she answers incorrectly, so the exam gives her a somewhat easier question, as it tries to gauge her level of understanding. After numerous questions of varying levels of difficulty, Sally's exam ends, perhaps with a passing score, perhaps not. Her exam included far more questions than Herman's did, because her level of understanding needed to be more carefully tested to determine whether it was at a passing level. When Rashad takes his exam, he answers his first question correctly, so he's given a more difficult question, which he also answers correctly. He's given an even more difficult question, which he also answers correctly. He then is given a few more very difficult questions, all of which he answers correctly. Shortly thereafter, his exam ends. He passes. His exam was short, about as long as Herman's.

Microsoft is also introducing more simulations into the exams. These simulations require that you complete a task or tasks on an element that looks just like the actual graphical interface of a Microsoft product. If you are familiar with the Microsoft product, you might find these questions to be a bit less abstract, and, therefore, slightly easier than similar questions presented in purely text format. Some tests (such as the IIS test) have many simulation-type questions while others (such as the current SQL Server 7 Administration test) have few or none.

Microsoft moved to adaptive testing for several reasons:

- It saves time by focusing only on the questions needed to determine a test-taker's specific abilities. This way an exam that took $1\text{-}\frac{1}{2}$ hours in the conventional format can be completed in less than half that time. The number of questions presented can be far fewer than the number required by a conventional exam.

- It protects the integrity of the exams. By exposing a smaller number of questions at any one time, it makes it more difficult for individuals to collect the questions in the exam pools with the intent of facilitating exam cramming.

- It saves Microsoft and/or the test delivery company money by cutting down on the amount of time it takes to deliver a test.

WARNING Unlike the previous test format, the adaptive format will not allow you to go back to see a question again. The exam goes forward only. Once you enter your answer, that's it; you cannot change it. Be very careful before entering your answer. There is no time limit for each individual question (only for the exam as a whole.) As your exam may be shortened by correct answers (and lengthened by incorrect answers), there is no advantage to rushing through questions.

What the SQL Server Administration Exam Measures

The System Administration for SQL Server 7 Certification Exam covers concepts and skills required for the support of SQL Server 7. It emphasizes the following areas:

- SQL Server hardware and software requirements
- Installing SQL Server
- Configuring SQL Server
- Creating databases and their devices
- Creating and managing transaction logs
- Backing up databases
- Backing up transaction logs
- Creating SQL Server users
- Managing database security
- Tuning SQL Server
- Replicating data
- Troubleshooting

If we had to create a single sentence to describe the test, it would be "Troubleshooting, upgrading to, creating databases on, backing up and restoring databases on, and managing security on SQL Server 7." You need to really understand topics on troubleshooting, installing and upgrading, creating databases, backing up and restoring databases, and security in order to pass the test.

Microsoft publishes a list of objectives that the test will cover. In this book, we have made it easy for you to find the information associated with each exam objective. Before the relevant discussion, you will see:

Microsoft **Exam** **Objective**   **Objective listed here.**

Exam objectives are subject to change at any time without prior notice and at Microsoft's sole discretion. Please visit Microsoft's Training & Certification Web site (www.microsoft.com/Train_Cert) for the most current exam objectives listing.

Tips for Taking the Administering Microsoft SQL Server 7.0 Exam

The exam focuses on fundamental concepts relating to Microsoft SQL Server operation. It can also be quite specific regarding how SQL Server administrative tasks are performed. This exam is often perceived as one of the more difficult of the Microsoft Certified Professional tests. Careful study of this book, along with hands-on experience with the operating system, will be especially helpful in preparing you for the exam.

Here are some general tips for taking the exams successfully:

- Arrive early at the exam center so you can relax and review your study materials, particularly tables and lists of exam-related information.

- Read the questions carefully. Don't be tempted to jump to an early conclusion. Make sure you know *exactly* what the question is asking.

- Don't leave any unanswered questions on standard tests. They count against you. If you are taking an adaptive test you cannot skip any questions, so if you have to guess make sure, the answer you have selected is your best guess.

- When answering multiple-choice questions you're not sure about, use a process of elimination to get rid of the obviously incorrect answers first. This will improve your odds if you need to make an educated guess.

- Because the hard questions will take up the most time, you may want to answer them quickly and mark them for later (on standard tests). You can move forward and backward through the exam on standard tests (unless the question specifically states that you cannot go back) and can see which items you have marked for later inspection.

- This test has some exhibits (pictures). It can be difficult, if not impossible, to view both the questions and the exhibit simulation on the 14- and 15-inch screens usually found at the testing centers. Call around to each center and see if they have 17-inch monitors available. If they don't, perhaps you can arrange to bring in your own. Failing this, some have found it useful to quickly draw the diagram on the scratch paper provided by the testing center and use the monitor to view just the question. You should always double-check your answer when looking at an exhibit in case you check the wrong answer when going back and forth.

- One of the keys to correctly answering Microsoft tests is figuring out just what it is that you are being asked. Most test questions are in the form of a story problem—cutting through the fluff and understanding the issue involved is most of the battle. You may want to look at the answer choices and "reverse-engineer" the question.

- Many of the Multiple Rating Items (MRI) questions that ask you "How well does this solution address the problem?" are very intimidating at first, because they are very long. Our strategy is to look at the solution and compare it against each desired outcome, keeping track of whether it works or doesn't. The available responses will sometimes consist of a count of the number of items that were successfully accomplished, which is the running total we have kept in our heads. Sometimes the question will end with a list of objectives, and you will be asked to specify whether they were fulfilled. We found these much easier, as we could look at the solution and see whether it fulfilled each individual objective.

- On simulations, do not change settings that are not directly related to the question. Also, assume default settings if the question does not specify or imply what they might be.

- This is not simply a test of your knowledge of Transaction SQL commands, but on how it is used to administer SQL Server 7 on Windows NT. You will need to know how to use the Transaction SQL language *and* the graphical utilities to perform your administrative tasks.

- A reminder: The adaptive format will NOT allow you to go back to see a question again. Be very careful before entering your answer. Because your exam may be shortened by correct answers (and lengthened by incorrect answers) there is no advantage to rushing through questions.

How to Use This Book   This book can provide a solid foundation for the serious effort of preparing for the SQL Server exam. To best benefit from this book, you might want to use the following study method:

1. Study a chapter carefully, making sure you fully understand the information.

2. Complete all hands-on exercises in the chapter, referring back to the chapter so that you understand each step you take.

3. Answer the exercise questions related to that chapter. (You will find the answers to these questions in Appendix A and on the CD.)

4. Note which questions you did not understand and study those sections of the book again.

5. Study each chapter in the same manner.

6. Before taking the exam, try the practice exams included on the CD that comes with this book. They will give you an idea of what you can expect to see on the real thing. Use resources available on the Internet to help supplement and update your training preparation. The best place to start is the Certification area on Microsoft's Web page, www.microsoft.com/mcp. When you are ready for more details about a particular test or objective list, the www.microsoft.com/train_cert Web site is another invaluable resource.

If you prefer to use this book in conjunction with classroom or online training, you have many options. Both Microsoft-authorized training and independent training are widely available. See Microsoft's Web sites (www.microsoft.com/mcp and www.microsoft.com/train_cert) for more information.

To learn all the material covered in this book, you will need to study regularly and with discipline. Try to set aside the same time every day to study, and select a comfortable and quiet place in which to do it. If you work hard, you will be surprised at how quickly you learn this material. Good luck.

What's on the CD? The CD contains several valuable tools to help you study for your MCSE exams:

- The Microsoft Train_Cert Offline Web Site is a good place to start. It provides an overview of Microsoft's training and certification program and the process of becoming an MCSE.

- The exercise questions and answers from each of the chapters in this book are included in a simple-to-use exam preparation program.

- The SQL Server 7 Evaluation Copy can help improve the quality of decision-making at all levels of your business with scalable business solutions, powerful data warehousing, and integration with Microsoft Office 2000.

Contact Information

To find out more about Microsoft Education and Certification materials and programs, to register with Sylvan Prometric, or to get other useful information, check the following resources. (Outside the United States or Canada, contact your local Microsoft office or Sylvan Prometric or VUE testing center.)

Microsoft Certified Professional Program — (800) 636-7544   Call the MCPP number for information about the Microsoft Certified Professional program and exams and to order the latest Microsoft Roadmap to Education and Certification.

Sylvan Prometric Testing Centers — (800) 755-EXAM   To register to take a Microsoft Certified Professional exam at any of more than 1000 Sylvan Prometric testing centers around the world, or to order this Exam Study Guide, call the Sylvan Prometric testing center.

VUE Testing Centers — (888) 837-8616   To register to take a Microsoft Certified Professional exam at a VUE testing centers, call the VUE registration center.

Microsoft Certification Development Team — Web: `http://www.microsoft.com/Train_Cert/mcp/examinfo/certsd.htm`   Contact the Microsoft Certification Development Team through their Web site to volunteer for one or more exam development phases or to report a problem with an exam. Address written correspondence to: Certification Development Team; Microsoft Education and Certification; One Microsoft Way; Redmond, WA 98052.

Microsoft TechNet Technical Information Network — (800) 344-2121
Use this number to contact support professionals and system administrators. Outside the United States and Canada, call your local Microsoft subsidiary for information.

Microsoft Related Training Resources

```
http://www.microsoft.com/train_cert/train/
http://www.cyberstateu.com/text/catalog/nt.htm
```

How to Contact the Authors

We welcome any of your comments, suggestions, and feedback. You can e-mail Lance Mortensen at:

LMSQL@aol.com

You can e-mail Rick Sawtell at:

Quickening@email.msn.com

Assessment Questions

1. SQL Server is capable of replicating to non-SQL Server databases as well as databases with different character sets and sort orders.

   A. True

   B. False

2. You can separate tables and their non-clustered indexes by placing each of these database objects on separate _____. (Fill in the blank.)

3. Temporary tables have a # or ## prefix depending on whether or not they are local or global objects. Local temporary tables are stored in the _____ (Tempdb, Local) database and global temporary tables are stored in the _____ (Tempdb, Local) database. (Fill in the blanks.)

4. The ORDER BY clause in a T-SQL SELECT statement is used to change the default order in which fields are displayed.

   A. True

   B. False

5. GibsonH created a table and gave ThompsonA permission to read it. Later ThompsonA created a view based on that table and gave Accounting permission to read the view. Will Accounting be able to read from the view?

   A. Yes, Accounting can read from the view

   B. No, Accounting cannot read from the view

6. True or False: Online transaction processing emphasizes fast reads.

   A. True

   B. False

7. True or False. Replication can usually fix itself in the event of a server going down.

   A. True

   B. False

8. Before replication can begin, both the publishing server and the subscribing server must be synchronized. Which agent performs this?

9. The SQL Setup utility can be used to do which of the following? (Select all that apply.)

   A. Add new components

   B. Add network protocols

   C. Upgrade from 6.5

   D. Rebuild the master database

10. You have set a disk mirror (RAID 1) for fault-tolerance. You want to be sure that the disk queues are not getting too high. What is the maximum you should set for Physical Disk: Average Disk Queue counter in Performance Monitor?

    A. One

    B. Two

    C. Three

    D. Four

11. You can have a database file (or log file) automatically grow by setting the _____ parameter. This parameter can be expressed in both _____ and _____. (Fill in the blanks.)

12. Three factors to consider when you are designing your replication strategy include autonomy, _____ and _____. (Fill in the blanks.)

13. Which of these is the correct syntax to back up to a file directly?

    A. `Backup database pubs to file = c:\mssql7\backup\pubs_backup.bak`

    B. `Backup database pubs to disk = 'c:\mssql7\backup\pubs_backup.bak'`

    C. `Backup database pubs to 'c:\mssql7\backup\pubs_backup.bak'`

    D. `Backup database pubs to c:\mssql7\backup\pubs_backup.bak fileonly`

14. To move large amounts of data from a flat file into SQL Server, you can use the _____ command line utility, or the _____ _____ Transact-SQL command. (Fill in the blanks.)

15. True or False: When you link to an ODBC database using the provider string parameter instead of a predefined system DSN, you still have to map the local login IDs to remote login IDs.

   A. True

   B. False

16. When you perform a bcp operation, _____ and _____ are always enforced while _____, _____ and _____ are always ignored. (Fill in the blanks.)

17. True or False: When your users perform distributed queries using both Informix and Microsoft SQL servers, SQL will be able to send the users NT security credentials to gain access to the Informix databases.

   A. True

   B. False

18. You can use the _____ _____ to move data, schema and object between two SQL Server 7 computers. (Fill in the blank.)

19. True or False: When a distributed query fails, it is usually a problem with connectivity or with object permissions in the linked database.

   A. True

   B. False

20. DTS packages have two types of security. To implement the security, you can use a _____ password which allows others to run the package, but not edit the package and a _____ password which allows others to edit and modify the package. (Fill in the blanks.)

21. True or False: When you link to an ODBC database using a predefined system DSN, you still have to map the local login IDs to remote login IDs.

   A. True

   B. False

22. True or False: A DTS task object is capable of running command executions, batch scripts and other DTS Packages.

    A. True

    B. False

23. True or False: When linking to an Oracle database from SQL Server 7, you must install the SQL*Net software to enable communications.

    A. True

    B. False

24. How many steps can a job have?

    A. One

    B. Five

    C. Ten

    D. Limited only by your resources

25. The SQL Client Network utility needs to be run only on the SQL Server because all SQL clients get their configuration information from the SQL Server itself.

    A. True

    B. False

26. True or False: Windows 95/98 is capable of being a publisher in a transactional replication scenario.

    A. True

    B. False

27. How can you edit a web publishing job?

    A. You can't

    B. Rerun the Wizard that made the job

    C. Edit the job directly

    D. Edit the row containing the job

28. Can you restore log files out of order?

    A. Yes

    B. No

29. When using transactional replication, your replicated transactions are stored in the _____ table in the distribution database. (Fill in the blank.)

30. What should you set the memory to in SQL Server 7 when SQL is the only program running on the server?

  A. Set it to (Total RAM-16 MB) for the amount

  B. Set it to 1 so SQL Server will automatically allocate it

  C. Set it to 0 so SQL Server will automatically allocate it

  D. Set it to the size of the physical RAM in the server

31. True or False: If the logreader agent quits running on the distribution server, then you will not be able to back up the transaction logs of publishing servers.

  A. True

  B. False

32. In SQL Server 7, _____ are 8 contiguous data pages. Each data page is ____KB in size. (Fill in the blanks.)

33. SQL Server 7 is part of which Microsoft Suite of applications?

  A. Office 97

  B. Office 2000

  C. Office Datamart

  D. BackOffice

34. True or False. SQL Server 7 has some wonderful new functionality that allows you to recover transaction logs out of sequence.

  A. True

  B. False

35. What rights does the SQLServerAgent require in order to manage the Distribution working folder?

36. True or False: By running the stored procedure `sp_configure 'query governor cost limit', '3'` you are telling SQL Server not to run more than three consecutive queries.

  A. True

  B. False

37. Which batch file is used to do an unattended removal?

    A. `sql70cli.bat`

    B. `sql70del.bat`

    C. `sql70cst.bat`

    D. `sql70rem.bat`

38. True or False: Data warehousing emphasizes fast reads.

    A. True

    B. False

39. Which of these four services is in charge of the others?

    A. Alert Manger

    B. Job Manager

    C. SQL Agent

    D. Event Manager

40. Which fixed server role should your users be members of if they are not supposed to have any administrative access?

    A. Admindenied role

    B. Standardusers role

    C. A custom fixed server role

    D. None of the above

41. When you run an upgrade from SQL Server 6.5 to 7, you should ensure that the Tempdb database is at least how many MB in size?

    A. 5MB

    B. 15MB

    C. 20MB

    D. 25MB

42. In SQL Server 7, the initial data file has a ._____ extension and additional data files have a ._____ extension, while transaction logs are stored in files with a ._____ extension. (Fill in the blanks.) See Chapter 4 for more information.

43. What is the command to restore a log?

    A. `Restore log`

    B. `Load log`

    C. `Restore transaction`

    D. `Load transaction`

44. How do you install just the SQL 7 client software?

    A. Run the `Client.exe` program

    B. Run the Setup program, choose Custom, and select just the client component.

    C. Run the Setup program and choose Install Client Software from the main menu.

    D. Run `Setup.exe` with the /CO switch.

45. You can use the DBCC _____ command to shrink all files that make up a database. (Fill in the blank.)

46. Replication in SQL Server 7 uses the following four agents: _____, _____, _____, and _____. (Fill in the blanks.)

47. True or False: When you perform a fast bulk copy, you remove the indexes and set the Select Into/bulk copy option to true. When the data is moved, it will be logged.

    A. True

    B. False

48. When trying to monitor your Physical Disk: Average Disk Queue counter in Performance Monitor on a non-RAID system, you notice that all the disk counters are zero. How can you fix this?

    A. From a command prompt, execute the `diskperf -y` command

    B. In Enterprise Manager, check the Enable Disk Monitoring check box on the Server Settings tab in the Server Properties dialog box

    C. Execute the stored procedure `sp_diskperf 'y'` from Query Analyzer

    D. Do nothing; it simply means your disks are not being used while you are monitoring them.

Answers to Assessment Questions

1. **Answer:** A. Replicating to heterogeneous databases is a new feature of SQL Server 7. Replicating to different character sets and sort orders is not typically recommended. See Chapter 9 for further information.

2. **Answer:** Filegroups. See Chapter 4 for more information.

3. **Answer:** Tempdb, Tempdb. See Chapter 7 for more information.

4. **Answer:** B. The ORDER BY clause selects which field to sort on. See Chapter 3 for more information.

5. **Answer:** B. Accounting cannot read from the view since the ownership chain is broken between the table, owner by GibsonH, and the view, owned by ThompsonA. See Chapter 5 for more information.

6. **Answer:** B. OLTP systems are usually concerned with entering new data—not reading old data. See Chapter 1 for more information.

7. **Answer:** A. Replication will normally pick up where it left off when a server is brought back online. If an extended period of time has passed, the subscribers may need to be resynchronized with the publishers. See Chapter 12 for more information.

8. **Answer:** The Snapshot agent performs this task. Once a copy of the data is made to the subscriber, replication can begin. See Chapter 9 for further information.

9. **Answer:** A, C. You add network protocols using the Network Support application and rebuild the master database using the `Rebuildm.exe` program. See Chapter 3 for more information.

10. **Answer:** D. The disk queue should be two per disk. See Chapter 10 for more information.

11. **Answer:** Filegrowth, megabytes, percentages. See Chapter 4 for more information.

12. **Answer:** Latency, transactional consistency. See Chapter 9 for further information.

13. **Answer:** B. You can specify a file (instead of a backup device) by using the `disk = 'path'` syntax. See Chapter 6 for more information.

14. **Answer:** `bcp`, `BULK INSERT`. See Chapter 7 for more information.

15. **Answer:** B. Part of the provider string parameter is the remote login ID and password to use when accessing this database. See Chapter 11 for more information.

16. **Answer:** Defaults, data types, rules, triggers, constraints. See Chapter 7 for more information.

17. **Answer:** B. Informix does not understand NT security credentials. You will need to use `sp_addlinkedsrvlogin` to tell SQL what account to use to gain access to the Informix server. See Chapter 5 for more information.

18. **Answer:** Transfer Manager. See Chapter 7 for more information.

19. **Answer:** A. You must successfully register and connect to your linked servers in order to run queries against them. When running queries, you must have appropriate object permissions. See Chapter 12 for more information.

20. **Answer:** operator, owner. See Chapter 7 for more information.

21. **Answer:** A. See Chapter 11 for more information.

22. **Answer:** A. True. See Chapter 7 for more information.

23. **Answer:** A. To link to an Oracle server, you need the SQL*Net software. See Chapter 11 for more information.

24. **Answer:** D. A job can have an unlimited number of steps, as long as you don't run out of system resources. See Jobs in Chapter 8 for more information.

25. **Answer:** B. Each client can be configured individually. See Chapter 3 for more information.

26. **Answer:** B. Windows 95/98 is incapable of supporting Named Pipes as a server. Named Pipes is required for transactional replication. See Chapter 9 for further information.

27. **Answer:** C. After you create a web publishing job, you can edit the job like any other job. See Chapter 8 for more information.

28. **Answer:** B. Transaction log files must be restored in the same sequence in which they were created. See Chapter 6 for more information.

29. **Answer:** `MSRepl_commands`. This folder has both marked (synchronized transactions which have been marked by the `sp_repldone` stored procedure) and unmarked transactions. When the distribution cleanup task runs, marked transactions are truncated. See Chapter 9 for further information.

30. **Answer:** C. Many settings in SQL Server 7 are automatically configured when they are set to 0. See Chapter 2 for more information.

31. **Answer:** A. This is a dangerous scenario. You should ensure that your logreader does not fail. A common reason for logreader failure is lack of space in the Distribution database. You should manage the distributor carefully. See Chapter 9 for further information.

32. **Answer:** Extents, 8. See Chapter 4 for more information.

33. **Answer:** A. BackOffice consists of SQL Server, SMS, Exchange, SNA, and other products that run on a server. See Chapter 1 for more information.

34. **Answer:** B. This is never true. If you do not recover your transaction logs in sequence and without skipping any, your database consistency is at issue. See Chapter 12 for more information.

35. **Answer:** Administrator or full control of the folder. See Chapter 9 for further information.

36. **Answer:** B. You are actually telling SQL Server not to run queries that are estimated to take longer than 3 seconds. See Chapter 10 for more information.

37. **Answer:** D. The batch file that Microsoft has written to help automate unattended removals of SQL 7 is `sql70rem.bat`. See Chapter 2 for more information.

38. **Answer:** A. Data warehousing is usually concerned with running queries on existing data. See Chapter 1 for more information.

39. **Answer:** C. The SQL Agent must be running before alerts, jobs, or events are handled. See Chapter 8 for more information.

40. **Answer:** D. The first two roles do not exist and it is not possible to create a custom fixed server role. If your users should not have administrative access to the server, do not add them to a fixed server role. See Chapter 5 for more information.

41. **Answer:** D. The Tempdb database should be at least 25MB in size to perform an upgrade. See Chapter 12 for more information.

42. **Answer:** MDF, NDF, LDF.

43. **Answer:** A. Although the `load transaction` command is still supported for backwards compatibility, the `restore log` command is the SQL Server 7 command to restore databases. See Chapter 6 for more information.

44. **Answer:** B. To install only the client software choose a Custom installation, and select just the client component. See Chapter 2 for more information.

45. **Answer:** `SHRINKDATABASE`. See Chapter 4 for more information.

46. **Answer:** Logreader, Snapshot, Merge, Distribution. See Chapter 9 for further information.

47. **Answer:** B. False. This not a logged transaction. See Chapter 7 for more information.

48. **Answer:** A. Execute the `diskperf -y` command to turn on disk counters. See Chapter 10 for more information.

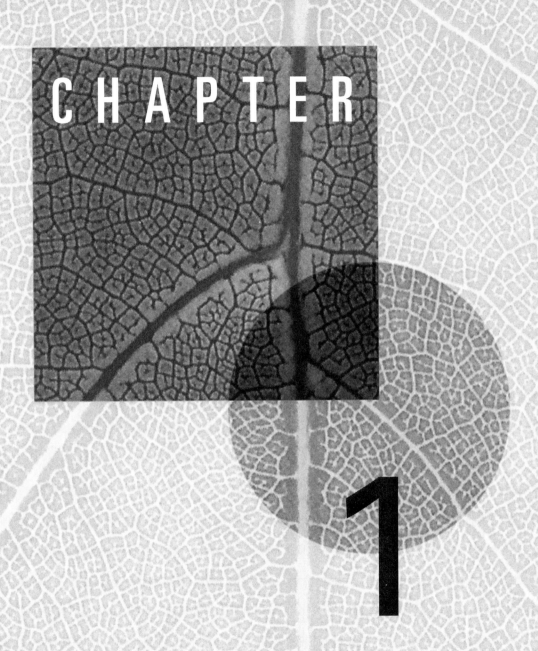

CHAPTER

1

Introduction to SQL Server 7 and
Relational Databases

SQL Server is a client/server-based relational database management system that runs on Windows NT Server, Workstation, or Windows 95/98 and is included in Microsoft's BackOffice suite. This chapter starts by defining a client/server environment, the types of databases involved, and what they contain. It then provides some background material on SQL Server and Windows NT, including the new features of SQL Server 7. The chapter finally discusses the tasks of the SQL Server developer and those of the SQL Server administrator.

What Is Client/Server?

Microsoft's SQL Server is a client/server database engine. SQL Server is the server part of the equation.

Client/server can be defined as an application that is split into at least two parts: One part runs on a server, and the other part runs on client computers, or workstations. The server side of the application provides security, fault-tolerance, performance, concurrency, and reliable backups. The client side provides the user interface and may contain such items as empty reports, queries, and forms.

In older, non-client/server database systems, the work is not shared between the server and workstation machines. For example, suppose that you have a 10MB database stored on your network server. When a client opens the database and runs a query, all 10MB are downloaded to the client, and then the query is processed at the client computer (Figure 1.1).

F I G U R E 1.1

In a non-client/server database system, the work is not shared between the server and the workstation computers.

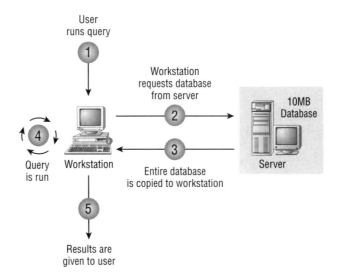

In contrast, when a query is run on a client/server system, the server searches the database, and then sends back to the client just those rows that match the search conditions (Figure 1.2). This not only saves bandwidth on your network, but (if the server is a powerful enough machine) is often faster than having the workstations do all the work.

F I G U R E 1.2

In a client/server application, the server and workstation share the work.

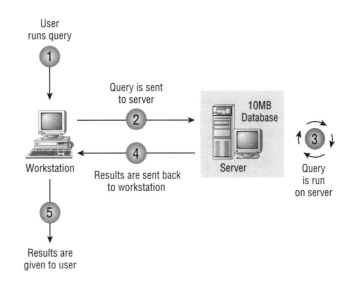

Types of Databases

A database can generally be thought of as a collection of related data that can be organized in various ways. The database can be designed to store historical data or changing data.

Relational Databases vs. Flat-File Databases

In earlier database products, a database was usually one file—something like `payroll.dbf` for an employee file or `patients.dbf` for use in a doctor's office. When all its information is stored in a single file, or *page*, and is accessed sequentially, the database resembles a spreadsheet and is considered a *flat-file database*. dBASE, Access, and other personal computer databases are examples of flat-file databases. Although flat-file databases are relatively easy to set up, those that contain complex data are more difficult to maintain. A *relational* database is composed of tables that contain related data. The process of organizing data into tables, (in a consistent and complete format), is referred to as *normalizing* the database.

Normalization of relational designs is a complex topic that will not be addressed in this book; it can be found in other books that are devoted to this topic. Before you implement your database design, however, you should start with a fully normalized view of the database.

In a relational database management system (RDBMS), such as SQL Server, a database is not necessarily tied to a file; it is more of a logical concept based on a collection of related *objects*. A database in SQL Server not only contains the raw data, it also contains the structure of the database, the security of the database, and any views or stored procedures related to that particular database.

A SQL Server database is composed of different types of objects (Figure 1.3).

F I G U R E   1.3

Common database
objects

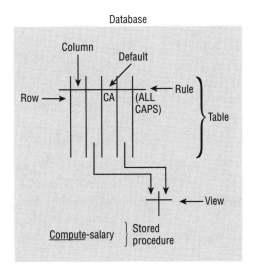

The following are some of the more common types of objects used in a database:

Object	Description
Table	This is the object that contains rows, columns, and the actual raw data.
Column	A column is a part of the table—the object that holds the data.
Row	A row is not a separate object, but rather a complete set of columns within a single table. Unlike the rest of the items discussed here, it is a logical construct, not a physically implemented object.
Datatype	There are various datatypes that can be used in columns, such as character, numeric, and date. A column can only hold data of a single datatype.
Stored procedure	A set of T-SQL statements that are combined to perform a single task or set of tasks. This object is like a macro, in that SQL code can be written and stored under a name. By invoking the name, you actually run the code.

Object	Description
Trigger	This object is a stored procedure that activates when data is added to, edited, or deleted from a table. Triggers are used to ensure that tables linked by keys stay internally consistent with each other. For example, an automobile dealer's database might include a trigger that makes sure that every time a car is added, the assigned salesperson actually exists.
Rule	This object is assigned to a column so that data being entered conforms to standards you set. For example, rules can be used to make sure that the state in a person's address is entered in uppercase and that phone numbers contain only numbers.
Default	This object is assigned to a column so that if no data is entered, the default value will be used. An example might be to set the state code to the state where most of your customers reside, so the default can be accepted for most entries.
View	A view is much like a stored query—you don't need to rewrite the query every time you'd like to run it; you can use the view instead. A view appears very much like a table to most users. A view usually either excludes certain fields from a table or links two or more tables together.

Data Warehousing vs. Transaction Processing

Databases fall into two general categories:

- Stored historical data that can be queried; this is often referred to as *data warehousing* or *decision support systems*. The main focus of data warehousing is the ability to quickly query existing data and perform complex analyses, usually looking for patterns or other relationships that are difficult to locate during the day-to-day operations of a company.

- Live, continually changing data. This type of database activity is referred to as a *datamart* or *OLTP* (Online Transaction Processing). In this case, the flexibility to expand and edit the database is the main focus.

Although these types of databases may appear to be the same at first glance, they are basically opposites. Data warehousing emphasizes reading the database with long-running transactions; OLTP emphasizes writing to the database with very quick transactions.

Although SQL Server makes a great server for both OLTP and data warehousing types of databases, if your company uses both types of databases, you may want to consider using two SQL Server machines—one for each function—in order to get optimal performance.

Another related (and rapidly growing) use of databases is to put the data into a Web page and publish it either internally on an intranet or to the public on the Internet. Again, the same basic types of databases are used: data warehousing if the data on the Web page is for historical reporting purposes, or OLTP if the customer can order from the Web page. Currently, most of the data is historical, or static, but that will change as the security and tools for transaction processing across the Internet improve.

Some Background on SQL Server

The release of SQL Server 7 for Windows NT (and Windows 95/98) is predicted to continue energizing the database market. While earlier versions of SQL Server have allowed many companies to downsize from mainframes to networks based on personal computers, SQL Server 7 adds many important new functions, including a vastly easier to use interface. More than two million copies of Microsoft's SQL Server have been sold since it was first introduced, and it is installed in a significant percentage of the companies that use some kind of database server.

SQL Server is one of the cornerstones of Microsoft's strategy for its BackOffice suite (Microsoft's line of client/server support applications). Microsoft's other BackOffice software includes Windows NT Server, Exchange (the e-mail server), IIS (the WWW server), SMS (Systems Management Server, the workstation management piece), Proxy Server (the firewall and caching server), and SNA (the IBM-protocol connectivity server) as well as other software that runs on Windows NT.

Every company has data, and almost every program generates even more data. The paperless office needs to store its data somewhere—usually in some kind of data server.

Before you work with SQL Server system administration, you need to understand its native language, history, and how it works with Windows NT and Windows 95/98.

History of the SQL Language

During the 1970s, IBM invented a computer language designed specifically for database queries. This language was called SEQUEL, which stood for Structured English QUEry Language. IBM released SEQUEL into the public domain, where it soon became known as SQL; it can be pronounced either as "sequel" or by its initials "S-Q-L."

Over time, the language has been expanded so that it is not just a language for queries, but can also be used to build databases and manage security of the database engine. Currently, there are various versions of the SQL language in use. Microsoft SQL Server uses a version called T-SQL or Transact SQL(both stand for Transaction SQL).

The T-SQL Language can be divided into two generic categories of commands:

- Database schema commands, also known as the Data Definition Language (DDL), are used to define the database, tables, and other objects that have to do with managing the structure of the database.

- Data management commands, also known as Data Manipulation Language (DML), are used much like the original commands of the SQL language, in that they manipulate, add to, or delete data in the database.

Although T-SQL is the programming language used by SQL Server, in this book our emphasis is on installing, maintaining, and connecting to SQL Server. In some cases, however, using T-SQL is one way to accomplish some of these tasks, such as creating and modifying SQL Server logons.

History of Microsoft's SQL Server on Windows NT

Microsoft initially worked with Sybase Corporation on a version of a SQL server system for OS/2. When Microsoft abandoned OS/2 in favor of its new network operating system, Windows NT, it decided to enhance the SQL server engine from Sybase and help modify the code for Windows NT. The resulting product was Microsoft SQL Server 4 for Windows NT, stabilizing at 4.21.

Over time, Microsoft took over more and more responsibility for the development of SQL Server; by version 6, Microsoft was in complete control of the software. Sybase engineers continued developing their database engine to run on Windows NT (Sybase version 10), while Microsoft developers continued enhancing SQL Server 6 (which quickly turned into version 6.5). Sybase continues to develop its product for Windows NT; Microsoft's current version of SQL Server (SQL Server 7) was officially launched in November of 1998.

A Brief History of Windows NT

Microsoft started developing Windows NT in 1990 when it became obvious that running a 16-bit version of Windows on top of MS-DOS could not provide the performance and security that businesses needed. Windows NT 4 came out in 1996, and NT 5 (now Windows 2000) was due in the second half of 1998 (see below).

Windows NT is a 32-bit operating system that has been designed with a familiar user interface (basically the same as the Windows 95/98 interface). One way to look at Windows NT is that it is much like a mainframe operating system under the hood, but the user interface is a friendly desktop. Windows NT has both server and client properties; that is, it can simultaneously function as a network server and as a client on the network. We'll talk more about client/server systems in the next section.

Windows NT comes in two versions:

- A Workstation version that is primarily used on desktop and laptop computers but can act as a server for up to 10 simultaneous connections at a time

- A Server version that is primarily used as a file/application server that can theoretically have thousands of simultaneous users connected to it

Windows NT is the ultimate general-purpose server. You can add functionality to the base server by installing services. SQL Server is implemented as a set of services on either Windows NT Workstation or Windows NT Server.

Windows NT 5 has recently been renamed Windows 2000. Other name changes include Windows 2000 Professional (formerly NT Workstation), Windows 2000 Server (NT Server), Windows 2000 Advanced Server (NT Server Enterprise version), and Windows 2000 Datacenter Server (a 16-CPU, SMP version of Windows 2000 Advanced Server designed for high-end data centers).

SQL Server 7 Basics

Although SQL Server 7 is similar to earlier editions in many respects, Microsoft has continued to modify and differentiate its several versions of SQL Server to meet the differing needs of various users.

SQL Server 7 not only adds a lower-end version (the Desktop version) but also adds support on the high end for various clustered NT Servers. SQL Server 7 continues the tradition of strong client support by providing backward-compatibility with older SQL clients while also adding new, enhanced client features.

Versions of SQL Server 7

SQL Server comes in four basic versions:

- Desktop
- Standard version
- Enterprise version
- Internet Connector

Desktop Version

SQL Server 7 can be run on the Windows 95/98 operating system. The Desktop version of SQL Server is meant to be used for traveling applications that occasionally link back to the primary network, and for ease of use in developing applications. The Desktop version (which can also be run on any version of Windows NT 4) installs and operates very much like the standard and Enterprise versions running on Windows NT.

This book assumes you are using the standard version of SQL Server 7 on Windows NT 4. When the Desktop version differs greatly from the full version it will be noted.

Standard Version

Windows NT was designed to address 4GB of RAM, with 2GB being allocated to Windows NT itself, and 2GB being reserved for applications to use (Figure 1.4).

FIGURE 1.4

Windows NT and RAM allocations

RAM reservations in Windows NT 4

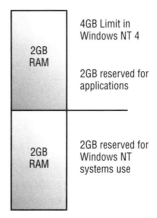

4GB Limit in Windows NT 4

2GB RAM

2GB reserved for applications

2GB RAM

2GB reserved for Windows NT systems use

Enterprise Version

Although 2GB of RAM were sufficient for almost every Windows NT application five years ago, the continued decline of hardware prices coupled with new, cache-hungry applications has pushed Windows NT into a new version: Windows NT Enterprise. SQL Server Enterprise Edition must be installed on Windows NT Enterprise Edition. While this version still addresses 4GB of RAM, it was designed to reserve only 1GB for NT, leaving 3GB for applications (Figure 1.5).

F I G U R E 1.5

Windows NT
Enterprise and RAM
allocations

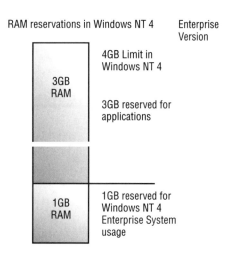

RAM reservations in Windows NT 4   Enterprise
Version

3GB
RAM

4GB Limit in
Windows NT 4

3GB reserved for
applications

1GB
RAM

1GB reserved for
Windows NT 4
Enterprise System
usage

Windows NT 2000 (previously known as Windows NT 5) will address more than 4GB of RAM (maybe 32GB or more) but until Windows 2000 comes out, SQL Server is limited by Windows NT 4.

Internet Connector Version

Although the Internet Connector version is basically a licensing rather than a software issue, it needs to be discussed because many sites connect to a SQL Server only via some sort of Web server. Instead of licensing concurrent connections, or a "super" connection from the Web server, the Internet Connector version allows you to pay a one-time fee that makes it legal for your web servers to provide SQL Server data to browser clients. Internet Connector is a per-processor license for Internet (not intranet) web servers that connect to SQL Server.

Clients Supported by SQL Server 7

SQL Server 7 supports the following clients directly:

- MS-DOS
- Windows 3.*x*, including Windows for Workgroups

- Windows 95/98

- Windows NT

 Because SQL Server 7 does not ship with 16-bit client support, you will have to use drivers from earlier versions of SQL Server.

 When SQL Server 7 is correctly linked to a WWW server, any client that can access the WWW server can also retrieve data from SQL Server 7.

SQL Server 7 Features

There are many features of SQL Server 7 that make it a compelling platform for client/server computing. Although a number of these features were present in the 6.5 version, they have been enhanced in 7.

- Support for both the Windows 95/98 and Windows NT operating systems

- Identical API (Application Programming Interface) support for both the Windows 95/98 and NT operating systems

- Integrated OLAP (Online Analytical Processing) server

- Integrated SNMP (Simple Network Management Protocol) support via Windows NT

- Integrated user-account support via Windows NT

- Automated task management

- Alert management

- Sophisticated replication support

- Query and index optimization wizards

- Database management wizards

- Full text-search capabilities

- OLE-DB (Object Linking and Embedding DataBase), ODBC, (Open Database Connectivity), SQL-DMO (SQL Data Management Objects), and DB-Library (Database Library) API support

- Dynamic enlarging and shrinking of databases

- Full and differential database backups

- Graphical query tools

- Improved, graphical import/export capabilities

- Graphical management tools using MMC (Microsoft Management Console) snap-ins

Although SQL Server 7 can run on both the Windows 95/98 and Windows NT platforms, there are some differences between the two types of installations:

Difference	Windows 95/98	Windows NT
SQL engine	Runs as an application	Runs as a service
Integrated security	No	Yes
Automated alerts	No	Yes
Maximum users (recommended)	5	Limited by hardware
Performance Monitor	No	Yes

Tasks of a SQL Server Developer

A SQL Server developer is responsible for designing, programming, and populating the database. Because the focus of this book is the administration rather than the development of SQL Server, the duties of the developer are not covered in detail. The developer's responsibilities can be summarized as follows:

- Analyze the business situation to see what type of system is required. Is a new system or an upgrade needed? Is it a small company at one location or a big corporation with multiple locations?

- Design the database, tables, and all objects. In the design process, the developer identifies objects and relationships and how those all fit together as logical entities; these are then translated into physical tables (normalized). The developer must then plan for the application design, including reports and queries, as well as other pieces, including access to Web pages.

- Design the security for the SQL Server and for individual databases. Implementing security is covered in Chapter 7, *Managing Your Data*.

- Design any data-replication scenarios. Replication, including scenarios and implementation, is covered in Chapter 11, *Working with Remote Data and Linked Servers*.

- Program the database, tables, and all objects. This involves working with the T-SQL language.

- Program the initial security of the database, possibly planning Windows NT groups to help ease ongoing SQL Server administration.

- Design the user interface, reports, and update screens. This is the front end of the system and will probably have the most impact on the users.

- Test the design, interface, reports, and update screens.

- Populate the database with live data from legacy systems and prepare the database to receive new data.

- Hand the project with appropriate documentation and training over to the administrator.

Tasks of a SQL Server Administrator

A SQL Server administrator is usually responsible for the day-to-day administration of the database. The administrator takes over where the programmer left off.

The tasks of the SQL administrator are the focus of this book. Microsoft has two separate SQL tests: one—the focus of this book—designed for the administrator, and the other—the implementation test—designed for T-SQL programmers.

In many companies, the lines between administrator and developer may become quite blurred, as the same person may be doing tasks related to both roles.

The administrator's duties can be summarized as the following:

- Back up the databases (see Chapter 6, *Implementing Database Backups and Restorations*).

- Restore the databases when necessary (see Chapter 6).

- Manage the databases (see Chapter 4, *Planning, Creating, and Managing a Database in SQL Server 7*; Chapter 5, *Security* and *SQL Server 7*; and Chapters 6 and 7).

- Set up and manage users for SQL Server (see Chapter 5).

- Manage security for new users and existing users (see Chapter 5).

- Setup and manage Tasks, Alerts, and Operators (see Chapter 8, *Implementing Proactive Administration in SQL Server 7*).

- Manage the replication environment (see Chapter 9, *Creating and Implementing a Replication Solution*).

- Tune the SQL Server system for the optimal performance (see Chapter 10, *Monitoring and Optimizing SQL Server 7*).

- Troubleshoot any SQL Server problems (see Chapter 12, *Troubleshooting SQL Server 7*).

Summary

Microsoft's SQL Server is a client/server-based relational database management system (RDBMS) that uses T-SQL as its dialect of the SQL language. Its ever-increasing popularity makes learning SQL Server 7 a wise career decision. A *client/server* database is an application that is divided into a part that runs on a server and a part that runs on workstations (clients). The server side provides security, fault-tolerance, performance, concurrency, and reliable backups. The client side provides the user interface.

A *relational* database is composed of tables that contain related data. The process of breaking a database into related tables is called *normalization*.

SQL Server developers have the responsibility for designing and implementing the databases. Designing a good database starts with understanding the client's requirements for the database. The data can then be grouped into related tables. SQL Server administrators have the responsibility for the day-to-day tasks of maintaining and managing the databases. SQL Server administration involves backing up databases and restoring them when necessary, setting up and managing users, managing database security, managing the replication environment, tuning the database system, and troubleshooting any problems that arise.

Review Questions

1. Which of the following is a database object? (Choose all that apply.)

   A. Table

   B. Index

   C. Rule

   D. Default

2. Who is responsible for backing up databases?

   A. The database administrator

   B. The database developer

   C. Database users

   D. The Windows NT administrator

3. Who is responsible for ongoing database security?

   A. The database administrator

   B. The database developer

   C. Database users

   D. The Windows NT administrator

4. Who is responsible for ongoing SQL Server optimization?

   A. The database administrator

   B. The database developer

   C. Database users

   D. The Windows NT administrator

5. What is the process of breaking related information into tables called?

   A. Fragmentation

   B. Database design

   C. Normalization

   D. Tabulating the data

6. When a query is run in client/server computing, who actually runs the query?

   A. The client

   B. The server

   C. Both the client and the server

   D. Neither; a "middleware" application runs the query.

7. SQL Server is an example of what kind of database system?

   A. Flat-file

   B. 3-D

    C. RDBMS

    D. Heirarchical

8. Data in relational databases is organized into:

    A. Fields

    B. Files

    C. Reports

    D. Tables

9. SQL Server 7 can run on which operating systems? (Select all that apply.)

    A. Windows for Workgroups

    B. Windows 95/98

    C. Windows NT Workstation

    D. Windows NT Server

10. SQL Server 7 uses which database language?

    A. DBMS

    B. T-SQL

    C. SQL

    D. QUERY

11. What is a view in SQL Server?

    A. Precompiled code

    B. A stored query

    C. A way of organizing like data

    D. A way of entering default values

12. Which version of SQL Server would you install if you wanted to access your SQL data running on NT Server only from a web server?

   A. The Desktop version on every client

   B. The Desktop version with Internet Connector licensing

   C. The standard version with per seat licensing

   D. The standard version with Internet Connector licensing

13. The standard version of SQL Server can run on which platforms?

   A. Windows 95/98

   B. Windows NT Workstation

   C. Windows NT Server

   D. Windows NT Enterprise Server

14. The Enterprise version of SQL Server can run on which platforms?

   A. Windows 95/98

   B. Windows NT Workstation

   C. Windows NT Server

   D. Windows NT Enterprise Server

CHAPTER

2

Installing, Upgrading, and
Configuring SQL Server 7

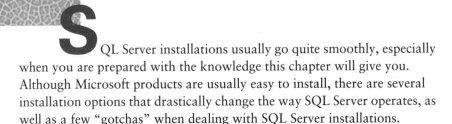

QL Server installations usually go quite smoothly, especially when you are prepared with the knowledge this chapter will give you. Although Microsoft products are usually easy to install, there are several installation options that drastically change the way SQL Server operates, as well as a few "gotchas" when dealing with SQL Server installations.

This chapter will walk you through an actual installation of SQL Server, paying attention to the various options along the way. We will look at the options available when upgrading from SQL Server 6.5, as well as automating the setup process.

Once the installation is complete, we will focus on configuring both the server and the clients.

Installing SQL Server 7

Like most Microsoft applications, the setup routine for SQL Server is both powerful and relatively intuitive. There are several decisions that, once made, are rather difficult to change, however, so before starting the installation, look at the various options available to you and plan accordingly.

Although this entire objective is covered in this chapter, the appropriate sub-objectives will be listed where they are covered in the chapter.

Microsoft Exam Objective

Install SQL Server 7.0.

- Choose the character set.
- Choose the Unicode collation.
- Choose the appropriate sort order.
- Install Net-Libraries and protocols.
- Install services.
- Install and configure a SQL Server client.
- Perform an unattended installation.
- Upgrade from a SQL Server 6.*x* database.

Before You Install

Although some of the SQL configurations can be changed after installation, several of the options cannot be changed. The configurations that must be chosen before doing an installation include:

- License mode
- Character set
- Sort order
- Unicode support
- Network libraries
- User accounts
- Installation path
- Upgrade vs. side-by-side installation
- Which components to install

License Mode

SQL Server supports per-seat and per-server licensing; there are advantages to both types. Most companies prefer per-seat licensing, but for companies who need only a limited number of users, per-server licensing may be a better fit.

Per-seat licensing means that you pay for every person in the company, whether or not they use SQL Server. The advantage here is that you can add additional SQL Servers for just the cost of Windows NT and SQL Server itself.

The desktop edition is only legally installable if you purchase per-seat licensing.

Per-server licensing requires a license for each SQL Server installed, and each server is limited to the purchased number of concurrent users. The advantage of this licensing is that everyone need not be licensed to use SQL Server if only a few people will use it.

Microsoft has added an Internet Connector license for SQL 7 (retailing at $2999 per processor) for those SQL Servers whose primary purpose is to hold data for WWW (IIS) servers.

Character Sets

SQL Server 7 supports several character sets The original use of 7 of the 8 bits of a byte provided 128 possible characters; using the 8th bit adds 128 more characters (called *extended characters*) for a total of 256 possible characters. Extended characters can be used to represent symbols, special letters of a foreign alphabet, or other such items. Although the first 128 characters of all character sets are the same (the fonts may differ), there are many extended character sets available. SQL Server supports the most common character sets.

Microsoft ✓ *Exam* *Objective*

Install SQL Server 7.0.

- Choose the character set.

The main thing to remember here is that *SQL Server can support only one character set at a time and that character set cannot be changed once SQL Server is installed.* SQL Server 7 adds support for Unicode characters that, because they take 2 bytes of data to hold, allow you to support more that 256 characters for any given character set. Unicode support is discussed below.

It is therefore crucial to pick a character set that will be recognized by the applications installed on the SQL Server. For instance, if an application wished to store the character ½, it would be able to do so only if certain character sets had been selected.

SQL Server supports the following character sets (this is not a comprehensive list):

- 1252 (ISO 8859, ANSI). This is the default character set for SQL Server 6.*x* and 7. It is compatible with the character sets used by Windows NT, and is the best choice, especially for multilingual companies and databases.

- 850 (multilingual). The old default character set, this is still in use in many databases, especially those upgraded from earlier versions of SQL Server. Although this character set supports most of the languages in use in the Americas and Europe, a better choice is 1252.

- 437 (US English). Although this is a popular character set because it contains support for graphic characters not normally supported by databases, its compatibility with other languages is limited.

If the applications use only the first 128 characters, the actual character set installed will probably not matter. Because it is very difficult to know which character set to use, we recommend that you always use the default character set, unless an application's installation instructions specifically say to choose a different one.

Sort Order

The sort order determines how data is stored, compared, and returned during queries. The available sort-order selections will be determined by the character set chosen.

Microsoft
✓ ***Exam***
Objective

Install SQL Server 7.0.

▪ Choose the appropriate sort order.

The main sort orders include the following:

Dictionary sort order, case-insensitive   This is the default sort order and treats upper- and lowercase characters the same for comparison purposes.

Dictionary sort order, case-sensitive   This sort order retains and enforces all cases in the database and when using SQL Server. For example, if the database is called "Pubs" (note the capital P and lowercase ubs), then a use pubs or use PUBS command would fail—only the use Pubs command would succeed.

Binary order   This sort order sorts everything by its binary representation of the data, not as a dictionary would sort characters.

If you choose a case-sensitive sort order, all SQL passwords are case-sensitive. If you choose a case-insensitive sort order, passwords (and all other key words) are also case-insensitive.

Unicode Support

SQL Server 7 supports Unicode character types. Unicode characters are represented by 2 bytes (rather than a single byte), enabling more than 64,000 possible characters for a given field.

Microsoft
✓ ***Exam***
Objective

Install SQL Server 7.0.

▪ Choose the Unicode collation.

The default Unicode support is for case-insensitive, width-insensitive, Kana (Japanese)-insensitive support. Use the default selection unless you have been specifically instructed to change it. If you need to support multiple languages but have to use the 850 or 437 character sets, you can choose the Unicode datatype when you create your columns.

Network Libraries

SQL Server doesn't automatically support every protocol that is installed on the computer—you need to configure SQL Server to support specific protocols, which must first be installed and correctly configured.

Microsoft
✓ Exam
Objective

Install SQL Server 7.0.

- Install Net-Libraries and protocols.

SQL Server supports the following protocols and standards:

TCP/IP   Support for this industry-standard protocol is enabled by default. SQL Server uses port 1433 as its default TCP/IP port. Because SQL Server uses configurations set by the operating system, TCP/IP connections to the SQL Server that do not function properly it may be caused by problems with the TCP/IP protocol and configurations and not with SQL Server.

IPX/SPX   Support for this protocol, used by NetWare servers and clients, is not enabled by default. Installing IPX/SPX on the SQL Server allows NetWare clients to connect to the SQL Server even if they don't have a Microsoft client installed. If you enable support for IPX/SPX you can also configure the name of the server that NetWare clients will see. Both NetWare and Microsoft clients should use the same server name to avoid confusion.

Named Pipes   Support for this networking standard is enabled by default. Named Pipes is a common method for connecting to a resource using a network. Note that Microsoft's NetBEUI, TCP/IP, and IPX/SPX support the Named Pipes specification natively.

Named Pipes is a REQUIRED protocol on NT—it can't be unselected during setup and is not available on Win95/98 as a server protocol.

Multi-Protocol   Support for this standard is enabled by default. Multi-Protocol support allows clients to connect via two or more methods, allowing encryption across TCP/IP and IPX/SPX.

AppleTalk   Support for this protocol is not enabled by default. Apple-Talk is used by Macintosh clients.

DecNet   Support for this protocol is not enabled by default. DecNet is used by some older Digital clients.

User Accounts

As with any service that connects to other computers and services, the SQL Server and Agent need a service account assigned to them. The account needs:

- The advanced Logon as a Service right
- User Must Change Password at Next Logon cleared
- Password Never Expires checked

The Logon as a Service right is needed so that the account can be used by a service. Since a service cannot change a password, you must clear the User Must Change Password at Next Logon box, and in order to keep the password from expiring you should select Password Never Expires.

You should make the user with Windows NT User Manager (Figure 2.1) before installing SQL Server. The SQL installation program will assign the Logon as a Service right but all the others need to be done by you.

F I G U R E 2.1

Creating a user account for SQL services

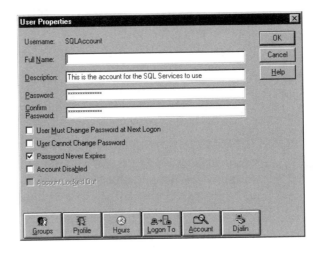

Installation Path

The default path is \MSSQL7 for both the program and database files on the system drive (where Windows is installed). You may choose a different path for the program files and/or database files.

Upgrading vs. Side-by-Side Installation

If SQL Server 6.5 is already installed on the server, the SQL Server 7 Setup program will attempt to upgrade the installation by default. SQL Server 6.5 requires Service Pack 3 or later in order to be successfully upgraded to SQL Server 7. If you choose to install SQL Server 7 in a different path, you can choose which version of SQL Server to start.

As with any upgrade, thoroughly backup all valuable databases in SQL Server 6.5 before attempting a live upgrade.

Selecting Components

A default SQL Server installation includes the MSSQLSERVER service (the actual database engine), the management software (Enterprise Manager and others), and the documentation. You can select any combination of software components by choosing a Custom installation.

The SQL Server 7 Installation

Although there are many steps to the installation, the process is fairly straightforward. Some general steps, such as installing the latest Windows NT Service Pack and version of Internet Explorer, should be done first. The Install Prerequisites option from the main setup screen allows you to install the required prerequisites for both Windows 95 and Windows NT.

Once the prerequisites have been installed, restart the SQL Setup program and select Install Database Components. This will list the different versions of SQL Server 7 that can be installed.

The Desktop version is designed for Windows 95/98, while the standard product is designed for Windows NT. Chapter 1, *Introduction to SQL Server 7 and Relational Databases,* provides more information on the differences between the two products. This book assumes that the standard product is installed.

The Setup program allows you to install SQL Server to the local computer, or, if you have administrative rights, to a remote computer. Normally, to save network use, you would run the installation routine on the computer you wish to be your SQL Server. Remote sites can easily be installed by choosing the remote installation option.

You will then get a screen prompting you to back up anything valuable on your system, in case the unexpected happens. After choosing Next you will see the license agreement form, which you must accept before being able to proceed.

The installation program will prompt you for a user and company after which you will be prompted if you want to run the SQL 6.5 to SQL 7 Upgrade Wizard. If you don't run the Wizard during the setup you can run it at a later time (recommended if you don't have reliable recent backups of your 6.5 databases).

The next screen is one of the most important ones, as it allows you to pick a custom setup routine. Custom setup routines allow you to change the sort order, character set, network support, and even whether the SQL engine or just the management tools will be installed. If you choose the Custom setup you will be taken to the Select Components screen where you can choose exactly which pieces of SQL Server will be installed. You will probably want to make sure the Full-Text Search Engine is selected (the default) in case you want to setup any text indexes later. Of course, you can always rerun the Setup program and add components after the initial installation.

The next screen allows you to change your sort order, character set, and Unicode collection. Note that you should leave these at the default settings unless you have a very good reason to change them.

The following screen allows you to select which network protocols to support. Note that Named Pipes, TCP/IP and Multi-Protocol support are selected by default. Select additional protocols as required.

You can assign a user account to the various SQL services at the next screen. You can choose to assign the same account to all three services (SQL Server, SQL Agent, and MS-DTC) or to create individual user accounts for the various services. This is the last screen to fill out before the installation begins.

The SQL installation program will let you know when SQL Server has been successfully installed.

In Exercise 2.1 you will install SQL Server 7, paying attention to the various options available during the installation. Although the exercise does a Custom installation, we will not change any of the default settings (basically doing what a Typical installation would).

EXERCISE 2.1

Installing SQL Server

1. Run the Setup program from the SQL Server 7 CD-ROM.

2. Install the prerequisites (if not already installed) by choosing the appropriate operating system from the main setup screen. Reboot after installing all prerequisites and rerun the Setup program.

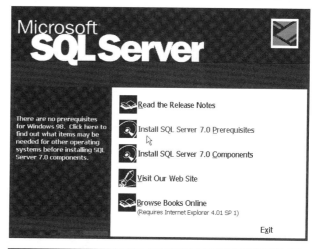

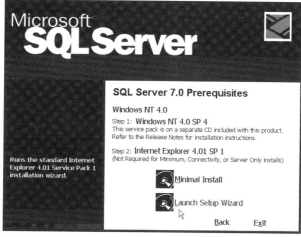

3. Select the appropriate version of SQL Server to install. Choose Desktop if on a workstation and Standard (full) if on a server. Choose Next.

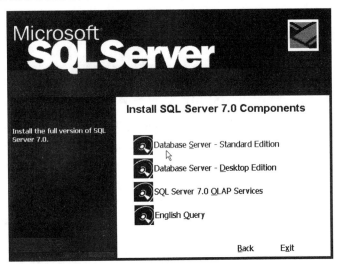

4. Select Local installation if you are running the Setup program on the computer you wish to become the SQL Server, otherwise choose Remote and supply the name of the remote server. Choose Next.

5. Select Next at the Introduction screen.

6. Select the appropriate license information, enter your CD key, and select OK, OK.

Note that if you had an earlier version of SQL 7 installed you will be asked whether you want to upgrade to the latest version. If so, the Setup program will skip to Step 9.

7. Enter your name and company name and select Next.

8. At the Upgrade Wizard prompt choose No (we will work with upgrades in a later exercise). Select Next.

9. Select Custom installation. Select Next to continue.

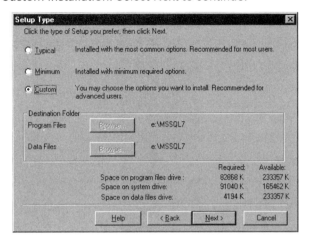

10. Select the Server Components, Management Tools, Client Connectivity, Books Online, and Full-Text Search check boxes. Select Next to continue.

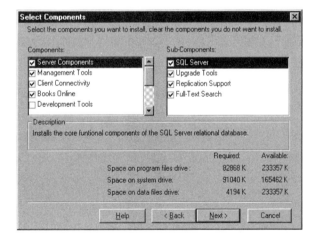

11. Leave the Sort Order, Character Set, Unicode Support, and Installation Folders at the default settings. Select Next to continue.

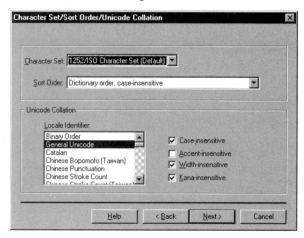

12. Leave Named Pipes, TCP/IP, and Multi-Protocol support selected. Select Next to continue.

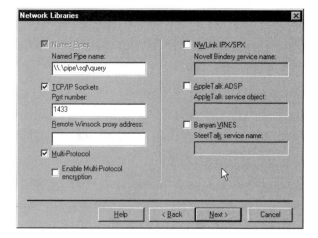

13. Enter the user account created earlier (see Figure 2.1) for the SQL Services to use. Select Next to continue.

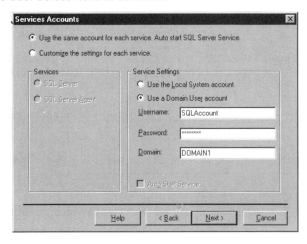

14. Click Next to go to the Licensing screen.

15. Enter your appropriate licensing information and choose Continue, checkmark the Agree box, and choose OK.

16. Review and adjust the installation settings as needed, then click Next to start the installation. The installation will take several minutes.

17. Choose OK when prompted that the installation has finished.

Unattended Installations

SQL Server can be installed without prompts by using various batch files and initialization files.

Microsoft ✔ *Exam* *Objective*

Install SQL Server 7.0

- Perform an unattended installation.

The SQL 7 CD-ROM contains sample batch files and initialization files as shown in Table 2.1.

T A B L E 2.1: Sample Batch and Initialization Files for SQL Server 7

Batch File	Initialization File	Action
Sql70cli.bat	Sql70cli.iss	Installs SQL Server administration tools
Sql70ins.bat	Sql70ins.iss	Installs a typical version of SQL Server
Sql70cst.bat	Sql70cst.iss	Installs all components of SQL Server
Sql70rem.bat		Uninstalls SQL Server

You can edit the sample initialization files to fit your site. You can also look at the initialization file that was created during an installation (stored as setup.iss in the \MSSQL7\install folder) and edit the file as needed. You can also run the SQL Setup program as

    Setupsql.exe k=Rc

which will generate the script file in the \Windows or \Winnt folder. Choose Cancel when prompted to copy files, or a full installation will take place.

Testing the Installation

Once SQL Server is installed you can easily and quickly test the installation. Start SQL Enterprise Manager (Figure 2.2) from the Microsoft SQL Server 7 group and open the SQL Server group.

F I G U R E 2.2

Starting Enterprise Manager

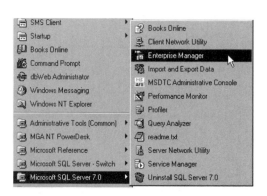

NOTE SQL 7 Enterprise Manager automatically registers a connection to the SQL Server using an integrated server account or the SA login account. The SA login account is the only SQL login account installed by default and has a blank password after the installation. You should choose a new password, making sure you don't forget or lose it.

Your server should be listed on the screen. Open it by clicking the + sign and you should see folders for the various databases, security settings, and so on for your SQL Server (Figure 2.3). If the server opens successfully it probably installed successfully.

FIGURE 2.3

Examining your SQL Server in Enterprise Manager

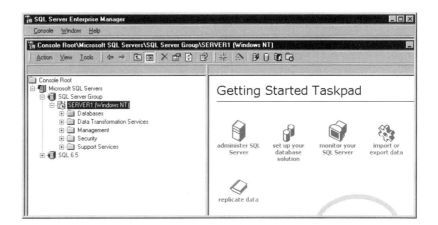

Another way to test the installation is by running a simple query in the Pubs sample database. To do this start the Query Analyzer by going to the Tools ➤ SQL Server ➤ Query Analyzer menu option from Enterprise Manager. You can also start the Query Analyzer separately by selecting its icon from the SQL Server group.

In Exercise 2.2, we will test the SQL installation by doing a simple query.

EXERCISE 2.2

Running a Simple SQL Query to Test the SQL Installation

1. Start the Query Analyzer from the Tools menu of Enterprise Manager or by selecting the icon in the SQL Server 7 group.

2. Enter the command

use pubs select * from authors

3. Click on the green arrow or enter Ctrl+E to run the query. You should get back 23 rows of authors for your results.

4. Close Query Analyzer. Answer No when prompted to save the output of the query.

SQL Server Services

SQL is composed of three separate services—MSSQLSERVER, SQLSERVER-AGENT, and MS-DTC—all of which install on a Windows NT computer. A SQL Server 7 installation on a Windows 95/98 computer does not include MS-DTC service, which is only available with the standard version of SQL Server. There is also a fourth service—MicrosoftSearch—that provides Full-Text indexes for SQL Server 7 (it is covered in detail in Chapter 3, *SQL Server Tools and Utilities*).

Microsoft
✓ Exam
Objective

Install SQL Server 7.0.

- Install services.

MSSQLSERVER The MSSQLSERVER service is the actual database engine. This service is required for any computer you wish to be a SQL Server.

To check whether the service has been installed, go to Control Panel ➤ Services and look for it by name.

SQLSERVERAGENT The SQLSERVERAGENT service is a helper service designed to take care of the automation involved in SQL Server. Although this service is not technically required, few, if any, sites run without it. You can check on its installation by going to Control Panel ➤ Services.

MS-DTC   The MS-DTC (Database Transaction Coordinator) service is an optional service designed to take care of transactions that span multiple servers. When a transaction is done across two or more servers, the MS-DTC service ensures that the transaction is done on all servers; otherwise the transaction is rolled back.

Microsoft Search   When you install Full-Text index support you install the Micrososft Search service, which is basically the same service supported by Microsoft's Index Server engine. Creating and managing Full-Text indexes are covered in Chapter 3.

Registry Settings

SQL Server creates a key in the Hkey_Local_Machine/ Software/ Microsoft as well as in the Hkey_Users key. Settings that apply to the SQL Server as a service are stored in the Hkey_Local_Machine/Software hive, while settings that apply to the management software configurations are stored (uniquely for each user) in the Hkey_Users key.

Installation Path

You can also check the installation path to see whether SQL Server has been installed correctly. There should be subdirectories under the /MSSQL7 folder as well as a `setup.out` file that was created during installation. Subdirectories under the main folder are shown in Table 2.2.

T A B L E 2.2:   Subfolders and Their Contents

Folder Name	Content
Backup	Default folder for backup files
Binn	EXE and Setup files
Books	Online documentation
Data	Default and system databases
DevTools	Sample code and applications
Html	Sample HTML pages and default folder for created web pages

T A B L E 2.2: Subfolders and Their Contents *(continued)*

Folder Name	Content
Install	Scripts used during installation
Jobs	Default folder for automated jobs
Log	Log files (including errors, version numbers, and FYI type messages) created by various SQL services
Repldata	Working folder for replication
Upgrade	Scripts and output used during upgrade

Upgrading SQL Server 6.*x* to 7

SQL Server 7 has a robust Upgrade Wizard that can easily convert a SQL Server 6.*x* system to a SQL Server 7 system. Because the upgrade is not reversible, there are several items to be aware of before you start.

Microsoft ✓ *Exam Objective*

Develop a migration plan.

- Plan an upgrade from a previous version of SQL Server.
- Plan the migration of data from other data sources.

NOTE Chapter 7, *Managing your Data,* has more details on migrating data from various data sources.

SQL Server 7 allows you to upgrade databases and entire servers from SQL Server 6.0 and 6.5, but does not support upgrades directly from earlier versions (4.21). SQL Server 7 has many available options when you upgrade from earlier versions, each with its advantages and disadvantages. The various methods and requirements when upgrading are discussed below.

Before You Begin the Upgrade

There are several items you need to decide on before upgrading; these include

- A one- vs. two-computer upgrade
- Upgrading vs. running side-by-side
- Prerequisites to upgrading
- How to upgrade databases successfully

 If you are upgrading servers involved in replication, you must upgrade the distribution server first, as SQL Server 7 has support for SQL Server 6.x replication tasks.

One-Computer vs. Two-Computer Upgrades

One of the major considerations is whether to leave the old SQL Server in place and migrate the data to a new server, or to upgrade the original 6.x server to SQL Server 7.

The main advantage of using a second box is that the original server is untouched during the upgrade and can quickly be brought back online if there is a problem with either the migration to the SQL 7 Server or the server itself. The major disadvantage here is that a second server at least as powerful as the original 6.x server must be purchased or leased.

Upgrading vs. Side-by-Side Installation

If you decide to upgrade a SQL 6.x server to SQL 7, you have one more decision to make. You can choose to install SQL 7 in the same folder that 6.x occupied, or you can install 7 in a different folder.

The advantage of installing 7 in a different folder than 6.x is that you can thoroughly test the 7 installation before converting your databases from 6.x to 7. In addition, the conversion process can be set to preserve the old databases. This allows you to use your 6.x server in the event of a problem during conversion. The disadvantage of installing SQL 7 in a new folder is that it will take significantly more hard drive space and requires manually converting your databases and settings.

Switching between 6.*x* and 7

You can only have one version of SQL Server running at any given time. SQL 7 comes with a program (Switch to SQL 6.5/Switch to 7) that can be run to rename various services so you can start either version of SQL Server. Note that some functions (such as using Performance Monitor to check a 6.5 server) will not work if you are switching back and forth.

Upgrade Prerequisites

Several prerequisites must be met in order to upgrade SQL Server 6.5 to SQL Server 7.

- Service Pack 4 for Windows NT

- Internet Explorer 4.01 Service Pack 1

- 32MB of RAM

- 180MB of free hard drive space (for full installation), plus free space equal to about 1.5 times the size of the databases being upgraded

- If upgrading SQL 6.5, Service Pack 3 (or higher) for SQL 6.5 is required

- If upgrading SQL 6.0, Service Pack 3 (or higher) for SQL 6.0 is required

- Named Pipes installed with the default pipe name: Pipe\SQL\Query

Because upgrades—especially live, in-place upgrades—have the chance of failing, always do a full backup of your 6.*x* server and databases first.

Upgrading Databases

Databases can be upgraded using the Upgrade Wizard. SQL Server 6.0 and 6.5 databases can be directly upgraded to SQL Server 7 with the Upgrade Wizard, while any SQL 4.21 databases must first be upgraded to SQL 6.*x* (6.5 is highly recommended) before you can upgrade them to SQL 7.

Microsoft
Exam
Objective

Install SQL Server 7.0.

- Upgrade from a SQL Server 6.*x* database.

Note that SQL Server 7 cannot load backups made from earlier versions of SQL Server. It must be able to read the live database in order to create a converted copy of it.

> **WARNING** If you have the Upgrade Wizard delete old SQL 6.*x* devices and databases, it deletes all devices and databases, whether or not they were upgraded. For this reason, if you have the Wizard delete old databases you should upgrade all user databases at the same time. Remember: Always back up before upgrading, regardless of the upgrade method used.

Upgrade Issues

When upgrading SQL Servers and databases there are some issues that you need to be aware of. One issue is when objects in the old databases cannot be created in the new database. This happens when:

- The object has been renamed with the sp_rename stored procedure.

- The accompanying text in syscomments is missing.

- Stored procedures have been created within other stored procedures.

- The owner of an object's login ID is not created at the new server.

- The older server was using integrated security but the new server is using mixed security and the NT groups have not been created at the new server.

Other issues that you may encounter when upgrading servers and databases include the following:

- The upgrade process will fail if @@Servername returns NULL.

- Stored procedures that reference or modify system tables will not be converted.

- Servers involved with replication should be upgraded in a certain order: the Distribution server must be upgraded first, and many SQL 7 replication functions will not be enabled until all involved servers are upgraded.

Configuring SQL Server 7

Although SQL Server follows the ANSI specifications for relational database engines, SQL Server also allows you to make changes to various internal settings to control the way SQL Server deals with issues such as the use of quotes " " or the use of the NULL character. You may want to make changes to the default settings to support legacy applications or for convenience when working with SQL Server.

Microsoft ✓ *Exam* *Objective*

Configure SQL Server.

- Configure SQL Mail.
- Configure default American National Standards Institute (ANSI) settings.

ANSI settings are discussed below. Configuring SQL Mail is covered in detail in Chapter 8, *Implementing Proactive Administration in SQL Server 7.*

SQL Server Settings

SQL Server 7 automatically configures the most common settings, including the memory used, the number of connections configured, and the percentage of cache devoted to procedures vs. data.

You can manually configure the most common items using Enterprise Manager, but for those items not shown in Enterprise Manager you will need to use the `sp_configure` command.

Configuring SQL Internal Settings

Configure SQL Server by highlighting the server and choosing Tools SQL Server Configuration Properties, or by right-clicking and choosing Properties.

In Exercise 2.3, we will look at the major configuration parameters of SQL Server.

EXERCISE 2.3

Configuring SQL Server

1. Start Enterprise Manager and connect to your SQL Server.

2. Highlight your server and go to Tools ➤ SQL Server Configuration Properties or right-click and choose Properties.

   From the main Properties sheet you can choose the startup parameters and whether the services autostart.

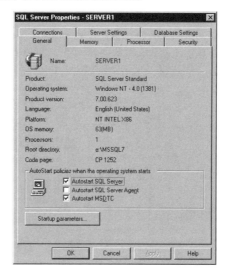

3. Go to the Memory tab to change the amount of RAM SQL Server uses. Note that SQL Server 7 dynamically allocates RAM and that you should be careful when adjusting this default.

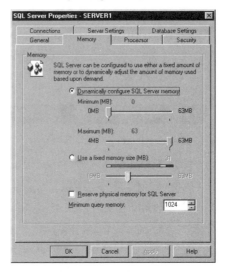

4. Go to the Processor tab. The number and priorities of the CPUs used by SQL Server can be controlled from the Processor tab. Note that Windows 95/98 (and thus SQL Server running on Win95/98) does not support more than one CPU. Do not boost SQL Server's priority unless it is on a dedicated server; an increase will slow all other processes.

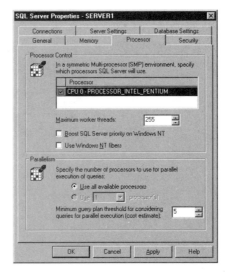

5. Go to the Security tab. This allows you to change SQL Server to use security that is integrated with NT. You can also assign a user account or change the account's password from this tab.

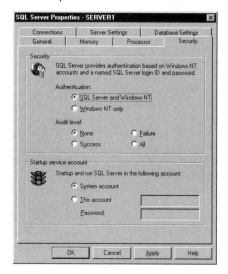

6. Go to the Connections tab. The Connections tab allows you to configure the number of connections that SQL Server will support. Because SQL Server 7 dynamically allocates connections as needed (Connections = 0), adjust the connections only if you want to limit them. Connections are not the same as users. For example, a user with Excel, Access (with three windows), and Crystal Reports open has five connections but only counts as one user. You need to license the number of users connected to SQL Server, but the number of connections is a function of how many applications they have open at any given time and does not affect licensing. It will, however, affect the hardware that the SQL Server runs on in order to maintain good response time, as more connections require a higher level of hardware for SQL Server.

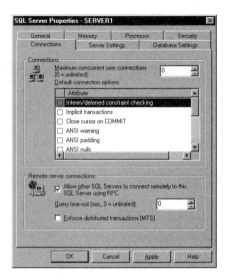

7. Go to the Server Settings tab. You can control the direct editing of system tables, allow nested triggers, and prevent runaway queries. You can also configure the SQL Mailsession here.

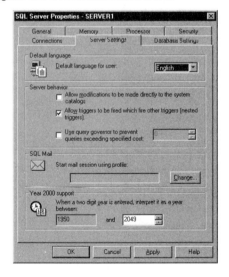

EXERCISE 2.3 (CONTINUED)

8. Choose the Database Settings tab. This allows you to set a default fill factor for indexes, a retry time for backups, and the recovery interval. Note that settings set to 0 are automatically configured by SQL Server.

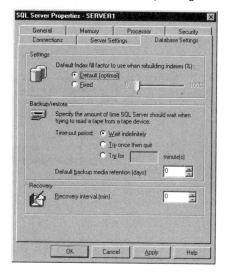

9. Choose OK to save your changes or Cancel to leave the Properties screen without saving them.

Configuring SQL Network Protocol Settings

SQL Server acts as a server separate from Windows NT and must be specifically configured to support the various protocols installed on Windows NT. Of course, protocols that are misconfigured (or not installed) in Windows NT will not work for SQL Server. In Exercise 2.4, we will configure protocols for SQL Server using the Server Network utility from the SQL Server program group.

EXERCISE 2.4

Configuring Protocols Supported by SQL Server

1. Start the Server Network utility from the SQL Server program group.

You will see a list of protocols and configurations that SQL Server currently supports.

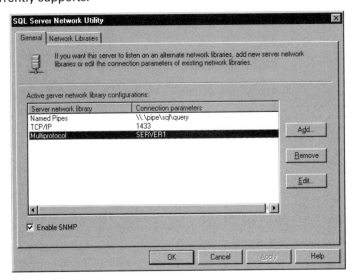

2. Add support for a new protocol by choosing Add. Pick the protocol you wish to add support for from the list, and choose OK. In our case we added support for the IPX/SPX protocol.

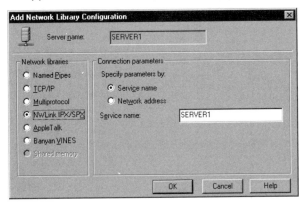

Many protocols have configurations that can be changed, such as the port for TCP/IP or the server name for IPX/SPX. You will be prompted for any changes when you add the protocol.

3. Change the properties of existing protocols by highlighting the protocol (we show TCP/IP) and choosing Edit from the main protocol screen.

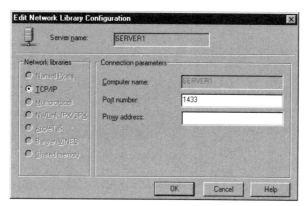

4. Choose OK, OK to save your changes when you have finished.

Configuring ANSI Settings

SQL Server 7 follows ANSI standards more closely than SQL Server 6.5 did. In SQL Server 6.5, for example, even though the ANSI standard is NULL, a column was considered NOT NULL unless you specified that the column should allow NULL data. SQL Server 7, however, allows all columns to contain NULL data unless you specify otherwise.

**Microsoft
Exam
Objective**

Configure SQL Server.

- Configure default American National Standards Institute (ANSI) settings.

Although most settings are global for SQL Server, some options are unique for each database. Database options are covered in detail in Chapter 4, *Planning, Creating, and Managing a Database in SQL Server 7*.

WARNING   If you upgrade a database from SQL Server 6.5 and leave the columns at the default (NOT NULL), the columns will allow NULL data after being converted to SQL Server 7. When creating columns and tables, you should always specifically state whether the column should allow NULL or NOT NULL. An upgrade to SQL Server 7 would then have no effect on the columns.

In Exercise 2.5, we will configure different ANSI standards for SQL Server.

EXERCISE 2.5

Changing ANSI Settings for SQL Server

1. Set the properties of SQL Server by opening Enterprise Manager, highlighting the server and choosing Tools ➤ Properties or by right-clicking and choosing Properties.

2. Go to the Connections option screen by clicking the Connections tab (see Exercise 2.3).

3. Set various options as desired. Choose OK to save your settings.

4. Set the desired database options by highlighting a database, right-clicking, and choosing Properties.

---

5. Go to the Options tab.

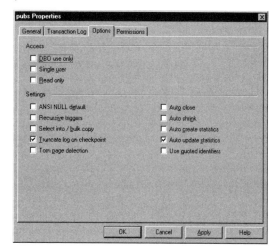

6. Set the various database options as desired. Choose OK to save your settings.

Installing SQL Server Clients

$\mathbf{S}$QL Server 7 supports various network clients, including MS-DOS, Windows 3.*x*, Windows 95/98, and Windows NT (although SQL Server only ships with 32-bit clients). Once you install the desired connectivity software, you can configure connections by using the ODBC Administrator (for ODBC connections) or the Client Network utility (for DB-Library and OLE-DB connections).

Microsoft ✓ *Exam* *Objective*

Install SQL Server 7.0.

- Install and configure a SQL Server client.

Many applications, such as Office 95/97 and IIS, install ODBC drivers for SQL Server. If client computers already have ODBC and SQL drivers installed, all you will need to do is configure the ODBC connections via the ODBC Data Sources applet of the Control Panel (see Figure 2.4).

F I G U R E 2.4

The ODBC Data
Sources applet of the
Control Panel

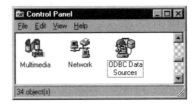

Once inside the ODBC applet you generally add one of two types of configurations:

- User DSN is usable only by the user who created it.

- System DSN is usable by any user and application contained on the computer.

When you install a SQL client you can install just the client piece (which lets the client connect to SQL Server), or you can install the SQL Server management tools (Enterprise Manager, Query Analyzer, etc.). To install the Client Connectivity software and/or the management tools, choose a Custom installation and leave only the management tools selected.

In Exercise 2.6, we will install the Client Connectivity software, and in Exercise 2.7, we will configure an ODBC connection.

EXERCISE 2.6

Installing SQL Server Client Connectivity Software

1. Start the installation by running the Setup program from the SQL Server CD-ROM.

2. Go through the steps for a normal installation, making sure you choose Custom installation (see Exercise 2.1).

3. From the Custom screen, clear all of the boxes except Client Connectivity and choose Next to install the client components.

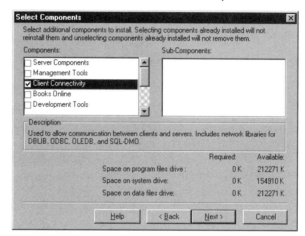

4. Select OK when the installation is complete. You may need to reboot the client if some sort of ODBC driver wasn't already installed.

Configuring an ODBC Connection

1. Start the Control Panel ➤ ODBC Data Sources applet.

2. Create a new User DSN configuration by choosing Add.

3. Select the SQL Server driver. Select Finish to continue.

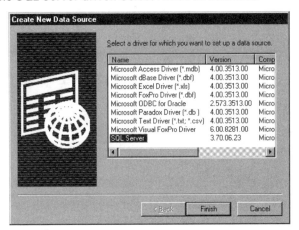

4. Enter a name for the connection and enter the name of the SQL Server. Select Next to continue.

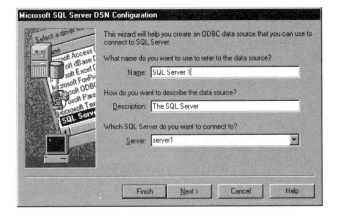

EXERCISE 2.7 (CONTINUED)

5. Enter the security information necessary to connect to the SQL Server. Select Next to continue.

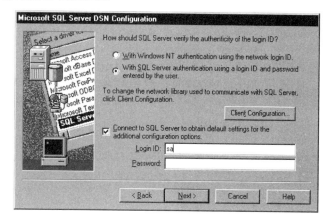

6. Select Next, Next to choose the default connection properties.

7. Select Test Data Source to test the configuration. You should get a screen similar to this.

8. Select OK, OK, OK to save the configuration and close the applet.

English Query Support

SQL Server 7 comes with English Query, an additional component that allows users to ask a question in simple English, such as "How many red cars did we sell in December?" The English Query module will convert it to an SQL query, send the query to SQL Server, and show the results.

To install English Query, simply choose it from the main SQL Server Setup screen. Configuring English Query is rather complex, however, and is beyond the scope of this book. For more information refer to the demonstration files as well as the online documentation for English Query.

OLAP Server Support

SQL Server includes an OLAP (Online Analytical Processing) server component that must be installed and configured separately. OLAP servers presummarize data to speed responses to queries running against a data warehouse. For example, an OLAP server can analyze and store sales totals based on salesperson, category of item, location of store, and day of week. Reports can easily be generated that look at data across three or more variables, such as "Show me the best salesperson for each store" or "Show me the lowest selling category for each month."

The OLAP server component is installed from the main SQL Server Setup screen. Configuring and using an OLAP server is beyond the scope of this book. Microsoft will have a separate test designed for data warehouse applications and the use of an OLAP server.

Neither English Query nor OLAP server is covered on the current Administration Exam.

Summary

SQL Server 7 is the latest generation of relational database servers from Microsoft. SQL 7 can be installed on a Windows 95/98 platform, as well as on Windows NT. Although the installations are similar, the functions that are limited to Windows NT computers (multiple CPU support, user accounts assigned to the SQL services, etc.) make the two installations different.

Before installing SQL 7 you must have the prerequisite hardware and software: at least 32MB of RAM, 70MB (minimal installation) to 160MB (typical) of hard-drive space, Service Pack 4 (if using Windows NT) and Internet Explorer 4.01 SP1.

If upgrading from SQL Server 6.5, you can choose to install 7 on top of 6.5, effectively doing a live upgrade. You can also install 7 in a different folder and switch between the two versions. Another option is to install 7 on a different server altogether. The Upgrade Wizard can be run again at any time and allows you to import 6.5 databases into 7.

Many configurations are automatically set by SQL Server 7, although you can take manual control by either using Enterprise Manager graphically, or by using the `sp_configure` stored procedure.

Clients are installed using the same Setup program that the server uses. Choose a Custom installation and deselect all the options except for the Client Connectivity components. Although many clients use ODBC to connect to SQL Server and may already have the SQL Server driver installed, you will probably have to configure the ODBC connection.

Review Questions

1. Which batch file is used to do an unattended installation?

   A. `sql70cli.bat`

   B. `sql70ful.bat`

   C. `sql70cst.bat`

   D. `sql70rem.bat`

2. If you do an unattended installation and do not specify which user account to be assigned to the SQL services, which account will be chosen?

   A. You must always specify an account to use

   B. The Administrator account

   C. The SA account

   D. The LocalSystem account

3. Which is the default folder for SQL 7?

   A. \MSSQL

   B. \MSSQL7

   C. \SQLServer

   D. \SQLServer7

4. Which is the default folder for databases in SQL 7?

   A. \DB

   B. \Devices

   C. \Data

   D. \Databases

5. In which Registry key will you find the majority of information on SQL Server 7 services?

   A. Hkey_Local_Machine\Software\SQLServer

   B. Hkey_Local_Machine\Software\Microsoft\MSSQLServer

   C. Hkey_Current_Config\Software\Microsoft\SQLServer

   D. Hkey_Current_User\Software\Microsoft\SQLServer

6. What is the default folder for error logs for SQL Server 7?

   A. \MSSQL\Errors

   B. \MSSQL\Log

C. \MSSQL7\Errors

D. \MSSQL7\Log

7. Which is the default login for SQL Server?

A. SQLAdmin

B. Administrator

C. Admin

D. SA

8. How do you change the configurations for SQL Server from within Enterprise Manager? (Select all that apply.)

A. Highlight the server, right-click, and choose Settings

B. Highlight the server, right-click, and choose Properties

C. Highlight the server and choose Tools ➣ Settings

D. Highlight the server and choose Tools ➣ Properties

9. What is the default port for TCP/IP and SQL Server?

A. 433

B. 520

C. 1020

D. 1433

10. How can you have two databases with different languages installed on the same server if you chose the English character set?

A. You can't

B. Choose a different sort order for each database

C. Choose the desired character set when you create the database

D. Choose the default Unicode character set, which allows different character sets in each database

11. How can you install SQL Server 7 so you can go back to 6.5 anytime you want? (Select all that apply.)

   A. Perform an in-place upgrade

   B. Install 7 in a different folder than 6.5

   C. Install 7 in the same folder as 6.5 and preserve your old settings

   D. Install 7 on a different server than 6.5 and upgrade the databases to SQL 7 across the wire

12. What is the name of the file that contains the initialization settings for your setup of SQL Server?

   A. setup.iss

   B. sql.iss

   C. sqlsettings.iss

   D. auto.iss

13. How can clients connect to SQL Server? (Select all that apply.)

   A. DB-Library

   B. ODBC

   C. OLE-DB

   D. SQL-DB

14. What utility is used to configure ODBC connections?

   A. ODBC Data Sources

   B. ODBC Setup

   C. ODBC Client Config utility

   D. SQL Client Config utility

15. You have your SQL Server set to a non-standard name. Which program would you use to configure the client to use the name?

   A. Enterprise Manager

   B. Server Network Utility

   C. Client Network Utility

   D. SQL Setup at the client

16. You have a SQL 6.5 Server with Service Pack 2 for SQL with 4GB of user databases on a Windows NT 3.51 Server with Service Pack 5. You have 2GB of free space. You wish to upgrade the computer in place into a SQL 7 Server. Which of the following will happen when you attempt to upgrade?

   A. The upgrade will work correctly

   B. The upgrade will not work because of a single problem

   C. The upgrade will not work because of two problems

   D. The upgrade will not work because of three problems

CHAPTER

3

SQL Server Tools and Utilities

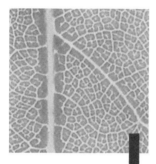

In this chapter you will examine some of the utilities that come packaged with SQL Server. Because you've already looked at many of these, we won't spend a great deal of time with them. You will also explore the SQL Enterprise Manager in more detail. The Enterprise Manager is so large and flexible that the different aspects of its management capabilities must be presented in succeeding chapters. In this chapter we will focus on creating and managing multiple servers and server groups. You will learn how to modify server options, configure SQL clients, and use the OSQL and Query Analyzer utilities. The chapter presents an overview of the Structured Query Language and discusses the SQL Profiler utility that allows you to track connections and disconnections from your SQL Server and determine which SQL scripts were run.

Although most of these utilities are not listed specifically in the objectives for the test, you will need to know what each utility does and when to use it for a given situation. The test contains many questions that require you to pick the best utility to use for a given situation, and many of the situations involve some form of troubleshooting. Troubleshooting SQL Server is also covered in Chapter 12, *Troubleshooting SQL Server 7*. You also need to know how to perform basic queries using Query Analyzer and OSQL.EXE, which will be discussed in this chapter.

The following utilities are packaged with SQL Server:

OSQL   This command-line utility provides you with an administrative interface to the SQL Server. You can run Transact-SQL (T-SQL) statements as well as stored procedures and DBCC (Database Consistency Checker) commands.

bcp   The Bulk Copy program is a command-line utility used for transferring information into and out of SQL Server.

Makepipe and Readpipe   These are command-line utilities that can be used to verify that the named-pipes protocol is working properly.

SQLSERVR   This is the actual .EXE file. You can start the SQL Server from the command line with special options that start it in troubleshooting mode.

SQLMaint   This utility can be used to create tasks that will take care of day-to-day administration of your SQL Server. This includes automating backups, updating statistics, and rebuilding indexes. Information generated here can be sent out in a report locally or to an e-mail operator.

Query Analyzer   This interactive SQL interface for Windows allows you to run all the same commands that the OSQL command line utility does. Its added advantage of being a Windows interface allows you to run multiple queries and view the results in their own separate windows.

MS Query   This utility is used to graphically create SQL statements for any ODBC-compliant data source.

SQL Client Network Utility   This utility is used to configure SQL Server clients' network libraries. It also reports on the network libraries that are in use for a particular client as well as the versions of the libraries.

SQL Enterprise Manager   This utility is used to manage nearly every aspect of one or more servers in your enterprise

SQL Performance Monitor   This captures statistical information on the performance of your SQL Server.

Books Online   An electronic version of the SQL Server manuals, this contains a fully cross-referenced search engine.

SQL Service Manager   This utility can be used to Start, Stop and Pause your SQL Server, SQL Agent, and the Distributed Transaction Coordinator

SQL Setup   The SQL Server Setup program can be used to upgrade your SQL Server or make other modifications to the system.

Profiler   This utility can be used to monitor what is being run on your SQL Server and by whom.

Enterprise Manager

Before you can manage SQL Servers in your enterprise, you must first register the servers in the SQL Enterprise Manager. In this section you will create server groups and then register SQL Servers to place into them.

Server groups are used to provide logical groupings for administrative purposes. Exercise 3.1 will take you through the steps for creating a new server group (for the Sales SQL Servers). You will then register a new SQL Server in the group.

Because Windows 95/98 does not support the server Named Pipes Net-Library, you must make sure your client is configured to use a different protocol (such as TCP/IP) so that Enterprise Manager will connect to the server. Note that because of the lack of support for Named Pipes, servers running on Windows 95/98 cannot be connected to by using the browser window—you will have to enter the name manually. Windows 95/98 clients making connections to a local (running on that computer) SQL Server use a "shared memory" net library so they can browse and see the server by name.

There are a few rules that you should be aware of before creating your servers and groups:

- Server groups can be created at the local server only. If you want the SQL Enterprise Manager running on other machines to have the same logical groups, you must go to each of those machines and repeat the same steps you did with the first server. You can get by this restriction by copying settings from a Registry of a computer that has registered servers.

- Group names must be unique at each server.

- SQL Server computer names can only be letters, numbers and these characters: _, #, $. Avoid using punctuation symbols as they have special meaning in the SQL Server environment.

EXERCISE 3.1

Using Enterprise Manager to Create Server Groups and Register to SQL Server

1. Start Enterprise Manager by going to Start ➢ Programs ➢ Microsoft SQL Server 7 ➢ Enterprise Manager.

2. Click on the + sign next to Microsoft SQL Servers to open the list of default SQL Server groups.

3. Note that there are two groups, SQL Server Group and SQL 6.5 (the SQL 6.5 group will only appear if you previously had SQL 6.5 on the computer). Click on the + sign next to SQL Server Group to open the group and get a list of the servers currently in the group. If you are running Enterprise Manager from your SQL Server, the server will automatically be a member of the group.

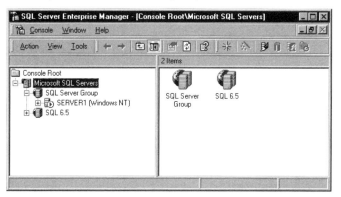

4. Create a new group called "Sales SQL Servers" by right-clicking on the Microsoft SQL Server item and choosing New SQL Server Group, or by going to the Action ➢ New SQL Server Group menu item. Choose OK after entering the name.

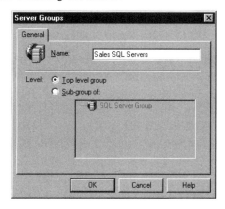

5. Register a server in the Sales SQL Servers group by highlighting the group, right-clicking, and selecting New SQL Server Registration or by choosing Action ≻ New SQL Server Registration.

6. Select the From Now On I Don't Want to Use the Wizard checkbox and choose Next.

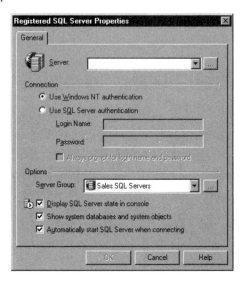

7. Enter the name of the server (SALES1) and either leave NT Authentication checked (if your NT user has sufficient rights in the SQL Server) or select Use SQL Server Authentication and enter the name and password of the account you wish to use.

8. You may want to select Show System Databases and Objects, which lets you see and manipulate the system objects using Enterprise Manager. Although this option is currently enabled by default, you should check this option when system databases and tables disappear.

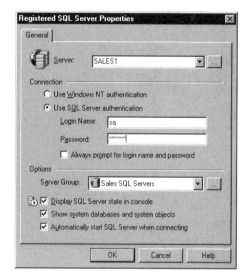

9. Select OK, and if your information is correct, the server will now be registered.

The Taskpad

Once you the server is registered, SQL Server provides various wizards and HTML help files that are very useful for the beginning user. These Wizards have been combined in a Taskpad, which is a good starting point for administering your SQL Server.

Many people do not like to use wizards. Microsoft has obliged the more experienced user by making all functions available with a right-click when in the SQL Folders (discussed below).

When you first highlight a SQL Server you will get the starting level of the Taskpad (Figure 3.1).

FIGURE 3.1

The Getting Started
Taskpad

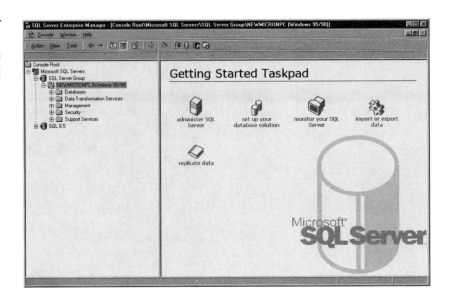

If you choose a category, specific Wizards will be shown. For example, if the Administer SQL Server task is chosen, a list of specific tasks that the Wizards can walk you through is shown (Figure 3.2).

FIGURE 3.2

The Administer SQL
Server tasks

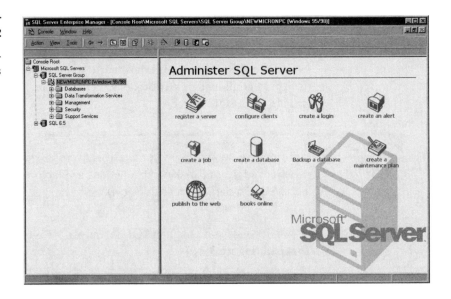

The Taskpad is especially useful for beginning administrators or for doing infrequent tasks, like creating a new stored procedure.

The main task categories, and their functions are shown below.

Administer SQL Server   Contains tasks such as registering servers; adding new users; and creating alerts, jobs, and databases as well as creating maintenance plans for existing databases.

Set up your Database Solution   Contains tasks such as creating databases, indexes, and stored procedures; restoring databases; and performing queries.

Monitor your SQL Server   Contains tasks such as creating alerts and traces, using the Profiler utility, and tuning indexes.

Import or Export Data   Contains tasks such as importing and exporting data using the Data Transformation Services.

Replicate Data   Contains tasks such as creating and managing push or pull publications and removing replication from a server.

The SQL Server Folders

Enterprise Manager allows you to "drill down" into your SQL Server in order to get quickly to the function you want to manage. By opening the subfolders listed under your server you can view and manage databases, data transformation services, the SQL Agent, backups and maintenance plans, security, and support service settings (Figure 3.3).

The various functions of Enterprise Manager will be covered in their respective chapters. For example, the Security folder and managing SQL Server security issues will be covered in detail in Chapter 5, *Security and SQL Server 7.*

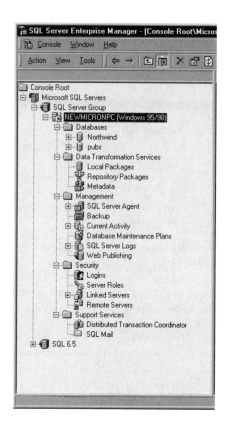

The Action Menu

The Action menu is context-sensitive to the highlighted server or folder. For example, if you highlight the Databases folder, you can choose to create, back up, or restore a database, as well as import or export data to or from a database. The Action menu items can also be called up by right-clicking when highlighting the desired folder.

The Tools Menu

The Tools menu allows you to quickly start many of the wizards and applications associated with SQL Server. For example, you can start the Query Analyzer from the Tools menu no matter where you are in Enterprise Manager.

SQL Setup Program

The SQL Setup program can be used to upgrade your SQL Server or add additional components; you will need the original CD-ROM. Choose to do a Custom Installation, and then check the additional components you wish to add (Figure 3.4).

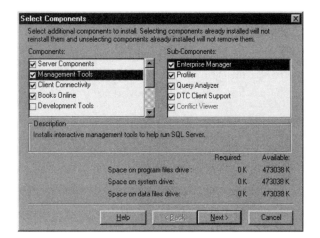

Many of the functions you had to do manually with the previous version of the Setup utility, such as changing the supported network protocols and security mode, are now done with new utility programs (such as Server Network Utility) or within Enterprise Manager.

Transact-SQL and the SQL Utilities

You use the Structured Query Language (SQL) to manipulate information stored in your database. These queries can be created and run from the OSQL or Query Analyzer utility or from program code in such external programs as Microsoft Access or Microsoft Visual Basic.

OSQL

The OSQL utility, which is accessed from the command prompt, allows you to establish a connection to the SQL Server so that you can execute T-SQL statements. OSQL is command-line driven, making it very useful for automating execution of scheduled statements; however, it is less friendly to use than a graphical interface. (Query Analyzer is a graphical front-end tool with functionality that is very similar to OSQL.)

Earlier versions of SQL Server included a similar utility called ISQL that used the DB-library to connect to SQL Server. Although ISQL still comes with SQL Server 7, OSQL is now recommended—mainly because it uses ODBC.

For a quick overview of the OSQL utility, follow the steps outlined in Exercise 3.2.

EXERCISE 3.2

The OSQL Utility

1. Go to a command prompt: Start button ➤ Programs ➤ MS-DOS.

2. From the command prompt, you must log in to a SQL Server. The command syntax is: osql /U<user id> /P<password> /S<server name>. If you do not supply a server name, you will be logged in to the local server. Remember that passwords are always case-sensitive. Type:

   osql /Usa /P

   You should now have a command prompt similar to this: 1>

3. To run a query, type it at the prompt and then execute the batch by adding the word "GO" on a line all by itself. For example, if you wanted to find out the name of your SQL Server, you could run:

   SELECT @@version
   GO

4. Your results will be similar to the following:

```
--------------------
Server1
(1 row(s) affected)
```

5. You can also run this next set of simple SELECT statements. You will quickly notice one of the major limitations of using the OSQL utility. Type in the following:

USE pubs
Go
SELECT * FROM authors
GO

6. Although you retrieved all the information from the authors' table in the pubs database, it scrolled past the top of your screen and word-wrapped in such a way that it made it difficult to read. For this reason, you will find the Query Analyzer utility to be much more useful.

7. To exit the OSQL utility and return to a command prompt, type in:

Exit

8. To exit the command prompt, type in again:

Exit

Query Analyzer

You can run all the same queries in the Query Analyzer interface as you can in OSQL. The Query Analyzer interface has the advantage of being an MDI (multiple-document interface). This allows you to run multiple queries in separate windows and then view the results in a separate window as well. The results window is especially advantageous in presenting all results in a single window. This allows you to scroll through the results and use the cut, copy and paste features as desired. Another of the many features of the Query Analyzer interface is the ability to retrieve and store SQL scripts.

Because Windows 95/98 does not support the server Named Pipes Net-Library, you must make sure your client is configured to use a different protocol (such as TCP/IP) so that Query Analyzer will connect to the remote SQL Servers. If you are connecting to a local server, this is not an issue.

There are two ways to open up the Query Analyzer utility. The first method is to start it as a stand-alone utility. This is done by clicking on Start button ➤ Programs ➤ Microsoft SQL Server 7➤ Query Analyzer. Using this method, you will be asked to provide a server name, login ID and password (Figure 3.5).

F I G U R E 3.5

The Query Analyzer login screen

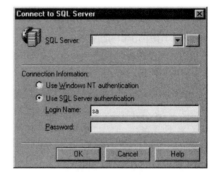

The second method is to enter through the SQL Enterprise Manager and choose the SQL Query Analyzer from the Tools menu. When you enter this way, there is no login screen: you are already logged in to a SQL Server. You can type your SQL statements directly into the Query panel (Figure 3.6).

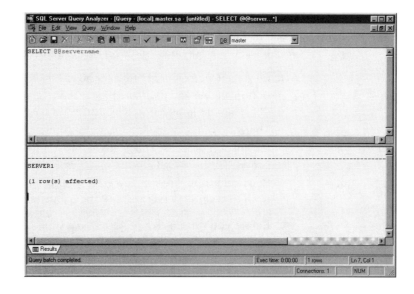

FIGURE 3.6

The Query Analyzer
window

Let's take a look at the different options available in the Query Analyzer utility. Exercise 3.3 will walk you through the use of the utility.

EXERCISE 3.3

The Query Analyzer Utility

The Create New Query button allows you to create a new query. It will open a new window for the query and a new connection to the SQL Server.

1. Start the Query Analyzer tool either from the Start button ➤ Programs ➤ Microsoft SQL Server 7 ➤ Query Analyzer (and log in), or from within the SQL Enterprise Manager ➤ Tools menu ➤ SQL Query Analyzer.

2. In the Query panel, enter the following:

   SELECT @@servername

3. Click the green arrow or press Ctrl+E or F5.

4. The query will execute and should give you the results in the Results panel (see Figure 3.6).

5. Click the New Query button. You will notice that you are now working in a new window. Now enter and execute the following query:

   SELECT @@version

6. The Results panel should show your current version. You can switch back to the previous windows by using the Windows menu.

7. Click the Open Query button (or go to File ➤ Open). The Open Query button allows you to browse for SQL scripts that you have saved. These are generally stored as ASCII text files with an .SQL extension. There are many prebuilt .SQL scripts that are used by the SQL Server Installation process. These are stored in the \MSSQL7\Install folder. Browse to the \MSSQL7\Install folder. From there, select the Inst-Pubs.sql script. You will now have a fairly extensive SQL script that is used to create/re-create your Pubs database.

8. Before you run this script, let's make sure that we can see some statistics as they are generated. Go to Query ➤ Current Connection Options and select Show Stats Time and Show Stats I/O (shown below).

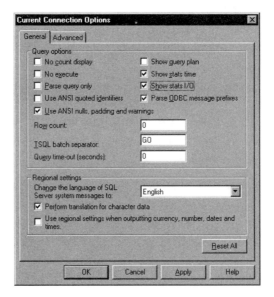

9. Execute the Query. This can take from half a minute to several minutes to run, depending on the hardware. If you look in the Current Query listbox, the world will be spinning while the query is running. You can stop this processing query by clicking the Stop button (the red square) next to the green arrow.

10. When the query has finished executing, click on the Messages tab. You will see the statistics generated during the running of this query.

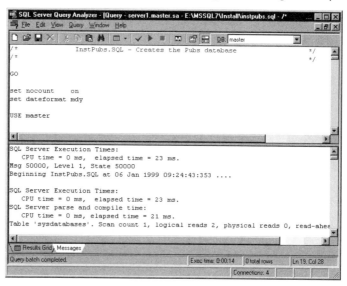

11. If you would like to review the results or even rerun an earlier query, simply select that query from the Windows menu. You can look at the saved result set by clicking on the Result panel, or you can reexecute the query and view the new results (which in this case will be the same as before).

The Save button allows you to save the current query as an .SQL (the default extension) ASCII text file. You can delete a query from the Current Query listbox by clicking on the Delete Query button. The Query Options button will allow you to modify the query options. These options are beyond the scope of this book; for more information, see the SQL Server Books Online.

So far you have been working with the master database. In this next example, you will learn two ways of switching to a different database and then running a query.

12. Start a new query. In the query window, type in the following query:

USE pubs
SELECT * FROM authors

13. Run this query. You will notice that the current database has been switched to pubs and the result set should look similar to this next window.

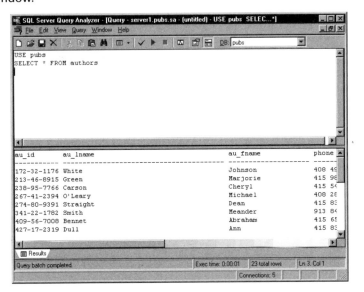

14. You could have run this query a bit differently. Open a new query.

15. In the Current Database listbox, select the pubs database.

16. Run the following query:

SELECT * FROM authors

17. You will get the same result set.

18. When you are finished, close the SQL Query Analyzer.

Simple *SELECT* Statements

Although the SELECT statement is not directly tested on the MCSE exam, being able to read simple SELECT statements and understand their functions will be helpful not only as you take the exam, but in your work as an administrator as well.

The SELECT statement can be used to retrieve specific rows and columns of information from one or more tables in one or more databases. There are three basic components to every SELECT statement: SELECT, FROM, and WHERE. Although the T-SQL utility is not case-sensitive when you are using SQL statements, we will present the SQL keywords here in upper case.

The syntax for a simple SELECT statement is:

```
SELECT <column_list>
FROM <table(s)>
WHERE <search_criteria>
```

One of the simplest SELECT statements is to select all columns from a single table. You use the *operator to do this. For example:

```
SELECT *
FROM authors
```

This will select all columns and all rows from the authors table and would look like this:

au_id	au_lname	au_fname	phone
172-32-1176	White	Johnson	408 496-7223
213-46-8915	Green	Marjorie	415 986-7020
238-95-7766	Carson	Cheryl	415 548-7723
267-41-2394	O'Leary	Michael	408 286-2428
274-80-9391	Straight	Dean	415 834-2919
341-22-1782	Smith	Meander	913 843-0462
409-56-7008	Bennet	Abraham	415 658-9932
427-17-2319	Dull	Ann	415 836-7128
472-27-2349	Gringlesby	Burt	707 938-6445
486-29-1786	Locksley	Charlene	415 585-4620

au_id	au_lname	au_fname	phone
527-72-3246	Greene	Morningstar	615 297-2723
648-92-1872	Blotchet	Reginald	503 745-6402
672-71-3249	Yokomoto	Akiko	415 935-4228
712-45-1867	delCastillo	Innes	615 996-8275
722-51-5454	DeFrance	Michel	219 547-9982
724-08-9931	Stringer	Dirk	415 843-2991
724-80-9391	MacFeather	Stearns	415 354-7128
756-30-7391	Karsen	Livia	415 534-9219
807-91-6654	Panteley	Sylvia	301 946-8853
846-92-7186	Hunter	Sheryl	415 836-7128
893-72-1158	McBadden	Heather	707 448-4982
899-46-2035	Ringer	Anne	801 826-0752
998-72-3567	Ringer	Albert	801 826-0752

(23 row(s) affected)

You can specify individual columns in the column list parameter. This is sometimes called vertical partitioning because you are selecting only certain columns. For example, if you wanted to get only the authors' last names and first names, you could run this query:

```
SELECT au_lname, au_fname
FROM authors
```

The result set would look like this:

au_lname	au_fname
---------------	---------------
White	Johnson
Green	Marjorie
Carson	Cheryl
O'Leary	Michael
...	...

```
Panteley          Sylvia

Hunter            Sheryl

McBadden          Heather

Ringer            Anne

Ringer            Albert

(23 row(s) affected)
```

You can also specify search criteria by using the WHERE clause. The WHERE clause is used to discriminate between rows of information. This is also known as horizontal partitioning, because you are selecting only certain rows of information. For example, if you wanted to get information on all authors whose last names begin with the letter *M* you could run this query:

```
SELECT *
FROM authors
WHERE au_lname LIKE 'M%'
```

```
au_id          au_lname        au_fname        phone

----------     ------------    ------------    -----------
               ---             --
724-80-9391    MacFeather      Stearns         415 354-7128

893-72-1158    McBadden        Heather         707 448-4982
```

```
(2 row(s) affected)
```

For more complex queries, you can join information from two or more tables and then extract the results. For example, to find out which authors publish which titles, you would need to join the authors table, titleauthor table, and titles table and then display results based on a matching title_id between the authors and titles table on a join table called titleauthor. For example:

```
SELECT authors.au_lname, authors.au_fname, titles.title
FROM authors, titleauthor, titles
WHERE titleauthor.au_id = authors.au_id
AND titles.title_id = titleauthor.title_id
```

Your results would look like the following:

au_lname	au_fname	title
Green	Marjorie	The Busy Executive's Database Guide
Bennet	Abraham	The Busy Executive's Database Guide
O'Leary	Michael	Cooking with Computers: Surreptitious Balance Sheets
MacFeather	Stearns	Cooking with Computers: Surreptitious Balance Sheets
Green	Marjorie	You Can Combat Computer Stress!
Straight	Dean	Straight Talk About Computers
Del Castillo	Innes	Silicon Valley Gastronomic Treats
DeFrance	Michel	The Gourmet Microwave
Ringer	Anne	The Gourmet Microwave
...	...	...
O'Leary	Michael	Sushi, Anyone?
Gringlesby	Burt	Sushi, Anyone?
Yokomoto	Akiko	Sushi, Anyone?

```
(25 row(s) affected)
```

You can also order your result sets in either ascending (default) or descending order. For example, if you wanted to list some author information in descending order by last name, you could run this query:

```
SELECT au_fname, au_lname
FROM authors
ORDER BY au_lname DESC
```

Your results would look like this table:

au_fname	au_lname
Akiko	Yokomoto
Johnson	White
Dirk	Stringer
Dean	Straight
...	...
Cheryl	Carson
Reginald	Blotchet-Halls
Abraham	Bennet

(23 row(s) affected)

MSQuery

You can also create queries using the MSQuery tool, which comes with Office 97 and many other applications. One of the nice features of the MSQuery tool is that you can visually create your queries and then cut and paste the SQL statements into your programs or into Query Analyzer. You simply add the tables you wish to work with and then drag and drop the fields you want into the lower panel. You can also paste the result into applications such as Word or Excel.

In order to use MSQuery you must have already set up an ODBC source. See Chapter 2, *Installing, Upgrading, and Configuring SQL Server 7,* for more details on configuring ODBC.

Exercise 3.4 will give you a general overview of how the MSQuery tool works.

EXERCISE 3.4

Using the MSQuery Tool

1. Start the MSQuery tool. If it is not installed run the Office Setup program and install it from there.

2. From the File menu, choose New Query. You will now be asked to provide a data source.

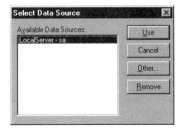

3. Use the LocalServer and add **sa** to your login id.

4. Click the Use button.

5. A password screen will now be displayed. Add your password and click OK to continue. You will now see the Add Table dialog box.

6. In the database listbox, switch from master to pubs. You will now see the tables in the pubs database.

7. Select the authors table and then click the Add button. This will add the table to the top panel for use in this query.

8. Add the titleauthor and titles tables.

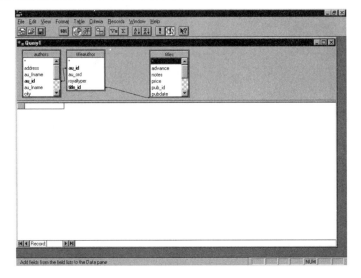

EXERCISE 3.4 (CONTINUED)

9. Click the Close button to close the Add Table dialog box.

10. Drag and drop the au_fname field from the authors table to the lower panel.

11. Do the same for the title field from the titles table.

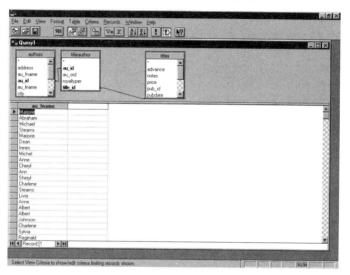

12. You can now view the actual SQL statement that has been created by clicking on the SQL button on the toolbar.

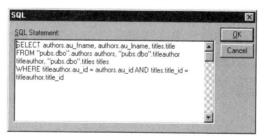

You can now cut and paste this SQL query into other applications like Visual Basic or the T-SQL utility. Although this was a relatively simple query, you can build extremely complex queries using the MSQuery tool.

The SQL Profiler Utility

The SQL Profiler utility can be used to track logins and logouts to your SQL Server, as well as track individual T-SQL commands; it will be discussed in detail in Chapter 10, *Monitoring and Optimizing SQL Server 7.*

Performance Monitor

You can get up-to-the-second information about the performance of your SQL Server through the SQL Performance Monitor. Using the Windows NT Performance Monitor to look at SQL Server will be covered in detail in Chapter 10.

Stored Procedures

Stored procedures are precompiled SQL statements that are stored on the SQL Server itself. There are three types of stored procedures:

- System stored procedures that are shipped with SQL Server and are denoted with an `sp_` prefix

- User-defined stored procedures, which can be can be registered with the system only by the system administrator

- Extended stored procedures, which work outside the context of SQL Server and are generally prefixed with an `xp_`

Because stored procedures are precompiled, they run more quickly and efficiently than regular queries do. The compiler doesn't have to determine how to run a stored procedure. The work order, or blueprint, is saved with the stored procedure, and all SQL Server has to do is load the information and run it.

You can run stored procedures from the T-SQL utilities. For example if you wanted to find out information about all databases you could run the following query:

```
EXEC sp_helpdb
```

```
master   9.25 MB    sa      1      Sep 26 1998   trunc. log on chkpt.
model    1.50 MB    sa      3      Dec  6 1998   select into/bulkcopy,
                                                 trunc. log
```

msdb		sa	4	Dec 6 1998	select into/bulkcopy, trunc. log
Northwind 3.94 MB		sa	6	Dec 6 1998	select into/bulkcopy, trunc. log
pubs		sa	5	Jan 6 1999	select into/bulkcopy, trunc. log
tempdb	8.50 MB	sa	2	Jan 5 1999	select into/bulkcopy, trunc. log

Installing an Extended Stored Procedure

Extended stored procedures are generally created in C or C++ and then compiled into a DLL file. You should then place the DLL in the same folder as the other SQL DLL files. Once you have done this, you can execute the `sp_addextendedproc`. This will register the procedure with the function and name of the DLL. The information will be stored in the syscomments and sysobjects tables as an extended stored procedure with *x* as the object type. You must do this for each extended procedure defined in the DLL. For example, if you have an extended procedure DLL, `FROGGER.DLL`, that has a function called `Leap` in it, you would execute the following stored procedure to register and install it:

```
EXEC sp_addextendedproc 'Leap', 'Frogger.dll'
```

DBCC Commands

DBCC commands are used to check the logical and physical consistency of your databases but are generally not used to fix the problems. Use stored procedures and SQL statements to resolve the problems reported.

As an administrator, you should become familiar with the DBCC commands. The following are a few that you should definitely be familiar with:

DBCC CheckCatalog   This will check for consistency between system tables.

DBCC CheckDB   This will check all tables in a database to see that index pages are correctly linked to their data pages. It will also make sure that the indexes are in sorted order and that the information on each page is reasonable.

DBCC CheckAlloc This makes sure that all pages in a database are correctly allocated and used.

DBCC SQLPerf(LogSpace) This will report on the currently used amount of transaction log space, expressed as a percentage.

DBCC SQLPerf(LRUStats) This will report on how your procedure and data caches are being used.

DBCC CheckFilegroup This will check all the tables held on a specific file group for damage.

Reading through and practicing the DBCC commands will allow you to diagnose problems with your SQL Server more quickly and efficiently and to optimize the system.

Client/Server Network Utilities

Each client can run the Client Network utility (see Chapter 2) to change the type of network connections used to connect to SQL Server. Two other utilities, MAKEPIPE and READPIPE, can be used for checking network connections.

Makepipe and Readpipe are almost always used together and are especially useful for tracking down network or security problems. The Makepipe utility is used at the server to make a temporary pipe, or network slot, while the Readpipe utility is used at the client end to attempt to connect to the server. If the connection is successful, the network and the associated protocols are OK. Note that neither Windows NT nor SQL Server security is used by the utilities, which is helpful when diagnosing security-related problems.

SQL Server uses Named Pipes, which is one method of communication between computers across a network.

Check your remote connection to SQL Server over Named Pipes by using the Makepipe and Readpipe utilities. Exercise 3.5 shows you how to use these utilities.

EXERCISE 3.5

Testing Named Pipes

1. To test Named Pipes, you will need a client and a server. On the server, go to a command prompt by selecting Start ➢ Programs ➢ MS-DOS.

2. At the command prompt, enter **makepipe**.

3. You should now see:

```
Making PIPE:\\.\pipe\abc
read to write delay <seconds>:0
Waiting for client to connect. . .
```

The server is waiting for a client to try to use the named pipe.

4. From a client machine, enter the following:

readpipe /S<*servername*> /D<*string*>

If your server's name is Gizmo and you want to send the message testing123 to the named pipe, enter:

readpipe /Sgizmo /Dtesting123

5. You should get something like this in response on the client machine:

```
SvrName:\\Gizmo
```

```
PIPE: :\\Gizmo\pipe\abc
DATA: :testing123
Data Sent: 1 testing123
Data Read: 1 testing123
```

6. On the server machine, you should see something like this:

```
Waiting for client to send . . . 1
Data Read:
Testing123
Waiting for client to send . . . 2
Pipe closed
Waiting for client to connect. . .
```

7. To close the pipe, close the Command Prompt window.

If this completes successfully, then you know that the Named Pipes protocol is working. If it doesn't work, you may need to look for other problems. For example, we would verify network connectivity by running a NET VIEW statement from a command prompt, or by double-clicking on the Entire Network icon in the Network Neighborhood. If something other than the computer shows up there, we know we can see the rest of the network.

If Named Pipes comes up successfully, but you still cannot connect, you probably have a DB-Library problem. You should verify that you have the same network library and DB-Library on both the server and the client computer. This can be done with the Setup program or with the Client Network utility as shown in Chapter 2.

The NT Event Viewer

The NT Event Viewer can be used to track SQL Server events and errors as well as the NT Application log. The disadvantage to SQL Server administrators of using this is that it logs not only SQL Server events, but also events from other applications running in Windows NT.

Each event is labeled with the level of its severity: informational, warning, or error. You can use the time stamp, severity, and source of the error to help determine whether it might have had an impact on your SQL Server. Exercise 3.6 will walk you through the use of the NT Event Viewer.

EXERCISE 3.6

Troubleshooting SQL Server with the NT Event Viewer

1. Navigate to the NT Event Viewer. Start Button ➢ Programs ➢ Administrative Tools ➢ NT Event Viewer.

2. The default log to be viewed is the System log. To change this to the Application log, choose Log ➢ Application.

3. If you see any red stop signs with a source of SQLAgent or MSSQLServer, double-click those items for more information.

Full-Text Search Service

SQL Server 7 includes a modified Index Server engine that allows you to index and search entire character and text fields.

Microsoft
Exam
Objective

Implement full-text searching.

Using full-text searches requires several initial steps:

1. Do a custom installation of SQL Server making sure to select the Full-Text Search Engine, which is not installed by default.

2. Create a Full-Text catalog. You will need to create the catalogs for the search engine using either Enterprise Manager or the `sp_fulltext_catalog` stored procedure.

3. Enable the Full-Text Search Engine by creating an index that will be contained in a catalog. Note that while a catalog can contain multiple indexes, a Full-Text index must always belong to a single catalog. Each database needs to be enabled to use the search engine. This can be done by using Enterprise Manager or the stored procedure `sp_fulltext_database`.

4. Select which columns you wish to be indexed by using Enterprise Manager or the `sp_fulltext_column` stored procedure.

5. Periodically update the indexes (*repopulate*). Full-Text indexes are not automatically updated when you add, change, or delete rows and need to be periodically updated. This can be done using Enterprise Manager or the `sp_fulltext_catalog` stored procedure. Note that tables containing a timestamp column can do incremental repopulations, while tables that do not contain a timestamp column will do full repopulations.

6. Back up the catalog files occasionally. Catalog files, which contain the Full-Text indexes, are stored as separate files; by default, they are not backed up when the database is backed up.

7. Periodically monitor the size of the catalogs by using Performance Monitor or by checking the size of the files using Explorer or My Computer.

Full-Text Search capabilities are not included with the Desktop version of SQL Server.

In Exercise 3.7 we will enable the Full-Text Search Service, create an index, select some columns to be indexed, and run a query.

EXERCISE 3.7

Enabling Full-Text Searches

1. Run the Setup program and ensure that the Full-Text Search engine is selected as shown below. Exit the Setup program when finished.

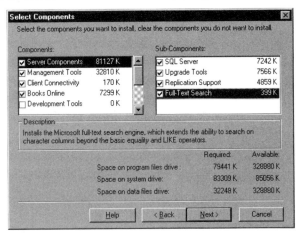

2. Start Enterprise Manager.

3. Highlight the pubs database and go to Tools ➤ Full-Text Indexing. This will start the Full-Text Indexing Wizard. Choose Next to proceed.

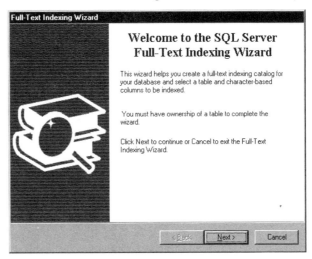

4. Select the Pubs database and choose Next.

5. Select the authors table and choose Next.

6. Select the default index and choose Next.

7. Select the au_fname, au_lname, address and city columns to be indexed.

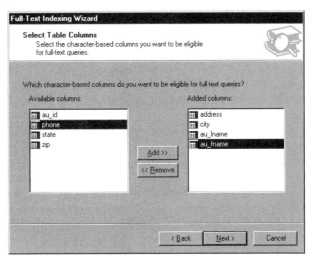

8. Create a new catalog (index) for the searches by entering a name for the new catalog. Note that if you had already created a catalog you could have chosen either to use a previous catalog or to create a new one. Choose Next when finished.

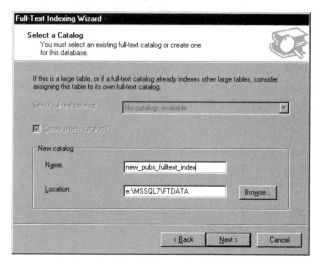

9. Schedule the catalog for periodic updates by selecting the New Schedule button and entering a name and schedule. Note that we have made the update recurring every week on Sunday at 12:00 A.M.

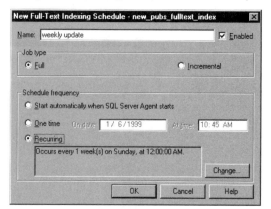

10. Choose OK and Next to save the schedule and go to the summary page.

EXERCISE 3.7 (CONTINUED)

11. Choose Finish to create the index. You should now see a note that the Wizard completed successfully. Note that the catalog will not be populated until it is updated manually or as scheduled.

12. Choose OK to close the screen.

13. To populate the index go to the Pubs database, highlight the Full-Text Catalogs folder, right-click, and choose Repopulate All Catalogs.

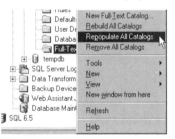

Summary

This chapter explored many of the utilities used for administering SQL Server and offered an overview of the T-SQL language. The chapter began with a look at implementing and managing multiple SQL Servers in different Server Groups, including creating Server Groups as well as registering new servers in the enterprise.

The SQL Setup utility can be used to add new components to SQL Server and to upgrade an earlier version of SQL Server.

Using the OSQL and Query Analyzer utilities requires a valid login ID and password. For the command-line version, remember that both the switches and password are case–sensitive.

The T-SQL utility is a very robust application that you will use extensively in SQL administration.

The T-SQL and OSQL section discussed the SELECT statement, the vertical and horizontal partitioning of tables, sorting the result set in either an ascending or descending fashion, and how to perform a simple query with multiple tables. The MSQuery tool, which is generally more useful to developers than to administrators, can be extremely helpful in learning some of the T-SQL language constructs.

There are many stored procedures in SQL Server. You can get help on the individual parameters these stored procedures require by running: `sp_help <procedure name>`. This section also discussed extended stored procedures and how to register them properly with SQL Server. The DBCC commands generally comment on the database itself, rather than making any changes to the database. These DBCC commands can be used to report on the current amount of log space being used, the consistency of the indexes, and many other things. All these statements can be run from the OSQL utilities.

Finally, the chapter explained how to install and configure the Full-Text Search Engine and create and update new indexes.

Review Questions

1. You have created a Full-Text index on a table with a timestamp column. What would you schedule on a regular basis to keep the index up-to-date?

    A. Rebuilds of the index

    B. Full repopulation of the index

    C. Incremental repopulation of the index

    D. Refreshes of the index

2. The SQL Client Network utility can be used to do which of the following? (Select all that apply.)

    A. Configure network libraries

    B. Add database libraries

C. Configure languages

D. Rebuild the Master database

3. Which of the following will start the OSQL command line utility and log you in?

A. `osql /Login sa /Pwd *****`

B. `osql /Lsa /S`

C. `osql /Usa /P`

D. `sqlservr /Usa /P`

4. You can specify the database you wish to work with in the Query Analyzer utility in which of the following ways? (Select all that apply.)

A. Use the `USE <databasename>` command in your SQL script

B. Click on the databases listbox and select your database

C. Just run the command; it will know which database you want to use

D. Drag and drop the database you wish to work with onto the window

5. `SELECT Employee.FirstName, Employee.LastName, WorkInfo .YearsExp FROM Employees, WorkInfo WHERE Employee.EmpID = WorkInfo.EmpID`. What does this T-SQL script do?

A. Displays all information in an employee record and all associated work information

B. Displays first name and last name in an employee record; if they have work experience, it will display that too

C. Displays all employees' first names and last names and their work experience where there are records that have a matching employee ID in the WorkInfo table

D. Displays all employees' first names and last names and their work experience whether or not they have a matching employee ID in the WorkInfo table

6. What are the benefits of stored procedures? (Select all that apply.)

   A. They are precompiled and therefore run more efficiently than normal queries

   B. They can be used in T-SQL batches

   C. They are not precompiled and therefore run more efficiently than normal queries as the optimizer can look at the current conditions and make the necessary optimizations real-time

   D. They are not used in T-SQL batches

7. Who can register an extended stored procedure?

   A. The SA

   B. Any DBO

   C. Any user

   D. The sysadmin role

8. How is Full-Text searching installed?

   A. By default

   B. By doing a Custom installation

   C. By doing a global installation and then enabling it table by table

   D. By doing a global installation and then enabling it database by database

9. SQL Server error messages can be viewed in the SQL Error log and which NT application?

   A. NT Performance Monitor

   B. NT Control Panel\Network

   C. NT Network Monitor

   D. NT Event Viewer

10. When do Full-Text Search indexes get updated?

   A. Never; you have to drop and rebuild the index

   B. Whenever you add or modify a row

   C. Whenever you schedule it to happen

   D. Whenever you trigger it manually

11. You have four SQL Servers in the same domain: Server1 is SQL 6.5 running on Windows NT Workstation, Server2 is SQL 7 running on Windows 98, Server3 is SQL 7 running on Windows NT Workstation, and Server4 is SQL 7 running on Windows NT Server. Which of these can you see in the browser window of the Query Analyzer? (Select all that apply.)

   A. Server1

   B. Server2

   C. Server3

   D. Server4

12. You have a database called Sales with a table called SalesTD. Which of these commands will perform a query on the table no matter which database you run it from?

   A. `Select all from SalesTD`

   B. `Select * from SalesTD`

   C. `Select * from Sales (SalesTD)`

   D. `Select * from Sales..SalesTD`

13. You have created a Full-Text index on a memo field that contains information about your clients. You add five clients on Tuesday, adding their occupation in the memo field. You notice that two of the new clients are dentists. On Wednesday you hurt your tooth and search for your clients that are dentists (using den*) but they don't show up. What is the probable cause?

A. You didn't specify occupation when you built the index

B. You built the index on the wrong column

C. The index hasn't been updated since the new clients were added

D. You misentered their occupation

14. You register your server and want to check on some system stored procedures but the Master database does not show up in the database folder. Why is that happening?

A. You are looking at SQL 7 running on Windows 95/98

B. You need to edit your registration properties to display system data

C. You need to edit your registration properties to connect with SA rights

D. The master database is not listed with other databases—it is listed in the Configuration folder

15. What is the best way to monitor the size of Full-Text catalogs?

A. Use Query Analyzer to run sp_catalog_size occasionally

B. Use Performance Monitor to watch the size of the catalog

C. Create a job that emails results from sp_fulltext_catalog

D. Create a job that emails results from sp_catalog_size

CHAPTER

4

Planning, Creating, and Managing a
Database in SQL Server 7

SQL Server 7 uses two types of files to store your database information: one or more database files and one or more transaction log files. As an administrator it is your responsibility to create and maintain these files. As part of your role as a database creator, you must decide how large to make these database files and what type of growth characteristics they should have as well as their physical placement on your system.

Microsoft
✓ *Exam*
Objective

Develop a SQL Server capacity plan.

- Plan the physical placement of files, including data files and transaction log files.
- Plan the use of filegroups.
- Plan for growth over time.
- Plan the physical hardware system.
- Assess communication requirements.

This chapter will examine these topics in more detail, first covering some planning issues then looking at how to create a database and transaction log. We will then learn how to manage these database objects by altering their various configuration options as well as by removing them from the SQL Server. The chapter also discusses database filegroups, which are used for optimization purposes in smaller systems and as an essential management concept in VLDBs (very large databases).

Database Planning Considerations

Database planning requires you to consider both the size and the physical location of your database files. To make an informed decision about these items, it is helpful to understand how memory is allocated in SQL Server. In this section, we will talk about how your database is created, where you should place the database, and the different internal memory management structures.

Database Files

In SQL Server 7, a new user database is really a copy of the Model database. Everything in the Model database will show up in your newly created database. Once the copy of the database has been made, it is expanded to the requested size. When you create a database in SQL Server 7, you must specify at least one file to store the data and hold your system tables and another file to hold the transaction log.

Microsoft
Exam
Objective

Develop a SQL Server capacity plan.

- Plan the physical hardware system.
- Assess communication requirements.

Database files have a default extension of .MDF. The transaction log is stored in one or more files, with a default .LDF extension. If you create a database that spans multiple database files, the additional database files have a default filename extension of .NDF. Additional transaction log files, however, don't change their extensions. There are several important things to remember about your data and log files:

- All data and log files that a particular SQL Server manages must reside on that SQL Server machine.
- Only one database is allowed per data file, but a single database can span multiple data files.

- Transaction logs must reside on their own file; they can also span multiple log files.

- Database files fill up their available space by *striping* across all data files in the filegroup. In this manner, you can eliminate hot spots and reduce contention in high volume OLTP (Online Transaction Processing) environments.

- Transaction log files do not use striping but fill each log file to capacity before continuing on to the next log file.

- When you create a database and don't specify a transaction log size, the transaction log will be resized to 25% of the size of your data files.

It is suggested that you place your transaction logs on separate physical hard drives. In this manner, you can recover your data up to the second in the event of a media failure.

When you create a database, you are allocating hard-disk space for both the data and the transaction log. Your data files can be stored in a variety of methods, depending on your hardware and software.

Database File Placement

Placing database files in the appropriate location is highly dependent on the available hardware and software. There are very few hard-and-fast rules when it comes to databases. In fact, the only definite rule is that of design. The more thoroughly you plan and design your system, the less work it will be later. Developing a capacity plan is no different.

There are several issues to keep in mind when you are attempting to decide where to place your database files. This includes planning for growth, communication, fault-tolerance, reliability, and speed.

Among the several measures you can take to ensure the reliability and consistency of your database—each with its own features and drawbacks—are the different levels of RAID (Redundant Array of Inexpensive Disks).

RAID 0 RAID 0 uses disk striping; that is, it writes data across multiple hard-disk partitions in what is called a *stripe set*. This can greatly improve speed as multiple hard disks are working at the same time. RAID 0 can be implemented through the use of Windows NT software or on third-party hardware. While RAID 0 gives you the best speed, it does not provide any fault-tolerance. If one of the hard disks in the stripe set is damaged, you lose all of your data.

RAID 1   RAID 1 uses disk mirroring. Disk mirroring actually writes your information to disk twice—once to the primary file, and once to the mirror. This gives you excellent fault-tolerance, but it is fairly slow, as you must write to disk twice. Windows NT includes the ability to mirror your hard disks. RAID 1 requires only a single hard-disk controller.

RAID 5   RAID 5—*striping with parity*—writes data to hard disk in stripe sets. Parity checksums will be written across all disks in the stripe set. This gives you excellent fault-tolerance as well as excellent speed with a reasonable amount of overhead. The parity checksums can be used to recreate information lost if a single disk in the stripe set fails. If more than one disk in the strip set fails, however, you will lose all your data. Although Windows NT supports RAID 5 in a software implementation, a hardware implementation is faster and more reliable, and we suggest that you use it if you can afford it.

RAID 10   RAID 10 (sometimes referred to as RAID 0 + 1) is the big daddy. This level of RAID should be used in mission-critical systems that require 24 hours a day, 7 days a week uptime and the fastest possible access. RAID 10 implements striping with parity as in RAID 5 and then mirrors the stripe sets. You still have excellent speed and excellent fault-tolerance, but you also have the added expense of using more than twice the disk space of RAID 1. Then again, we are talking about a situation that can afford no SQL Server downtime.

The other issue you need to keep in mind when working with databases is communication. SQL Server can only have database files on what it deems a local hard disk. Your local hard disks can be on your local machine, or on a hardware device that is connected directly to the SQL Server machine (like a hardware RAID array). Although you have this limitation with your active database files, this rule does not apply to your backups. Backups can be placed anywhere in your enterprise, including a named pipe, local hard disks, networked hard disks, and tape.

Microsoft suggests a combination of RAID 5 and RAID 1. In their scenario, you place your data files on the RAID 5 array for speed and redundancy. You place your transaction log files on the RAID 1 drives so that they can be mirrored.

Data Storage Structures

There are two main types of storage structures in SQL Server 7: extents and data pages.

Extents

An extent is a block of eight pages totaling 64KB in size. Because the extent is the basic unit of allocation for tables and indexes and all objects are saved in a table of some kind, all objects are stored in extents.

When a table or an index needs additional storage space, another extent is allocated to that object. A new extent will generally not be allocated for a table or index until all pages on that extent have been used. This process of allocating extents rather than individual pages to objects serves two useful purposes.

First, the time-consuming process of allocation is done in one batch rather than forcing each allocation to occur whenever a new page is needed. Second, it forces the pages allocated to an object to be at least somewhat contiguous. If pages were allocated directly, on an as-needed basis, the likelihood is quite high that pages allocated to different objects would be next to each other in physical order. This arrangement would have a significant negative impact on performance. When pages for a single object are contiguous, reads and writes can occur much more quickly.

Pages

At the most fundamental level, everything in SQL Server is stored on an 8KB page. The page is the one common denominator for all objects in SQL Server. There are many different types of pages, but every page has some factors in common. Pages are always 8KB in size and always have a header, leaving about 8060 bytes of usable space on every page.

There are five primary types of pages in SQL Server:

- **Data Pages** Data pages hold the actual database records. Although 8060 bytes are free for use on a data page, records are limited in length to no more than 8060 bytes.

- **Index Pages** Index pages store the index keys and levels making up the entire index tree. Unlike data pages, there is no limit to the total number of entries that can be made on an index page.

- **Text/Image Pages** Text and Image pages hold the actual data associated with text, ntext, and image datatypes. When a text field is saved, the record will contain a 16-byte pointer to a linked list of text pages that hold the actual text data. Only the 16-byte pointer inside the record is counted against the 8000-byte record-size limit.

The page is the smallest unit of I/O in SQL Server. Every time data is either read from or written to a database, this occurs in page units. Most of the time this reading and writing is actually going back and forth between data cache and disk. Data cache is divided into 8KB buffers, intended solely for the purpose of holding 8KB pages. This is an important part of database capacity planning.

Estimating Storage Requirements

All storage space in SQL Server is preallocated. Databases can be both expanded and contracted. This used to pose an interesting dilemma for database administrators. How large should your databases be? They need to be large enough to accommodate your data needs without excessive expansion, yet making them too large will simply waste space. When estimating storage requirements, we must go to the basic level of data storage, the table and the index. Let's look at how storage space can be estimated by using these objects.

Estimating Table Storage Requirements

Tables are really nothing more than templates specifying how data is to be stored. All data stored in a table must adhere to a datatype. You can follow a specific process to estimate the space required by a table.

1. Calculate the space used by a single row of the table.

2. Calculate the number of rows that will fit on one page.

3. Estimate the number of rows the table will hold.

4. Calculate the total number of pages that will be required to hold these rows.

Calculating Row Size

Datatypes are of various shapes and sizes and allow you incredible control over how your data is stored. Table 4.1 lists some of the most common datatypes.

T A B L E   4.1:   Datatypes and Sizes

Datatype Name	Description	Size
TinyInt	Integer from 0 to 255	1 byte
SmallInt	Integer from -32,768 to 32,767	2 bytes
Int	Integer from -2,147,483,648 to 2,147,483,647	4 bytes
Real	1-to-7-digit precision, floating-point	4 bytes
Float	8-to-15-digit precision, floating-point	8 bytes
Smalldatetime	1/1/1900 to 6/6/2079 with accuracy to the minute	4 bytes
Datetime	1/1/100 to 12/31/9999 with accuracy to 3.33 milliseconds	8 bytes
Smallmoney	4-byte integer with 4-digit scale	4 bytes
Money	8 byte integer with 4-digit scale	8 bytes
Char	Character data	1 byte per character

When calculating storage requirements for a table, we simply add the storage requirements for each datatype in the table plus an additional 2 bytes per row of overhead. This will give us the total space that is occupied by a single row. For example, if a table in a database has three fields defined as

Char(10), Int, and Money, the storage space required for each row could be calculated as follows:

- Char(10) = 10 bytes
- Int = 4 bytes
- Money = 8 bytes
- Overhead = 2bytes
- Total = 24 bytes

A row is limited to 2 bytes of overhead only when no variable length datatypes (varchar, nvarchar, and varbinary) have been used and no columns allow nulls. If variable-length columns are used or nulls are allowed, additional overhead must be added. The amount will depend on the datatype and number of columns.

Calculating Rows per Page

Once you have a number indicating the total bytes used per row, you can easily calculate the number or rows that will fit on a single page. Because every page is 8KB in size and has a header, about 8060 bytes are free for storing data. The total number of rows per page can be calculated as 8060 ÷ RowSize. The resulting value is truncated to an integer.

In our example, each row requires 24 bytes of space to store. We can calculate the rows per page as follows: 8060 ÷ 24 = 335.

In our example, we rounded down the result to the nearest whole number.

Special Considerations   When calculating rows per page, there are some additional factors that you will need to consider. Remember that rows can never cross pages. If there is not enough space on a page to complete the row, the entire row will be placed on the next page. This is why we had to truncate the result of our calculation.

In addition, the number of rows that can fit on one page may also be dependent on a *fill factor* that is used for the clustered index. Fill factor is a way of keeping the page from becoming 100% full when the index is created. Using a fill factor may reduce the amount of space used on a page when the index is built, but since fill factor is not maintained, the space will be eventually used.

As an example, if a clustered index were built on our table with a fill factor of 75%, this means that the data would be reorganized such that the data pages would be only 75% full. This means that instead of 8060 bytes free on each page, we could use only 6045 bytes.

Estimating the Number of Rows for the Table

There is no magic secret to estimating the number of rows used in your table. You have to know your data to estimate how many rows your table will eventually hold. When you make this estimate, try to consider as well as possible how large you expect your table to grow. If you do not allow for this growth in your estimates, the database will need to be expanded. This entire exercise in projecting storage requirements will then be at least somewhat wasted effort.

Calculating the Number of Pages Needed

Calculating the number of pages needed is another simple calculation as long as we have reliable figures of the number of rows per page and the number of rows you expect the table to hold. The calculation is number of rows in table ÷ number of rows per page. Here, the result will be rounded up to the nearest whole number.

In our example we saw that 335 rows would fit in a single page of the table. If we expected this table to eventually hold 1,000,000 records, the calculation would be:

- 1,000,000 ÷ 335 = 2985.07

- Round the value to 2985 Pages

Now we can extend our calculation to determine the number of extents that must be allocated to this table to hold this data. Since all space is allocated in extents, we again need to round up to the nearest integer when calculating extents. Remember that there are eight 8KB pages per extent. Our calculation would be:

- 2985 ÷ 8 = 373

Since a megabyte can store 16 extents, this table would take about 23.2MB of space to store. Add a little bit of extra space "just in case" and you are ready to proceed to the next table.

Estimating Index Storage Requirements

Indexes in SQL Server are stored in a B-Tree format; that is, we can think of an index as a large tree. You can also think of an index as a table with a pyramid on top of it. The ultimate concept here is that for every index, there is a single entry point: the root of the tree or the apex of the pyramid.

When estimating storage requirements, the base of this pyramid can be thought of as a table. You go through the same process in estimating the "leaf" level of an index as you would in estimating the storage requirements of a table. Although the process is very similar, there are a few issues that are important to consider.

1. You are adding the datatypes of the index keys, not the data rows.

2. Clustered indexes use the data page as the leaf level. There is no need to add additional storage requirements for a clustered-index leaf level.

The toughest part of estimating the size of an index is estimating the size and number of levels you will have in your index. While there is a fairly long and complex series of calculations to determine this exactly, we usually find it sufficient to add an additional 35% of the leaf-level space estimated for the other levels of the index.

Creating Databases

In this section we will look at creating, expanding, shrinking, and dropping databases. The approaches demonstrated will use both the Enterprise Manager and Transact-SQL (referred to as T-SQL in the remainder of this chapter). This section discusses the following exam objectives:

<hr>

Microsoft
✓ *Exam*
Objective

Create and manage databases.

- Create data files, filegroups, and transaction log files.
- Specify growth characteristics.

<hr>

Develop a SQL Server capacity plan.

- Plan the physical placement of files, including data files and log files.
- Plan for growth over time.

Let's start with the more difficult way of creating a database, using T-SQL. When you create a database, you should specify the logical name of the database, the physical filename where the database file will reside, and the size of the database file. Optional parameters include the maximum size to which the database is allowed to grow, as well as the growth characteristics. You can also specify the logical and physical filenames of the transaction log as well as its maximum size and growth characteristics. Here is the basic syntax of the CREATE DATABASE statement:

```
CREATE DATABASE db_name
[ON { [PRIMARY]
(NAME = logical name,
 FILENAME = 'physical filename',
 [SIZE = initial size,]
 [MAXSIZE = maxsize,]
 [FILEGROWTH = [filegrowth MB | %])} [...n]]
[LOG ON
{(NAME = logical name,
 FILENAME = 'physical filename',
 [SIZE = initial size],
 [MAXSIZE = maxsize],
 [FILEGROWTH = filegrowth MB | %])} [...n]]
[FOR LOAD | FOR ATTACH]
```

The following explains the uses of the listed parameters:

- *db_name* This is the name that you are going to give this database. It must follow the rules for SQL Server identifiers.

- **PRIMARY** This parameter, the name of the filegroup, defaults to PRIMARY (Filegroups are an advanced topic that we will cover later in this chapter.) In short, filegroups allow you to place individual database objects in separate files. For example, you might place a large table on one filegroup and the table's index on another filegroup. In this manner, writes to the table do not interfere with writes to the index. These are used with the ALTER DATABASE statement, not the CREATE DATABASE statement.

- *logical name* This is the logical name of the database file, which you will use to reference this particular database file while in SQL Server.

- *'physical filename'* This is the complete path and filename of the file you are creating. Note that it is surrounded by single quotation marks.

- **Initial Size** This is the initial size of the database expressed in either kilobytes or megabytes. Keep in mind that this will allocate hard-disk space.

- **Maxsize** This is the maximum size to which the database can grow. This is useful when you specify filegrowth options. This parameter is specified in kilobytes or megabytes.

- **Filegrowth** This option specifies the size of the increments by which a given database file should grow. It can be expressed in either kilobytes or megabytes or as a percentage. If not specified, the default is 1MB.

- **FOR LOAD** This option marks the database for DBO (Database Owner) use only and is used for backward compatibility with SQL Server 6.5. This means that the database is not marked online, but is waiting for data to be loaded into it through a select into/bulk copy operation or through the restoration of a backup.

- **FOR ATTACH** This option reattaches the files that make up a database. It essentially recreates entries in the system tables regarding this database file.

Let's take a look at a few examples of using the CREATE DATABASE statement. In this first example, we will create a very simple database with no growth characteristics.

```
CREATE DATABASE Simple
ON PRIMARY
(NAME = 'Simple_Data',
 FILENAME = 'C:\MSSQL7\Data\Simple_Data.mdf',
```

```
   SIZE = 5MB)
LOG ON
(NAME = 'Simple_Log',
 FILENAME = 'C:\MSSQL7\DATA\Simple_Log.ldf',
 SIZE = 2MB)
```

The size of this database is 7MB. 5MB are used to store the data and system tables, and 2MB are used to store the transaction log. The file does not have any filegrowth parameters and therefore will not grow automatically.

You can use the ALTER DATABASE statement to specify new database growth parameters. This simplifies altering the MAXSIZE and FILE-GROWTH properties.

Now look at a more complex database. In this example, we will create a database that has data spanning two files and a transaction log. We will also set the autogrowth and maxsize parameters.

```
CREATE DATABASE Complex
ON PRIMARY
(NAME = Complex_Data1,
 FILENAME = 'C:\MSSQL7\Data\Complex_Data1.mdf',
 SIZE = 5MB,
 MAXSIZE = 10MB,
 FILEGROWTH = 1MB),
(NAME = Complex_Data2,
 FILENAME = 'C:\MSSQL7\Data\Complex_Data2.ndf',
 SIZE = 2MB,
 MAXSIZE = 10MB,
 FILEGROWTH = 2MB),
LOG ON
(NAME = Complex_Log1,
 FILENAME = 'D:\Logs\Complex_Log1.ldf',
 SIZE = 2MB,
 MAXSIZE = 8MB,
 FILEGROWTH = 1MB)
```

This creates a database with an initial size of 9MB—5MB for the first file, 2MB for the second file, and 2MB for the log. The database has a maximum size of 28MB.

You should always specify a maximum size for data and transaction log files that have an autogrowth feature. If you do not, it is possible for the file to fill the entire hard-disk partition. If this happens, Windows NT will no longer allow you to use that partition. If the partition also has the Windows NT system files on it, you will no longer be able to use Windows NT until the situation is remedied.

Follow the steps outlined in Exercise 4.1 to create a new database called "Sample" with an initial database size of 4MB, and a transaction log of 1MB. You will also set the maximum size of the database to 10MB and the maximum size of the log to 4MB. Both will have a filegrowth of 10%.

EXERCISE 4.1

Create a Database Using T-SQL

1. Open the SQL Server Query Analyzer. Do this through the SQL Enterprise Manager by selecting Tools ➢ SQL Query Analyzer or by choosing Start ➢ Programs ➢ Microsoft SQL Server 7 ➢ SQL Query Analyzer.

2. Enter the following query:

```
CREATE DATABASE Sample
ON [PRIMARY]
(NAME = 'SampleData',
 FILENAME = 'C:\MSSQL7\Data\SampleData.MDF',
 SIZE = 4,
 MAXSIZE = 10,
 FILEGROWTH = 10%)
LOG ON
(NAME = 'SampleLog',
 FILENAME = 'C:\MSSQL7\Data\SampleLog.LDF',
 SIZE = 1,
 MAXSIZE = 4,
 FILEGROWTH = 10%)
```

EXERCISE 4.1 (CONTINUED)

3. Execute the query. You should receive notification that the query successfully completed and that the two new database files were created. It should look something like this:

```
The CREATE DATABASE process is allocating 4.00 MB on disk
'SampleData'. The CREATE DATABASE process is allocating
1.00 MB on disk 'SampleLog'.
```

Now that you have created a database using T-SQL, let's do it with the Enterprise Manager. Follow the steps outlined in Exercise 4.2 to create a database called "Sybex." There will be two data files, each 2MB in size, with a filegrowth of 1MB and a maximum size of 20MB. You will also create a transaction log with a size of 1MB, a filegrowth of 1MB, and no maximum size.

EXERCISE 4.2

Creating a Database Using the SQL Enterprise Manager

1. Start the SQL Enterprise Manager by selecting Start ➤ Programs ➤ Microsoft SQL Server 7 ➤ Enterprise Manager.

2. Connect to your SQL Server

3. Expand your Databases folder as shown here.

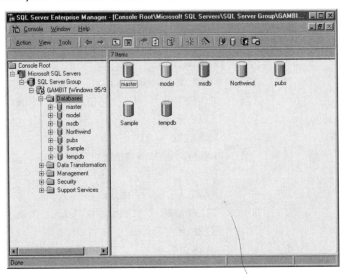

4. Right-click either the Databases folder in the console tree, or in the white space in the right pane and choose New Database from the context menu.

5. You should now have the General tab of the Database Properties dialog box as shown below. Type in the database name **Sybex**. Notice that the database filename automatically fills in as Sybex_Data.mdf.

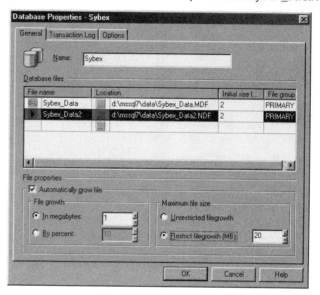

6. Fill in the other boxes as shown above. Set the File Name field to Sybex_Data2. Use the default value for the Location field. For both the Sybex_Data file and the Sybex_Data2 file, set the Initial Size field to 2MB. Set the Automatically Grow File option to true (checked) and set the File Growth increment to 1MB. Set the Restrict Filegrowth option to 20MB.

7. Now click the Transaction Log tab. Set the option as shown here. The File name should be Sybex_Log. Use the default value for the Location field and set the Initial Size to 1MB. Set the Automatically Grow File option to true (checked) and set the File Growth parameter to 1MB. Set the Maximum File Size to Unrestricted Filegrowth.

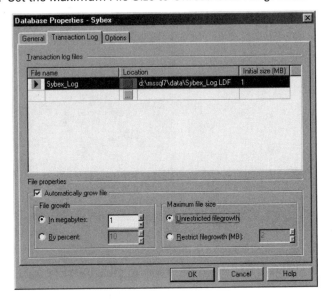

8. Click OK when you are finished. You should now have a new Sybex database.

Gathering Information about Your Database

Now that you have successfully created a couple of databases, it is time to learn how to gather more information about them. There are two ways to gather information about your database; you can use the Enterprise Manager or the Query Analyzer.

Let's start with the graphical tool first. Using the Enterprise Manager, you can gather a wealth of information about your database. This includes the size of the database, its current capacity, any options that are currently set, etc. If you click on your database in the console tree, you will receive summary information in the right pane as shown in Figure 4.1.

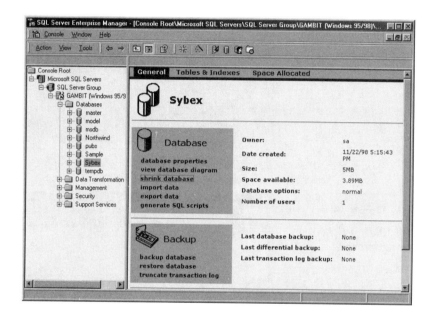

The various items listed in the right pane are all hyperlinks to the designated areas. For example, if you click on the Database Properties item, you will see the screens used to create the database in Exercise 4.2.

You can also use system stored procedures to gather information about your database. The sp_helpdb stored procedure used by itself will give you information about all databases in your SQL Server. You can gather information about a particular database by using the database name as a parameter. Figure 4.2 shows the sp_helpdb stored procedure and its result set.

Notice that both the Sample and the Sybex databases are 5MB in size. Like the other databases shown, they show an owner of **sa**, their creation dates, database IDs (dbid), and their status. The status parameter describes which database options have been set. For example, the Master database has the Truncate Log on Checkpoint database option enabled. We'll talk about the database options later in this chapter.

If you switch to the Sybex database and run the sp_helpfile stored procedure, you can gather information about the data and log files that are used for the Sybex database (Figure 4.3).

FIGURE 4.2

The sp_helpdb stored
procedure

FIGURE 4.2

The sp_helpdb stored
procedure

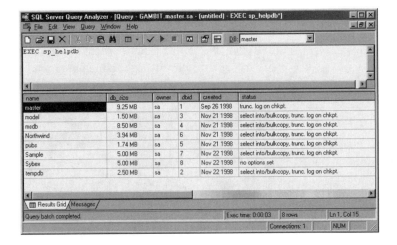

FIGURE 4.3

The sp_helpfile
stored procedure

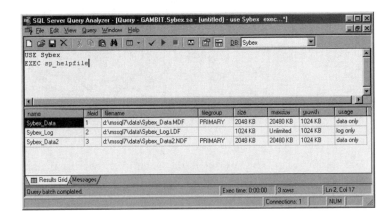

As you can see from Figure 4.3, you can gather information about file
sizes and locations, the filegroup they are a member of, and the database file
use (either data or log).

Managing Your Database

In this section, you will learn more about the various methods used to
manage your database. This includes database options and their effects,
altering the database by adding additional database files, and removing a
database from your system.

Working with Database Options

Database options allow you to specify how your database will behave in given situations. You can view and modify database options using the Enterprise Manager or the `sp_dboption` stored procedure. The `sp_dboption` stored procedure includes database options that are not available through the GUI.

Let's take a look at the database options currently set on your Sybex database that was created earlier today. Start the Enterprise Manager and move down through the console tree until you see your database. Right-click on your database and choose Properties. From the Database Properties dialog box, click the Options tab as shown in Figure 4.4.

F I G U R E 4.4

The Database
Options tab

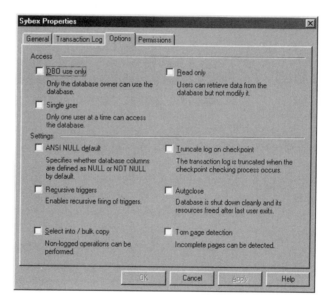

The database options are broken into separate categories for Access and Settings. This is what the different settings mean:

- **DBO Use Only**   Only members of the db_owner fixed database role have access to this database. This option is frequently used when performing a restoration or other tasks where you do not want to allow non-owners in the database.

- **Single User** Only one user at a time can access the database and with only a single connection.

- **Read Only** This option marks the database as read only. No changes to the database will be allowed.

- **ANSI NULL default** This option specifies that new columns created or added to tables have a default value of NULL. Although this is a default setting for the entire database, you can override this value by specifying either NULL or NOT NULL when you create your columns.

- **Recursive Triggers** This option allows recursive triggers to fire. Unlike SQL Server 6.5, you can have as many triggers per table as you wish. Recursive triggers occur when one trigger fires a trigger on another table, which in turn fires another trigger on the originating table.

- **Select Into/Bulk Copy** This option allows you to perform non-logged operations. This includes the use of the bcp (bulk copy) command-line program as well as statements that create or fill tables using the SELECT INTO SQL statements. Note: Since non-logged operations do not write to the transaction log, you should back up your database after performing these actions.

- **Truncate Log on Checkpoint** This option specifies that the inactive portion of the transaction log should be truncated at the checkpoint process. Every minute, the checkpoint process is activated and checks each database in SQL Server. If it finds a database with 5 minutes' worth of changes, it flushes the modified data pages in cache to the hard disk. When dirty pages have been written to disk as well as to the transaction log, you have a known point of consistency. This option is useful if you do not want to keep an active transaction log. We use it often during the development stages of a database.

- **Torn-Page Detection** This option allows SQL Server to detect when a partial-page write to disk has occurred. Because this is a form of data corruption that should be avoided, we suggest you enable this option.

- **Auto Close** This option safely closes your database when the last user has exited from it. This can be a useful option for optimization. It decreases the amount of resources that SQL Server needs to consume in order to maintain user information and locks.

- **Autoshrink**   This option will automatically shrink both data and log files. Log files will be shrunk after a backup of the log has been made. Data files will be shrunk when a periodic check of the database finds that the database has more than 25% of its assigned space free. Your database will then be shrunk to a size that leaves 25% free.

- **Auto Create Statistics**   This option will automatically generate statistics on the distribution of values found in your columns. The SQL Server Query optimizer uses these statistics to determine the best method to run a particular query.

- **Auto Update Statistics**   This option works with the auto-created statistics mentioned above. As you make changes to the data in your database, the statistics will be less and less accurate. This option periodically updates those statistics.

- **Use Quoted Identifiers**   This option allows you to use double quotation marks as part of a SQL Server identifier (object name). This can be useful in situations in which you have identifiers that are also SQL Server reserved words.

When you have made your selections, simply click OK to apply them and continue using SQL Server. You can also use the sp_dboption stored procedure to accomplish these same tasks. For example, to mark the Sybex database as read only, you could enter this code:

```
use master
go
exec sp_dboption sybex, 'Single User', true
```

When you run this command, you should get the following data back:

```
DBCC execution completed. If DBCC printed error messages,
contact your system administrator.
The database is now single user.
```

To verify, you could run the sp_helpdb system stored procedure and check the status of the database. You can also review the database in the Enterprise Manager. In the Enterprise Manager, you should now see a face icon superimposed on your database in the console tree as shown in Figure 4.5. If the icon is missing, right-click on your databases folder and choose Refresh. You may also find that changes you make in the Query Analyzer do not show up in the Enterprise Manager. Here too, right-click on the object you are viewing and choose Refresh. This will refresh the information displayed.

FIGURE 4.5

Single-User Database
option has been set on
the Sybex database.

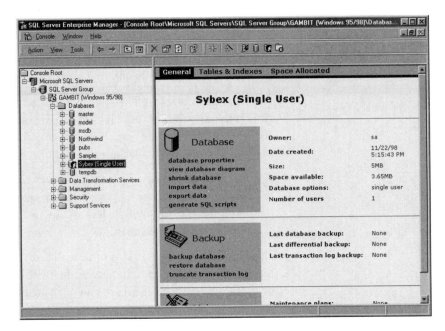

The `sp_dboption` stored procedure includes the following additional database options that are not available through the Enterprise Manager:

- **Concat Null Yields Null**   This option specifies that anything you concatenate to a null value will return a null value.

- **Cursor Close on Commit**   This option automatically closes any open cursors when the transaction that created the cursor completes. (Cursors are the results from a query.)

- **Default to Local Cursor**   This option creates cursors that are local in nature and available only to the local batch, trigger, or stored procedure that generated the trigger. This option can be overridden by using the GLOBAL keyword when creating the cursor.

- **Merge Publish**   This option allows a database to be a publisher as part of merge replication.

- **Offline**   This option takes a database offline and shuts it down. When a database has been taken offline, it can be placed on removable media like CD-ROM.

- **Published** This option specifies that the database is allowed to publish data for use in replication.

- **Subscribed** This option specifies that the database can participate in the subscriber side of replication.

Altering Databases

There may be times that you wish to make changes to your database or the database files. These include expanding your data files or adding more data files, shrinking the database, or even removing the database from your system. This section discusses all these topics. Let's start with the ALTER DATABASE statement itself, then cover expanding, shrinking, and removing databases and data files.

Here is the basic syntax of the ALTER DATABASE statement:

```
ALTER DATABASE db_name {
ADD FILE <file_spec> [,…n] [TO FILEGROUP <filegroup_name>]
| ADD LOG FILE <file_spec> [,…n]
| REMOVE FILE <logical_name>
| ADD FILEGROUP <filegroup_name>
| REMOVE FILEGROUP <filegroup_name>
| MODIFY FILE <file_spec>
| MODIFY FILEGROUP <filegroup_name, filegroup property> }
```

The File_spec option includes the following syntax you saw earlier in the CREATE DATABASE statements:

```
(NAME = logical name,
 FILENAME = 'physical filename',
 [SIZE = initial size,]
 [MAXSIZE = maxsize,]
 [FILEGROWTH = [filegrowth MB | %])} […n]]
```

With the ALTER DATABASE command, you can add or expand data and log files. You can add or modify filegroups, and you can remove data files, log files, and filegroups.

Expanding Databases

You can expand databases in SQL Server by using the SQL Enterprise Manager or the ALTER DATABASE statement. When you expand a database, you can make the current database files larger, or you can add additional database files. This is a relatively straightforward task when using the Enterprise Manager—and just a little more tricky when using ALTER DATABASE statements in T-SQL. First, let's look at expanding databases using the Enterprise Manager.

Expanding Databases Using the Enterprise Manager   In Exercise 4.3, you will expand the Sample database by increasing the size of the data files and the log files by 2MB. You will also increase the maximum size of the data files by 10MB.

EXERCISE 4.3

Expanding a Database Using the Enterprise Manager

1. Start the SQL Server Enterprise Manager.

2. Drill down through the console tree to the Sample database.

3. Right-click on the Sample database and choose Properties.

4. In the Database Properties window, change the current data file size from 4MB to 6MB.

5. Increase the maximum size from 10MB to 20MB as shown here.

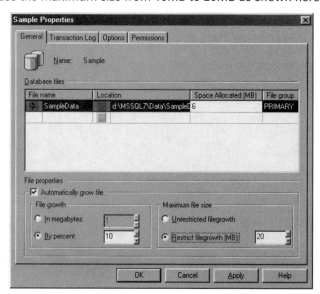

6. Now switch to the Transaction log tab and increase its initial size from 1MB to 3MB and increase the Restrict Regrowth parameter from 4MB to 14MB.

7. Click OK when you are finished.

8. If you now right-click your database in the console tree and choose Refresh, you will see that your database has increased in size from its old 5MB to a new size of 9MB, as shown here.

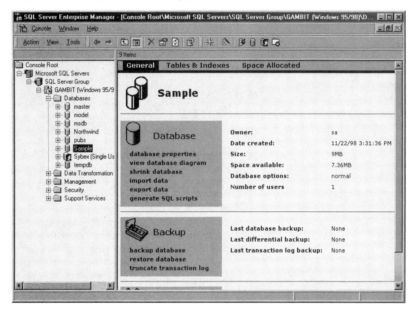

You can add additional data files as well as log files from the Database Properties window. Simply click in a new box and fill in the new logical name, physical location, initial size, and other properties.

Expanding Databases Using T-SQL   Now let's do some modifications using the ALTER DATABASE statements. In this example, you will add a new log file to the Sample database. The log file will have the following characteristics:

Option	Value
Name	Sample_Log2
Physical Name	C:\MSSQL7\Data\Sample_Log2.ldf

Option	Value
Size	4MB
Maxsize	10MB
Filegrowth	2MB

Follow the steps outlined in Exercise 4.4 to complete this example.

EXERCISE 4.4

Expanding a Database Using T-SQL

1. Open the SQL Server Query Analyzer.

2. Enter the following code to alter the Sample database:

```
ALTER DATABASE Sample
ADD LOG FILE
(NAME = Sample_Log2,
 FILENAME = 'C:\MSSQL7\Data\Sample_Log2.ldf',
 SIZE = 4MB,
 MAXSIZE = 10MB,
 FILEGROWTH = 2MB)
```

3. When you have completed the command, you should get something similar to the following information:

```
Extending database by 4.00 MB on disk 'Sample_Log2'.
```

4. Run the sp_helpdb and the sp_helpfile stored procedures discussed earlier in this chapter.

There are certain advantages and disadvantages to having multiple database files as opposed to just enlarging your current database files. The main disadvantage of multiple database files is administration. You need to be aware of these different files, their locations, and their use. There are advantages, however. For example, you can place these files on separate physical hard disks (if you are not using striping), avoiding the creation of "hot spots" and thereby improving performance. When you use database files, you can back up individual database files rather than the whole database in one session. If you also take advantage of filegroups, you can improve performance by explicitly placing tables on one filegroup and the indexes for those tables on a separate filegroup. A filegroup is a logical grouping of database files used for performance and to improve administration on VLDBs. We will discuss filegroups later in this chapter.

Shrinking Databases

When you wish to shrink your database, you can choose to shrink individual files within the database or all files in the database. There are three methods you can use to shrink your database: the DBCC SHRINKDATABASE or DBCC SHRINKFILE commands, the Enterprise Manager, and the Autoshrink Database option.

To understand what is really happening in your database when it is being shrunk, let's first take a look at the database consistency checker statements.

Shrinking Databases Using T-SQL   To shrink a database using T-SQL, you can use the DBCC SHRINKDATABASE command, which will attempt to shrink all files in the database, or the DBCC SHRINKFILE command, which will attempt to shrink a specific database file. Here is the syntax of the SHRINKDATABASE command.

```
DBCC SHRINKDATABASE {
(db_name,
[target_percent],
[{NOTRUNCATE | TRUNCATEONLY}])}
```

The following lists the arguments and their meanings:

- **db_name**   The logical name of the database that you wish to shrink.

- **target_percent**   The percentage of free space left in the database after it has been shrunk.

- **NOTRUNCATE**   Does not release the free space back to the operating system.

- **TRUNCATEONLY**   Releases all free space back to the operating system. Note that when you use TRUNCATEONLY, the target_ percent parameter is ignored.

Understanding how the SHRINKDATABASE statements work is very tricky (see Books Online). When you use the SHRINKDATABASE statement, it attempts to shrink all data files in the database to a new size. When you run DBCC SHRINKDATBASE (db_name) by itself, it will tell you how much your database can be shrunk.

The target percentage parameter is used to specify how much free space you wish to have in your database after it is shrunk. Let's say that you have a 100MB database, currently using 50MB for data storage, with the other 50MB as free space. To shrink the database and leave yourself with 10MB of free space, you must determine what percentage of 100MB (the current size of the database) is 10MB (the desired amount of free space). The answer in this case is 10%. This is your target percentage. Run the following command:

DBCC SHRINKDATABASE (Foo, 10%)

You should end up with a database that is 60MB in size: 50MB for the used data pages and 10MB of free space. You should be aware of some additional issues. For example, you cannot set the target percentage to a value that is larger than the current database. Using our 100MB database with 50MB free and 50MB used, setting the target percentage to 60% and doing the calculations would give the following numbers: 60% of 100MB is 60MB. The current data size is 50MB, which is 50% of the database. Since 50% plus 60% is more than 100%, this cannot be done.

This example is fairly straightforward, but what happens if you have a 817MB database with 709MB used, and you want to shrink it and leave 30% free space as your target percentage? This would not work, because 30% of 817 is roughly 245MB. Adding 245MB to the existing 709MB gives us 954MB—which is more than 817MB. The maximum percentage you could set Would be considerably less: 817MB – 709MB = 108MB. Dividing 108MB by 817MB gives us 13%. While this would not shrink the database at all, the statement would complete successfully.

When using a SHRINKDATABASE or SHRINKFILE statement, it is important to understand the functions of the TRUNCATEONLY and NOTRUNCATE options as well as what is happening to the data within the database files.

The SHRINKDATABASE and SHRINKFILE statements work in a fashion similar to the disk defragmenter. Keep in mind that data is striped across multiple data files automatically. When you issue one of the shrink commands, the data in the stripes is consolidated; the free space that was between the data in the stripe sets is also consolidated and moved to the bottom of the stripe set.

- The TRUNCATEONLY clause will ignore the target percentage parameter and shrink the database to the size of data. It will also release all of the freed-up disk space back to the operating system.

- The NOTRUNCATE option just consolidates the data into one area and the free space into another area without releasing any free space back to the operating system. For obvious reasons, the NOTRUN-CATE ignores the target percentage parameter also.

Figure 4.6 shows a before-and-after representation of a SHRINKDATABASE command with the NOTRUNCATE option. As you can see, all of the data (the shaded blocks) was consolidated and the free space was moved to the end of the files.

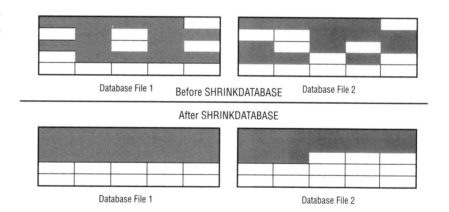

F I G U R E   4.6

Effects of the SHRINK-DATABASE command with NOTRUNCATE

Database File 1   Before SHRINKDATABASE   Database File 2

After SHRINKDATABASE

Database File 1   Database File 2

The SHRINKFILE command allows you to shrink a single database file. Here is the syntax:

```
DBCC SHRINKFILE {
(filename | file_id}
[, target_percentage]
[, {EMPTYFILE | NOTRUNCATE | TRUNCATEONLY}])}
```

The filename or file_id parameters are used to specify the individual database file you wish to shrink. The file_id can be found by first running an sp_helpdb stored procedure. The other new parameter is the EMPTYFILE option, which is used in conjunction with a filegroup. You can use this option to move all data stored on a particular file to other files in the filegroup. EMPTYFILE will then mark the file as empty. Once a file has been marked empty, you can remove it from the filegroup using the ALTER DATABASE command with the REMOVE FILE parameter.

Here is an example of what you would see if you used the SHRINKFILE command and then the REMOVE FILE commands. In this example we will assume you have a filegroup with three files in it. The files are named fgTest_Data1 through fgTest_Data3. The database is named Test. We will first empty the fgTest_Data3 file and then remove it.

```
USE Test
GO
DBCC SHRINKFILE (fgTest_Data3, EMPTYFILE)
GO
```

This is what your output might look like:

DbId	FileID	CurrentSize	MinimumSize	UsedPages	EstimatedPages
12	7	256	256	0	0

```
(1 row(s) affected)
```

Now you can drop the file, as it has been emptied and marked as empty:

```
ALTER DATABASE Test
REMOVE FILE fgTest_Data3
```

Your output should be similar to this:

```
DBCC execution completed. If DBCC printed error messages,
contact your system administrator.
The file 'fgTest_Data3' has been removed.
```

If you now run sp_helpdb on the Test database, you will see that the file has successfully been removed. There is an easier way to achieve the same results.

Shrinking Databases Using the Enterprise Manager You can use the Enterprise Manager to shrink your databases. Another nice feature of the Enterprise Manager is the ability to have the database shrink automatically over time. We'll take a look at that in a minute, but first let's see how to shrink a database one time.

To shrink a database using the Enterprise Manager is not particularly intuitive. (Right-clicking your way to the Properties sheet and entering a smaller value for the Initial Space option will not shrink the database: it will actually run either the CREATE DATABASE command or the ALTER DATABASE command.) Enterprise Manager works it a little differently. Follow the steps outlined in Exercise 4.5 to shrink the Sample database.

EXERCISE 4.5

Shrinking a Database Using the Enterprise Manager

1. Open the Enterprise Manager.

2. Drill down to the Database folder and click on the Sample database. You should now see some general information about your Sample database as shown below.

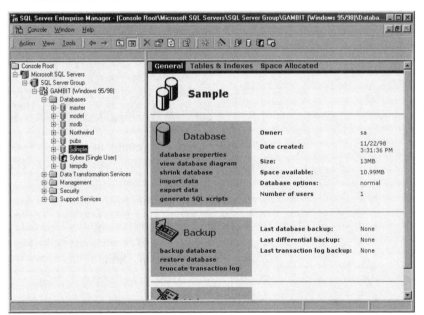

3. Notice that the current size of the Sample database is 13MB and that there is about 11MB of free space. We will attempt to shrink the database down to 7MB or so. To do this, right-click on the Sample database in the console tree and choose All Tasks ➤ Shrink Database.

4. You should now see something similar to the graphic shown here. Since we want to shrink the 13MB of database down to about 7MB, click Shrink database by % and change the value to 50. Click OK when you are finished.

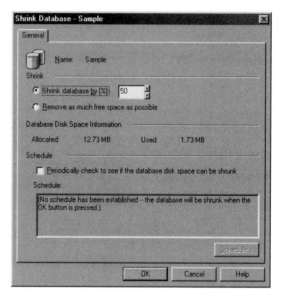

5. You should get a confirmation message that tells you that the database has been successfully shrunk to 13MB. This unchanged figure illustrates an excellent point: you cannot shrink a database to a size smaller than its initial size.

6. There are two other important options. The default shrinking option is to shrink the database as much as possible and release all that free space back to the system. This is similar to the DBCC SHRINKDATABASE with the TRUNCATEONLY option enabled.

7. The other option allows you to set your database up to shrink itself automatically over time. When this option is enabled, the scheduler will create a job that will check the database. Whenever it find that the database has more than 25% of its space free, it will automatically shrink the database to reflect a database with 25% free space.

Renaming a Database

During your tenure as a SQL Server administrator you may find it necessary to change the name of a database because of a departmental shift, turning a development database into a production database, or for any other reason.

To rename a database in SQL Server 7, is as simple as running the sp_renamedb stored procedure. There are several restrictions that you should be aware of when you do this:

- The database must be set to single-user.
- You must be in the master database to run the sp_renamedb stored procedure.
- You must be a member of the sysadmin fixed server role.
- Data files and filegroups are not affected.
- Fully qualified database object names may be affected. A fully qualified object name is in the form:
  servername.databasename.owner.object.–
- For example: HomePC.Sample.dbo.Table1.

Follow the steps outlined in Exercise 4.6 to rename the Sample database to NewSample. Keep in mind that we are changing just the logical name of the database, nothing else.

Renaming a Database Using T-SQL

1. Open the SQL Server Query Analyzer

2. In the query window, enter the following:

```
USE master
GO
EXEC sp_dboption 'Sample', 'Single User', True
EXEC sp_renamedb 'Sample', 'NewSample'
EXEC sp_dboption 'NewSample', 'Single User', False
GO
```

```
DBCC execution completed. If DBCC printed error messages,
contact your system administrator.
The database is now single user.
(1 row(s) affected)
DBCC execution completed. If DBCC printed error messages,
contact your system administrator.
The database is renamed and in single user mode.
A member of the syadmin role must reset the database to
multiuser mode with sp_dboption.
DBCC execution completed. If DBCC printed error messages,
contact your system administrator.
The database is now multiuser.
```

3. You can now run the sp_helpdb stored procedure to see the new NewSample database in the output.

4. Close the Query Analyzer when you are finished.

Dropping Databases

When you no longer need a database it can be dropped from your server, freeing up disk space for other database files. Only the owner of a database has the authority to drop a database. Dropping a database is a very simple task, with both the Enterprise Manager and T-SQL. Although the process is easy, remember that dropping a database is permanent. If you need to recover your database later, you will need to restore it from a backup.

When using the Enterprise Manager to drop databases, simply locate the desired database in the console tree and press the Delete key on your keyboard or right-click and choose Delete. You will be asked to confirm the deletion, after which the database will be dropped.

With T-SQL, databases are dropped using the DROP DATABASE statement. The syntax is:

```
DROP DATABASE database_name [, database_name...]
```

Notice that according to the above syntax statement, multiple databases can be dropped at once using this statement. Just separate the database names with commas.

There are three databases that cannot be dropped: the Master, Model, and Tempdb databases. You are free to drop the Pubs and the Northwind databases if you wish. Although you can drop the Msdb database, doing so will render the SQLServerAgent service and replication completely unusable. It will also cause errors to be reported whenever you do a backup or restore, as the system will attempt to write information to the detail and history tables in the Msdb database.

Working with Filegroups

A final feature of database management is the filegroup. In this section, you will learn more about filegroups, how they are created and modified and how they affect your overall database strategy.

Microsoft Exam Objective

Develop a SQL Server capacity plan.

- Plan the use of filegroups.

When you use filegroups, you can explicitly place database objects onto a particular set of database files. For example, you can separate tables and their non-clustered indexes onto separate filegroups. This can improve performance as modifications to the table can be written to both the table and the index at the same time. This can be especially useful if you are not using striping with parity (RAID 5). Another advantage of filegroups is the ability to back up only a single filegroup at a time. This can be extremely useful for a VLDB as the sheer size of the database could make backing up an extremely time-consuming process. Another advantage is the ability to mark the filegroup and all data on the files that are part of it as either READONLY or READWRITE. There are really only two disadvantages to using filegroups. The first is the administration that is involved in keeping track of the files in the filegroup and the database objects that are placed in them. The other disadvantage is that if you are working with a smaller database and have RAID 5 implemented, you may not be improving performance.

The two basic filegroups in SQL Server 7 are the primary, or default, filegroup that is created with every database, and the user-defined filegroups created for a particular database. The primary filegroup will always contain the primary data file and any other files that are not specifically created on a user-defined filegroup. You can create additional filegroups using the ALTER DATABASE command or the Enterprise Manager.

Filegroups have several rules that you should follow when you are working with them:

- The first (or primary) data file must reside on the primary filegroup

- All system files must be placed on the primary filegroup

- A file cannot be a member of more than one filegroup at a time

- Filegroups can be allocated indexes, tables, text, ntext, and image data

- New data pages are not automatically allocated to user-defined filegroups if the primary filegroup runs out of space

Creating Filegroups with the Enterprise Manager

Creating new filegroups and adding data files to them is a relatively straightforward task when using the Enterprise Manager. You can create the filegroups when you create a new database or when you alter an existing database. Follow the steps in Exercise 4.7 to create a new filegroup and add two new database files to it. You will be using the NewSample (formerly the Sample database) to do this.

EXERCISE 4.7

Creating a Filegroup with Enterprise Manager

1. Open the Enterprise Manager

2. Drill down in the console tree to the NewSample database

3. Right-click on the NewSample database and choose Properties from the context menu.

4. You are now looking at the NewSample database properties dialog box.

5. Add a new data file called fgTable_Data1, with a filename of C:\MSSQL7\ Data\fgTable_Data1.dat, 5MB in size, and then set the File Group box to Table.

6. Add another new data file called fgIndex_Data1, with a filename of C:\MSSQL7\Data\fgIndex_Data1.dat, 2MB in size, and then set the File Group box to Index.

7. Click OK when you are finished. Your database properties screen should look similar to the graphic shown here.

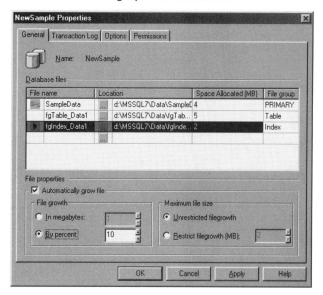

Creating Filegroups with T-SQL

As might be expected, using T-SQL to create a filegroup is a bit trickier. To add a filegroup and then to add data files to the filegroup, you need to use the ALTER DATABASE statement that we covered earlier in this book.

In this example, we will create a new filegroup called Testing on the Dummy database. You will also see the results of the query.

```
ALTER DATABASE Dummy
ADD FILEGROUP Testing
GO

The command(s) completed successfully
```

You can verify your filegroups by running the `sp_helpfilegroup` stored procedure. For example, you could enter the following command on the NewSample database.

```
USE NewSample
GO
EXEC sp_helpfilegroup
```

Your results might look like this

Groupname	Groupid	filecount
Index	3	1
PRIMARY	1	1
Table	2	1

Now let's add another data file to the Table filegroup on the NewSample database. Follow the steps outlined in Exercise 4.8. You will be creating a new table called `fgTable_Data2`, which will be 2MB in size and be a part of the Table filegroup. You will then verify the table using the `sp_helpfile-group` stored procedure.

EXERCISE 4.8

Adding a Data File to a Filegroup Using T-SQL

1. Open the Query Analyzer

2. Run the following query. Note the square brackets around the Table filegroup. This was done to ensure that SQL Server doesn't confuse the Table keyword with the filegroup of the same name.

```
USE NewSample
GO
ALTER DATABASE NewSample
ADD FILE
(NAME = fgTable_Data2,
 FILENAME = 'C:\MSSQL7\Data\fgTable_Data2.ndf',
 SIZE = 2MB)
TO FILEGROUP [Table]
GO

Extending database by 2.00 MB on disk 'fgTable_Data2'.
```

You can verify your new file by running the sp_helpfilegroup stored procedure.

```
USE NewSample
GO
EXEC sp_helpfilegroup
```

You should get the following results:

Groupname	Groupid	filecount
Index	3	1
PRIMARY	1	1
Table	2	2

Removing a Filegroup

To remove a filegroup, you must first ensure that all the files that make up the filegroup have been removed. You cannot move a data file from one filegroup to another. Keep in mind that files can be resized or deleted.

Once the files have been removed, you can remove the filegroup using the ALTER DATABASE statement. Follow the steps in Exercise 4.9 to remove the table data files and the table filegroup as well as the index filegroup from the NewSample database.

EXERCISE 4.9

Removing Files and Filegroups

1. Open the Query Analyzer

2. Run the following query, which will remove the files and then the filegroup:

```
USE NewSample
GO
ALTER DATABASE NewSample
REMOVE FILE fgTable_Data1
GO
ALTER DATABASE NewSample
REMOVE FILE fgTable_Data2
GO
ALTER DATABASE NewSample
REMOVE FILE fgIndex_Data1
GO

The file 'fgTable_Data1' has been removed.
The file 'fgTable_Data2' has been removed.
The file 'fgIndex_Data1' has been removed.
```

3. Now that the data files have been removed, you can remove the filegroups themselves. Run the following query:

```
USE NewSample
GO
ALTER DATABASE NewSample
REMOVE FILEGROUP [Table]
GO
ALTER DATABASE NewSample
REMOVE FILEGROUP [Index]
GO
The filegroup 'Table' has been removed.
The filegroup 'Index' has been removed.
```

4. To verify that the filegroups have been removed, you can run the sp_ helpfile, or the sp_helpfilegroup stored procedure, or you can look at the database properties in the Enterprise Manager To use the Enterprise Manager, drill down in the console tree to your database. Right-click on the database and choose Refresh. Once the database properties have been refreshed, take a look at them.

5. Right-click the NewSample database and choose Properties. You should now see something similar to graphic shown here.

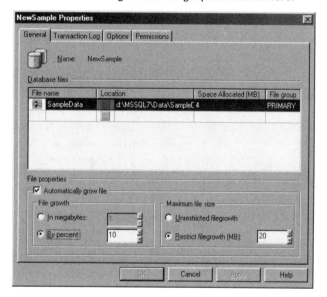

We have given you a broad overview of the uses and simple implementation of database filegroups (filegroups are very similar to segments in SQL Server 6.5). While this database structure can be a key component of your database optimization tasks, it is beyond the scope of this book. For further information on filegroups, see the SQL Server Books Online, or pick up a book on performance tuning and optimization in SQL Server.

Summary

There is much more to data storage in SQL Server than meets the eye. SQL Server data storage structure is more than just a file or a collection of files. It is an entire internal architecture designed for one purpose alone: to extract and modify your data as quickly and efficiently as possible.

In this chapter we defined a database. We discussed data files and the transaction log and how they work together to ensure data consistency as well as database files and their placement as it relates to fault-tolerance. We looked at the different levels of RAID and their advantages and disadvantages. For most installations, RAID 5 is the most inexpensive choice for maximizing fault-tolerance and performance, with a small price in additional storage.

The CREATE DATABASE statement and its many options are a powerful new part of SQL Server 7. This includes the ability to have your database automatically grow as needed and the importance of setting the MAXSIZE parameter so that the data or log file doesn't fill an entire disk partition.

Gathering information about a newly created database includes the sp_helpdb and sp_helpfile stored procedures. A number of database options can be set using the sp_dboption stored procedure or through the Enterprise Manager. While working with the Enterprise Manager is more straightforward than using T-SQL, strong knowledge of the administrative features of the T-SQL language will allow you to write batch scripts that can be scheduled to run whenever you need them.

Databases can be altered by adding files and modifying or removing files that are already part of the database. Databases can be made smaller with the DBCC SHRINKDATABSE or DBCC SHRINKFILE commands or through the All Tasks ➤ Shrink Database choices in the Enterprise Manager.

Renaming a database does not affect the data and log files that make up the database. Although in essence, you are just changing the logical name of the database, such a change could have adverse effects on the objects within the database.

Databases can be removed using the DROP DATABASE statement or the Enterprise Manager. Keep in mind that in order to drop a database, you must be the database owner or a member of the sysadmin fixed server role.

Filegroups are used to optimize your database by placing database objects on specific filegroups. The most common use of filegroups is to place tables on one filegroup and the table's corresponding indexes on a separate filegroup. In this manner, modifications to the data and writes to the database happen in two separate areas, which can improve performance. The autoshrink and autogrowth characteristics of a SQL Server 7 database make capacity planning less of a factor than previously. You should still try to keep these resource-intensive operations to a minimum by doing the best possible job in your capacity planning.

Review Questions

1. Which of the following system tables is used to store information about your databases?

   A. Sysdatabases

   B. Sysdevices

   C. Sysusages

   D. Sysfragments

2. Using the Query Analyzer, you have just created a new database called Accounting with an initial size of 100MB and no Filegrowth options set and no transaction log information provided. What is the default size of the transaction log for this database?

   A. 10MB

   B. 15MB

   C. 20MB

   D. 25MB

3. What is the most granular unit of storage in SQL Server 7?

   A. Record

   B. Page

   C. Extent

   D. Allocation Unit

4. Indexes and tables can share a(n) _____ when they are first created. As these database object grow, they will be allocated their own _____. (Fill in the blanks.)

   A. Page, pages

   B. Extent, extents

   C. Table, tables

   D. Record, records

5. When you create or alter your database, you can specify a size parameter for the Filegrowth option. This size parameter can be expressed as which of the following? (Choose all that apply.)

   A. Megabytes

   B. Kilobytes

   C. Bytes

   D. Percentage of current database size

6. You have just taken over responsibility for an installation of SQL Server 7. The former database administrator did not keep good notes on the server. Which of the following stored procedures will give you information about the size, location, name, and type of data (data or log) of all files that a particular database is using?

   A. sp_help

   B. sp_helpfile

   C. sp_helpfilegroup

   D. sp_helpdb

7. What is the maximum size of a row in SQL Server 7?

   A. 2000 bytes

   B. 4000 bytes

   C. 8060 bytes

   D. 16,000 bytes

8. You have a database in SQL Server that stores all the transactions posted every month. The database spans three database files. Normal operation shows that this database grows from approximately 10MB at the beginning of the month to about 400MB by month end. You wish to shrink the database at the end of each month back to an initial size of 10MB. You decide to move the data to a history database on another SQL Server machine. Once this is done, you have about 398 MB of free space in your database. What command can you use to reclaim that free space and return it back to the operating system?

    A. Use the `DBCC SHRINKDATABASE` command with a percentage parameter and the TRUNCATEONLY parameter.

    B. Use the DBCC SHRINKDATABASE command with a percentage parameter and the NOTRUNCATE parameter.

    C. Use the `DBCC SHRINKDATABASE` command with the TRUNCA-TEONLY parameter.

    D. Use the `DBCC SHRINKDATABASE` command with the NOTRUN-CATE parameter.

9. You are estimating the storage requirements for a table defined with the following fields: Char(15), Int(4), Float(8), Char(10). How many bytes will be used to store each row, assuming no fields allow nulls? (Remember to include 2 bytes of overhead for your row.)

    A. 33

    B. 35

    C. 37

    D. 39

10. You have a very large database and cannot make a full database backup in the time allotted. What database objects will allow you to perform a partial database backup and still ensure consistency?

    A. Multiple data files

    B. Multiple log files

    C. Filegroups

    D. There is nothing that you can do that will backup a portion of the database and ensure data integrity.

11. You are a database developer and have been working on a database in the development environment called "devFamTree." You have finished developing and testing the database and would like to put it into production as "FamilyTree." You must first put the database into single-user mode. Which of the following commands would do this?

A. `ALTER DATABASE devFamTree, 'Single User', True`

B. `MODIFY DATABASE devFamTree, 'Single User', True`

C. `EXEC sp_changedbowner, 'devFamTree', 'single user'`

D. `EXEC sp_dboption devFamTree, 'Single User', True`

12. You are a database developer and have been working on a database in the development environment called "devFamTree." You are finished developing and testing the database and would like to put the database into production as "FamilyTree." You have placed the database into Single-User mode and now wish to change the database name. Which of the following commands would do this?

A. `ALTER DATABASE devFamTree, FamilyTree`

B. `MODIFY DATABASE devFamTree, FamilyTree`

C. `EXEC sp_renamedb devFamTree, FamilyTree`

D. `EXEC sp_changedb devFamTree, FamilyTree`

13. You are evaluating hardware for your SQL Server database system. Your database must be up and running 24 hours a day, 7 days a week. You have a limited budget so new hardware is out of the question. You must ensure fault-tolerance, but you also want to optimize speed and storage. You decide to implement Windows NT's disk striping with parity, or RAID 5. How would you rate this solution?

A. This is a poor solution and does not fit the requirements

B. This is a poor solution although it appears to fit the requirements

C. This is good solution, but doesn't fit all of the requirements

D. This is an excellent solution and fits all of the requirements

14. You have just created several new databases on your system and are worried about recovery. You decide to make backups of each of these databases. What other database should you back up?

A. Master

B. Model

C. Msdb

D. Tempdb

15. You are getting ready to create a new database that will be 25GB. You have 6 hard disks, each of which is 10GB in size. Which of the following data storage schemas will result in the fastest performance with the best fault-tolerance?

A. Use RAID 5, striping with parity across all 6 hard disks, and place both the transaction log and data files on the RAID array.

B. Use RAID 5, striping with parity across 4 of the 6 hard disks, and place your data files on them. Use RAID 1, disk mirroring on the other 2 hard disks, and place the transaction log on them.

C. Use RAID 0, striping only across all 6 hard disks, and place both the transaction log and data files on them.

D. Use RAID 0, striping only across 4 hard disks, and place the data files on them. Use RAID 1, mirroring on the other 2 hard disks, and place the transaction log on them.

16. You are getting ready to create a new database that will be 20GB. You have 6 hard disks, each of which is 10GB in size. Which of the following data storage schemas will result in the fastest backup performance while maintaining a high level of fault-tolerance and recoverability?

   A. Use RAID 5, striping with parity across all 6 hard disks. Create a single 20GB file for your data. Place the transaction log and data file on the RAID array.

   B. Use RAID 5, striping with parity across 4 of the 6 hard disks. Use RAID 1, disk mirroring on the other 2 hard disks, and place the transaction log on them. Create four 5GB filegroups and place them on the stripe set.

   C. Use RAID 1, mirroring for 2 of the hard disks, and place the transaction log there. Create four 5GB filegroups and place each filegroup on an individual hard disk.

   D. Create twenty 1GB data files and place them on a RAID 5 system. When you do your backups, back up a single file each day on a rotating 20-day cycle.

CHAPTER

5

Security and SQL Server 7

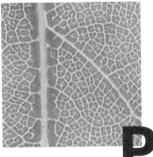

Protecting information, guarding access to an organization's data, is much like protecting a physical structure. For example, imagine that you own a business and the building that houses it. You do not want the general public to gain access to your building—only your employees. Even here, however, you need restrictions on the areas to which your employees have access. Because only accountants should have access to the accounting department, and almost no one should have access to your office, you must put various security systems in place to ensure this.

Protecting SQL Server (your "building") holds true to this concept: no one gets in unless granted access, and once inside, various security systems keep prying eyes out of sensitive areas. In this chapter we will discuss the methods used to apply security to SQL Server.

Understanding Security Modes

To continue our analogy, in order for your employees to gain access to the building, they will need some sort of key, whether a metal key or an electronic access card. In order for your users to gain access to SQL Server, you will need to give them a key as well. The type of key you give them largely depends on the type of lock—*authentication mode*—you use.

Although this entire exam objective is covered in this chapter, individual sub-objectives are covered throughout the chapter, and thus just the sub-objective will be shown where appropriate.

*Microsoft
Exam
Objective*

Develop a security strategy.

- Assess whether to use Microsoft Windows NT accounts or Microsoft SQL Server logins.
- Assess whether to leverage the Windows NT group structure.
- Plan the use and structure of SQL Server roles. Server roles include fixed server, fixed database, and user-defined database.
- Assess whether to map Windows NT groups directly into a database or to map them to a role.
- Assess which Windows NT accounts will be used to run SQL Server services.
- Plan an *n*-tier application security strategy, and decide whether to use application roles or other mid-tier security mechanisms such as Microsoft Transaction Server.
- Plan the security requirements for linked databases.

An authentication mode is how SQL processes user names and passwords. There are two such modes in SQL 7: Windows NT Authentication mode and Mixed Mode.

Windows NT Authentication Mode

In this mode, a user can simply sit down at their computer, log on to the Windows NT domain and gain access to SQL Server. Here's how it works:

1. The user logs on to a Windows NT domain; the user name and password are verified by NT
2. The user then opens a *trusted connection* (Figure 5.1) with SQL server.
3. SQL will then try to match the user name or group membership to an entry in the Sysxlogins table.
4. Since this is a trusted connection SQL does not need to verify the user password; that is, SQL trusts NT to perform that function.

F I G U R E 5.1

Trusted connection to
SQL Server

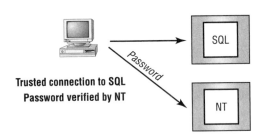

The main advantage to Windows NT Authentication mode is that users do not have to remember multiple user names and passwords. That will vastly increase security since there is less danger of users writing their passwords down and storing them in an unsafe place (like a sticky note on their monitor). This mode also gives you tighter reign over security since you can apply NT password policies that will do such things as expire passwords, require a minimum length for passwords, keep a history of passwords, and so on.

One of the disadvantages is that only users with a Windows NT account can open a trusted connection to SQL Server. That means that someone like a Novell client running the IPX net library cannot use Windows NT Authentication mode. If it turns out that you have such clients, you will need to implement Mixed Mode.

Mixed Mode

Mixed Mode allows both NT Authentication and SQL Authentication. In SQL Authentication:

1. The user Logs on to their network, NT or otherwise.

2. Next, the user opens a *non-trusted* (Figure 5.2) connection to SQL Server using a separate user name and password.

3. SQL then matches the username and password entered by the user to an entry in the Sysxlogins table.

F I G U R E 5.2

Non-trusted connec-
tion to SQL Server

The primary advantage here is that anyone can gain access to SQL using Mixed Mode, regardless of the net library used. This means that Mac users, Novell users, Banyan Vines users, and the like can gain access. You could also consider this to be a second layer of security, since hacking into the network in Mixed Mode does not mean that someone has automatically hacked into SQL at the same time.

Ironically, multiple passwords be a problem as well as an advantage. Consider that users will have one user name and password to log on to the network and a completely separate user name and password to gain access to SQL. When users have multiple sets of credentials they tend to write them down and thus breach the security system you have worked so hard to set up.

Setting the Authentication Mode

As an administrator you will probably set the authentication mode no more than once, at installation time. The only other time you might need to change the authentication mode would be if you changes were made to your network. For example, if you had set your SQL Server to Windows NT Authentication mode and needed to include Macintosh clients, you would need to change to Mixed Mode.

It is interesting to note that although most things in SQL can be done through either the Enterprise Manager or Transact-SQL (T-SQL), setting the authentication mode is one of the rare things that can be done only through the Enterprise Manager. Exercise 5.1 takes you through the steps of setting the authentication mode.

EXERCISE 5.1

Setting the Authentication Mode

1. Open the Enterprise Manager, right-click your server (either your server name or Local) and select Properties.

2. Select the Security tab.

3. In the Authentication section, select SQL Server and Windows NT. This will set you to Mixed Mode for the rest of the exercises.

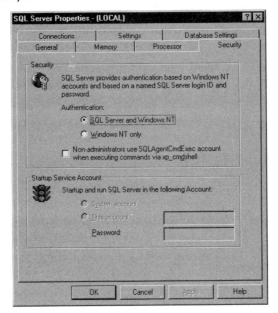

4. Click the OK button to close the Properties dialog box.

Now that you have set the proper authentication mode it is time to move forward and give your users a "key" to your building with SQL Server Logins.

SQL Server Logins

Once you have decided what type of "lock" (authentication mode) to use on your "building" you can start handing out "keys" so that your employees can gain access. A real key will give your employees access to the building as a whole but to none of the resources (like filing cabinets) inside. In the same way, a SQL Server "key", a *login*, will give your users access to

SQL Server as a whole but not to the resources (like databases) inside. If you are a member of the sysadmin or securityadmin *fixed server roles* (discussed later), you will be able to create one of two types of logins: standard logins (like the metal key in our analogy) and Windows NT logins (like the newer electronic access card).

Microsoft
✓ *Exam*
Objective

Develop a security strategy.

- Assess whether to use Microsoft Windows NT or Microsoft SQL Server logins.
- Assess whether to leverage the Windows NT group structure.

Microsoft
✓ *Exam*
Objective

Assign SQL Server access through Windows NT accounts, SQL Server logins, and built-in administrator logins.

Standard Logins

We learned earlier that only clients with a Windows NT account can make trusted connections to SQL (SQL trusts NT to validate the user's password). If the user (such as a Macintosh or Novell client) for whom you are creating a login cannot make a trusted connection, you must create a standard login for them (as discussed in Exercises 5.2 and 5.3).

While you can create standard logins in Windows NT Only authentication mode you won't be able to use them. If you try, SQL will ignore you and use your NT credentials instead.

EXERCISE 5.2

Creating and Testing a Standard Login Using Enterprise Manager

1. Open Enterprise Manager and expand your server by clicking the + sign next to the icon named after your server.

2. Click the Logins Icon just below the *Your_server_name* icon.

3. Click the Action Menu and select New Login.

4. In the Name box, type **SmithB**.

5. In the Authentication section select SQL Server Authentication.

6. In the Password text box, type **password**.

7. Under Defaults, select Pubs as the default database.

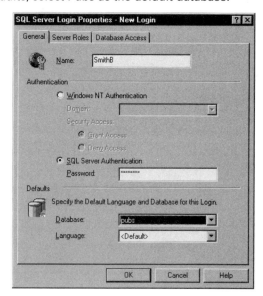

8. Click the OK button.

9. In the Confirm New Password text box, type **password**.

10. Click OK and notice your new Standard Type login in the contents pane.

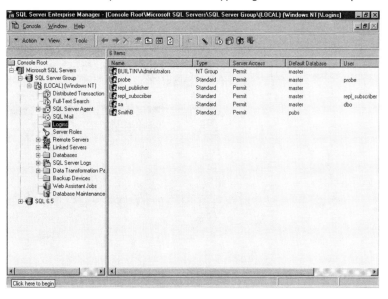

11. To test the new login, open Query Analyzer.

12. Under Connection Information select Use SQL Server Authentication.

13. In the Login Name box, type **SmithB**.

14. In the Password Box, type **password**.

15. Click OK and notice the title bar. It should read "sqlserver.pubs.SmithB."

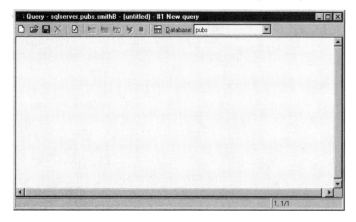

EXERCISE 5.3

Creating and Testing a Standard Login Using T-SQL

1. Open Query Analyzer and log in using Windows NT Authentication

2. Execute the following query to create a standard login for GibsonH:

   sp_addlogin @loginame='GibsonH'**, @passwd=**'password'**,
   @defdb=**'pubs'

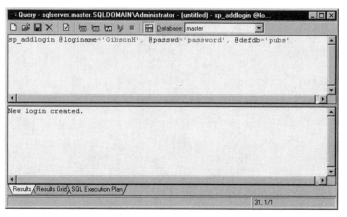

3. On the File menu select Disconnect.

4. On the File menu select Connect.

5. Log in using SQL Authentication with a username of GibsonH and a password of password. You were able to log in because you successfully created GibsonH.

6. For further verification, close Query Analyzer and open Enterprise Manager.

7. Select Logins and notice the new Standard Type user GibsonH.

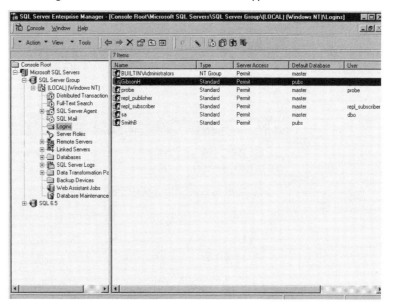

 A standard login, sa, is created at installation time with a blank default password. Since the system administrator (SA) has godlike power over the system, you must choose a new password immediately.

Windows NT Logins

Creating Windows NT Logins (as described in Exercise 5.4) is not much different from creating Standard Logins. While Standard Logins applied to only one user, however, a Windows NT Login can be mapped to one of the following:

- A single user

- A Windows NT group an administrator has created

- A Windows NT *builtin* group (e.g., Administrators)

Before you create a Windows NT Login you must decide which of these three you want to map it to. Generally you will want to map to a group that you have created. This will help you a great deal in later administration. For example, suppose you have an Accounting database to which all 50 of your accountants require access. You could create a separate login for each of them, which would require you to manage 50 SQL logins. On the other hand, if you create a Windows NT group for these 50 accountants and map your SQL Login to this group, you will have only one SQL Login to manage.

EXERCISE 5.4

Creating Windows NT-to-SQL Logins Using Enterprise Manager

1. Open User Manager, click on the User menu, and select New User.

2. Create six new users with the criteria from the following table:

Username	Description	Password	Must Change	Never Expires
MorrisL	IT	Password	Uncheck	Check
ThompsonA	Administration	Password	Uncheck	Check
JohnsonK	Accounting	Password	Uncheck	Check
JonesB	Accounting	Password	Uncheck	Check
ChenJ	Sales	Password	Uncheck	Check
SamuelsR	Sales	Password	Uncheck	Check

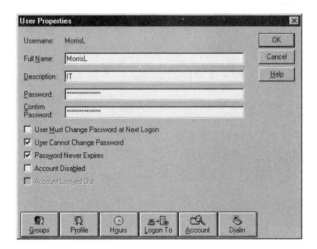

3. While in User Manager, create a Local group called Accounting.

4. Add the new users you just created with a Description of Accounting.

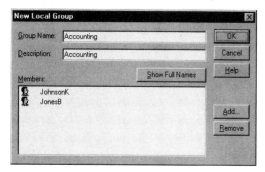

5. While still in User Manager, create a Local group named Sales.

6. Add all the users with a Description of Sales.

7. While still in User Manager, click the Policies menu and select User Rights.

8. Select Log on Locally from the Rights list and add Everyone.

9. Click OK to return to User Manager.

10. Close User Manager and open Enterprise Manager.

11. Expand your server and click the Logins folder.

12. On the Actions Menu select New Login.

13. In the Name box, type **Accounting** (the name of the Local group created earlier).

14. Select Windows NT Authentication and select your domain from the drop-down list next to Domain.

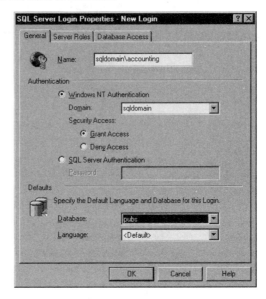

15. Click OK and notice the Accounting Login of Type NT Group.

16. Go back into the New User dialog by selecting New User from the Action menu.

17. Fill in the Name field with **ThompsonA**.

18. Select Windows NT Authentication and select your domain from the list.

19. Under Defaults, select Pubs as the default database.

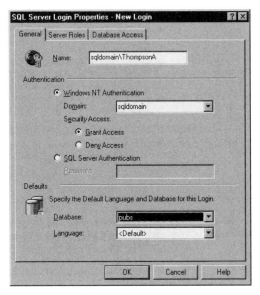

20. Click OK and notice the new login for ThompsonA of Type NT user.

21. Log off Windows NT and log back on as JonesB.

22. Open Query Analyzer and select Use Windows NT Authentication. Notice the title bar displays "sqlserver.pubs.sqldomain\accounting." This is because JonesB is a member of the NT Accounting group.

23. Close Query Analyzer, log off NT, and log back on as ThompsonA.

EXERCISE 5.4 (CONTINUED)

24. Open Query Analyzer and select Use Windows NT Authentication. The title bar displays "sqlserver.pubs.sqldomain\ThompsonA," because we created an account specifically for ThompsonA rather than making him a member of the Accounting group.

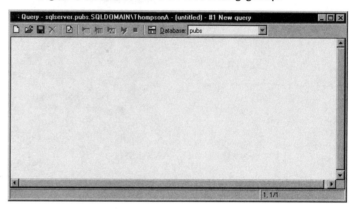

Exercise 5.5 will show you how to create Windows NT logins using T-SQL.

EXERCISE 5.5

Creating Windows NT Logins to SQL Using T-SQL

1. Open Query Analyzer and log in using Windows NT Authentication.

2. Execute the following query to create a Windows NT Login for the Sales group; note that the command is different than that used in creating a Standard Login:

```
sp_grantlogin @loginame='sqldomain\sales'
```

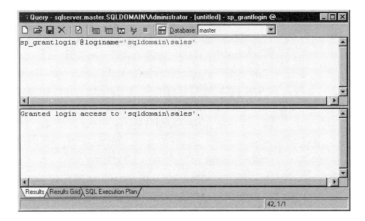

3. On the Query menu select Clear Window and do not save the changes.

4. Execute the following query to create a Windows NT Login for MorrisL:

   sp_grantlogin @loginame='sqldomain\MorrisL'

5. Close Query Analyzer and open Enterprise Manager.

6. Expand your server by clicking the + next to the server name.

7. Select Logins and notice the two new logins for Sales and MorrisL.

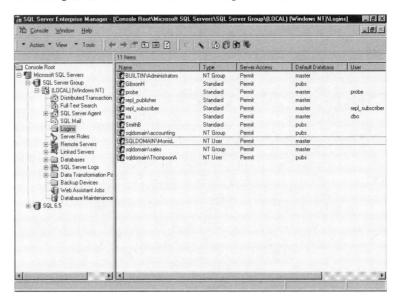

Items Common to All Logins

You may have noticed that some things are common to all the logins that we created.

The first is the default database. When a user first logs in to SQL they will connect to the default database. This is just a starting point, since users can't use the default database without a database user account: all they can do is connect to it. If you do not set the default database, it will be Master—which is not the best place for your users to get started. You will want to change that to a different database, for example, an Accounting database if you are working with an accounting user. You can also set a default language, which will not need frequent changing since the default is the server's language. A different language can be set here for users who require it.

In all types of logins, you can grant database access at create time. On the Database Access tab in the Enterprise Manager New Login dialog box, all you need to do is check the database to which this login will require access; this automatically creates a database user account. Although, we didn't do that in the exercises, as an administrator, you will want to grant access to databases at create time.

WARNING If you create a Windows NT login using sp_grantlogin you cannot set the default database or language.

In addition, you can add users to a fixed server role at the time you create them; this is done on the Server Roles tab in Enterprise Manager. Fixed server roles—limitations on access—are discussed next.

Fixed Server Roles

Back to our analogy: As the owner, when you walk into your building, you are allowed to do whatever you want (after all, you do own it). When members of the accounting department walk in, however, they are limited in what they can do. For example, they are not allowed to take keys away from other workers, but they may be allowed to do other administrative tasks like signing checks.

Microsoft ✓ *Exam Objective*

Create and assign SQL Server roles. Server roles include fixed server, fixed database, public, user-defined database, and application.

Microsoft ✓ *Exam Objective*

Develop a security strategy.

- Plan the use and structure of SQL Server roles. Server roles include fixed server, fixed database, and user-defined database.
- Assess whether to map Windows NT groups directly into a data-base or to map them to a role.

That is what fixed server roles are used for, to limit the amount of administrative access that a user has once logged in to SQL Server. Some users may be allowed to do whatever they want, whereas other users may only be able to manage security. Exercises 5.6 and 5.7 will show you how to assign users to a fixed server role.

EXERCISE 5.6

Assigning a User to a Fixed Server Role Using Enterprise Manager

1. Open Enterprise Manager and select Server Roles.

EXERCISE 5.6 (CONTINUED)

2. Double-click System Administrators to open the Sysadmin Server Role Properties dialog box.

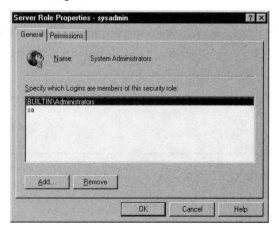

3. Click Add, select MorrisL, and click OK.

4. Click the Permissions tab and notice the extensive list of permissions granted to this role.

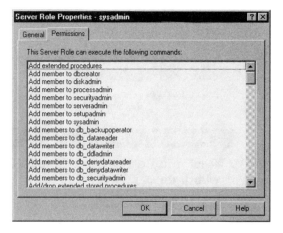

5. Click OK to exit the Server Role Properties dialog box.

EXERCISE 5.7

Assigning a User to a Fixed Server Role Using T-SQL

1. Open Query Analyzer and log in using Windows NT Authentication.

2. Execute the following query to add a member to the serveradmin fixed server role:

```
sp_addsrvrolemember @loginame='GibsonH',
@rolename='serveradmin'
```

3. Close Query Analyzer, open Enterprise Manager, expand your server, and select Logins.

4. Double-click GibsonH and notice that it has been added to the server-admin fixed database role.

There are seven server roles to which you can assign users. The following list starts at the highest level and describes the administrative access granted:

Sysadmin   Members of the sysadmin role can do whatever they want in SQL Server. Be careful whom you assign to this role; people who are unfamiliar with SQL can accidentally create serious problems. This role is only for the database administrators (DBAs).

Serveradmin   These users can set serverwide configuration options, like how much memory SQL can use or how much information to send over the network in a single frame. If you make your assistant DBAs members of this role you can relieve yourself of some of the administrative burden.

Setupadmin   Members here can managed linked servers.

Securityadmin   These users manage security issues such as creating and deleting logins, reading the audit logs, and granting users permission to create databases. This too is a good role for assistant DBAs.

Processadmin   SQL is capable of multitasking; that is, it can do more than one thing at a time by executing multiple processes. For instance, SQL might spawn one process for writing to cache and another for reading from cache. A member of the Processadmin group can end (called *kill* in SQL) a process. This is another good role for assistant DBAs and developers. Developers especially need to kill processes that may have been triggered by an improperly designed query or stored procedure.

Dbcreator   These users can create and make changes to databases and also restore backups. This may be a good role for assistant DBAs as well as developers (who should be warned against creating unnecessary databases and wasting server space).

Diskadmin   These users manage files on disk. They do things like mirroring databases and adding backup devices. Assistant DBAs should be members of this role.

If you do not want users to have any administrative authority, do not assign them to a server role. This will limit them to being just normal users.

Builtin\Administrators is automatically made a member of the sysadmin server role, giving SQL administrative rights to all of your NT administrators. Since not all of your NT administrators should have these rights, you may want to create a SQLAdmins group, add your SQL Administrators and your SQLAgent service account to that group. Afterward you should remove Builtin\Administrators from the sysadmin role.

Creating Database User Accounts

Now that your employees have access to your building as well as the proper administrative access once they are inside, they will need access to other resources to do their work. For example, if you want to give your accounting department access to the accounting files, you need to give them a new key—one to the file cabinet. Your employees now have two keys, one for the front door and one for the file cabinet.

In much the same way, we need to give users access to databases once they have logged in to SQL. This is accomplished by creating database user accounts and then assigning permissions to those user accounts (permissions are discussed later). Once complete, your SQL users will also have more than one key, one to for the front door (the login) and one for each file cabinet (database) to which they need access.

Exercises 5.8 and 5.9 describe how to create database user accounts.

Microsoft *Exam* **Objective**

Assign database access to Windows NT accounts, SQL Server logins, the **guest** user account, and **dbo** user account.

EXERCISE 5.8

Creating Database User Accounts Using Enterprise Manager

1. Open Enterprise Manager and expand your server.

2. Expand Databases by clicking on the + sign next to the icon.

3. Expand the Pubs database.

4. Click the Database Users icon.

5. From the Action menu select New Database User.

6. In the Login Name box view all the available names; note that only logins that you have already created are available.

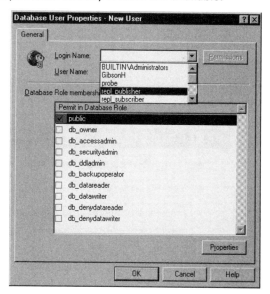

7. Select Sqldomain\accounting.

8. In the Login Name box leave Sqldomain\accounting.

9. Click OK. You now have a new user named Sqldomain\accounting.

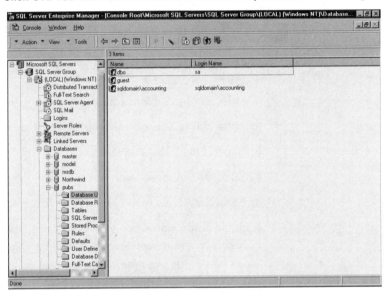

10. Repeat steps 5 through 9 for Sales, ThompsonA, MorrisL, and SmithB.

Creating Database User Accounts Using Transact SQL

1. Open Query Analyzer and log in using Windows NT Authentication.

2. In the Database drop-down list at the top right of the Query window select the Pubs database. This sets Pubs as the active database.

3. Execute the following query to create a new user account:

```
sp_grantdbaccess @loginame='GrantH'
```

4. On the Query menu select Clear Window and do not save the changes.

5. Execute the following query to create a database user account for the Sales group; the database user name will be different from the login name:

```
sp_grantdbaccess @loginame='Sales', @name_in_
db='SalesUsers'
```

6. Close Query Analyzer, open Enterprise Manager and expand your server, then expand Databases.

7. Select Users; you have two new users: GrantH and SalesUsers.

You may have noticed that one user account already exists in your database: Dbo. Members of the sysadmin fixed server role automatically become the DBO (database owner) user in every database on the system. In this way they can perform all the necessary administrative functions in the databases, such as adding users and creating tables. *Guest user* is a catch-all term used for people who have a SQL login but not a user account in the database. These users can log in to SQL as themselves and access any database where they do not have a user account. The guest account should be limited in function since anybody with a SQL login can make use of it.

Whenever a member of the sysadmin fixed server role creates an object (like a table) it is not owned by that login. It is owned by the DBO. If MorrisL created a table, it would not be referred to as MorrisL.table, but as dbo.table instead.

Now that you have created user accounts for everyone, you need to restrict what they are capable of doing with the database. This is done by assigning permissions directly to the users or by adding the users to a database role with a predefined set of permissions.

Understanding Permissions

To continue our business analogy, it would be unthinkable for the sales department to go over to the accounting department and start writing themselves large checks. In most businesses today, the sales department does not have permission to use the checkbook. Even further, not all the people in the accounting department have full access to the checkbook; some only have permission to read from it while others have permission to write checks from it.

We see the same situation in SQL Server. Not all your users should be able to access the accounting or human resources databases, since they contain sensitive information. Even users who are allowed in should not necessarily be given full access. To enforce these restrictions you need to grant permissions.

Microsoft ✓ ***Exam*** ***Objective***   **Grant to database users and roles the appropriate permissions on database objects and statements.**

Statement Permissions

In your building, do you allow the contractors who constructed it to come in and use your files and copiers and various other resources? No, you gave them permission to construct the building initially and to make renovations over time—but not to use the files and other such resources inside.

In SQL, this constraint would be akin to granting the contractors statement permissions. Statement permissions have nothing to do with the actual data; they allow users to create the structure that holds the data. It is important not to grant these permissions haphazardly, however—it can lead to such problems as *broken ownership chains* (discussed later) and wasted server resources. It is best to restrict these permissions to DBAs, assistant

DBAs, and developers. The following are the statement permissions (Exercises 5.10 and 5.11 show how to apply them):

- Create Database
- Create Table
- Create View
- Create Procedure
- Create Rule
- Create Default
- Create Backup Database
- Create Backup Log

The Create Database permission can be granted only on the master database.

EXERCISE 5.10

Granting Statement Permissions Using Enterprise Manager

1. To prepare SQL for the following exercises, we need to remove permissions from the public role. Open Query Analyzer and execute the following query:

```
use pubs
revoke all from public
```

2. Close Query Analyzer and do not save the changes.

3. Open Enterprise Manager and expand your server, then expand Databases.

4. Right-click the Pubs database and select Properties.

5. In the Properties dialog box select the Permissions tab.

6. Grant ThompsonA the Create Table permission by clicking the check box under Create Table until a black check appears.

7. Grant Accounting the permission to Backup DB and Backup Log.

8. If the Guest user has any permissions granted, remove them by clicking each check box until it is cleared.

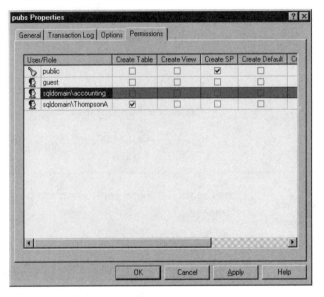

9. Log off Windows NT and log back on as JonesB.

10. Open Query Analyzer, log in using Windows NT authentication, and type the following query:

```
Use pubs
Create table Statement1
(column1varchar(5)not null,
column2varchar(10) not null)
```

11. On the Query pull-down menu select Execute Query and notice that the query is unsuccessful because JonesB (a member of the Accounting group) does not have permission to create a table.

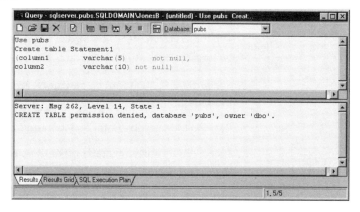

12. Close Query Analyzer, log off Windows NT, and log back on as ThompsonA.

13. Repeat step 8 and execute the query. This time it is successful since ThompsonA has permission to create tables.

Granting Statement Permissions Using T-SQL

1. Open Query Analyzer and log in using Windows NT authentication.

2. Execute the following query to grant GibsonH permission to create tables:

   ```
   use pubs
   GRANT create table to GibsonH
   ```

3. On the File Menu select Disconnect.

4. On the File Menu select Connect and log in using SQL authentication. Enter **GibsonH** as the username and **password** as the password.

5. Execute the following query to verify that GibsonH has the Create Table permission:

```
Use pubs
Create table Statement2
(column1varchar(5)not null,
column2varchar(10) not null)
```

6. For further verification, close Query Analyzer and open Enterprise Manager.

7. Right-click the Pubs database icon and select Properties.

8. Select the Permissions tab and notice that GibsonH has been granted the Create Database permission.

Object Permissions

Once the structure exists to hold the data, you need to give users permission to start working with the data in the databases by granting your users object permissions. Using object permissions you can control who is allowed to read from, write to, or otherwise manipulate your data. Exercises 5.12 and 5.13 will instruct you in the ways of setting the following object permissions.

Select   When granted, allows users to read data from the table or view. When granted at the column level this will allow users to read from a single column.

Insert   Allows users to insert new rows into a table.

Update   Allows users to modify existing data in a table. When granted on a column, users will be able to modify data in that single column.

Delete   Allows users to remove rows from a table.

References   When two tables are linked with a foreign key, this allows the user to select data from the primary table without having Select permission on the referenced table.

Execute   This allows users to execute the stored procedure where the permission is applied.

EXERCISE 5.12

Assigning Object Permissions Using Enterprise Manager

1. Open Enterprise Manager, expand your server, then Databases, and select Pubs.

2. Select Tables in the right pane, right-click Authors, and select Properties.

3. Click the Permissions button.

4. Grant Salesusers Select permission by clicking the check box under Select until a black check appears.

5. If the guest user has any permissions granted, remove them by clicking each one until all check boxes are clear.

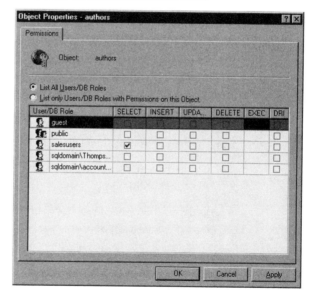

6. Click OK and close Enterprise Manager.

7. Log off Windows NT and log back on as JonesB.

EXERCISE 5.12 (CONTINUED)

8. Open Query Analyzer and select Windows NT Authentication.

9. Execute the following query. It fails since Accounting does not have Select permission:

```
use pubs
select * from authors
```

10. Close Query Analyzer and repeat steps 7 through 9 for ChenJ. The query succeeds this time since Sales (of which ChenJ is a member) has Select permission.

11. Log off Windows NT and log back in as Administrator.

EXERCISE 5.13

Assigning Object Permissions Using T-SQL

1. Open Query Analyzer and log in using Windows NT Authentication.

2. Execute the following query to grant Select permissions to SmithB:

```
use pubs
grant select on authors to SmithB
```

3. On the File menu select Disconnect.

4. On the File menu select Connect and log in as SmithB using SQL Authentication.

5. Verify that SmithB has Select permission on the Authors table to execute the following query:

```
use pubs
select * from authors
```

6. Close Query Analyzer.

Although granting permissions to single users will be useful from time to time, it is better, faster, and easier to apply permissions en masse. This requires understanding database roles.

Database Roles

Continuing our business analogy, your accountants need to write corporate checks. You could give them permission to do so in one of two ways. First, you could give each of the accountants their own checkbook drawn from a single account with permission to write checks from it. That would be an accounting nightmare—trying to keep track of all the checks that had been written during the month. The better way to accomplish this is to get one corporate account with one checkbook, and give the accountants as a group permission to write checks from that one book.

> ***Microsoft***
> ✓ ***Exam***
> ***Objective***
>
> **Create and assign SQL Server roles. Server roles include fixed server, fixed database, public, user-defined database, and application.**

In SQL when several users need permission to access to a database, it is much easier to give them all permissions as a group rather than trying to manage each user separately. That is what database roles are for, granting permissions to groups of database users, rather than granting them to each database user separately. There are three types of database roles to consider: fixed, custom, and application.

Fixed Database Roles

Fixed database roles have permissions already applied; that is, all you have to do is add users to these roles and they inherit the associated permissions. (That is different from custom database roles, as you will see later.) There are several fixed database roles in SQL Server that can be used to grant permissions (Exercises 5.14 and 5.15 show how to assign users to these roles):

Db_owner   Members of this role can do everything the members of the other roles can do as well as some administrative functions.

Db_accessadmin   The users have the authority to say who gets access to the database by adding or removing users.

Db_datareader   Members here can read data from any table in the database.

Db_datawriter   These users can add, change, and delete data from all the tables in the database.

Db_ddladmin   Data Definition Language administrators can issue all DDL commands; this allows them to create, modify, or change database objects without viewing the data inside.

Db_securityadmin   Members here can add and remove users from database roles and manage statement and object permissions.

Db_backupoperator   These users can back up the database.

Db_denydatareader   Members cannot read the data in the database.

Db_denydatawriter   These users cannot make changes to the data in the database.

Public   The purpose of this group is to grant users a default set of permissions in the database. All database users automatically join this group and cannot be removed.

EXERCISE 5.14

Assigning Users to Fixed Database Roles Using Enterprise Manager

1. Open Enterprise Manager, expand your server and Databases, then select Pubs.

2. Click Database Roles.

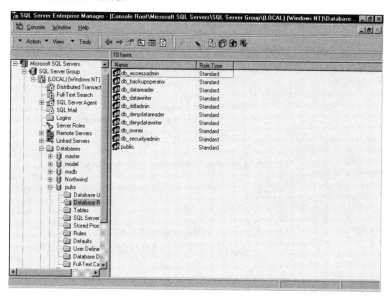

3. In the contents pane, double-click Db_denydatawriter.

4. Click the Add button.

5. Select SmithB and click OK.

6. Click OK again to go back to Enterprise Manager.

7. Open Query Analyzer and select Use SQL Server Authentication.

8. In the User Name box, type **SmithB**; in the Password box, type **password**.

9. In the following query you will try to update information in the Authors table; it fails since SmithB is a member of the db_deny-datawriter role:

```
Update authors
Set authors.au_fname='Mike'
Where au_fname='Michael'
```

10. Close Query Analyzer.

EXERCISE 5.15

Assigning Users to Fixed Database Roles Using Transact-SQL

1. Open Query Analyzer and log in using Windows NT Authentication.

2. Execute the following query to add GibsonH to the db_denydata-reader role.

```
use pubs
sp_addrolemember @rolename='db_denydatareader'
@membername='GibsonH'
```

3. On the File menu select Disconnect.

4. On the File menu select Connect and log in using Windows NT Authentication.

5. Execute the following query to verify that GibsonH does not have the permission to read data because of his membership in the db_deny-datareader role:

```
use pubs
select * from authors
```

6. Close Query Analyzer.

 If you use the sp_addrolemember stored procedure to add a user to a database role, you do not need to create the user account first. SQL will create it for you.

Custom Database Roles

There will, of course, be times when the fixed database roles do not meet your security needs. You might have several users who need Select, Update, and Execute permissions in your database and nothing more. Because none of the fixed database roles will give you that set of permissions, you can create a custom database role. When you create this new role, you will assign permissions to it and then assign users to the role; then the users will inherit whatever permissions you assign to the role. That is different from the fixed database roles where you did not need to assign permissions but just added users. Exercises 5.16 and 5.17 explain how to create a database role.

You can make your custom database roles members of other database roles. This is referred to as *nesting roles.*

EXERCISE 5.16

Creating Custom Database Roles Using Enterprise Manager

1. Open Enterprise Manager and expand your server, then Databases, and select Pubs.

2. Click Database Roles.

3. On the Action Menu select New Database Role.

4. In the Name box, type **SelectOnly.**

5. Under Database Role Type, select Standard Role and click Add.

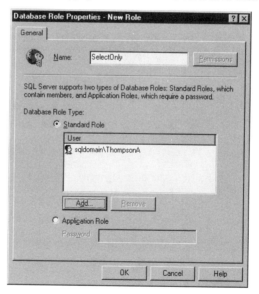

6. Select ThompsonA and click OK.

7. Click OK to go back to Enterprise Manager and notice the new role in the contents pane.

8. Double-click the Role and then click the Permissions button.

9. Locate the Tables entry and check the corresponding Select check box to grant Select access to all tables in the database.

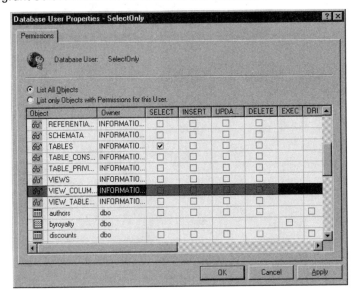

10. Click OK to go back to the previous dialog box.

11. Click OK once more to go back to Enterprise Manager.

12. Close all programs, log off Windows NT, and log back on as ThompsonA.

13. Open Query Analyzer and use Windows NT Authentication.

14. Notice that the following query succeeds since ThompsonA is a member of the new SelectOnly role:

```
use pubs
select * from authors
```

15. Now notice the failure of the next query since ThompsonA is a member of a role that is allowed to select only

```
Update authors
Set authors.au_fname='Mike'
Where au_fname='Michael'
```

16. Close all programs, log off NT, and log back on as Administrator.

Creating Custom Database Roles Using T-SQL

1. Open Query Analyzer and log in using Windows NT Authentication.

2. Execute the following query to create the UpdateOnly database role in the Pubs database:

   use pubs
   sp_addrole @rolename='UpdateOnly'

3. On the Query Menu select Clear Windows and do not save the changes

4. Execute the following query to grant Update permission to the new role:

   grant update on authors to updateonly

5. On the Query Menu select Clear Windows and do not save the changes.

6. Execute the following query to add Sales to the UpdateOnly database role:

   sp_addrolemember @rolename='UpdateOnly',
   @membername='Sales'

7. Close Query Analyzer, log off Windows NT, and log back in as ChenJ (a member of the Sales group).

8. Open Query Analyzer and log in using Windows NT Authentication.

9. Execute the following query and note its success since the Sales group's membership in the UpdateOnly role provides update permissions:

```
use pubs
update authors
set authors.au_fname='Mike'
where au_fname='Michael'
```

10. On the Query menu select Clear Window and do not save any changes.

11. Execute the following query and note its failure since the Sales group does not have any permissions other than update:

```
select * from authors
```

12. Close Query Analyzer, log off Windows NT, and log back in as Administrator.

Application Roles

Suppose that your human resources department uses a custom program to access their database, and you don't want them using any other program for fear of damaging the data. You can set this level of security by using an *application role*. With this special role, your users will not be able to access data using just their SQL login and database account; they will have to use the proper application.

Once you've created the application role described in Exercises 5.18 and 5.19, the user logs on to SQL, is authenticated, and opens the approved application. The application executes the sp_setapprole stored procedure to enable the application role. Once the application role is enabled, SQL no longer sees users as themselves; it sees users as the application and grants them application role permissions.

EXERCISE 5.18

Creating Application Roles Using Enterprise Manager

1. Open Enterprise Manager and select Database Roles in the Pubs database.

2. On the Action Menu select New Database Role.

3. In the Name box, type **EntAppRole**.

4. Under Database Role Type, select Application Role.

5. In the Password box, type **password**.

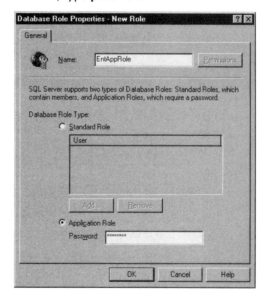

6. Click OK to get back to the Enterprise Manager.

7. Double-click the EntAppRole and click the Permissions button.

EXERCISE 5.18 (CONTINUED)

8. Grant Select permissions on Authors by clicking on the Select check box next to the Authors line until a black checkmark appears.

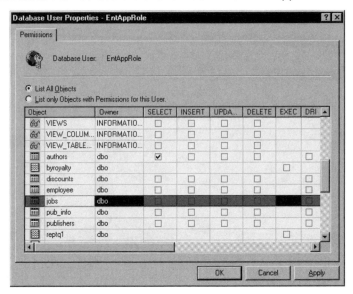

9. Click OK to get back to the previous dialog box and click OK again to return to Enterprise Manager.

10. Close Enterprise Manager and open Query Analyzer.

11. Use SQL Authentication and log on as GibsonH.

12. Notice that the following query fails since GibsonH has been denied Select permissions because of membership in the db_denydatareader database role:

```
use pubs
select * from authors
```

13. To activate the application role execute the following query:

```
sp_setapprole @rolename='EntAppRole', @password='password'
```

EXERCISE 5.18 (CONTINUED)

14. Clear the query window and do not save the changes; repeat step 16 without opening a new query, and notice that the query is successful this time. This is because SQL now sees you as EntAppRole, which has Select permission.

15. Close Query Analyzer.

EXERCISE 5.19

Creating Application Roles Using T-SQL

1. Open Query Analyzer and log in using Windows NT Authentication.

2. Execute the following query to add an application role to the Pubs database:

```
sp_addapprole @rolename='TsqlAppRole',
@password='password'
```

3. Close Query Analyzer, open Enterprise Manager, and select Database Roles in the Pubs database. Note the new application role that was just added.

Grant, Revoke, and Deny, Oh My!

Permissions can be granted, revoked, or denied. Exercises 5.19 and 5.20 will give you hands-on experience with these three states of permission:

Grant Granting allows users to use a specific permission. For instance, if you grant SmithB Select permission on a table, he can read the data within. A granted permission is signified by a black checkmark on the Permissions tab.

Revoke   In this state, while users are not explicitly allowed to use a revoked permission, if they are a member of a role that is allowed they will inherit the permission. That is, if you revoke the Select permission from SmithB, he cannot use it. If he is a member of a role that has been granted Select permission, SmithB can read the data just as if he had the Select permission. Revocation is signified by a blank check box on the Permissions tab.

Deny   If you deny a permission, the user does not get the permission—no matter what. If you deny SmithB Select permission on a table then, even if he is a member of a role with select permission, he cannot read the data. Denial is signified by a red X on the Permissions tab (Figure 5.3).

FIGURE 5.3

States of Permissions in Enterprise Manager

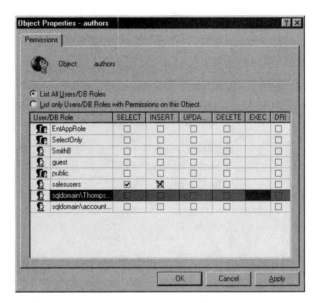

EXERCISE 5.20

Granting, Revoking, and Denying Permissions Using Enterprise Manager

1. Open Enterprise Manager, expand your server and Databases, then select the Pubs database.

EXERCISE 5.20 (CONTINUED)

2. Select Database Users, double-click SmithB, and click the Permissions button.

3. Grant SmithB Select permission on the Authors table by clicking the check box in the Select column on the Authors line until a black check box appears (this may already be completed from a previous exercise).

4. Click OK to go back to the previous dialog box and click OK again to return to Enterprise Manager.

5. Open Query Analyzer and log in as SmithB using SQL Authentication.

6. Execute the following query; it is successful since SmithB has Select permission on the Authors table:

```
use pubs
select * from authors
```

7. Leave Query Analyzer open and return to Enterprise Manager.

8. Double-click the SmithB user in the Pubs database and click the Permissions button.

9. Revoke the Select permission on the Authors table by clicking on the check box in the Select column next to Authors until the check box is blank.

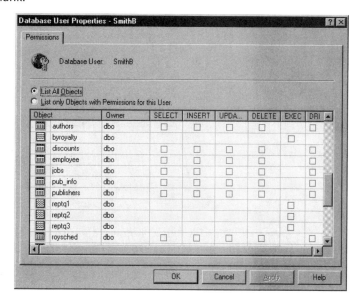

10. Return to Query Analyzer and execute the query in step 6. It fails because SmithB does not have explicit Select permission.

11. Leave Query Analyzer open and return to Enterprise Manager.

12. Double-click user SmithB in the Pubs database again and this time add him to the Db_datareader role by clicking the check box next to Db_datareader until a checkmark appears.

13. Return to Query Analyzer and rerun the same query. Now it is successful. This is because SmithB has inherited the Select permission from the Db_datareader role and does not need to have it explicitly applied.

14. Leave Query Analyzer open and return to Enterprise Manager.

15. Select Tables under the Pubs database and double-click the Authors table in the contents pane.

16. Click the Permissions button.

17. Deny SmithB Select permission by clicking on the check box in the Select column next to SmithB until a red X appears.

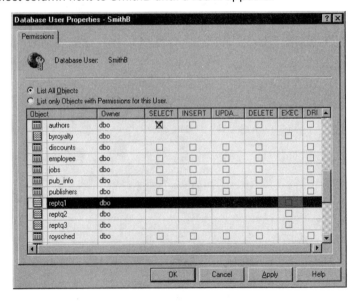

18. Click OK then OK again to return to Enterprise Manager.

EXERCISE 5.20 (CONTINUED)

19. Return to Query Analyzer and again run the query from step 6. It fails this time because we have specifically denied SmithB access and therefore he can no longer inherit the Select permission from the Db_ datareader role.

20. Close Query Analyzer and return to Enterprise Manager.

21. Select Tables under the Pubs database and double-click the Authors table in the contents pane.

22. Click the Permissions button.

23. Return the Select permission for SmithB to the revoked state by clicking on the check box in the Select column next to SmithB until it becomes blank.

24. Click OK, then OK again to return to Enterprise manager.

25. Double-click user SmithB in the Pubs database remove him from the Db_datareader role by clicking the check box next to Db_datareader until it is blank.

26. Click OK to return to Enterprise Manager.

EXERCISE 5.21

Granting, Revoking, and Denying Permissions Using T-SQL

1. Open Query Analyzer and log in using Windows NT Authentication.

2. Execute the following query to grant SmithB Select permission on the Authors table:

```
use pubs
grant select on authors to SmithB
```

3. On the File menu select Disconnect.

4. On the File menu select Connect and log in as SmithB using SQL Authentication.

5. Execute the following query and note its success since SmithB has been granted Select permission:

```
use pubs
select * from authors
```

6. On the File menu select Disconnect, then select Connect and log in using Windows NT Authentication.

7. Execute the following query to revoke the Select permission from SmithB:

```
use pubs
revoke select on authors from SmithB
```

8. On the Query menu select Clear Window and do not save the changes.

9. Execute the following query to add SmithB to the db_datareader database role:

```
use pubs
sp_addrolemember @rolename='db_datareader',
@membername='SmithB'
```

10. On the File Menu select Disconnect.

11. On the File menu select Connect and log in as SmithB using SQL Authentication.

12. Execute the following query and note its success. SmithB is a member of the db_datareader database role and therefore inherits the Select permission from that role.

```
use pubs
select * from authors
```

13. On the File menu select Disconnect.

14. On the file menu select Connect and log in using Windows NT Authentication.

15. Execute the following query to deny Select permission to SmithB:

```
use pubs
deny select on authors to SmithB
```

16. On the File menu select Disconnect.

17. On the File menu select Connect then log in as SmithB using SQL Authentication.

18. Execute the following query and notice that it fails. This is because SmithB has now been explicitly denied permission and cannot inherit permission from the Db_datareader role.

```
use pubs
select * from authors
```

19. Close Query Analyzer.

With a better understanding of how and where permissions are applied we can look into one of the problems generated when permissions are applied improperly: the broken ownership chain.

Ownership Chains

In the physical world, people own objects—things—that they can do with as they please, including lending or giving them to others. SQL understands this concept of ownership. When a user creates an object, they own that object and can do whatever they want with it. For example, if ThompsonA creates a table, he can assign permissions as he chooses, granting access only to those users he deems worthy. That is a good thing until you consider what is known as an ownership chain.

An object that is on loan still belongs to the owner; the person who has borrowed it must ask the owner for permission before allowing another person to use it. Acting without such permission would be much like a *broken ownership chain.*

Suppose that ThompsonA creates a table and grants permissions on that table to Accounting (Figure 5.4). Then one of the members of Accounting creates a view based on that table and grants Select permission to SmithB. Can SmithB select the data from that view? No, because the ownership chain has broken. SQL will check permissions on an underlying object (in this case the table) only when the owner changes. Therefore, if ThompsonA had created both the table and the view there would be no problem since SQL would check only the permissions on the view. Because the owner changed from Accounting (who owned the view) to ThompsonA (who owned the table) SQL needed to check the permissions on both the view and the table.

How can you avoid broken ownership chains? The first way is to make everyone who needs to create objects a member of the sysadmin fixed server role; then everything they create will be owned by the DBO user rather than by the login. For example, since MorrisL is a member of the sysadmin fixed server role, everything he creates in any database will be owned by the DBO, not MorrisL. While this is technically possible, it is a poor method since it grants a great deal of administrative privilege over the server to people who do not need it.

A much better way to avoid broken ownership chains is to make all the users who need to create objects members of either the db_owner or db_ddladmin fixed database roles. Then if they need to create objects, they can specify the owner as DBO (i.e., `create table dbo.table_name`). This way the DBO would own all objects in the database, and since the ownership would never change, SQL would never need to check any underlying permissions.

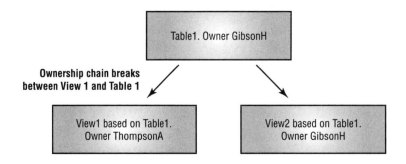

FIGURE 5.4

Example of a broken ownership chain

When a db_owner or db_ddladmin member creates an object as another user, it can be any database user, not just the DBO.

Now you have a good understanding of local security, but what if you have to access data on more than one server? Let's look at how to implement security in a distributed environment.

N-Tier Security

Let's return to our business analogy: Your business is prospering, and you have had to expand into two buildings. This means that your employees will need access to resources in both buildings, which in turn means you will need to give your users a key to the new place so they can gain access.

Microsoft ✓ Exam Objective

Develop a security strategy.

- Plan an *n*-tier application security strategy, and decide whether to use application roles or other mid-tier security mechanisms such as Microsoft Transaction Server.

- Plan the security requirements for linked databases.

You have the same concerns when your resources are spread across multiple SQL servers, your users may need access to resources on multiple, or *n* number of, servers. This is especially true of something called a *distributed query* (Figure 5.5), which returns result sets from databases on multiple servers. Although you might wonder why you would want to perform distributed queries when you could just replicate the data between servers, there are practical reasons for doing the former. Don't forget that because SQL Server is designed to store terabytes of data, some of your databases may grow to several hundred megabytes in size—and you really don't want to replicate several hundred megabytes under normal circumstances.

FIGURE 5.5

Distributed queries

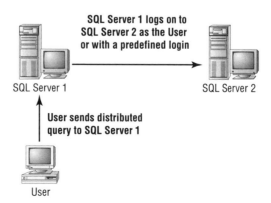

The first step is to inform SQL that it will be talking to other database servers by running the `sp_addlinkedserver` stored procedure. The procedure to link to a server named AccountingSQL looks something like this: `sp_addlinkedserver @server='AccountingSQL', @provider='SQL Server'`.

Your users can then run distributed queries by simply specifying two different servers in the query. The query: `select * from SQLServer.pubs.dbo.authors, AccountingSQL.pubs.dbo.employees` would access data from both the SQLServer (the server the user is logged in to, or sending server) and AccountingSQL server (the remote server) in the same result set.

The security issue here is that the sending server must log in to the remote server on behalf of the user to gain access to the data. SQL can use one of two methods to send this security information: security account delegation or linked server login mapping. If your users have logged in using Windows NT Authentication, and all of the servers in the query are capable of understanding Windows NT domain security, you can use account delegation. Here's how it works:

1. If the servers are in different domains you must make certain that the appropriate Windows NT trust relationships are in place. The remote server's domain must trust the sending server's domain.

2. Add a Windows NT login to the sending server for the user to log in with.

3. Add the same account to the remote server.

4. Create a user account for the login in the remote server's database and assign permissions.

5. When the user executes the distributed query, SQL will send the users Windows NT security credentials to the remote server, allowing access.

If you have users who access SQL with standard logins, or if some of the servers do not participate in Windows NT domain security, you will need to add a linked login. Here's how to do it:

1. On the remote server, create a standard login and assign the necessary permissions.

2. On the sending server, map a local login to the remote login using the `sp_addlinkedsrvlogin` stored procedure. To map all local logins to the remote login RemUser, type: **sp_addlinkedsrvlogin @rmtsrvname='AccountingSQL', @useself=FALSE, @local-login=NULL, @rmtuser='RemUser', @rmtpassword='password'**

3. When a user executes a distributed query, the sending server will login to the AccountingSQL (remote) server as RemUser with a password of "password."

It is essential to monitor your office to be sure that no one is trying to bypass security; this can be done with the SQL Profiler.

Monitoring SQL Logins with SQL Profiler

Most people have at one time or another had to pass through a security checkpoint. At that checkpoint sat a security guard watching monitors and searching packages. Why was this guard there? Because you can have the most advanced security system in the world, but without someone keeping watch it will eventually fail. A thief would simply need to probe the system systematically for weak spots and, once they were found, take advantage of them to break in. With the guard watching, this becomes a great deal more difficult.

The same is true for SQL. You cannot simply put a security system in place and then leave it. You must keep watch, just like the security guard, to make certain no one is probing for weak spots and attempting to break in. This task of keeping watch has been delegated to Profiler.

 Profiler is discussed in more detail in Chapter 10, *Monitoring and Optimizing SQL Server 7.*

Profiler is used to track and record activity on the SQL Server, which is done by performing a *trace* (as seen in Exercise 5.21). A trace is a record of the data captured about events, which can be a stored in a database table; a trace log file that can be opened and read in Profiler; or both. Two types of traces exist, shared and private. Shared traces are viewable by anyone, whereas private traces are viewable only by the owner. While your security trace should be private, your optimization and troubleshooting traces can be shared.

Microsoft
Exam
Objective

Audit server and database activity.

The actions that are monitored on the server are known as *events* and those events are logically grouped together in *event classes*. Not all of these events have to do with security; in fact, most of them have to do with optimization and troubleshooting. The following lists the classes and events that are important from a security standpoint:

Event Class Misc

Loginfailed   This will tell you if someone has tried to log in unsuccessfully. If you notice someone repeatedly failing to log in it means either the user forgot their password or someone is trying to hack in using that account.

ServiceControl   This monitors SQL Server starts, stops, and pauses. If you note a stop or pause and you are the only administrator, it means there is a problem with the server itself—or someone has hacked in with an administrative account.

Event Class Objects

Object:Deleted   This will tell you if an object, like a table, has been deleted. From a security standpoint, this is after the fact, since the damage may have already been done. By monitoring this, however, you will be able to catch the culprit if something is improperly deleted.

Event Class SQL Operators

Delete   This is logged just before a delete statement is executed. It does not stop delete statements from executing; it just records them. This event will again be useful in catching a hacker if something is illicitly deleted.

EXERCISE 5.22

Monitoring Login Failures with Profiler

1. Open Profiler in the SQL Server 7 Program group.

2. On the File menu select New, then Trace.

3. In the Trace Name box, type **Security**.

4. For Trace Type select Private.

5. Next to SQL Server select Local.

6. Click the check box next to Capture to File and click OK to select the default file name.

7. Click the check box next to Capture to Table, and use the following criteria to fill in the subsequent dialog box:

   Server: **Local**

   Database: **Pubs**

   Owner: **Myself**

   Table: **Security**

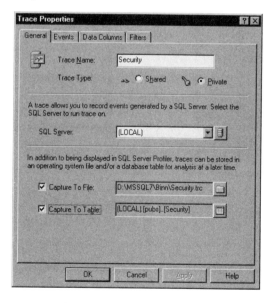

8. Click OK to return to the previous dialog box.

9. Select the Events tab.

10. Under Selected Events, select Sessions and click Remove.

11. Under Selected Events, select T-SQL and click Remove.

12. Under Available Events, expand Misc and click on Loginfailed.

13. Click Add to move Loginfailed to the Selected Events column.

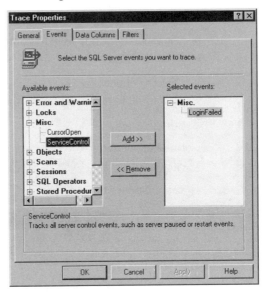

14. Click OK to start the trace.

15. To test the trace, leave Profiler open and open Query Analyzer.

16. Log in using SQL authentication with the username SmithB with a password of coconut. This will fail since you have supplied the wrong password.

17. Return to Profiler and notice that a login failure has been recorded for user SmithB.

18. Go back to Query Analyzer and log in as SmithB with a password of password. This will succeed since you have entered the correct password.

19. Close Query Analyzer and return to Profiler. Notice that there is no successful login record for SmithB since we are only monitoring failed logins.

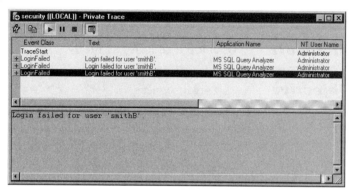

20. On the File menu select Close.

21. On the File menu select Open and then Trace File.

22. Open the Security.trc file and notice that all the events just recorded have been saved for later viewing.

23. Close Profiler, open Query Analyzer, and log in using Windows NT Authentication.

24. Execute the following query to view the newly created Security table:

    use pubs
    select * from security

25. On the File Menu select Disconnect and do not save any changes.

26. On the File menu select Connect and log in as SmithB using SQL Authentication.

27. Execute the query from step 24 and notice that it fails. This is because you created a private trace that SmithB does not have permission to view.

28. Close Query Analyzer and do not save any changes.

SQL Server System Accounts

Before SQL Server can interact with outside applications, a user account must be assigned to the various SQL Services.

Microsoft ✓ **Exam Objective**

Develop a security strategy.

- Assess which Windows NT accounts will be used to run SQL Server services.

Although creating SQL Server service accounts was covered in Chapter 2, *Installing, Upgrading, and Configuring SQL Server 7,* this section will cover why and how to create the accounts.

As a security precaution, the service needs a user account assigned to it whenever a service attempts to gain network access. This is to prevent hackers from writing a program that could compromise your network. Microsoft assumes that you are managing and controlling your user accounts carefully so that any unauthorized accounts would be detected and locked out. Accounts that are created primarily for services to use are called *service accounts*. Most services need at least one service account created for them, such as Systems Management Server and Exchange. SQL Server also benefits from having a service account assigned to it, as SQL Server can interact with Exchange servers (or other MAPI-compatible e-mail servers) and can connect to other SQL Servers for replication or job-management purposes.

When you create a service account for SQL Server you can create a single account for all SQL Server services to use or you can create separate accounts for the individual services.

While the service account assigned to the SQL Agent needs administrative rights, the account assigned to the other SQL Server services doesn't. You may want to create and assign separate accounts to limit the rights of the accounts assigned to the MSSQLSERVER service and also to help in auditing security issues.

Any account you create needs rights to the \MSSQL7 folder and user rights on the domain, and must be a domain user.

Creating a Security Plan

Let us suppose that you have just been hired as Database Administrator for AlsoRann Inc., a small company that relies heavily on their SQL server. A great deal of the data on the SQL Server is proprietary and therefore must be secured. You realize, however, that jumping right in and randomly applying permissions to databases is going to result in a mess—if not a disaster—so you take a more logical approach: you develop a security plan.

A good security plan is always the first step in applying security to any type of system. Here are a few things that you will need to consider in your plan:

Type of users   If all your users support trusted connections you can use NT accounts. If you have the authority to create groups in NT, you may be able to create NT groups and then create logins for those groups rather than individual accounts. If not all your users support trusted connections (like Novell or Macintosh) then you will need to use Mixed Mode authentication and create some standard logins.

Fixed Server Roles   Once you have given users access to SQL, how much administrative power, if any, should they be given? If your users need administrative authority, you will add them to one of the fixed server roles; if not, there is no need to add them.

Database access   Once logged in, to which databases will your users have access? It is highly unlikely that every user will need a user account in every database.

Type of Access   Once the user has a database user account, how much authority will they have in the database? For example, can all users read and write, or is there a subset of users who are only allowed to read?

Group Permissions   It is usually best to apply permissions to database roles and then add users to those roles. There are some exceptions in every system, though, and you may need to apply some permissions directly to users, especially those who need to be denied access to a resource.

Creating   Figure out who needs the authority to create objects, such as tables and views, and group them together in either the db_owner or db_ddladmin role. Doing this will allow users to create objects as the DBO instead of themselves. In this way you can avoid broken ownership chains.

Public Access   Remember that all database user accounts are members of the public role and cannot be removed. Whatever permission the public role has will be given to your users. Limit the permissions on the Public group.

Guest Access   Do you want users with no database user account to be able to access databases through a guest account? For some databases, like a catalog, this may be acceptable. In general, however, this can be considered a security risk and should not be used on all databases.

Table 5.1 shows the employees of AlsoRann Inc. and their security needs. The first thing you may notice is that there are two Novell network users. This means you need to create at least two standard logins, means you need to implement Mixed Mode authentication.

The next thing you may notice is that some of the users—specifically Accounting and Sales—are already grouped together in NT. Rather than creating accounts for each individual member of these departments, you can instead add a Windows NT Group login for the whole lot of them. Because ThompsonA and MorrisL are not members of an NT group, they will need Windows NT User logins.

Next, look at the administrative rights that each user will need over the system. Since GibsonH needs to be able to configure server settings like memory use, he should be added to the serveradmin fixed server role. And since MorrisL needs full administrative access to the entire system, she should be added to the sysadmin fixed server role.

To make the processes of writing a bit simpler, AlsoRann has only one database. Look at the permissions that everyone needs on that database. As a customer service rep, SmithB needs permission to read the data but not to write any data; the db_denydatawriter fixed database role will fit those needs well.

As a developer, GibsonH needs permission to create objects in the database, but he should not be able to read the data. Making GibsonH a member of the db_ddladmin role so that he can create objects as DBO and avoid broken ownership chains. We could have made him a member of the db_ owner group and achieved the same effect, but then he would be able to do whatever he wanted in the database, including reading the data.

ThompsonA needs to be able to select, insert, and update data, but he should not be able to delete any data. There is no fixed database role that grants these three permissions together. You could apply all of these permissions directly to ThompsonA, but what if you hire more people that need the same permissions? It might be a better idea to create a custom database role, grant that role the Select, Insert, and Update permissions and make Thompson A a member of that role. The same is true of the Sales group, which needs permission to read and update; they will require a custom role.

For Accounting it will be easiest just to add them to the db_datareader and db_datawriter roles, that way they receive permissions to read and write to the database. MorrisL will not need to be a member of any role; since she is a member of the sysadmin fixed server role, she is automatically considered the DBO in every database on the server.

T A B L E   5.1:   The Employees of AlsoRann Inc.

Name	NT Group	Department	Network	Admin	Permissions
SmithB	N/A	Service	Novell	None	Read, no Write
GibsonH	N/A	Development	Novell	Server Configuration	Write, Create, no Read
ThompsonA	None	Administration	NT	None	Select, Insert, Update
MorrisL	None	IT	NT	All	All
JohnsonK	Accounting	Accounting	NT	None	Read, Write
JonesB	Accounting	Accounting	NT	None	Read, Write
ChenJ	Sales	Sales	NT	None	Read, Update
SamuelsR	Sales	Sales	NT	None	Read, Update

In the real world, of course, a security plan is not going to be nearly this simple. There will be hundreds, if not thousands, of users to deal with from a variety of networks, each needing different permissions. To sum up, although developing a security plan is probably more work than the actual implementation, you cannot do without it.

Summary

SQL Server 7 has a sophisticated security system that allows you to carefully implement your security plan. SQL Server can operate in mixed security mode, which means that Windows NT users and groups can be given access directly into SQL Server, or separate, unique accounts can be created that reside only in SQL Server. If SQL Server is running in NT Authentication mode, every user must first connect with a preauthorized Windows NT account.

This chapter examined the processes of creating and managing logins, groups, and users. You learned how to create a Standard login and a Windows NT user or group login using Enterprise Manager or T-SQL and when each type is appropriate. If you have a well-designed security plan that incorporates growth then managing your user base can be a painless task.

To limit administrative access to SQL at the server level, you learned that you can add users to a fixed server role. For limiting access in a specific database, you can add users to a database role, and if one of the fixed database roles is not to your liking, you can create your own. You can even go so far as to limit access to specific applications by creating an application role.

Each database in SQL Server 7 has its own independent permissions. You looked at the two types of user permissions, statement permissions, which are used to create or change the data structure; and object permissions, which manipulate data. Remember that statement permissions cannot be granted to others.

The next section described the database hierarchy. You looked at the permissions available to the most powerful user—the SA—down through the lower-level database users.

You then learned about chains of ownership. These are created when you grant permissions to others on objects you own. Adding more users who create dependent objects creates broken ownership chains, which can become complex and tricky to work with. You learned how to predict the permissions available to users at different locations within these ownership chains. You also learned that to avoid the broken ownership chains, you can add your users to either the db_owner or db_ddladmin database role and have them create objects as the DBO.

Permissions can be granted to database users as well as database roles. When a user is added to a role they inherit the permissions of the role, including the public role of which everyone is a member. The only exception is when the user has been denied permission, since Deny takes precedence over any other right, no matter the level at which the permission was granted.

We then looked at remote and linked servers and at how security needs to be set up to make remote queries work. We finished with a look at *n*-tier security and applications.

Review Questions

1. You have several types of clients on your network: Novell, Macintosh, and Windows. What authentication method should you implement?

 A. Standard Only

 B. Windows NT Only

 C. Mixed Mode

2. Archie Thompson needs permission to read data from the payroll table in the Accounting database, but he should not be able to read data from any of the other tables. To which fixed database role should he be added?

 A. Db_dataselect

 B. Db_datareader

 C. Db_dataaccess

 D. None of the above

3. Several of your users need Select, Update, and Insert permissions on a database. They should be members of which of the following database roles?

 A. Db_datareader

 B. Db_datawriter

 C. Db_datareader and db_datawriter

 D. Create a custom role

4. TomR is a member of the Windows NT Sales group. The Sales group has been granted access to SQL server with a Windows NT Group type account. The Sales login is a member of the db_datareader fixed database role in the Accounting database. TomR has also been given his own Windows NT User type login and has been denied Select permission on the tables in the Accounting database. Can TomR select data from the Accounting database?

A. Yes; TomR can select from the Accounting database since he is a member of the Sales group, which is a member of the db_datreader fixed database role

B. No; TomR cannot read from the Accounting database since he has been specifically denied Select permission on the database

C. TomR cannot have a separate login since he is a member of the Windows NT Sales group, which already has a login

D. Yes; but only when he connects to SQL Server as Sales instead of as himself

5. Several of your users need to be able to create objects in your database. What is the best way to avoid broken ownership chains?

A. Make all the users who need to create objects members of the db_ddladmin fixed database role

B. Make all the users who need to create objects members of the db_owner fixed database role

C. Make all the users who need to create objects members of the sysadmin fixed server role

D. Create a custom fixed server role with the proper object permissions and make those users members of this new role

6. Some of your users need permission to create databases. What is the best way to grant this permission?

A. Make those users members of the db_ddladmin role

B. Make those users members of the sysadmin server role

   C. Grant those users the Create Database permission on the master database

   D. Make those users members of the diskadmin server role

7. On your network you have the authority to administrate both Windows NT and SQL accounts. Some of your users need access to a database that will be used for a short-term project. What is the best way to grant them permissons on the database?

   A. Add all the users to a Windows NT group, create a Windows NT Group login in SQL, create a user account for the login in the database, and grant permissions to the account

   B. Create separate Windows NT User logins and separate database user accounts for each user; then grant permissions to each user

   C. Create separate logins for each user account, create database user accounts for each role, and add those accounts to a database role

   D. Assign them security equivalence to the SA account

8. True or False: When you add a user to a database role using Transact-SQL (T-SQL) you do not need to create the user account first.

   A. True

   B. False

9. What are the results of the following query: `sp_grantlogin @loginame='domain\jordenj', @defdb='pubs'`

   A. A Windows NT login is created for JordenJ and the default database is set to Pubs

   B. A Standard login is created for JordenJ and the default database is set to Pubs

   C. A Windows NT login is created for JordenJ but the default database is not set

   D. The query fails

10. True or False: GaryR is a member of the sysadmin fixed server role. When GaryR creates a table in the Sales database the owner is DBO not GaryR.

    A. True

    B. False

11. You are worried about default permissions in user databases in SQL Server. You propose removing everyone from the Public group and selectively adding them back in as necessary. What will the results be?

    A. Your method will work, but will not fix the problem

    B. Your method will work and will fix the problem

    C. Your method will not work, so will not fix the problem

    D. Your method will not work, but there was no problem to begin with

12. Security at your site is a major issue. You want SQL Server to interact with an Exchange server and you also have replication occurring. How would you configure the service accounts?

    A. Create a domain administrative account and assign it to both SQL services

    B. Create a local administrative account and assign it to both SQL services

    C. Create separate accounts for the SQL Server and SQL Agent services. Assign the domain administrative account to SQL Server and the local administrative account to the SQL Agent

    D. Create separate accounts for the SQL Server and SQL Agent services. Assign the domain administrative account to SQL Agent and the local administrative account to the SQL Server

13. You have a database called PhoneNumbers that everyone in your company needs to be able to run queries against. You create a user called guest in the database and make it a member of db_datareader. You then assign the Windows NT group Domain Guests to SQL Server. Can all your Windows NT users access the database?

    A. Yes, it works fine as is

    B. It will work after you make Domain Guests members of the database

    C. It will work after you make the guest user a member of the public role in the database

    D. It will not work

14. You have a payroll database that should only be modified by the payroll application. Which of these steps should you take to ensure that users can modify data only when using the payroll application?

    A. Create an application role for the database

    B. Assign appropriate rights to the application role

    C. Modify the application so that it triggers the application role when the application is started

    D. Put the appropriate users in the application role

CHAPTER

6

Implementing Database
Backups and Restorations

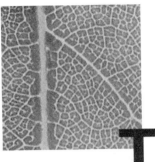

This chapter looks at various options for protecting your data, an area of crucial importance. It discusses the reasons for backing up data and planning and choosing appropriate backup strategies. It shows you how to perform various types of backups and how to restore databases when necessary.

Why Back Up?

Having fault-tolerant disk drives doesn't mean you don't have to do backups. Data can be corrupted by a variety of problems, including:

- Hard-disk-drive failure
- Hard-disk-controller failure
- Motherboard failure
- Power outage or spike
- Virus attack
- Accidental change or deletion of data
- Malicious change or deletion of data

Creating (and testing) regular backups is an integral part of any good administrator's maintenance plan. The words you never want to hear are "The hard drive is dead and the backups are bad."

Developing a Backup Plan

Because you will probably be the one in charge of scheduling and verifying backups, there are several issues besides that of doing the routine backups that must be looked at before a backup plan can be designed and properly implemented.

Microsoft
✓ ***Exam***
Objective

Develop a data availability solution.

- Choose the appropriate backup and restore strategy. Strategies include full database backup; full database backup and transaction log backup; differential database backup with full database backup and transaction log backup; and database files backup and transaction log backup.
- Assess whether to use a standby server.
- Assess whether to use clustering.

To this end, consider the following:

- How often will the backups occur?
- To what medium will the backups be made?
- Who is responsible for the backups?
- How will the backups be verified?
- What are the policies for backing up non-logged operations?
- Does a standby server makes sense for the installation?
- Will Windows NT's capabilities (such as clustering, drive mirroring, or RAID 5) be used to help protect data?

How Often Will the Backups Occur?

A backup is much like a spare tire—you may never need it, but it is a lifesaver when you do. The frequency of making backups is directly related to how much data you will lose if the system suffers a major catastrophe. If you only back up once a week on the weekends, any crash suffered late in the week could mean many days of data will be lost. Conversely, if you back up the transaction log every hour, the most data you will lose will be an hour's worth.

The following recommendations are general ones—feel free to customize them for your situation.

Master Database Schedule it for weekly backups and perform a manual backup after major modifications to your databases, devices, or users.

Msdb Database Schedule it for weekly backups and perform a manual backup after major changes to tasks, events, operators, or alerts.

Tempdb Database Don't bother backing it up, as it is automatically cleared every time SQL Server is stopped and started.

Model Database You should make a baseline backup of this, and then manually back it up whenever it changes (which won't be very often).

Pubs Database Don't bother backing it up, as it is simply a sample database that gives you live data to practice on. The only reason for backing it up would be to test your scheduling or restore procedures.

User Databases Schedule these so that changed data is backed up at least every night. One option is to do an entire database backup every night. Another option is to do an entire database backup on the weekends, and back up just the log on weeknights. While you can schedule the log to be backed up during the day (in case of failure), backing up the entire database during production hours may cause a slowdown on a heavily used server and be harder to track and restore from.

To What Medium Will the Backups Be Made?

SQL Server can back up databases to tape or to a dump device (a file). If a tape drive is used, it must be on the Windows NT HCL (Hardware Compatibility List) and installed in the computer running SQL Server.

SQL Server 7 and Windows NT now use compatible file formats for tape backups. You can use the same tape drive and tape to perform both SQL Server and Windows NT backups (unlike earlier versions of SQL Server).

Who Is Responsible for the Backups?

The scariest thing in the world is when two coadministrators both think the other one took care of the backups. Have a plan in place for the person in charge, and detail what is to happen on that person's day off.

How Will the Backups Be Verified?

Trusting the backups you've made without verifying them is like trusting your spare tire to be in good condition—it *probably* is, but.... The purpose of a backup is not simply to have something backed up, but to be able to restore it in a reasonable manner.

One of the best ways to verify that your backups are working is to restore them to a separate computer. Not only does this verify the integrity of your backups, it helps prepare you in case you have to bring up a spare server quickly.

What Are the Policies for Backing Up Non-Logged Operations?

Most transactions are logged by SQL Server in the transaction log. There are some transactions that are not logged, which means that if a database had to be restored, any and all of the non-logged operations that happened since the last backup would be lost.

Non-logged operations include:

- Fast bulk copies when Select Into/Bulk Copy is enabled
- Select Into commands when Select Into/Bulk Copy is enabled

Bulk copies and the Select Into command are covered in Chapter 7, *Managing your Data.*

Back up the database before starting a non-logged operation, in case you need to restore the database to its previous state quickly.

Protecting Your SQL Data Using NT

The ultimate goal of designing and implementing a disaster recovery plan is to plan for, and protect the data in case of a major catastrophe. Windows NT has several options that can protect data in case of hard drive failure, effectively keeping SQL Server from knowing that there has been a problem.

Disk Administrator is the Windows NT program used to create mirrored, duplexed, striped, and striped-with-parity drives (RAID 5). For more information see *MCSE: Windows NT Server Study Guide*.

Disk Mirroring

One protective option is to mirror the hard drive partitions so that all data writes are made to two separate physical hard drives (Figure 6.1). In case of a hard drive failure, Windows NT simply uses the remaining hard drive until you replace the broken hard drive and re-mirror the system again. Disk mirroring is transparent to SQL Server—you set up disk mirroring through Windows NT, and then install SQL Server normally.

FIGURE 6.1

Disk mirroring

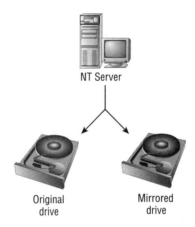

NT Server

Original drive

Mirrored drive

Disk Duplexing

Disk mirroring eliminates the hard drive as a single point of failure, but it still uses only one hard disk controller card. If the controller happens to fail, both the original and mirrored hard drives will contain corrupt data. Disk duplexing attempts to solve this potential problem by using two controller cards (Figure 6.2).

FIGURE 6.2

Disk duplexing

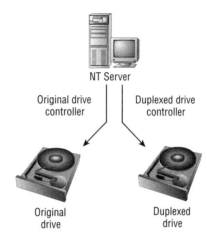

Disk duplexing is basically a fancier (and more reliable) way of doing disk mirroring. Simply install disk duplexing with Windows NT, and then install SQL Server normally on the duplexed drives. In case of either a controller or hard disk failure, Windows NT will use the remaining controller and drive until a replacement can be made.

 Make sure you use SCSI and not IDE or EIDE drives when you do your mirroring or duplexing. SCSI drives are independent, and a failure of one will not affect the others, while IDE and EIDE drives are linked in a master/slave relationship, where failure of one drive will probably keep the remaining drive from working.

Disk Striping

Windows NT supports the creation of a stripe set, which is the fastest way you can set up your drives. Stripe sets run vertically across two or more physical drives, so that more than one hard drive participates in writing and reading data (Figure 6.3).

FIGURE 6.3

Disk striping

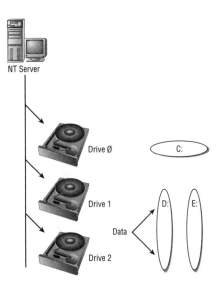

Stripe sets write in 64KB blocks of data and then move to the next drive for the next block of data. To use striped drives with SQL Server, create the striped drive first with Windows NT, and then install SQL Server normally.

Stripe sets have no redundancy built into them. If a hard drive that is part of a stripe set fails, none of the data in the strip set (even on hard drives that are still good) will be usable. For data protection (at a cost of some speed) use striped-with-parity drives (RAID 5 drives).

Disk Striping with Parity (RAID 5)

Windows NT supports striped-with-parity drives, commonly referred to as RAID 5, or just RAID, drives. When creating a striped-with-parity drive, Windows NT will use one of the hard drives for a parity or check bit that can be used to recover the data in case a hard drive fails.

Figure 6.4 shows a striped-with-parity drive, with all the hard drives working. Figure 6.5 shows the same figure, with hard drive 2 having failed. Windows NT can reconstruct hard drive 2 in memory, by using the parity bits spread across the remaining drives (Figure 6.6).

F I G U R E 6.4

Striped-with-parity (RAID 5) drive

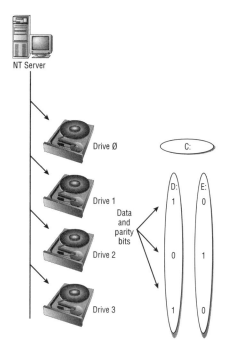

F I G U R E 6.5

Single hard drive failure on a striped-with-parity drive

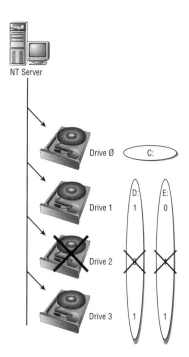

F I G U R E   6.6

Reconstructing the
lost drive

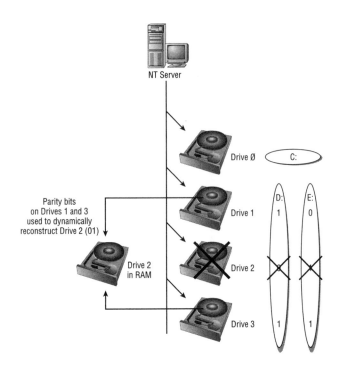

 Although striped-with-parity drives aren't as fast as a pure striped drive, they do provide redundancy in case of hard disk failure.

To use striped-with-parity drives with SQL Server, simply create them using Windows NT, and then install SQL Server normally.

 Most high-end servers support hardware-level RAID, and may even provide a hot-backup hard drive (e.g., a spare hard drive already installed and connected) in case of failure. Hardware RAID, while faster than the software RAID that Windows NT supplies, is more expensive; it may also be proprietary.

NT Clustering

Windows NT 4 has an optional component that allows you to have a drive array shared between two file servers. The advantage of an NT cluster is two-fold. First, you have fault tolerance in case of a physical problem with the server; second, you have increased performance if the bottleneck is not caused by the hard-drive array.

NT Clustering is built into Windows NT 4 Enterprise Edition and will also be supported by Windows 2000 Advanced Server and DataCenter editions.

Standby Servers

A standby server can easily be set up to receive periodic copies of the data from the primary server. If the primary server goes down, the standby server can be renamed as the primary server and rebooted; it will then look and act like the primary server. Making a standby server work correctly involves a few steps:

1. Create the primary server as usual.

2. Create the secondary server with a unique name.

3. Do periodic full backups of the databases on the primary server.

4. Restore the backup files to the standby server.

5. Do frequent backups of the transaction log on the primary server.

6. Restore the backups of the transaction log to the standby server using the Standby switch if you wish to make the standby database read-only, or with the No Recovery switch.

7. If you have the time to prepare to switch servers, perform a transaction log backup of the primary server and restoration on the standby server and take the primary server offline.

8. Set the databases on the standby server for real use by using the Recover switch.

9. Rename the standby server as the primary server and reboot the standby server.

10. Use the standby server normally until the primary server is ready to come back online; then simply follow steps 1 through 9 again.

Protecting Your Data Using SQL Server

$\mathbf{S}$QL Server has both automatic database recovery and support for user-initiated backups and restores. The automatic recovery feature is designed so that databases won't become corrupt if the server is unexpectedly stopped. The manual recovery features are supported to allow critical databases to be backed up and restored in case of failure or user error.

Automatic recoveries happen every time SQL Server is started, and SQL Server allows you to back up your databases dynamically (while they are in use). These two features are extremely helpful, as databases won't get corrupted even during unexpected outages, and users can stay connected to the server while a backup is being run.

Database Consistency Checker (DBCC)

One of the more unpleasant features of SQL Server is that the backup routines are more tolerant of errors than the restore routines. Because of this, backups may appear to work, but the backups are in fact worthless, as they contain errors that cause the restore procedure to fail. There are various commands that check the database for errors. These should be run on a regular basis to ensure that the database is in perfect working order.

DBCC CheckDB   This command checks the database for errors. This is the command that you will probably run most often, as it checks for common errors in the linkage of tables and index pages.

DBCC CheckAlloc   This command checks allocation pages for errors and shows how extents have been allocated in the database.

DBCC CheckCatalog   This command checks the system tables for allocation and corruption errors.

The maintenance wizard (covered below) not only allows you to run the DBCC commands, but can be set to stop the backup process if an error is found.

Transactions and Checkpoints

In order to understand backups and which part of the database is getting backed up with different commands, we must discuss transactions and checkpoints. A transaction is one or more commands that need to be processed as a whole in order to make sense. For example, withdrawing cash from an ATM is a transaction made up of two distinct parts—subtracting an amount from your account and delivering it to you as cash (Figure 6.7). If only part of the transaction is performed, a system that is designed correctly will roll back, or throw out, the first part of the transaction.

F I G U R E   6.7

A two-step transaction

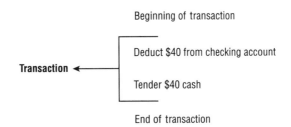

SQL Server treats each statement as a separate transaction by default, but SQL programmers can easily establish the starting and ending points of a transaction with the words BEGIN TRANSACTION and COMMIT TRANSACTION, respectively. If the transaction is interrupted, SQL Server will roll back to the state it was in before the transaction was started. The SQL program itself can roll back the transaction by issuing a ROLLBACK TRANSACTION command at any time (such as when the user pushes the Cancel button).

SQL Server doesn't write every single transaction to the database immediately; instead, transactions are cached and written to the database later. Because cached data is vulnerable to power outages, SQL Server also logs each transaction in the transaction log. In this way, SQL Server provides the best of both worlds by combining the speed of a cache with the data integrity of logged transactions. SQL Server flushes the cache to the database with a *checkpoint;* that is, it periodically writes modified data to the database. The DBO of a database can also issue a checkpoint at any time.

Automatic Recovery of Transactions

SQL Server incorporates a safety feature—the automatic recovery of databases—that runs whenever SQL Server is restarted, and cannot be disabled. This feature ensures that not only is the database brought up-to-date, but that only clean, completed transactions are put into the database.

In Exercise 6.1, we will look at the SQL Server error log and examine the entry for the automatic recovery of the Master database.

EXERCISE 6.1

Examining the Error Log for Automatic Recovery Entries

1. Start Enterprise Manager and connect to your server.

2. Open the error log by opening the Management folder, opening the SQL Server Logs folder, and highlighting the Current log file.

3. Examine the log for transactions that were rolled forward. You should find transactions for both the Master database and all the user databases.

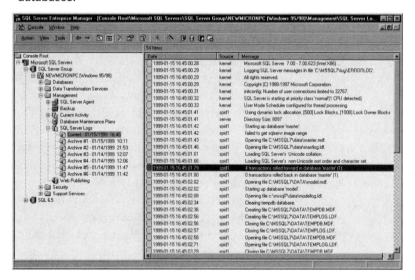

4. Close the error log.

Exercise 6.2 examines the Recovery Interval and Recovery Flag settings.

EXERCISE 6.2

The Recovery Interval and Recovery Flag Settings

1. Open the Configurations screen by highlighting and right-clicking the server and choosing Properties, or choose Action ➢ Properties from the main menu when highlighting the server.

2. Choose the Database Settings tab.

3. The Recovery Interval is at the bottom. Note that the default is 0, which means that SQL Server will automatically adjust the recovery interval so that restores are faster.

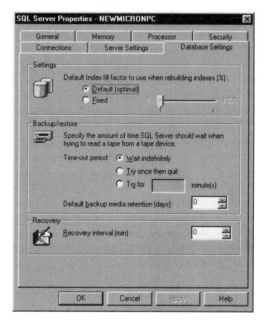

4. Close the screen by choosing Cancel or by choosing OK if you made a change.

SQL Backups

You have several choices when backing up your data, including the following:

Full Database Backups   Here the entire database is backed up. Although they are the easiest to implement and restore from, full database backups may not be practical because of the amount of time required for very large databases.

Transaction Log Backups   Because the transaction log records all changes made to a database, backing up the log (after performing an occasional full database backup) allows you to re-create the database without having to do a full database backup every time.

Differential Database Backups   New with SQL 7, differential backups back up only data that has changed since the last full backup. This could be more efficient than transaction log backups for databases with existing data that changes often. For example, if a person's bank account changed 10 times in one day, the transaction log backup would contain all 10 changes while the differential backup would contain just the final amount.

Filegroup Backups   Also new with SQL 7, filegroup backups allow you to back up different pieces of the database, based on the various files that make up the database. Usually filegroup backups are done when the time required to perform a full database backup is prohibitive.

Microsoft ✓ *Exam Objective*   **Back up system databases and user databases by performing a full database backup, a transaction log backup, a differential database backup, and a filegroup backup.**

One of the best features of SQL Server database backups is that they are dynamic. That is, users do not have to disconnect from the server or even from the database while a backup is in progress. SQL Server 7 has dramatically reduced the overhead when doing database backups. Various tests from Microsoft show about a 5% to 20% performance decrease when doing database backups.

Although databases can be backed up dynamically, various operations are not allowed when backing up a database. They include:

- Creating or rebuilding indexes
- Creating or modifying tables
- Creating or modifying columns

Creating a Backup Device

SQL Server backs up databases to a *backup device* (called a *dump* in earlier versions). SQL, however, has no built-in backup devices—you will need to create them yourself and configure your backups in order to have regularly backed up databases.

You can create backup devices that point to files, or you can back up directly to tape. SQL Server 7 uses the same tape format that various Windows NT backup programs use, so you can leave a single tape in the computer for both SQL and Windows NT backups.

If you use a tape drive, it should be listed on the Windows NT compatibility list, as well as being mounted in the SQL Server. Some third-party backup software allows the tape drive to be in a remote server, but SQL Server's native tape software doesn't.

As the majority of people back up to a file, and then back the file up to tape as part of their Windows NT backup, we will focus primarily on backing up to files. Most of the principles for backing up to tape are the same.

Because SQL Server keeps the database files open while SQL Server is running, the databases are not backed up during regular Windows NT backups. In addition, because the default settings in SQL Server will not back up any of your databases, you need to configure SQL Server backups. Once a backup has been made to a backup device, the device is closed, and will be backed up normally during Windows NT backups.

Exercise 6.3 attempts to rename the Master device to demonstrate NT's inability to back up the open device file.

This exercise will not be able to rename the MASTER.MDF file as long as SQL Server is running. If your SQL Server is not running, the database files are like any other files and can be renamed. If this happens, simply rename it back to MASTER.MDF before restarting SQL Server.

EXERCISE 6.3

Attempting to Rename the MASTER.MDF Database File

1. Go to Explorer and find the Master device—it will probably be in the \MSSQL7\DATA path, and be called MASTER.MDF.

2. Highlight the file and attempt to rename it MASTER.MDX. You should get an error message like the following:

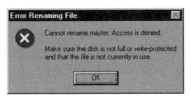

3. Choose OK and rename the file back to MASTER.MDF.

Creating a Backup Device Using *Sp_addumpdevice* Backup devices can be created with the sp_addumpdevice command. The syntax for the command specifies the logical name for the device and the path to the file that will be created after the backup is completed:

```
Sp_addumpdevice 'type', 'logical name', 'path'
```

Follow the steps in Exercise 6.4 to make a backup device to which we can later back up the Master database.

EXERCISE 6.4

Creating a Backup Device Using T-SQL Commands

1. Create a new folder called C:\SQL7_Backups or locate the \MSSQL7\BACKUPS folder.

EXERCISE 6.4 (CONTINUED)

2. Open a Query Analyzer session.

3. Enter the command:

   sp_addumpdevice '**disk**', '**master_backup**', '**c:\sql7_ backup\master.bak**'.

   You can substitute the path to the \MSSQL7\BACKUP folder if you wish.

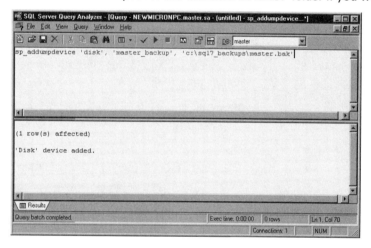

4. The results returned should say 'Disk' Device Added.

5. Verify the creation by opening the Backup folder under the Management folder (you may have to choose Refresh to have the device appear).

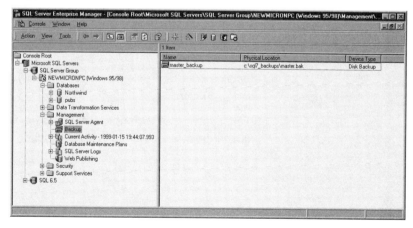

Creating a Backup Device Using Enterprise Manager   Backup devices can be created quite easily using Enterprise Manager. To create a backup device, simply open the Backup folder and choose New Backup Device by clicking the right mouse button, or choose New Backup Device from the Action menu.

Follow the steps in Exercise 6.5 to create backup devices for Pubs, Northwind, and Msdb databases.

EXERCISE 6.5

Creating Backup Devices Using Enterprise Manger

1. Open the Backup folder (under Management) inside Enterprise Manager.

2. Right-click and choose New Backup Device or choose Action ➢ New Backup Device.

3. Create a device called pubs_backup and point it to the \MSSQL7\BACKUP\pubs_backup.bak file.

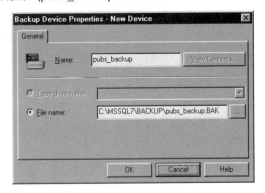

4. Choose OK to make the device.

5. Create devices for the Northwind and Msdb databases using the same naming convention.

6. Create a device for the pubs transaction log with the name of pubs_log with the path of \MSSQL7\BACKUP\pubs_log.bak.

EXERCISE 6.5 (CONTINUED)

7. Verify that all devices were made by looking in the Backup folder.

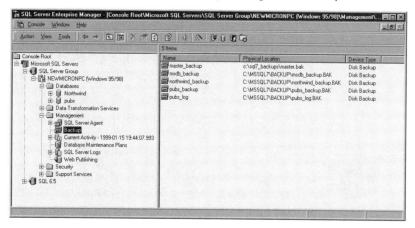

A backup device is essentially a pointer that SQL Server uses so that it knows where to put the backup file when the backup is actually done. Because of this, files are not created until the backup is actually performed.

Performing Full Database Backups

The actual process of backing up the database is relatively straightforward. SQL Server allows a database to be backed up to a single backup device or to multiple devices. The latter (when a database or transaction log is backed up across two or more devices) is called a *parallel striped backup*.

For example, backing up a database to tape may take an hour. If we had three tape drives in the SQL Server box and backed up the database across all three devices, the backup would take approximately 20 minutes.

Another feature of striped backups is that they don't have to be restored simultaneously. A database that had been backed up on three different tape devices could be restored onto a SQL Server that had only one tape drive. We would restore the tapes in order: first, second, and third.

When a database backup is started, SQL Server will first do a checkpoint of the database and bring it up-to-date with all the completed transactions. SQL Server then takes a snapshot of the database and backs up the entire database. If users are trying to update pages, they will be temporarily blocked by SQL Server as it jumps ahead of the updates.

Any transactions that were not completed when the backup started will not be in it. Because of this, even though backups can be done during normal business hours, backing up the databases at night will help ensure that there is a clear understanding of what is in the backup as well as what didn't make it.

Backing Up the Database Using T-SQL Commands   Databases can be backed up by either issuing T-SQL commands or using Enterprise Manger. The syntax for the command that backs up databases is

```
Backup Database <name> to <device> (with init)
```

Earlier versions of SQL Server used the Dump Database command to back up databases. While this older syntax is still supported in SQL Server 7, it may be phased out in later versions and so is not recommended.

Exercise 6.6 shows how to back up the Master database using T-SQL commands.

EXERCISE 6.6

Backing Up Databases Using T-SQL Commands

1. Open a Query Analyzer session.

2. Enter the following command:

   Backup Database Master to master_backup with init

3. The results should look something like this:

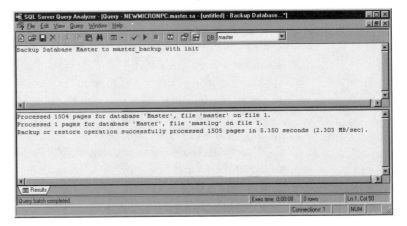

Backing Up the Database Using Enterprise Manager   Using Enterprise Manager to do full database backups is quite easy and intuitive, as shown in Exercise 6.7.

Backing Up Databases Using Enterprise Manager

1. Highlight the Pubs database.

2. Go to the Backup screen by either right-clicking and choosing All Tasks ➤ Backup Database or going to the Tools menu and choosing Backup Database; you can also select Backup Database from the Backup section of the right screen.

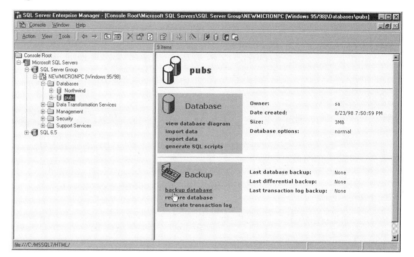

3. Select Add for the destination, choose Backup Device, select Pubs_ backup, and choose OK.

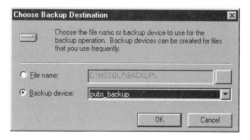

4. Select the Overwrite Existing Media option from the Overwrite portion of the screen.

Note that the default for backups is to append onto the existing backup file. You will need to select Overwrite Existing Media in order to overwrite any previous backups.

5. Select OK to start the backup. You should see blue bars go across the screen as the backup proceeds. The Pubs database should only take a few seconds to back up.

6. After the backup completes, choose OK from the Confirmation screen to close the Backup screen.

Performing Parallel Striped Backups   Follow the steps in Exercise 6.8 to perform a parallel striped backup of the Northwind database.

EXERCISE 6.8

Performing a Parallel Striped Backup

1. Create two new backup devices—northwind_a_backup and northwind_b_backup (see Exercise 6.5).

2. Highlight the Northwind database and go to the Backup screen by right-clicking and choosing All Tasks ≻ Backup Database, or go to the Tools menu and choose Backup Database; you can also select Backup Database from the Backup section of the right screen.

3. Select Add for the destination, choose Backup device, select the Northwind_a_backup device and choose OK.

4. Repeat step 3, this time selecting the Northwind_b_backup device.

5. Select the Overwrite Existing Media option from the Overwrite portion of the screen.

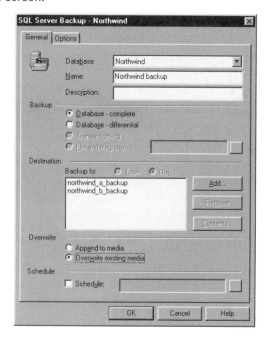

6. Select OK to perform the backup.

7. Select OK to close the Backup screen.

Backing Up and Restoring Directly to or from Files

SQL Server 7 has the capability to back up or restore directly to or from a file without having to specify a backup device first.

The syntax in SQL Server 7 to back up directly to a file is an extension of the Backup Database command, using a To keyword in front of the specified path and file instead of the device name. For example, to back up Pubs2 to a file, enter the following:

```
Backup Database Pubs2 to disk = 'C:\MSSQL\Dumps\Pubs2.dmp'
```

The `Restore` command works similarly, with the `From` switch added:

```
Load Database Pubs2 From disk = 'C:\MSSQL\DUMPS\PUBS2.DMP'
```

Enterprise Manager can also be used to back up to a file directly. Instead of selecting a backup device simply enter the path of the file you wish to use, as shown in Figure 6.8.

FIGURE 6.8

Using Enterprise Manager to back up to a file directly

Backing Up Transaction Logs

If the database is not set to Truncate Log on Checkpoint the transaction log can be backed up and restored apart from the database.

The transaction log is a running total of all the transactions that have occurred in that particular database. One of the features of SQL Server is that the transaction log is truncated (cleaned out) only after a successful backup of the log. Many companies have run SQL Server for two or three months with no problems until they suddenly find that no new transactions can be recorded because the transaction log filled up.

The good news is that the transaction log will be cleaned out by SQL Server as part of a normal transaction log backup. The bad news is that SQL Server doesn't do this by default—all backups (and thus the cleaning, or truncating, of the log) must be configured by the administrator.

Although the Truncate Log on Checkpoint option will automatically keep the log clean, it is not recommended for production environments because you cannot recover transactions that happened between database backups. You will also not be able to perform transaction log backups. If you do use the Truncate Log on Checkpoint option, make sure you perform frequent (at least nightly) database backups.

Another advantage of backing up the transaction log is that it can be restored up to a certain point in time. For example, if you had a backup of the transaction log for Wednesday and you later discovered a major error had occurred at 4:05 P.M., you could restore the data up to 4:04 P.M.

The log can be backed up by issuing the command

```
Backup log <database> to <device>.
```

This command backs up the log and cleans it out.

Exercise 6.9 adds a new employee to simulate activity in the database and then backs up the log.

EXERCISE 6.9

Backing Up the Transaction Log

1. In Enterprise Manager, clear the Truncate Log on Checkpoint option on the Pubs database by highlighting the database, right-clicking and choosing Properties, and then going to the Options tab. Click OK to save the change.

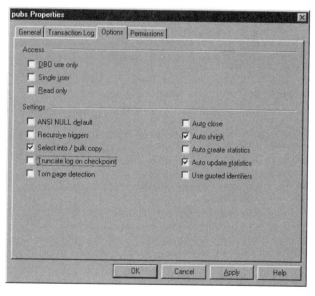

2. Simulate activity in the database by issuing the following command from a Query Analyzer window in the Pubs database:

```
INSERT EMPLOYEE VALUES ('KRM52936F', 'Katie', 'R',
'Mortensen',~CA DEFAULT, DEFAULT, DEFAULT, DEFAULT)
```

3. Go to the Backup screen by highlighting the database in Enterprise Manager; select Backup Database or right-click and choose Backup Database.

4. Back up the transaction log by selecting Transaction log for the backup type; remove any previous devices, and add the Pubs_log device (defined earlier). Select Overwrite Existing Media and choose OK to start the backup.

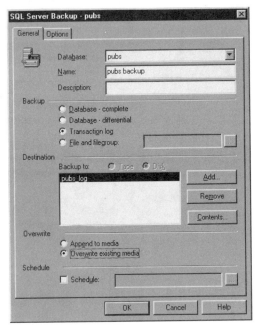

5. Select OK to close the window.

Various switches can be added to the command to change the way the backup works:

Truncate_Only This switch is used only to clean out the log. If the database is backed up in its entirety every night, maintaining a backup of the log would be redundant, yet the log still needs to be cleaned out. If this switch is used on a regular basis, you might want to set the database to Truncate Log on Checkpoint.

No_Truncate   This switch does the opposite of the `truncate_only` switch—it backs up the log without cleaning it out. The main purpose of this switch is to make a new backup of the transaction log when the database itself is either too damaged to work—or is completely gone.

Note that with SQL Server 7 you must have at least one .MDF file (database file) still working in order for the `no_truncate` switch to back up data successfully from the transaction log.

Differential Database Backups

SQL Server 7 adds the ability to create a differential database backup, which records the final state of any added, edited, or deleted rows since the last full database backup.

Differential backups, unlike transaction log backups, cannot be restored to a particular point in time, since only the final state of the data is recorded. You may wish to combine differential backups with transaction log backups so you have the advantages of both types of backups.

To perform a differential backup using T-SQL syntax, simply open a Query Analyzer window and issue the following command:

Backup Database <*database*> to <*device*> with differential

You can also use Enterprise Manager to perform differential backups, as demonstrated in Exercise 6.10.

EXERCISE 6.10

Performing a Differential Database Backup

1. Start Enterprise Manager and go to the Management/Backup folder.

2. Make a new device for the differential backups by creating a device called pubs_diff_backup.

EXERCISE 6.10 (CONTINUED)

3. Highlight the Pubs database and choose Backup Database.

4. Select Differential Backup, remove any previous devices, choose the Pubs_diff_backup device, and select Overwrite Existing Media. Choose OK to start the backup.

5. Choose OK to close the Backup screen.

Filegroup Backups

SQL Server 7 also allows you to back up files and filegroups independent of the database. For example, suppose you have three data volumes (N:, O:, P:) and three filegroups (Employees, Customers, Orders), each residing on a different data volume. If the entire database took too long to back up you could back up the Employees file on Monday, the Customers file on Tuesday, and the Orders file on Wednesday. Because backing up files or filegroups does not back up the transaction log, make sure you also perform a transaction log backup after backing up the filegroup.

To perform the filegroup backup using T-SQL, issue the following command:

```
Backup database <database>
file=<filename>,filegroup=<filegroup> to <device>
```

Enterprise Manager can also be used to perform a filegroup backup. In Exercise 6.11 we will perform a filegroup backup of the Pubs database.

EXERCISE 6.11

Performing a Filegroup Backup

1. Start Enterprise Manager and go to the Management/Backup folder.

2. Make a new device for the Filegroup backup by creating a device called pubs_filegroup_backup.

3. Highlight the Pubs database and choose Backup Database.

4. Select to do a File and Filegroup backup and select the Primary (the default) filegroup. Choose OK.

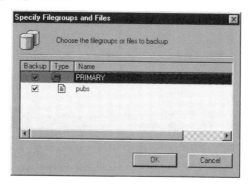

5. Remove any previous devices and select the Pubs_filegroup device; select Overwrite Existing Media. Choose OK to start the backup.

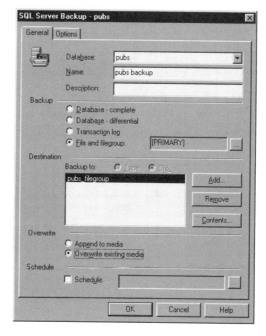

6. Choose OK to close the Backup screen.

Scheduling Backups

SQL Server has built-in scheduling that allows you to set a recurring time for your backups. By scheduling backups you are simply creating SQL Server tasks, which are handled by the SQL Executive service. Creating, editing and deleting tasks are covered in detail in Chapter 8, *Implementing Proactive Administration in SQL Server 7*.

In Exercise 6.12, we will schedule a backup of the Master database to occur nightly.

EXERCISE 6.12

Scheduling Backups

1. Start Enterprise Manager. Open the Databases folder. If the Master database is shown, right-click it and choose Backup Database.

   If the Master database does not appear, you can change your settings to make it appear by highlighting the server, going to Action ➢ Edit SQL Server Registration Properties or by right-clicking the server and choosing to edit the registration. Select Show System Databases and Objects and choose OK. You can also leave the system databases hidden in the Databases folder and simply select the Master database from the Backup screens.

2. Go to the Backup screen by highlighting the Database folder and choosing Action ➢ All Tasks ➢ Backup Database or by highlighting the Master database and selecting to back it up.

3. Select to do a complete backup (the only possible choice for the Master database), select to go to the Master_backup device, select Overwrite Existing Media, and check the Schedule box.

EXERCISE 6.12 (CONTINUED)

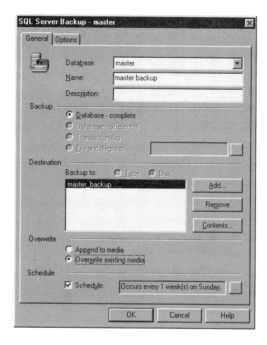

4. Note that the default schedule is set for once a week on Sunday. Change the schedule by selecting the box to the right of the Schedule.

5. Note that the scheduling box allows for a task to be started at various times, including on a regular basis. Change the time for the task by selecting the Change button (at the bottom right).

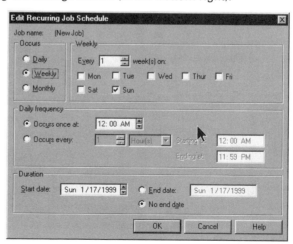

EXERCISE 6.12 (CONTINUED)

6. Change the time as needed and select OK, OK, OK to save your scheduled task. Note that to edit your task you will need to go to the Management ➤ SQL Server Agent ➤ Jobs folder.

Backup Device Information

There are several different ways to get information about the backup devices and the dates and contents of the backups stored on them.

The sp_helpdevice command can be used, with the particular database device specified. In Exercise 6.13, we will run the sp_helpdevice command and look at the dump devices in more detail.

EXERCISE 6.13

The Sp_helpdevice **Command**

1. Start the Query Analyzer.

2. Go to the Query menu and select Results Grid.

3. Enter the command **sp_helpdevice**.

You should see something like the following:

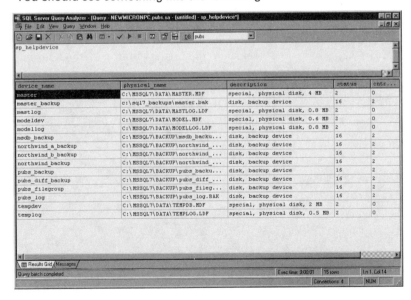

EXERCISE 6.13 (CONTINUED)

4. Enter the command **Restore headeronly from pubs_backup**. You should be able to see the contents of the Pubs_backup device. You will probably have to scroll to the right to see all the fields.

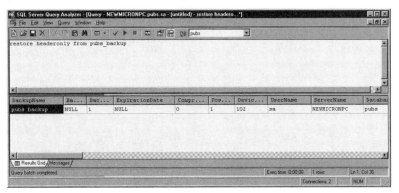

5. Close the Query Analyzer

Enterprise Manager can also be used to see the contents of backup devices. Exercise 6.14 shows how to examine backup devices.

EXERCISE 6.14

Examining Backup Devices Using Enterprise Manager

1. Start Enterprise Manager.

2. Go to the Management ≻ Backup folder.

3. Highlight the Pubs_backup device, right-click, and choose Properties.

4. Select the View Contents button.

5. You should see the same type of information that the Restore Headeronly command gave, including the database backed up, the type of backup, and the date of the backup, among other things. Note that you will probably have to scroll to the right to see all of the fields.

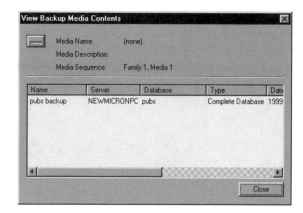

6. Choose Close and Cancel to go back to Enterprise Manager.

The Maintenance Wizard

The Database Maintenance Plan Wizard (first added to SQL Server 6.5) does a great job of scheduling backups. The Wizard is started from the menu or by choosing the Wizard icon. Exercise 6.15 will walk you through using the Wizard to schedule regular backups of the Pubs database.

EXERCISE 6.15

The Database Maintenance Plan Wizard

1. Start the Wizard by going to Administer SQL Server Tasks, selecting Tools ➤ Wizards, opening the Management folder, and selecting the Database Maintenance Plan Wizard. You can also start it by selecting the Wizard icon to open the list of Wizards.

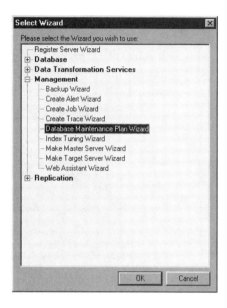

2. Highlight the Database Maintenance Plan Wizard and choose OK.

3. Choose Next on the Introduction screen.

4. Select the databases on which you wish to run the Wizard. For this exercise, we will run it only on the Pubs database. Select Next to continue.

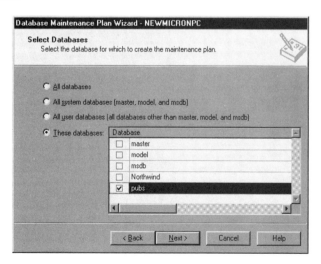

5. Select Reorganize Data and Index Pages to optimize the data and index pages. Select Next to continue.

If you select Remove Unused Space from Data Pages, you are choosing to autoshrink the database. Note that you can change the default schedule for the reorganization by using the Change button.

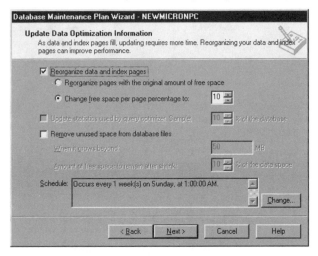

6. On the next screen you can check the database for errors and auto-matically fix any errors found. Select Check Database Integrity to perform the tests. This screen gives the same functionality as the DBCC command. Select Next to continue.

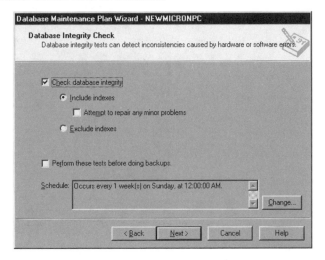

7. The choices on the next screen allow you to schedule the database backup. Note that you can turn off the Verify option, although that is not recommended for beginning users. Select Next to continue.

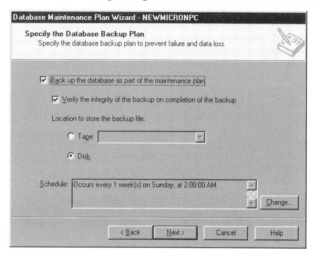

8. The next dialog box allows you to pick the location for the database backups. You can also set the automatic deletion of backups that are older than a specified number of weeks. Select to Remove the files that are older than 4 weeks so that old backup files do not fill your hard drive. Note that files will be created with the `Database_type_time-stamp.bak` file-naming convention. Select Next to continue.

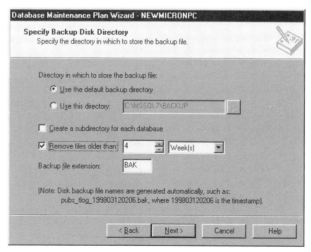

9. The next dialog box is similar to that in step 8, except that this one pertains to the transaction logs of the database. Select Next to continue.

10. Here you can generate reports and even have the maintenance report e-mailed to a specified person (providing you have e-mail support configured correctly). Select Next to continue.

11. The Maintenance History dialog box allows you to configure how much history will be kept about the maintenance job and where the information will be kept. (You can also specify that the history be kept on a remote server.) Select Next to continue.

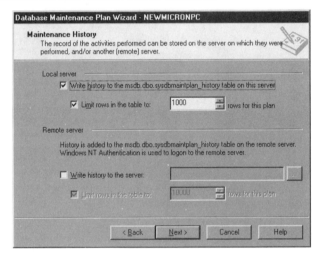

12. You will get a final confirmation screen about the maintenance plan. Select Finish to save the plan and OK at the Creating Confirmation screen.

13. To monitor, edit, or delete the plan, go to the Management ➤ Database Maintenance Plan folder—your plan should be listed. To edit the plan, simply double-click it.

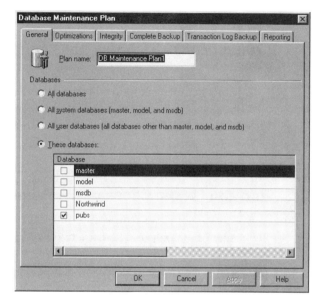

14. Choose OK to save changes to the plan or Cancel to back out of any changes.

Restoring Databases

The process of restoring SQL databases can be summed up in the following steps:

- Attempt to back up the transaction log

- Find and fix the cause of the failure.

- Drop all the affected databases.

- Restore the database from a database backup or from a file or filegroup backup.

- Restore the transaction log from a log backup or restore the differential database backup.

The older syntax of Load Database and Load Transaction can be used in place of the Restore Database and Restore Log commands, but they are not recommended because support for these older commands could be dropped with any newer version of SQL Server.

Attempt to Back Up the Transaction Log

You should always try to create a transaction log backup after a database failure in order to capture all the transactions up to the time of the failure. You should use the no_truncate switch, which backs up the log when the database is unusable. If you successfully back up transactions to the point of the failure, simply restore this new transaction backup set after you restore the other transaction log backups.

Find and Fix the Cause of the Failure

This step involves troubleshooting NT and/or SQL Server to determine the cause of the failure. There are two basic reasons for determining the cause—obviously, the first is to fix the problem and the second is to take the appropriate steps to prevent it from happening in the future.

Drop the Affected Databases

Before the database can be re-created, it should first be dropped so that any references to bad hardware are deleted. You can delete it using either Enterprise Manager or the T-SQL Drop Database <database> command. If hardware was not the reason you are restoring, you do not need to drop the database.

Restore the Database

Enterprise Manager can restore databases quickly. Simply highlight the database to be restored, select the backup, and choose Restore. You can also restore a database without having to re-create it as the restoration procedure will create the database if it doesn't already exist. To automatically re-create the database simply choose a backup set to restore from, and if the database doesn't exist it will be re-created. If a database by the same name as that in the backup set already exists it will be overwritten. If you wish to restore a backup set to a differently named database use the Replace switch (discussed below).

Although the syntax to do a restoration starts out simple, there are many options that let you control exactly what is restored from which backup set. The syntax to do a restoration is:

`Restore Database <database> from <device> <options>.`

The most common options are:

Dbo_only   Tags the restored database as Read_Only.

Recovery   Recovers any transactions and allows the database to be used. This is the default if not specified.

No_recovery   Allows additional transaction logs to be restored, and also does not allow the database to be used until the Recovery option is used.

If you use this option by mistake (or end up not having any logs to restore) you can issue the command `Restore Database <database> Recovery` to activate the database.

Replace   Required when the name of the database being restored is different than the one that was backed up.

Standby   Allows the database to be read-only between log restores. This is used for standby servers or for other special purposes, such as testing the data contained in each transaction backup set.

Restart   Usually used with tape backups. Restart allows you to restart an operation at the point of failure. For example, suppose you have 5 tapes, and on the last tape you insert the wrong one. By using the Restart switch, you can simply insert tape 5 and quickly finish the job.

SQL Server wipes out the old database when you restore a full backup of a database—there is no merging of data.

Exercise 6.16 will have you restore the Pubs database from a full database backup.

EXERCISE 6.16

Restoring Databases Using Enterprise Manager

1. Restore the Pubs database by highlighting it and selecting Restore Database from the right screen, or by right-clicking and choosing All Tasks ➢ Restore Database.

2. On the list of backups, make sure that you only have the first backup (the full backup) selected.

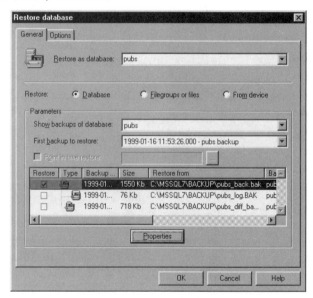

3. Go to the Options tab. Make sure that the Recovery completion state is set to Leave Database Nonoperational so we can restore the transaction log later.

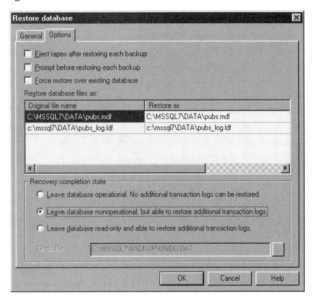

4. Select OK to start the restoration. Select OK at the Restoration Confirmation screen.

5. Go back to the Databases folder. The Pubs database should be grayed out and say (Loading) next to it.

Restore the Log

Enterprise Manager or the `Restore Log` command can be used to restore transaction logs. Restoring transaction logs can be thought of as reapplying all the transactions just as they occurred.

The T-SQL command to restore the log is

```
Restore Log <database> from <device> <options>
```

All the options that apply to the `Restore Database` command also apply to the `Restore Log` command, with the exception of the Replace option, which is not supported for log restorations.

Unlike restoring the entire database, restoring transaction logs literally reapplies all the transactions that took place between the time of the full database backup and the time of the transaction log backup, appending any changes to the database.

To restore transaction logs using Enterprise Manger, highlight the database you want restored and choose Restore Database. Exercise 6.17 shows you how to restore the log files for the Pubs database and looks at the results.

EXERCISE 6.17

Restoring Transaction Logs Using Enterprise Manager

1. Restore the Pubs database by highlighting it and selecting Restore Database from the right screen, or by right-clicking and choosing All Tasks ➤ Restore Database.

2. Select From Device and Add, Pubs_log to specifically restore just the transaction log.

3. Make sure you select Transaction Log from the Restore Backup Set menu.

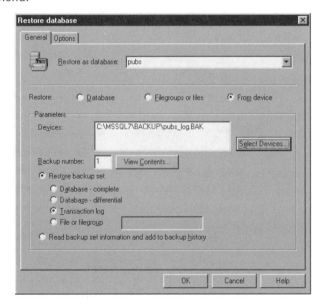

If you have been appending backups to the backup devices, use the View Contents button to select the correct backup set to restore.

4. Select OK to restore the transaction log. Select OK to close the Confirmation window.

5. Test the restoration by opening a Query Analyzer window, going to the Pubs database and do a `select * from employee` command. The row added earlier (Katie Mortensen) should appear.

Restoring to a Certain Time   SQL Server can restore transaction log backup up to a certain point in time. To do this, just choose a date and time from the Restore window as shown in Figure 6.9.

FIGURE 6.9

Restoring to a certain point in time

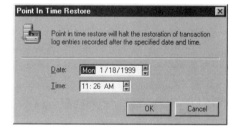

Restore Differential Backups

Restoring a differential backup works very much like restoring transaction log backups. You must first do a full database restoration, then select the most recent differential backup to restore.

The T-SQL syntax to restore a differential backup is the same as for restoring the entire database.

Restore Filegroups

Restoring filegroups can be done by using either Enterprise Manager or T-SQL syntax. It is done in Enterprise Manager in much the same fashion as full database restorations.

The T-SQL syntax for restoring files and file groups is

```
Restore Database <database> from <device> File=<logical
filename> Filegroup=<logical filegroup name>
```

Restoring the Master Database with a Valid Backup

Because the Master database contains all the settings for SQL Server, restoring the Master database is not only more complicated, but impossible to do accidentally. In order to restore the Master database you must start SQL Server with the -m switch, which causes SQL Server to start in single-user mode.

When you rebuild the Master database, the Msdb, Model, and Distribution databases also are rebuilt (reset). You should restore these database from your most recent backups or the scheduled jobs, alerts, operators, and ongoing replication will all disappear.

In Exercise 6.18, we will start SQL Server in single-user mode, and restore the Master database from a backup.

EXERCISE 6.18

Restoring the Master Database

1. Stop SQL Server.

2. Open a command prompt.

3. Start SQL Server from a command prompt by issuing the following command: **SQLSERVR -m.**

4. Minimize the command prompt.

5. Start Enterprise Manager (SQL Server will show a red stop light even though it is running).

6. Highlight the Master database.

7. Go to the Restore screen.

8. Select the Master_backup device, and choose Restore Now.

9. After the Master database is restored, the command prompt should automatically stop SQL Server return to a regular C:\ prompt.

10. Restart SQL Server normally.

Restoring the Master Database without a Backup

If the master database becomes corrupt and a current backup is unavailable, there is a procedure that will allow you to re-create the Master database so that your user databases reappear. The steps are as follows:

Find and fix the cause of the failure   Just as noted above, you will need to find and fix the hardware or software failure that caused the Master database to become corrupted.

Rebuild the master database   Use the `Rebuildm.exe` program to rebuild the Master database.

WARNING   Rebuilding the Master database does not fix the existing one—it creates a completely new Master database—just as though you reinstalled SQL Server.

Attach valid database files to the master database by running the `sp_attach_db` command for each file   You can attach and detach databases without losing the data in the databases by using the `sp_attach_db` and `sp_detach_db` procedures. Because a newly rebuilt Master database will not know about any of your previous databases, you will need to run `sp_attach_db` for each of them.

Re-create the settings for SQL Server   Because the rebuilt Master database holds all the settings for SQL Server, they will revert to the defaults. You will need to reconfigure SQL Server with its previous settings, and probably stop and restart SQL Server to have them take effect. See Chapter 2, *Installing, Upgrading, and Configuring SQL Server 7,* for more details on changing settings.

Re-create the users and security for each database   Because the rebuilt Master database will only have the default SQL logins, you will need to re-create all of the logins. See Chapter 5, *Security and SQL Server 7,* for more details.

Restore the Msdb, Model, and Distribution databases   Rebuilding the Master database also rebuilds the Msdb database. Any tasks, alerts, and operators you have created will have to be re-created by hand if a current backup of the Msdb database is unavailable.

Summary

Preserving data under less than ideal situations is one of the primary responsibilities of a database administrator. There are several options to consider in protecting your data. Windows NT has several features that provide data protection, including disk mirroring, disk duplexing, and striped-with-parity drives (RAID 5 drives). Although a pure striped drive doesn't provide any data protection, it is the fastest way to set up your drives.

Because SQL Server database devices are locked when SQL Server is running, normal NT backups will not back up any data. The solution is to define backup devices, which are files that contain a backup of databases and transaction logs. After the backup process is complete, these devices are closed by SQL Server and can be backed up normally by NT.

Backups can be performed using T-SQL commands or through Enterprise Manager. Backups can also be scheduled to happen on a regular basis, in which case a SQL Executive task is created.

Restoring a database deletes all the previous data and objects, while restoring a transaction log merely reapplies all the transactions. Transaction logs can also be restored up to a certain date and time, making recovery from errors easier.

Rebuilding the Master database resets it to a pristine new Master, which wipes out any users, devices, databases, and settings you may have had. The Master database can be restored only while SQL Server is run with the -m switch, which starts it in single-user mode.

Review Questions

1. What is the SQL Server 7 command to back up databases?

   A. Backup database

   B. Dump database

   C. Backup device

   D. Dump device

2. How do you edit a recurring (scheduled) backup?

   A. You can't—you have to delete and re-create it

   B. From the Database/Jobs screen

   C. From SQL Agent/Jobs screen

   D. From the Management/Database Maintenance Plan screen

3. What is the SQL Server 7 command to back up a transaction log?

   A. Dump database /log

   B. Dump log

   C. Dump transaction

   D. Backup log

4. What does the no_recovery switch do?

   A. There is no such switch

   B. It cleans out (truncates) the log without making a backup

   C. It makes a backup of the log without cleaning it

   D. It loads a backup of a database but leaves the database offline so you can continue restoring transaction logs

5. When do you need to use the `replace` switch?

   A. There is no such switch

   B. When you are restoring into a database with data

   C. When you are restoring into a database that is marked read-only

   D. When the database you are restoring into has a different name than the originally backed up database

6. What is the most efficient (as in spaced used) form of disk fault tolerance?

   A. Stripe set

   B. Mirror set

   C. Duplex set

   D. Striped-with-parity set

7. Windows NT supports which of the following?

   A. Mirroring

   B. Duplexing

   C. Stripe

   D. Striped with parity

8. What program allows you to do backups graphically?

   A. Transfer Manager

   B. Backup Manager

   C. Security Manager

   D. Enterprise Manager

9. What is the command to restore a database in SQL Server 7?

    A. Restore database

    B. Run database

    C. Load database

    D. Undo database

10. What feature of SQL Server allows backups to run faster?

    A. SCSI support

    B. Striped backups

    C. Mirror backups

    D. Parallel striped backup

11. You have a recent full backup file of your database. Your hard drive that contained the database files (but none of the SQL system database files) crashed. After fixing the hard drive, which of these steps is redundant?

    A. Using the `sp_attach_db` command

    B. Creating the database

    C. Restoring the database

    D. Rebuilding the Master database

12. You wish to move a database to another SQL Server. You stop the first SQL Server and move the .MDF and .LDF files to the second server. What step must you take on the second server to install the database?

    A. Restore the database from the .MDF and .LDF files

    B. Run the `sp_db_mount` command to bring the database online

    C. Create a new database and specify the path to the .MDF and .LDF files

    D. Run the `sp_attach_db` command

13. You need to be able to restore your databases to any given time, but you have a very large database with many inserts and updates that takes three hours to do a full backup. You implement the following steps: You schedule a full backup every week, with differential backups every night. You set the Truncate Log on Checkpoint option on to keep the log small, and schedule transaction log backups every hour. Will this solution work?

A. This solution works very well

B. This solution will not work because you cannot combine differential backups with transaction log backups

C. This solution will not work because you cannot schedule transaction log backups with full database backups

D. This solution will not work because you cannot schedule transaction log backups when you have selected Truncate Log on Checkpoint

14. You have three filegroups (FilesA, FilesB, FilesC). You are rotating your filegroup backups so that they get backed up every third night. You are also doing transaction log backups. The files in FilesB get corrupted. Which steps would you do, and in what order do you do the restoration?

A. Restore the transaction log files

B. Restore FilesB filegroup

C. Back up the log with the `no_truncate` switch

D. Restore the entire database

15. You have an OLTP application that is mission-critical, but can have up to 15 minutes of unscheduled downtime. You have an adequate—but not unlimited—budget. You also run daily reports on the server that currently have to be run at night for performance reasons, but you would like to run them during the day. Which solution should you recommend?

A. RAID 5 drives for your server

B. A standby server with frequent transaction backups

C. An NT cluster server

D. Replication to another server

16. You have a 100GB database with a 25GB transaction log. You have ten 25GB drives and two hard-drive controllers. You want to minimize the time it takes to do backups and ensure fault-tolerance in case any drive fails. You also want to ensure maximum performance for your OLTP database. Which of these is the best solution?

A. Create a 125MB RAID 5 set for the data and log. Create a single .MDF file for the data and a single .LDF file for the log. Schedule full database backups every week and transaction log backups every night.

B. Create a 125MB RAID 0+1 set for the data and log. Create a single .MDF file for the data and a single .LDF file for the log. Schedule full database backups every week and transaction log backups every night.

C. Create a 100MB RAID 5 set for the data and a 25MB RAID 0+1 set for the log. Create three filegroups for the data. Schedule a full backup every week, rotate filegroup backups during the week, and do a transaction log backup every night.

D. Create a 100MB RAID 5 set for the data and a 25MB RAID 0+1 set for the log. Create a single .MDF file for the data and a single .LDF file for the log. Schedule full database backups every week and transaction log backups every night.

17. Which of these operations can you do while performing a full database backup?

A. Create a new index

B. Update columns

C. Import in a large number of rows

D. Create a new table

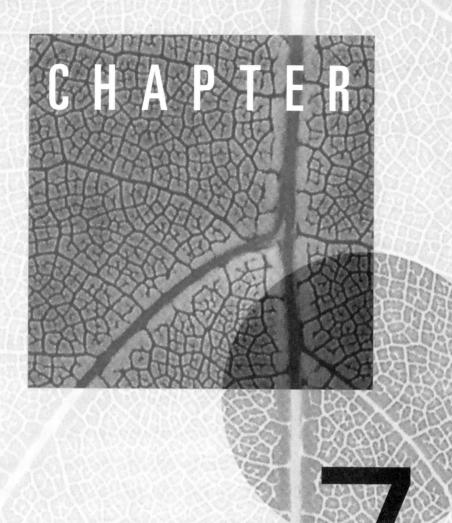

CHAPTER

7

Managing Your Data

Managing your data will be reflected in many different areas of your SQL Server administration duties. This includes the migration of data from other sources as well as working with data from your local SQL Server. There are many different activities that you can perform when it comes to managing data. These include adding new records to a table through the INSERT and SELECT INTO statements. You can add data from a flat file or move SQL Server data to a flat file using the bcp (bulk copy) utility, or the Transact-SQL (T-SQL) command BULK INSERT. You can move and transform data from any OLE-DB or ODBC sources and destinations using the integrated Data Transformation Services (DTS). Transformations include such things as converting a character field into a numeric value, or splitting an EmployeeName field into a FirstName and a LastName field. Managing data may also include the use of HDR (Host Data Replication), which will be covered in the Chapter 9, *Creating and Implementing a Replication Solution in SQL Server 7.*

You may also wish to move both data and database schema from one SQL Server 7 computer to another SQL Server 7 computer. In this chapter we will also discuss the issues involved with the upgrade and movement of your data from an older version of SQL Server. Two other activities that involve your data are backup and restoration (addressed in Chapter 6, *Implementing Database Backups and Restorations*) and replication (see Chapter 9, as noted above).

The first half of this chapter has been designed to discuss the following Exam Objective.

Microsoft
Exam
Objective

Load data by using various methods. Methods include the INSERT statement, the SELECT INTO statement, the bcp utility, Data Transformation Services (DTS), and the BULK INSERT statement.

Let's look at our first section on using the INSERT statement to add data to your SQL Server.

Loading Data with *INSERT* Statement

When you use the INSERT statement, you will add a single row of data to your table. There are variations of the INSERT statement that will allow you to add multiple rows of data by selecting data from another table. You can also use the SELECT INTO statement to move data from one location to another.

Before you can use the INSERT statement, you must know a little about the structure of the table into which you wish to insert data. You should know the number of columns in the table, the datatypes of these columns, the column names, and any defaults or constraints (e.g., IDENTITY) that are on a particular column.

To gather this information, you can use the Enterprise Manager or the sp_help stored procedure. To use the Enterprise Manager, simply navigate through the console tree to the desired database. Open the database and then click on Tables as shown in Figure 7.1. The tables are now displayed in the right pane. Right-click on a table and choose Properties. You are now looking at the Categories Table Properties for the Northwind database, as shown in Figure 7.2.

FIGURE 7.1

The Tables pane

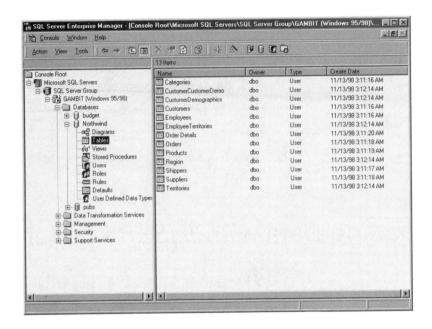

FIGURE 7.2

Table properties

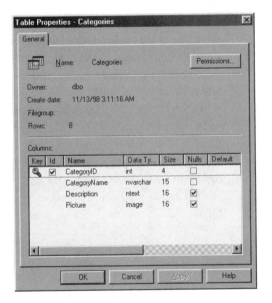

Open up the Query Analyzer and run the following code:

```
USE MASTER
GO
EXEC sp_help Categories
```

You should be given a wealth of information regarding the name of the table and its owner as well as information regarding the name of each column, its datatype, length, precision and scale, nullability, and constraints.

The easiest way to work with the INSERT statement is to specify data for each column in the table that requires data, in the same order in which the columns were defined. In the Categories table, the CategoryID field is an IDENTITY column and will automatically generate a value for us. We need to specify the CategoryName, Description, and Picture fields. You can add a new record to the Categories table by running the code shown in Exercise 7.1. Note the last set of quotation marks is a placeholder for the Picture field, which we are not adding.

EXERCISE 7.1

Using the *INSERT* Statement

1. Open the SQL Query Analyzer. Choose Start ➤ Program Files ➤ SQL Server 7 ➤ Query Analyzer.

2. In the query analyzer, add the following code:

```
INSERT INTO Categories VALUES
('Beer', 'Beers of the World!', '')
```

3. This will add a single row to the table. To verify your new row of data, run the following query:

```
SELECT * FROM Categories
```

4. You should now see item number 9 in the output list as shown here.

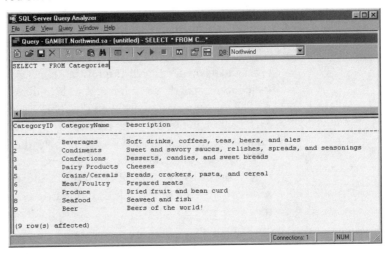

When you are inserting character data, you must enclose the characters in single quotation marks. When you are inserting numeric data, you do not use quotation marks.

There is much more information that we could cover with the INSERT statement, but that is related much more to the SQL Server developer than it is to the administrator. For the exam, you really need to know when it is appropriate to use the INSERT statement rather than the SELECT INTO statement or DTS or bcp and so on.

Remember these facts about the INSERT statement:

- It generally adds a single record at a time.

- The inserted record is a logged transaction.

- If there is an index, it will be updated as well.

- You must have INSERT permission on the table to which you wish to add records. Let's move on to the SELECT INTO statement and see how it affects your data management.

Copying Tables with *SELECT INTO*

The SELECT INTO statement is used to create new permanent tables or new temporary tables filled with data from another table. It is essentially a copy table command.

To use the SELECT INTO command to create a permanent table in your database, you must first enable the Select Into/Bulk Copy database option. This can be done either in the Enterprise Manager or through the sp_dboption stored procedure. To create a temporary table, you must precede its name with the octothorpe symbol (#)—which most of us call the pound sign or the number sign (unless you are in Australia—then it's the hash mark). This is used to create a local temporary table. You can also create global temporary tables by using two octothorpes, as in ##MyGlobalTempTable.

When you create a local temporary table, only the user connection that created it has access to it. When the session ends, the temporary table (which is stored in the Tempdb database) will be released. Global temporary tables can be accessed by any user connection and are available until the table is dropped or all connections to SQL Server are removed.

Spaces and Naming Conventions

You can use spaces in your naming conventions. To do this, you must enclose the identifier in square brackets. For example, a table named Order Details would be referred to as [Order Details]. Although you can use spaces in your naming conventions, we strongly suggest that you use the underscore (as in Order_Details) or mixed case. Mixed case pushes all the words together and uses both upper- and lowercase characters to make it more readable, as in OrderDetails.

When you set the Select Into/Bulk Copy database option, you are specifying that you are about to perform a non-logged insert of data. To set this option from Enterprise Manager, navigate through the console tree to the database of your choice. Right-click on the database and choose Properties. From the properties window, click the Options tab. In Figure 7.3, the Options tab for the Northwind database has been selected and the Select Into/Bulk Copy database option has been enabled.

FIGURE 7.3

The Database Options
screen

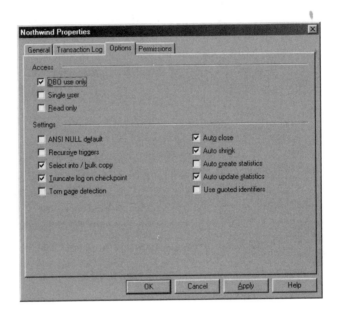

Exercise 7.2 will generate a new table called tblNewCategories in the Northwind database and fill it with the data from the old Categories table. Note that the script I am using the `sp_dboption` stored procedure to both enable and then disable the Select Into/Bulk Copy database option.

EXERCISE 7.2

Using the *SELECT INTO* Statement

1. Open the Query Analyzer.

EXERCISE 7.2 (CONTINUED)

2. Run the following code:

```
USE Northwind
GO

EXEC sp_dboption 'Northwind', 'select into/bulkcopy', True
GO

SELECT * INTO tblNewCategories
FROM Categories
GO

EXEC sp_dboption 'Northwind', 'select into/bulkcopy',
False
GO
```

3. To verify that the script really created a new table and filled it with data, you can run the following query. You should see a list of 9 items that were transferred during the SELECT INTO procedure.

```
USE NORTHWIND
GO

SELECT * FROM tblNewCategories
GO
```

WARNING As with any non-logged transaction, the recoverability of your database is at issue. You should perform a backup of your data as soon as possible.

Keep these things in mind when you are working with the SELECT INTO statement:

- To create a permanent table, you must have the Select Into/Bulk Copy database option enabled.

- To create local temporary tables, you must prefix your table name with an octothorpe (#).

- To create global temporary tables, you must prefix your table name with two octothorpes (##).

- To run the SELECT INTO command you must have CREATE TABLE permissions in the database.

- To set the Select Into option, you can use the sp_dboption stored procedure.

- Running a SELECT INTO statement performs a non-logged operation, and you should ensure your data by backing up afterward.

Copying Data with bcp

Bulk copy, or bcp, is a lightning-fast command-line utility for moving data between a flat file and your SQL Server 7 database. The upside of bcp is its speed and compatibility. If you do not have indexes created on your tables and you have the Select Into/Bulk Copy database option set, reading an ASCII file into your server is very quick. There are several downsides, however, including the cumbersome interface. Because it is a command-line utility, it requires you to remember a number of different switches as well as case-sensitivity. Another disadvantage is that bcp transfers data only. It will not transfer other database objects like tables, views, and schema. The last downside is the fact that bcp cannot do data transformations. These are such functions as converting a text string to a numeric value or vice-versa, splitting a Name field into a FirstName and a LastName field, and many other types of transformations.

Microsoft ✓ ***Exam*** ***Objective***

Develop a migration plan
- Plan an upgrade from a previous version of SQL Server.
- Plan the migration of data from other data sources.

With bcp, you can append data to an existing table just as you would if you were using a third-party utility like Visual Basic, but the bcp program is generally much quicker. When you export data using bcp, you will always overwrite the old flat file (if it exists).

When you use bcp to move data out of SQL Server, you should specify a name for the flat file. There are several common extensions:

bcp   Native-mode data files

csv   Comma-separated files

err   Error output files

fmt   bcp format files

txt   ASCII text files

To use bcp, you must have the appropriate permissions. When you wish to move data from a flat file into SQL Server 7, you must have Read permissions on the file itself (if using NTFS) and you must have INSERT permissions on the SQL Server table into which you would like to move the data.

To use bcp to move data from SQL Server to a flat file you must have NTFS permissions for either Change or Full Control on the directory and the file. If you are using a FAT or FAT32 partition, this is not an issue, as neither of these file systems supports permissions. Within SQL Server, you must have SELECT permissions on the table or view from which you want to pull your data.

Here is the syntax for bcp:

```
Bcp [[databasename.]owner.]tablename | view_name | "Query"}
{in | out | queryout | format } datafile
[/6]
[/a packet_size]
[/b batchsize]
[/c]
[/C code_page]
[/e errfile]
[/E]
[/f formatfile]
[/F firstrow]
[/h "hint [,…n]"]
[/i inputfile]
[/k]
[/L lastrow]
[/m maxerrors]
[/n]
```

```
[/N]
[/o output_file]
[/P password]
[/q]
[/r row_term]
[/S server_name]
[/t field_term]
[/T]
/U login_id
[/v]
[/w]
```

Following is an explanation of each parameter. Note that the only required parameters are `tablename, in/out/queryout/format, datafile,` and login ID `'/U'`.

databasename.owner.tablename or view_name or query Specifies the name of the table you want to export from or import to. This can be a temporary table, a view, or a query. If you don't specify the databasename or the owner, these values will default to the current database and the username in the database who is running the bcp command. For example, you were logged in as AcctMgr in the Budget database and wanted to import into the tblBgtSummary table, you would specify Budget.AcctMgr.tblBgtSummary for this parameter.

in/out/queryout/format Specifies whether you are loading data into SQL Server 7 or extracting data out to a flat file.

datafile Specifies the name of the flat file you wish to work with. You must specify the full file and path name. If you do not, it will default to the local directory from which you run the bcp program. If you do not specify a filename, bcp will go into format file mode. This allows you to create a format file that can be reused later. The format file is simply a template for bulk-copying data into or out of SQL Server 7.

/6 This option specifies that you are working with data from a SQL Server 6.*x* file.

/a packet size This option allows you to specify the size of the packets you are going to be transferring across the network. The default is 4096 bytes.

/b batch size   This option specifies how many records you are going to transfer in a single batch. SQL Server will treat each batch as a separate transaction. If this option is not specified, the entire file will be loaded as a single batch.

/c   This option is used to specify that the data being moved will be all be converted to the character data type rather than the internal SQL Server datatypes. When used for export, it will create a tab delimited flat file.

/C   This option (note the capital C) allows you to specify a code page for the data file. For example, you can generate a file with the code page 850, which was the default code page for SQL Server 6.

/e errfile   This option is used to create a path and filename containing the rows of data that bcp could not import or export properly. This can be very useful when you are troubleshooting your bcp operation. If you do not specify an error file, none will be generated. We suggest that you use the .ERR file extension.

/E   The capital E specifies that identity columns in your SQL Server 7 table should be temporarily turned off. This allows the values in the source file to replace the automatically generated identity values in the SQL Server table during the bulk copy. Identity columns are similar to the autonumber feature in Microsoft Access.

/f formatfile   This option allows you to specify the path and filename of the format file you wish to use during an insertion or extraction from SQL Server 7. If you do not specify the formatfile portion of this option, bcp will prompt you for formatting information and then create a format file called `bcp.fmt`.

/F firstrow   The capital *F* and firstrow value allow you to specify a row, other than the first row, to begin reading into SQL Server 7.

/h "hint"   This option allows you to specify any hints you wish to use. For example, you might create hints about check constraints or sort orders.

/i inputfile   This allows you to specify all these input parameters and store them in a file. When you run bcp again, all you need to do is specify this input file and all the stored parameters are used. As always, specify the full file and pathname.

/k   This option specifies that empty columns will retain their NULL values rather than having some default value applied to them.

/L This option is used to specify the last row to load from the data file into SQL Server. If this is not specified, SQL Server will load all rows from the data file.

/m maxerrors This option allows you to specify the maximum number of errors SQL Server will allow before the bulk copy process is canceled. You should specify this option if you are importing large data files. The default value is 10 errors.

/n This option is used to specify that the data being transferred is in native format. In other words, the data being moved around retains its SQL Server 7 datatypes. This option is especially useful when you are moving data from one SQL Server to another SQL Server.

/N This option specifies that you will be using Unicode for character data and native format for all non-character data.

/o outputfile This option specifies the name of the file that will receive any messages generated by the bulk copy. This option is useful when you run bcp from a batch file and later want to review what was processed.

/P password This option is used to specify the password you wish to use when logging into SQL Server from bcp. If you do not specify a password, bcp will prompt you for one.

/q This option is used to specify that quoted identifiers are being used. When this option is set, all identifiers (table name, column names, etc.) must be specified within double quotation marks.

/r row_term This specifies the value that bcp will use to determine where one row ends and the next row begins. This is normally the \n switch, which specifies both a carriage return and line feed.

/S servername This option is used to specify the SQL Server to which you are connecting. If you don't specify a servername, bcp will assume the local SQL Server. Note: If you are connecting to a local server, bcp will run more quickly if you do not set this option, since setting this option forces bcp to go through the network interface rather than through an anonymous pipe.

/t field_term This option is used to specify the field terminator. In many cases this will be the comma or a tab character.

/T This capital *T* specifies that the bulk copy utility will connect to SQL Server over a trusted connection.

/U   This option specifies the login ID that you will use to gain access to SQL Server and is a required parameter.

/v   This option will report which DB-Library version is being used for the bulk copy process.

/w   This option specifies that the data will be transferred using Unicode.

There are a few other items to keep in mind when you are using bcp. Character mode is the most flexible method of bulk copy because all data is treated as characters. This means that both SQL Server and most other applications can work with the data. When you use character mode to export data, it will be stored as an ASCII text file. Native mode uses the internal SQL Server datatypes and can be faster for data transfers from one SQL Server to another SQL Server database. In fact, when you use the Transfer Manager (discussed later in this chapter) it uses bcp to move data from one SQL Server 7 computer to another SQL Server 7 computer.

When you are working with the data files, bcp needs to know where one field ends and another begins. bcp also needs to know where one row of data ends and another begins. To do this, we specify a common character to be a terminator. You can use the following common characters as either field or row terminators:

\0   Specifies an ANSI NULL

\n   Specifies a new line

\r   Specifies a carriage return

\t   Specifies a tab

****   Specifies a backslash

When you perform a bulk copy to import data, you can do it in normal mode, which means every insert is logged, or in fast mode, in which inserts are not logged. To operate in fast mode, you must enable the Select Into/Bulk Copy database option and you must drop all indexes that are affected by the data transfer. Once you have done this, you can quickly add your data using bulk copy. When you do a bulk copy, you should also be aware that defaults and datatypes will always be enforced and rules, triggers, and constraints will always be ignored.

Since rules, triggers, and constraints are ignored during a fast bulk copy, you should check the validity of your data by running queries or other stored procedures. A simple way to check your constraints is to run an UPDATE statement and set a particular field equal to itself. This will force all constraints to be checked against the new data. It will also fire off any update triggers associated with the table.

Once you are happy with your data, you should re-create your indexes and then backup your database as it is now unrecoverable (because the import was not logged).

Exercise 7.3 will use bcp to create an output file. You will use this output file in the next exercise involving the BULK INSERT statement.

EXERCISE 7.3

Creating an Output File Using bcp

1. Since bcp is a command-line utility, we will create a batch file to run our bcp command. Open the Notepad utility. Click Start ➤ Program Files ➤ Accessories ➤ Notepad

2. From within the Notepad program, save the File as **bcpOrdDet.bat** in the C:\MSSQL7\Data folder.

3. Add the following code to the file. Be sure you do not add any extra characters or hit the Enter key. (While our code will span several lines on the page, yours should not.) Make sure everything is on one line. Replace the *<servername>* listed in this example with your servername.

   ```
   bcp "Northwind..Order Details" out
   c:\mssql7\data\bcpOrdDet.txt -c -q -SServerName -Usa -P
   <servername> -Usa -P
   ```

4. When you are finished, save the file again and close Notepad.

5. Now it's time to run the bulk copy. Navigate to the bcpOrdDet.bat file and double-click on it. It should run for a second or so and complete. It should then tell you that 2155 rows were copied.

6. If you navigate to the C:\MSSQL7\Data folder, you will see the bcpOrd-Det.txt file there at about 55KB. If you open the bcpOrdDet.txt file you will see your data. It is tab-delimited. We chose the –c option, which automatically chooses the tab \t for a field terminator and the newline \n character for a row terminator. The –q parameter sets the quoted identifier value to on. We did this because the Order Details table has a space in it and therefore needed to be enclosed in quotation marks.

Using *BULK INSERT*

T he BULK INSERT command is a new T-SQL statement in SQL Server 7. The BULK INSERT command treats data files like OLE-DB recordsets. Since SQL Server thinks the file is an OLE-DB recordset, it can move multiple records per step. You can move the entire file in one batch or in several batches.

One major difference between bcp and BULK INSERT is that BULK INSERT cannot move data from SQL Server to a file. Essentially, BULK INSERT gives you bulk copy capabilities through the use of T-SQL. Since bcp is a command-line utility, it can be placed into batch files; BULK INSERT cannot. You must be a member of the sysadmin server role to use the BULK INSERT command.

It is important to read through the BULK INSERT syntax and parameters at least once before the exam:

```
BULK INSERT [[database_name.][owner].]{table_name
FROM data_file}[WITH (
[BATCHSIZE = batch_size]]
[[,] CHECK_CONSTRAINTS]
[[,] CODEPAGE [= 'ACP' | 'OEM' | 'RAW' | 'code_page']]
[[,] DATAFILETYPE [= {'char' | 'native'| 'widechar' |
'widenative'}]]
[[,] FIELDTERMINATOR [= 'field_terminator']]
[[,] FIRSTROW [= first_row]]
[[,] FORMATFILE [= 'format_file_path']]
[[,] KEEPIDENTITY]
[[,] KEEPNULLS]
[[,] KILOBYTES_PER_BATCH [= kilobytes_per_batch]]
[[,] LASTROW [= last_row]]
[[,] MAXERRORS [= max_errors]]
[[,] ORDER ({column [ASC | DESC]} [,…n])]
[[,] ROWS_PER_BATCH [= rows_per_batch]]
[[,] ROWTERMINATOR [= 'row_terminator']]
[[,] TABLOCK])]
```

Here are the parameters:

database_name.owner.table_name   The fully qualified table into which you BULK INSERT data.

data_file   The path and filename from which you wish to import

CHECK_CONSTRAINTS   Specifies that constraints will be checked during the BULK INSERT.

CODEPAGE   This option specifies which codepage was used to generate the data file.

DATAFILETYPE   This option is used to specify in which format the data in the file has been stored. This could be character data, bcp native, Unicode character, or Unicode native.

FIELDTERMINATOR   This option specifies which character has been used as a field terminator. As with bcp, the default is a tab character (often shown as \t).

FIRSTROW   This option specifies the row with which you want to begin the BULK INSERT process. The default is the first row.

FORMATFILE   This option is used to specify the full file and pathname of a format file to be used with the BULK INSERT.

KEEPIDENTITY   This option is used to specify that IDENTITY values copied from the file will retain them rather than having SQL Server generate new values.

KEEPNULLS   This option is similar to the KEEPIDENTITY option. It specifies that NULL values in the data file will remain NULL values when loaded into the table.

KILOBYTES_PER_BATCH   This option allows you to specify the number of kilobytes to be move in each step. By default, this is the size of the entire file.

LASTROW   This option specifies which row you to want to use to end the BULK INSERT process. By default, it is the last row in the file.

ORDER   This option allows you to specify a sort order in the data file. This can improve performance in situations where the data file and SQL Server use different sort orders.

ROWS_PER_BATCH   This option specifies how many rows of data to move in each step of the batch. If you use the BATCHSIZE option, you do not need to use this option. By default, all rows are moved in a single batch.

ROWTERMINATOR   This option allows you to specify the end of a single row of data. The default value is the newline character \n.

TABLOCK   This option specifies that a table lock, which will lock the entire table, should be used during the BULK INSERT procedure. No other users may make changes to data in the table during the upload. This can improve the BULK INSERT performance, but it will decrease performance for the other users.

In Exercise 7.4, you will use the BULK INSERT command to load your data from the bcpOrdDet.txt file we created in Exercise 7.3. To truly test the BULK INSERT command, we will first make a backup of the Order Details table using the SELECT INTO statement. We will then truncate the table, removing all data from the table in a single transaction. We will then use the BULK INSERT command to copy data from our text file back into SQL Server.

EXERCISE 7.4

Loading Data Using the *BULK INSERT* Command

1. Open the Query Analyzer

2. Run the following query to create a backup table of our Order Details items.

```
USE Northwind
GO
EXEC sp_dboption 'Northwind', 'select into/bulkcopy', True
GO
SELECT * INTO tmpOrderDetails
FROM [Order Details]
GO
EXEC sp_dboption 'Northwind', 'select into/bulkcopy',
False
GO
```

3. You should be notified that 2155 rows were affected. Let's double-check that the rows were moved. Run the following:

```
SELECT * FROM tmpOrderDetails
GO
```

4. You should receive confirmation that there are 2155 rows in the temporary table. Now let's truncate the Order Details table. Run the following code and verify that there are no records left in the table by running the code sample shown after the GO keyword below.

```
TRUNCATE TABLE [Order Details]
GO
SELECT * FROM [Order Details]
GO
```

5. You should now have an empty Order Details table. Let's run the BULK INSERT command and move our data stored in the bcpOrdDet.txt file into the Order Details table. Run the following code:

```
BULK INSERT Northwind.dbo.[Order Details]
FROM 'c:\mssql7\data\bcpOrdDet.txt'
```

6. You should see that 2155 rows were transferred. To verify, run the SQL code shown here:

```
SELECT * FROM [Order Details]
GO
```

Using Data Transformation Services

Most companies store their data in a variety of locations and a variety of formats. This includes Access databases, AS-400 mainframe systems, spreadsheets, and ASCII text files, among others. With DTS, you can import and export data between these sources and destinations. When you are working with data from two SQL Server 7 computers, you can also transfer database objects and schema. This includes the stored procedures, views, permissions, table layouts, and other information and can be accomplished through the Transfer Manager.

SQL Server can move data through any OLE-DB- or ODBC-compliant data source and data destination. The DTS interface itself is a set of COM (Component Object Model)-based objects. These COM -based objects allow you to:

- Transfer data to and from Access, Excel, SQL Server, Oracle, DB2, ASCII text files, and other sources.

- Create DTS packages that are integrated with other COM-compliant third-party products.

- Schedule DTS packages.

Since COM-based objects are language independent, any computer language that supports COM can be used to interact with your DTS packages. This includes scripting languages like VBScript, JavaScript, and PerlScript. You can also use full-fledged programming languages like Visual Basic and C++ to interact with the DTS packages you create.

In the following sections, we will break down DTS into four distinct areas:

Packages   A DTS package encompasses all the components needed to perform an import, export, or transformation. This includes the tasks and the steps.

Import/Export Wizard   These Wizards quickly walk you through the process of creating a DTS package. Once you become more familiar with the Wizard process, you can use the `dtswiz` and `dtsrun` commands from the command line to bypass most of the Wizard's dialog boxes.

DTS Designer   This is a desktop environment similar to that found with Access or Visual Basic. You have palettes and toolboxes that allow you to visually create DTS packages.

Transfer Manager   The Transfer Manager is used to move data, schema, and objects (indexes, stored procedures, etc.) from one SQL Server 7 computer to another SQL Server 7 computer.

DTS Packages

DTS Packages are a set of tasks designed into a workflow of steps. These steps and tasks are then grouped together into a package. You can create packages using the Import and Export Wizards, through a scripting language, from the command line using dtswiz and dtsrun, or visually through the DTS Designer.

Once you have created a package, it becomes a completely self-contained COM object. You can interact with this object through the Enterprise Manager Task Scheduler as well as the command line and COM-compliant languages. You can store your DTS Packages in a number of formats and enforce several security mechanisms.

Let's first go through the components that are used to create a package. This includes:

- Task objects
- Step objects
- Connection objects
- Data pump

Task Objects

A DTS Package is made up of steps that are associated with task objects. Each task defines a particular action that should be taken or some type of processing that should be done. Task objects can be used to perform the following activities:

- Move data from one OLE-DB- or ODBC-compliant data source to an OLE-DB- or ODBC-compliant data destination. This is often referred to as a Data Pump task.
- Run a T-SQL statement.
- Run a T-SQL batch.
- Execute external programs, batch files, or commands.
- Execute another DTS package.
- Execute COM-compliant scripts (VBScript, JScript, and PerlScript are currently supported within DTS itself).
- Gather results from other running DTS Packages.
- Send e-mail using SQL Mail.

Step Objects

Step objects are used to coordinate the flow of tasks. While task objects are self-contained units, a task object that does not have an associated step object will not be executed. Essentially, we use step objects to structure our workflows.

Step objects can be executed in several different situations:

- Run step only when the prior step completes successfully.

- Run step only when the prior step fails to complete.

- Run step after prior step completes, regardless of success or failure.

This type of relationship between the different steps is known as *precedence constraints*. In other words, a later step has a precedence constraint on the prior step. Once all precedence constraints for a step are satisfied, the next step can begin execution.

Here is a quick example. Suppose you have three steps in your package. Step 1 calls a task that creates a new table. Once the new table has completed, you can run Step 2; this runs a task that runs a bcp batch to load the new table with data. Step 3 could then run a task to create new indexes on the newly created table. Step 2 has a precedence constraint on Step 1. Step 3 has a precedence constraint on Step 2.

Since task objects are separate from step objects, you can assign the same task to multiple steps.

Although task objects can be associated with multiple steps, a particular task can have only one instance of itself running at any given time.

As explained above, step objects can be executed conditionally based upon precedence constraints; another important feature of step objects is their ability to run in parallel. If a particular set of step objects have no precedence constraints, they will all run simultaneously. In Figure 7.4, you can see that steps 1 through 3 will run in parallel as none of them has a precedence constraint. Steps 4 and 5 will execute once steps 1 and 2 have completed. Steps 4 and 5 have precedence constraints. Step 6 will execute if Step 5 fails for some reason.

FIGURE 7.4

Steps can run in parallel

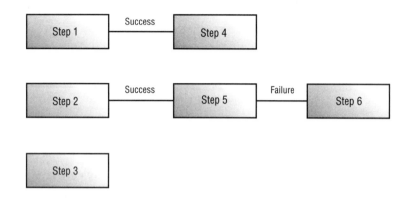

Precedence constraints are assigned by specifying that the next step will execute in one of several situations:

On Success This specifies that the next step will wait until the first step has completed successfully before beginning.

On Failure This specifies that the next step will wait until the first step issues a failure and then begin processing.

Unconditional This option specifies that the next step will execute regardless of success or failure of the previous step.

Return Codes This option requires you to gather the return codes generated by calling a scripting language module. The scripting language allows you far more flexibility for working with your steps.

Connection Objects

In order to move data around, you must connect to both a data source and a data destination. DTS uses connection objects to accomplish this. These connection objects contain all the information necessary to make a connection, including the login Ids, passwords, filenames, locations of the data, format of the data, etc. There are two types of connection objects:

Data file A data file connection object specifies the location and data format of an ASCII file that will be used during the DTS process.

Data source A data source connection object is used to specify OLE-DB- or ODBC-compliant data source and destination servers. This includes the server location, data format, login credentials, and passwords.

Connections remain dormant until they are invoked. Once invoked, the connection will remain active until the DTS package has completed.

Data Pump Object

The DTS data pump object is an OLE-DB service provider that takes care of your importing, exporting, and the data transformation. It is an in-process COM server that runs in the process space of the SQL Server 7 application. The data pump gathers data from one or more data sources and can transform the data before sending it out to one or more data destinations.

Since the DTS data pump is a COM-based object, you can greatly enhance the transformation services available by using COM-compliant scripting languages such as JavaScript, PerlScript, and VBScript. Figure 7.5 demonstrates the data flows from a data source through the data pump object and any of its transformations and then out to a data destination.

FIGURE 7.5

The DTS data flow

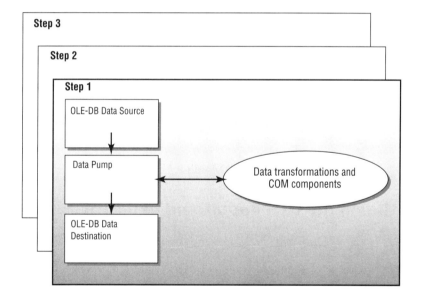

DTS Storage and Security

DTS packages can be stored in three locations. You can store them with SQL Server in the Msdb database, in the SQL Server repository or as a COM-based object. Each of these has advantages.

When you store packages in the Msdb database, other SQL Servers can connect to the packages and use them. This has an advantage over the repository, in that the storage requirements are lower. This in turn means that access time to the package is reduced.

Packages stored in the repository become available to other SQL Server 7 computers. The repository can also make metadata (data about data) available to other applications. For example, it is possible to learn how many times a particular package has been run or how many packages there are. This creates a lineage, or history, of transformations that have been applied to your data. You can view the data sources and destinations as well as the transformations that have been applied. You can also see the changes to the transformations over time.

When you store packages in COM-structured storage, they are stored as data objects and data streams. A data object is similar to a folder, while a data stream is similar to a file within that data object. These data-stream objects have an advantage in that they are easily disseminated throughout your network file servers or through e-mail. Keep in mind that any COM-compliant programming language can now manipulate your DTS package when it is stored as a COM data stream. Another advantage of a COM storage structure is the ability to encrypt your package and all its components. The only structures that are not encrypted are the VersionID, ID, Name, Description, and CreationDate.

Two types of security are applied to your packages: DTS Owner and DTS operator passwords. A user or application who has the DTS Operator password has the ability to execute the package but cannot modify or view the package components. A user or application with the DTS Owner password has complete access to the package. By default, when you store a package with an owner password, it will be encrypted; otherwise it is not.

Using the DTS Import and Export Wizards

In this section, we will walk through the Import Wizard process as an exercise. (Because the Export Wizard is nearly identical to the Import Wizard, it will not be covered.) In Exercise 7.5, we will import the pubs-authors table into the Northwind database.

The DTS Wizard has the following capabilities:

- Copy tables

- Copy query results, including the ability to create queries with the Query Builder Wizard

- Specify data connection objects for both the source and destination

- Create and schedule DTS packages

- Transform data

- Run scripting languages

- Save packages in SQL Server, the repository, and COM-structured storage

- Transfer database schema and objects using Transfer Manager from one SQL Server 7 database to another SQL Server 7 database.

EXERCISE 7.5

Importing a Table Using the DTS Import Wizard

1. Open the Enterprise Manager and connect to your SQL Server.

2. Right-click the Data Transformation Services folder and choose All Tasks, then Import Data... from the context menu.

3. You should now be at the Import Wizard Welcome screen. Click Next to continue.

4. You are now presented with the Choose a Data Source screen. Choose (local) for the Server. Enter **sa** as your Username and choose the Pubs database for the database option. If Pubs does not show up in the drop-down listbox, click the Refresh button and try again. The Import Wizard is verifying that the data source and database really exist. If you click on the Source listbox, you can see all the types of data sources and destinations currently supported in SQL Server 7. When you are finished you should have your options set as shown here.

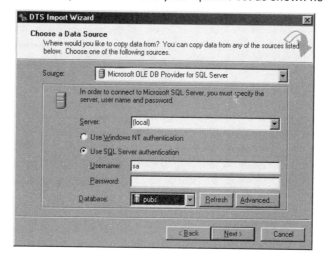

5. Click the Advanced button to display the Advanced Properties that you can work with as shown here.

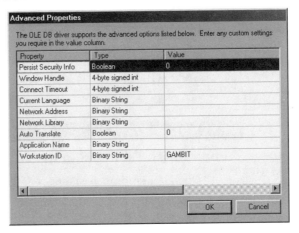

6. Click Next to work with the Data Destination screen. Fill in the options as you did earlier, but change the database to Northwind as shown here. Click Next to continue.

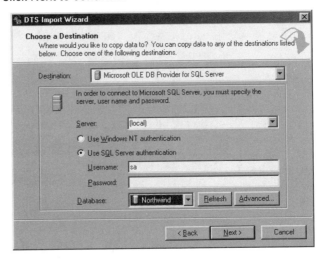

7. You are now presented with the Specify Table Copy or Query dialog box. If you choose Table Copy, it will move an entire table. The Query will allow you to specify a query and use the query builder. Since we selected a SQL Server 7 data source and destination, the Transfer Objects option is available. This is the Transfer Manager interface. Select the Query option as shown here. Click Next to continue.

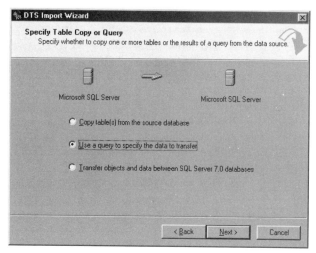

8. You are now presented with the Type SQL Statement screen as shown here. You can type in a query or use the Query Builder button, or load a query stored in a file. Once a query has been added, you can check it for syntax by clicking the Parse button. Click the Query Builder button.

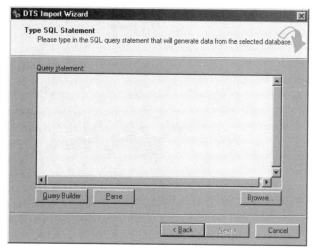

EXERCISE 7.5 (CONTINUED)

9. The Query Builder screen shows the tables in the source database. Expand the authors table and then click the au_lname field, then click the button with the > character on it. Do the same for the au_fname and state fields. When you are finished, you should see something similar to the graphic shown here. When you are finished, click Next to continue.

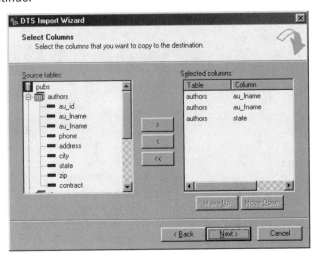

10. You are now presented with the Specify Sort Order screen. Select the au_lname field and click the right arrow again. We will be sorting this new table by the authors' last names as shown here. When you are finished, click Next to continue.

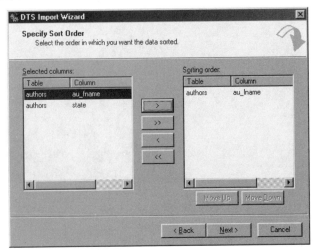

11. You are now presented with the Specify Query Criteria screen as shown below. Click Next to continue.

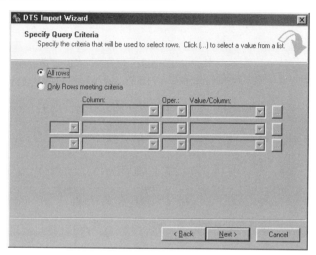

12. You should now be back at the Type SQL Statement screen, but now it has a query in it, as shown here. Click Next to continue.

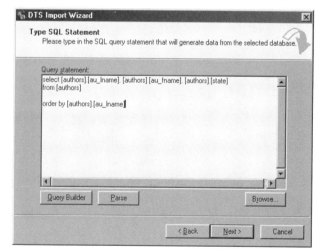

13. You should now see the Select Source Tables screen pictured below. Notice that the Source Table is Query and the Destination Table is called Results. You can change that if you like. There is also an ellipsis (…) in the Transform field. We are going to make some minor changes here. Let's take a look at some of the more advanced transformations that you could work with and then make our simple change. Click the ellipsis in the Transform field.

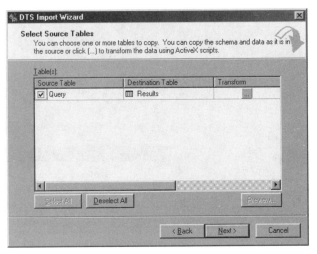

14. You are now presented with the Column Mappings and Transformations screen shown here. Select the Create Destination Table and the Drop Existing Table options.

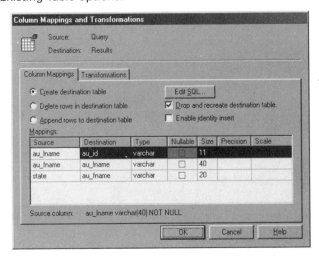

EXERCISE 7.5 (CONTINUED)

15. We are also going to edit the `Create Table SQL` statement. Click the Edit SQL button. Delete all rows from the Create Table command except for the au_lname, au_fname, and state fields, as shown here.

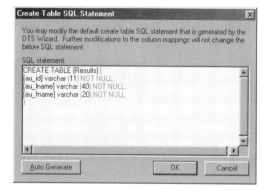

16. When you are finished, click OK. You are now back at the Column Mappings tab.

17. If you click the Transformations tab and then choose the Transform Information as it Is Copied to the Destination option, you can specify your own custom transformations using one of three scripting languages as shown here.

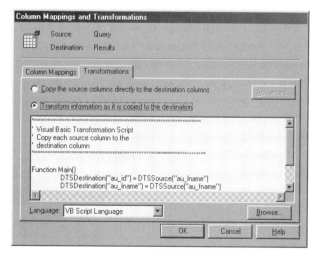

18. Click the OK button to return to the Select Source Tables screen. Click Next to continue processing.

19. You are now presented with the Save, Schedule and Replicate Package screen shown here. The Run Immediately option will run the package as soon as it has completed. You can also choose to make the package available for replication and to set up a schedule for automatic execution. Select the Save DTS Package option as well. When you are finished, click Next to continue.

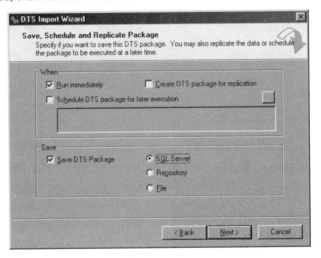

20. You are now presented with the Save DTS Package screen. Fill in the package name with **Authors**. Fill in the package description with **Authors and their home state** as shown below. Do not add a password or change any other options. Click Next to continue.

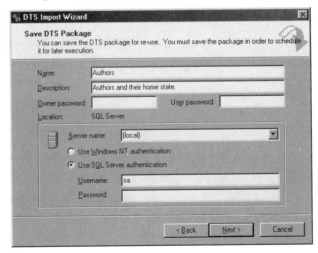

21. You are now presented with the Finish screen. Click Finish. You will see the package executing. You may be prompted with another dialog informing you that the package ran and completed successfully.

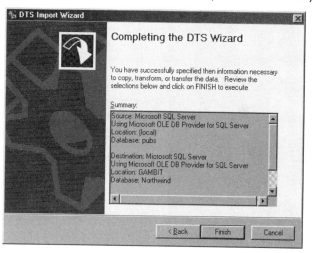

Transfer Manager

Through the Data Transformation Services Import and Export Wizards, you can transfer objects, security, and/or data from one database to another. When you use this method, the objects, data, and security in the original database are unaffected; they are copied to the receiving database, not actually moved.

In SQL Server 6.5, the Transfer Manager interface was a stand-alone component incorporated into the Enterprise Manager. In 7, this component has been incorporated into the DTS Import and Export Wizards.

Because new objects are being created, the user performing the transfer needs SELECT permissions in the source database and DBO permissions in the destination database.

Since this moves not only data, but schema from one SQL Server 7 computer to another SQL Server 7 computer, this is ideal for situations where you want to transfer data from one platform to another. For example, you may wish to move both data and schema from a 7 server on an Intel platform to a 7 server on an Alpha platform. Another nice feature of the transfer manager is that you can move data with one character set or sort order to another server with a different character set or sort order.

In Exercise 7.6, we will create a new database and then use the Transfer Manager to move the Pubs database to it.

EXERCISE 7.6

Copying a Database Using the Transfer Manager

1. Open the Enterprise Manager and drill down through the console tree to the Data Transformation Services icon. Right-click on the icon and select All Tasks. From the All Tasks menu, select Export Data.

2. You are now at the same introduction screen that you saw for the DTS Import in Exercise 7.5. Click Next to continue.

3. Fill in the Choose a Data Source screen as shown here. Your Server should be entered as (local), your Username as **sa**, and your Database as **pubs**. If you don't see the Pubs database, click Refresh and look again.

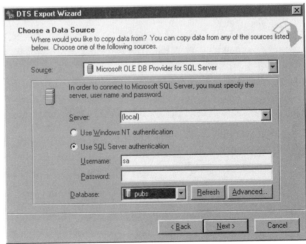

4. When you have filled in the information click Next to continue. You are now looking at the Data Destination screen. Enter **(local)** for the server again and **sa** as the login; on the Database drop-down listbox, enter **<new>**.

5. You should now see the small Create Database screen shown here. Fill in the name as **NewPubs**. The Data File Size should be 2MB and the Log File Size should be 1MB. Click OK when you are finished.

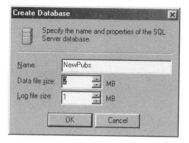

6. Your Choose a Destination screen should now look like this. Choose Next to continue.

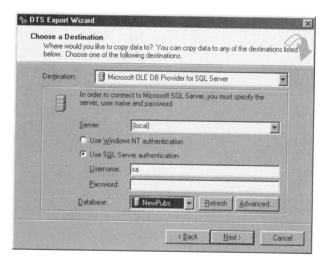

7. In the Specify Table Copy or Query screen, select the Transfer Objects... option and click Next.

8. You are now presented with the Select Objects to Transfer screen. As you can see, you can choose the following options:

- **Create Destination Objects**   This option allows you to have SQL Server generate scripts that will then create your destination objects. Optional parameters include the ability to drop those objects first if they already exist in your destination database.

- **Copy Data**   You can also have the data (rather than just the database schema) copied. When you copy the data, you need to specify whether you are going to replace the existing data or just append the copied data to it.

- **Transfer all Objects**   You can also transfer all database objects—views, stored procedures, indexes, etc—and use the default options to do so.

- **ScriptFile Directory**   This allows you to specify the directory in which you want the scripts files generated by this transfer to reside.

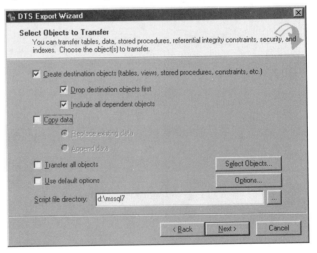

9. You should also take a closer look at the default options and the transferred objects. Deselect the Transfer All Objects and Use Default Options checkboxes as shown above.

10. Click the Select Objects button. You should now see the Select Objects screen. You can choose which objects you wish to transfer, as well as which objects you wish to see in the list. As shown in the graphic, choose all the options at the top of the screen. Click the Select All button to highlight all the objects listed. Click on Check, which will put a checkmark next to each object. Click OK when you are finished.

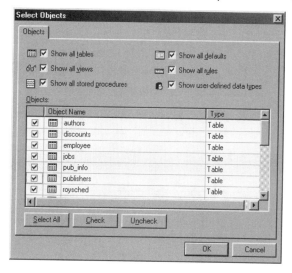

11. Click the Options button. You are now looking at the various options used for the transfer of your data.

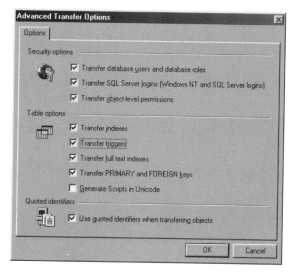

12. Leave all the selected options and click OK to return to the Transfer screen.

13. Click Next to continue.

14. You now have the option of deciding when you wish to run the package and whether or not you wish to save it. We are going to run the package immediately and then take a look at what it does. Click Next to continue.

15. Click Finish to complete the process. You will see the package being processed and data being moved. When it is all finished, select Close or Done to end the process.

16. You should now have a new database called NewPubs with all the data, stored procedures, views, and other items found in the original. If you don't see it in the Enterprise Manager console, right-click on the Databases folder and choose Refresh.

If you navigate to the C:\MSSQL folder, you will see a list of script files that the Transfer Manager generated. Table 7.1 lists the files and their associated properties. You should note that the naming convention for these files is `ServerName.DatabaseName.Extension`.

In this table, the server's name is Gambit. There are also bcp files created by the Transfer Manager to move the data from one file to the next. These have the format `dbo.table.bcp`.

T A B L E 7.1: Log and Script Files Created by the Transfer Process

File Name	Purpose
`Gambit.Pubs.LOG`	Log of errors and warnings about the source database
`Gambit.NewPubs.LOG`	Log of errors and warning about the destination database
`Gambit.Pubs.BND`	Table bindings

T A B L E 7.1: Log and Script Files Created by the Transfer Process *(continued)*

File Name	Purpose
Gambit.Pubs.DEF	Script used to create defaults
Gambit.Pubs.DP1	Script used to drop table constraints
Gambit.Pubs.DP2	Script used to drop database objects
Gambit.Pubs.DR1	Script used to add primary keys to tables
Gambit.Pubs.DR2	Script used to add defaults, rules, and other constraints
Gambit.Pubs.FKY	Script used to add foreign keys to tables
Gambit.Pubs..GRP	Script used to add roles (groups) to the database
Gambit.Pubs.ID1	Script used to create clustered indexes
Gambit.Pubs.ID2	Script used to create non-clustered indexes
Gambit.Pubs.LGN	Script used to create SQL Server logins
Gambit.Pubs..PRC	Script used to create stored procedures
Gambit.Pubs.PRV	Script used to create permissions
Gambit.Pubs.RUL	Script used to create rules
Gambit.Pubs.TAB	Script used to create tables
Gambit.Pubs.TRG	Script used to create triggers
Gambit.Pubs.UDT	Script used to create user-defined datatypes
Gambit.Pubs.USR	Script used to create user names and statement permissions
Gambit.Pubs.VIW	Script used to create views

DTS Designer

The DTS Designer is a GUI-based utility you can use to create and edit your DTS packages. Although the details of the GUI are beyond the scope of this book, we would like you to take a look at it. Follow the steps outlined here:

1. Open the SQL Enterprise Manager

2. Drill down through the console tree into the Data Transformation Services folder.

3. Click on the Local Packages Icon. You should now see the Authors package we created earlier.

4. Right-click on the Authors package and choose Design as shown in Figure 7.6.

FIGURE 7.6

Opening the package designer

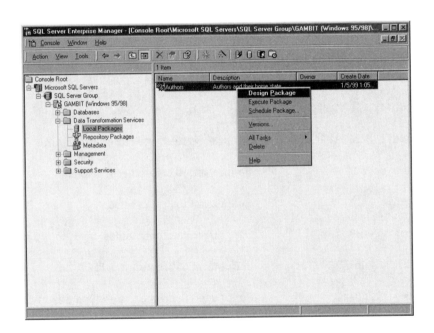

5. You should now see the DTS Designer screen with a similar layout to what is displayed in Figure 7.7.

6. Right-click any of the objects or connections to view their information.

7. Close the package designer when you are finished.

F I G U R E 7.7

DTS Designer

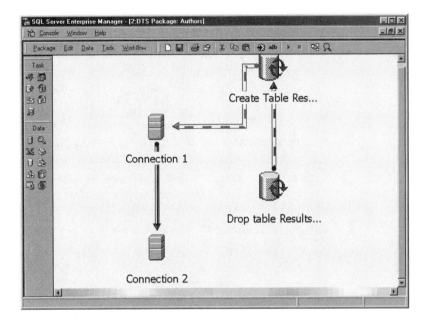

Summary

In this chapter we covered many different aspects of managing your data in SQL Server. We looked at migrating data from other data source, using bcp, BULK INSERT, and DTS. We also looked at some other data management techniques including the use of the INSERT and SELECT INTO statements.

The INSERT statement is generally used to add one record at a time. When you use this statement, you must have INSERT permission on the table to which you are trying to add data and you must know something about the table's layout and design. INSERTs are logged transactions.

The SELECT INTO statement is essentially a copy-table command. When you use this statement, you can have data or portions of data from one table placed into either a new permanent table or a temporary table. As you may recall, temporary tables are stored in the Tempdb database. Local temporary tables have a # prefix, and global temporary tables have a ## prefix. For a SELECT INTO statement to work, you must first enable the Select Into/Bulk

Copy database option. This option can be enabled through the Enterprise Manager, or through code using the `sp_dboption` stored procedure. `SELECT INTO` statements are not logged transactions. If you plan to keep the table you create with the `SELECT INTO` statement, you should back up your database at the earliest opportunity as recoverability is not possible.

The bcp (bulk copy) utility is a command-line program that can move data from a flat file (generated by any number of programs) into SQL Server or from SQL Server to a flat file very quickly. Learning how to use the bcp options is a bit painful at first, but with a little practice, this utility can become a very fast and useful tool. To perform a fast bulk copy, you should drop indexes on the table into which you are moving data. You should enable the Select Into/Bulk Copy database option and then run the bcp program. Keep in mind that defaults and datatypes will be enforced during the bulk copy, but triggers, rules, and default values will be ignored. You should run some type of query to check the new data for clarity and accuracy. Once you have done that, we suggest you re-create your indexes and then back up your database since a fast bulk copy is a non-logged operation.

One of the best new features of SQL Server 7 is the `BULK INSERT` T-SQL command. The `BULK INSERT` statement is very similar to a T-SQL-based bulk copy command. One of the advantages of the `BULK INSERT` command is that it treats the flat file as an OLE-DB recordset. This allows records to be moved very quickly and efficiently into SQL Server. Note that `BULK INSERT` only inserts records. The quickest way to move data out of SQL Server to a flat file is to run a bcp command.

Data Transformation Services (DTS) is an important new interface. You can create fairly complex import and export packages that can then be executed on a scheduled basis. You can move data from any OLE-DB- or ODBC-compliant source to an OLE-DB- or ODBC-compliant destination. The transformations you can perform on your data are nearly limitless. With the addition of the COM-compliant scripting languages, you can really do just about any type of data manipulation that you desire. The packages you create can be saved and scheduled for reuse. You can store your packages in the SQL Server or the repository or as a COM-structured storage object. Each of these storage locations has some advantages. Remember that the repository allows you to track the lineage of your data as well as the changes made to the DTS package itself. COM-structured storage makes the package simple to distribute through e-mail or a central server. Storing it in the SQL Server takes less memory, and other SQL Servers can access the package and run it.

Accessing and running a SQL Server package brings up the security issues. By default, the packages have no security and are not encrypted. Placing a password on the package encrypts it. With an operator password in place, others who know the password can execute the package, but cannot work with the package internals. When an owner password is used, others can execute the package as well as edit it.

When you want to transfer data or schema or database objects from one SQL Server 7 computer to another SQL Server 7 computer, your best choice is the Transfer Manager. All the other utilities discussed in this chapter move data only. The Transfer Manager is capable of moving objects as well as data and schema, and it allows you to specify exactly which objects or data you want to move. Remember that the Transfer Manger builds script files that actually recreate the specified objects. If you use the Transfer Manager to move data as well, bcp files will also be generated for the transfer. Look at the `*.LOG` files created by the Transfer Manger. These files will store information about errors encountered during the transfer itself.

Review Questions

1. Which of the following is true regarding the `INSERT` statement?

    A. You must have SELECT permissions in the table to which you wish to add records

    B. INSERT statements add only one record at a time

    C. An INSERT is usually logged

    D. You must have INSERT permissions in the table to which you wish to add records

2. You decide to run the following `SELECT INTO` statement: `SELECT * INTO ##SomeTable FROM Northwind..Orders`.

    Where does this new table reside?

    A. In the Northwind database as Orders

    B. In the Northwind database as ##SomeTable

    C. In the Tempdb database as Orders

    D. In the Tempdb database as ##SomeTable

3. Which of the following is true regarding the SELECT INTO statement?

   A. You must have the Select Into/Bulk Copy database option enabled

   B. You must be a member of the sysadmin database role

   C. SELECT INTO statements are logged transactions

   D. You must have CREATE TABLE permissions in the database

4. Your environment includes a SQL Server 7 computer and an AS-400 running DB2. Only three people in your organization have access to the AS-400, but nearly 200 need access to the data. The AS-400 currently dumps large ASCII flat files to your computer. Since you are the SQL Server administrator, it is up to you to make the data available to those 200 users. Which of the following data management techniques could be used to move the ASCII files into your SQL Server computer?

   A. You can use the bcp utility

   B. You can use the BULK INSERT statement

   C. You can use the SELECT INTO statement

   D. You can use the INSERT statement

5. Your environment includes a SQL Server 7 computer and an AS-400 running DB2. Only three people in your organization have access to the AS-400, but nearly 200 need access to the data. The AS-400 currently dumps large ASCII flat files to your computer. Since you are the SQL Server administrator, it is up to you to make the data available to those 200 users. You decide that you want to use the Bulk Copy command-line utility. You also want the transfer to be as fast as possible. Which of the following will accomplish this task?

   A. You must drop all indexes on the affected tables to avoid transaction logging

   B. You must drop all data in the affected tables to avoid transaction logging

    C. You must enable the Select Into/Bulk Copy database option to avoid transaction logging

    D. You must enable the Truncate Log on Checkpoint database option to avoid transaction logging

6. Which of the following is true about the bulk copy operation?

    A. Defaults and datatypes are always ignored

    B. Defaults and datatypes are always enforced

    C. Rules and triggers are always ignored

    D. Rules and triggers are always enforced

7. You decide that you want to use the Bulk Copy command-line utility. Which permissions are required for you to perform this bulk copy operation?

    A. When copying data in to SQL Server, you must have READ permissions on the file (if it is on an NTFS partition)

    B. When copying data in to SQL Server you must have INSERT permissions on the table which is affected

    C. When copying data out of SQL Server you must have SELECT permission on the affected tables

    D. When copying data out of SQL Server you must have SELECT INTO permissions on the affected tables

8. When you bulk copy data out of SQL Server, you wish to create a flat file that uses tabs for field terminators and newline characters for the end of a row. Which of the following switches accomplish this?

    A. /t \t

    B. /r \n

    C. /F {Tab}

    D. /R {Newline}

9. Which of the following is true about the BULK INSERT statement?

    A. It is a command-line utility

    B. It is a T-SQL command

    C. It only reads one record at a time

    D. It is reads all records in a flat file as if they are an OLE-DB recordset

10. You have many users who want to work data from your SQL Server 7 computer by accessing a centrally located flat file. You decide to create a character-based flat file on a central server. Which of the following utilities can be used to create this character-based flat file?

    A. bcp

    B. BULK INSERT

    C. The DTS Export Wizard

    D. The SELECT INTO statement, with a flat file specified

11. You wish to use the BULK INSERT command to add a large amount of data from a flat file into SQL Server. Which of the following is true about this command?

    A. You can specify a batch size to load the data in several smaller chunks, thus speeding up the transfer

    B. You must be the database owner to run the BULK INSERT command

    C. You must be a member of the sysadmin fixed database role to run the BULK INSERT command

    D. The flat file must reside on your local hard disk to perform a BULK INSERT

12. You have a large SQL Server 7 computer running a quad-processor Alpha-AXP computer. The server currently holds about 3 terabytes of data. For administrative reasons, you want to distribute portions of that data to SQL Server 7 computers running on Intel Pentium IIs throughout your organization. As part of the distribution process, you wish to include some tables, many of the views, and several of the stored procedures. You do not want to keep the security setting, however. You decide to use the DTS Import and Export engine to move the information. Which of the following is true about this solution?

A. This is a poor solution as only data will be transferred, but not the views and stored procedures

B. This is a poor solution as all data will be transferred, including the rules, defaults, triggers, constraints, and security information

C. This is a fair solution; however, all security information will be transferred

D. This is an excellent solution and fits all the required parameters

13. You have a large SQL Server 7 computer running a quad-processor Alpha-AXP computer. The server currently holds about 3 terabytes of data. For administrative reasons, you want to distribute portions of that data to SQL Server 7 computers running on Intel Pentium IIs throughout your organization. As part of the distribution process, you wish to include some tables, many of the views, and several of the stored procedures. You do not want to keep the security setting though. You decide to use the Transfer Manager to move the information. Which of the following is true about this solution?

A. This is a poor solution as only data will be transferred, but not the views and stored procedures

B. This is a poor solution as all data will be transferred including the rules, defaults, triggers, constraints, and security information

C. This is a fair solution; however, all security information will be transferred

D. This is an excellent solution and fits all the required parameters

14. You have a large DB2 database running on an AS-400. The server currently holds about 3 terabytes of data. For administrative reasons, you want to distribute portions of that data to SQL Server 7 computers running on Intel Pentium IIs throughout your organization. Which of the following can be used to transfer the data?

    A. You can use the DTS Import and Export Wizards

    B. You can have the AS-400 dump an ASCII file and then you can use bcp

    C. You can have the AS-400 dump an ASCII file and then you can use BULK INSERT

    D. You can use the Transfer Manager to move the data

15. You have a DTS package object that contains a login ID, password, file name, and location as well as information about the format in which the data is stored. Which DTS package object is this?

    A. Data pump object

    B. Connection object

    C. Step object

    D. Task object

16. The Task object in a DTS package can perform which of the following?

    A. Move data from a source to a destination

    B. Run a T-SQL statement or batch

    C. Execute external programs like .CMD files or .BAT files

    D. Execute another DTS package

    E. Execute COM-compliant scripts like VBScript

17. The step object in a DTS package can run in parallel when there are no precedence constraints on it. Which of the following are Step object precedence constraints?

A. On Success

B. On Failure

C. Unconditional

D. Return Codes

18. You have used a third-party program in the past to move and transform your data from one location to another. The program worked well for you, but you had no method to track the lineage of your data (e.g., you wish to track the changes made to your data over time as well as changes made to the program.) You now want to use DTS within SQL Server rather than having an external program. You port most of your transformation code from the program into your DTS package. The DTS package runs perfectly for you. Where should you save your DTS package so that you can track the data lineage?

A. Store the package in the SQL Server DTS packages area

B. Store the package in the SQL Server repository

C. Store the package as a COM-based object

D. Store the package as an ASCII file

19. You want create a DTS package that can access and work with sensitive data. When you store the package, you want to give some people the ability to run the package and others the ability to edit it. For security reasons, you also want the package encrypted. Which of the following steps should you take to accomplish these goals?

A. Supply an owner password for the package

B. Supply an operator password for the package

C. Select the encrypt option for the package

D. Do nothing. Only the sysadmin can work with packages

20. DTS packages can transform your data using a COM-compliant scripting language. Which of the following scripting languages is currently supported in the DTS Import/Export Wizards?

    A. JScript

    B. VBScript

    C. PerlScript

    D. None of the above

21. You are currently running SQL Server 6.5 and are thinking about upgrading to SQL Server 7. On your SQL Server 7 computer, you wish to use a different character set and sort order. You decide to upgrade the SQL Server 6.5 computer to 7 using the current 6.5 sort order and character sets. You then install another version of SQL Server 7 on the network with the new sort orders and character set. Which of the following methods of data transfer is the best choice to move your data from the recently upgraded SQL Server?

    A. Re-create the objects in the destination database and use bcp to move your data

    B. Re-create the objects in the destination database and use DTS to transfer your data

    C. Use the Transfer Manager to move all objects and data from the source database to the destination database

    D. You cannot transfer data with different character sets and sort orders

CHAPTER

8

Implementing Proactive Administration in SQL Server 7

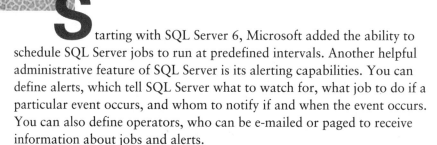

tarting with SQL Server 6, Microsoft added the ability to schedule SQL Server jobs to run at predefined intervals. Another helpful administrative feature of SQL Server is its alerting capabilities. You can define alerts, which tell SQL Server what to watch for, what job to do if a particular event occurs, and whom to notify if and when the event occurs. You can also define operators, who can be e-mailed or paged to receive information about jobs and alerts.

The database that holds all of the jobs, alerts, and operators you've defined is the Msdb database. This database is installed by default, although there are no jobs or operators defined by default.

This chapter begins with a discussion of the Msdb database, including its system tables and information on how to back it up and restore it. It next covers the SQLServerAgent, the overall controlling service for jobs, alerts, operators, and events.

The chapter explains how to create and manage alerts, operators, and jobs, showing how to set each of these up and how to make changes as necessary.

The Msdb Database

The Msdb database is a system database that is automatically created when you install SQL Server. Because the Msdb database contains all your jobs, alerts, and operators, it should be backed up on a regular basis. Once a week should be sufficient. If you make many changes to your jobs, alerts, or operators during the week, you may want to back up the database promptly after you've made the changes.

The backup process for the Msdb database is the same as for any other database. You need to define a backup device for the Msdb database, and you will probably want to schedule a backup job to back up this database on a regular basis. (See Chapter 6, *Implementing Database Backups and Restorations,* for details about backing up and restoring databases, as well as scheduling backup jobs.)

Backups are important because you may need to restore the Msdb database if you delete an important job, alert, or operator, or if the database gets corrupted. You can restore the Msdb database in the same way that you restore other databases: In SQL Enterprise Manager, highlight the database, select Backup/Restore from the Context menu or Tools menu, choose a valid backup on the Restore tab, and click on the Restore Now button.

Rebuilding the Msdb Database

If disaster strikes (for example, if you don't have a valid backup of the Master database, or you wish to change the character set or sort order), you may be forced to rebuild your Master database.

When you choose to rebuild the Master database, you (without any warning or note) rebuild the Msdb database as well. Like the rebuilt Master database, the rebuilt Msdb database has all the default settings that came with SQL Server installation. This means that not a single job or operator is defined. You will need to restore all your Msdb data from a valid backup. If there is no valid backup, you will need to re-create your jobs, alerts, and operators by hand.

You can rebuild just the Msdb database by running the `instmsdb.sql` and `web.sql` scripts from the MSSQL7\Install folder.

The SQL Agent

The SQL Agent can be thought of as an optional helper service for SQL Server. Nothing it does is technically required to make SQL Server work, but it does enough that you will probably want to enable it.

The SQL Agent service is in charge of finding and carrying out jobs and alerts, and notifying operators on the success and/or failure of those jobs and alerts.

Configuring the SQL Agent

The SQL Agent is installed by default. This installation may not be entirely successful, because it uses the account you are logged in as its service account when you may want it to use a different account. The SQL Setup program's attempt to correctly configure the service for your system might encounter problems as well.

Microsoft ✓ ***Exam Objective***

Automate administrative tasks.

- Define jobs.
- Define alerts.
- Define operators.
- Set up SQLAgentMail for job notification and alerts.

Two main settings are required for the SQL Agent to work properly:

- A user account, with appropriate rights, should be assigned to the service.

- The service should be configured to start automatically (if it is set to manual, you will have to start it by hand every time you reboot your server).

- While most services don't require a user account assigned to them in order to function correctly, services that go beyond the physical box and connect to other servers on the network (as the SQL Agent may do) usually need a user account assigned. This is so they have an account to be authenticated with on the remote server. Otherwise they connect with "NULL" security credentials and by default will be denied access.

Setting Up the User Account

As explained in Chapter 2, *Installing, Upgrading, and Configuring SQL Server 7*, you can set up your SQL Agent user account before you install SQL Server, and then configure the account correctly during the installation process. If you didn't do this at installation time, don't worry—you can still set up the account and configure it.

When using the Desktop version of SQL Server with Windows 95/98, you cannot assign an account to the SQL Agent; it uses the current logged-in account. Not assigning an account to the agent will not affect any jobs or alerts on the local computer. The major limitation on Windows 95/98 computers is that they cannot be assigned as job managers for other servers.

There are three parts to setting up the SQL Agent user account: creating the user in Windows NT, giving the user appropriate rights, and assigning the user to the service. Here is the procedure:

- Create the user account using the Windows NT User Manager or User Manager for Domains utility, just as for any other user. Clear the User Must Change Password at Next Logon option, and check the Password Never Expires option. It may also be a good idea to set the User Cannot Change password option.

- Give the user account appropriate rights. Make the user account for the SQL Agent a member of the Administrators group, and also of the Domain Administrators group if you want that account to be usable on any and all SQL Servers in the domain. Assign the Log on as a Service right to this account. This right is in the Advanced Rights dialog box (choose User Rights from the User Manager for Domains Policies menu and check the Advanced Rights box). Add the account you've created to the list of accounts that already have this right by selecting Add, then pick the appropriate account from the list.

The Services applet of the Control Panel will usually assign the Log on as a Service right to a user account if it is needed and isn't already assigned.

- Assign the user to the service. The user account can be assigned to the SQL Agent in several different ways: during the initial installation (see Chapter 2), from the Services applet of the Control Panel, from Server Manager (by selecting Services from the Computer menu), and from Enterprise Manager (by right-clicking on SQL Executive and selecting Configure from the context menu).

Starting the Service Automatically

You can set SQL Server to start automatically, either by choosing this option during installation (see Chapter 2) or later, through the Enterprise Manager's Server Options dialog box. If you set autostart, the MSSQLServer service will start when the server boots; no one needs to be logged on in order to make things happen.

It makes sense that if you have SQL Server set to start automatically, then you should also set the SQL Agent to start automatically. You can set this auto start option in the same way that you set auto start for the SQL Server service—during installation of SQL Server or through the Server Configuration/ Options dialog box (Server Options tab). However, if you don't have the SQL Server service start automatically, you should also have the SQL Agent set to start manually. Then you will need to manually start both services.

Changing the SQL Agent Password

You may occasionally want to change the password assigned to the SQL Agent (for example, after an employee who had access leaves). You'll need to change the password in two areas:

- Change the password using Windows NT's User Manager for Domains.

- Change the password assigned to the SQL Agent.

In the Windows NT User Manager for Domains utility, you change the password through the user's Properties dialog box. Replace the old password with the new one, and then confirm the new password.

WARNING   Passwords, unlike usernames, are case-sensitive in Windows NT.

Once you have changed the password, you need to tell the SQL Agent about it. There are several ways to reconfigure the service: through the Services Control Panel, the Server Manager's Services option on the Computer menu, or Enterprise Manager's SQL Executive Configure option (on the Context menu).

Understanding Alerts, Jobs, and Events

The SQL Agent is the overall controlling service for jobs, alerts, operators, and events. There are separate engines for jobs, alerts, and events, but the SQL Agent is the controller for these engines.

Let's look at what happens to a common error before and after the SQL Agent has been configured. Suppose that the Pubs2 database log fills up and generates an 1105 error (the standard error code generated for a full log). SQL Server's own internal error generator will create the 1105 error, but without SQL Agent to watch for and handle the error, the problem will need to be fixed by hand. And until you resolve the problem, users will not be able to access the database. Figure 8.1 illustrates how errors are handled without jobs and alerts.

F I G U R E 8.1

Flowchart of standard SQL Server error messages

With a predefined alert and job, the alert engine will be looking for the 1105 error in the Windows NT application log, and will be ready to trigger a backup job that will truncate (clean out) the log, as illustrated in Figure 8.2. Now when SQL Server generates an 1105 error, the alert engine finds it, and then acts on it by triggering the job. The database log is truncated, and users can resume using the database normally. If the backup failed to work, another error would be generated. At that point, the operator could be sent an e-mail message and/or paged.

FIGURE 8.2

Flowchart of SQL
Server error mes-
sages, alerts, and jobs

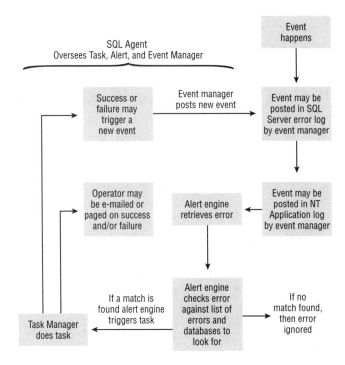

Creating and Managing Jobs

Earlier versions of SQL Server (4.21a and earlier) could schedule backups, but that was the extent of their scheduling capabilities. Beginning with version 6, SQL Server's scheduling capabilities have been greatly expanded. In SQL Server 7, you can schedule jobs to run at regular intervals or when an alert is triggered. Replication is also supported through regularly scheduled jobs.

Microsoft
✓ *Exam*
Objective

Automate administrative tasks.

- Define jobs.

Types of Jobs

SQL Server supports four general types of jobs:

TSQL jobs   These jobs are written using T-SQL commands. They are often used to back up the database, rebuild indexes, and perform other various routine database maintenance activities.

CmdExec jobs   These jobs literally open a command prompt and run some sort of batch file or executable file. Common CmdExec jobs are those created by the Database Maintenance Plan Wizard or by the SQL Server Web Assistant.

Replication jobs   These jobs deal with replication. Normally you would use the Replication wizards and prompts to help set up replication jobs, although monitoring these jobs is an important step in maintaining replication.

Active Script jobs   These jobs can run Visual Basic or Java scripts at a regular interval.

Multiserver Jobs

SQL Server 7 adds the ability to create jobs that run on multiple servers. In order to create multiple server jobs you must do the following:

- Ensure that all servers involved are running SQL Server 7 on Windows NT.

- Designate one server as the master server (MSX).

- Designate a master server operator (MSX Operator).

- Designate one or more servers as target servers when you create the job.

Note that a target server can report to only one master server at a time and that the SQL Agent needs to be set up to use a service account (not set for the local account). You should also choose the MSX Operator carefully, since that account is the only one that will be notified about multiserver jobs. Another feature of multiserver jobs is that target server will automatically upload its job completion status to the master server.

Creating Jobs

The required elements of a job are the name, schedule, and command to be executed during one or more steps. There are various ways to create and schedule jobs. The following are the most common ways:

- You can create your own jobs manually, through the Management folder in Enterprise Manager.

- You can use the Job Wizard to step you through the process.

- You can let Enterprise Manager create jobs for you. Enterprise Manager can create certain jobs, the most common of which is the backup job. In Chapter 6, we used the Enterprise Manager's Database Backup/Restore dialog box to create a backup job.

- The Database Maintenance Plan Wizard can create jobs to handle routine maintenance and database backup. In Chapter 6, we explained how to create a backup job using the Database Maintenance Plan Wizard.

 The Database Maintenance Plan Wizard creates one or more jobs for a given plan. For any given plan, you will probably see separate jobs for the optimizations, integrity checks, and backups.

- When you use the SQL Server Web Assistant to set up updates to a Web page that happen on a regular interval, it creates a recurring job. The SQL Server Web Assistant is covered below.

- When you install and set up replication, various jobs are created to make replication work. Replication is covered in Chapter 9, *Creating and Implementing a Replication Solution in SQL Server 7*.

Jobs can be scheduled in one of four ways:

When the SQL Agent starts A job can be created that automatically executes whenever the SQL Agent starts. This would be good for an automated system of some kind.

When the CPU is idle A job can be scheduled to start after the CPU has been idle a certain amount of time, which is configurable in the Properties screen of the SQL Agent.

One time only A one-time-only job is usually created for a special purpose; it executes only once on its scheduled date and time.

Recurring A recurring job happens on a regular basis. The job's frequency can be daily, weekly, or even monthly.

In Exercise 8.1, we will manually create a T-SQL job and schedule it as a recurring job. This new job will back up the Pubs database on a daily basis.

EXERCISE 8.1

Creating a Job Manually

1. In Enterprise Manager, open the Management window and open the Jobs window. This should show you any jobs you have previously made (like the backup and maintenance jobs from Chapter 6).

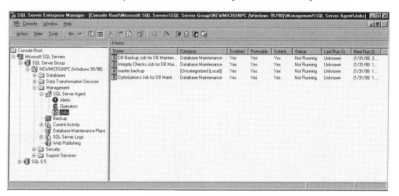

2. Click the New button (it looks like a star) on the toolbar or right-click the Jobs folder and choose New Job.

3. In the New Job dialog box, enter a name for the job, such as Back up Pubs database every night.

Note that you can pick target servers for this job if you have enlisted this server as a master server and have designated one or more target servers from the bottom right of the screen.

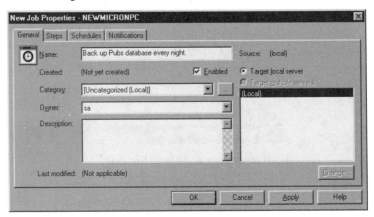

4. Go to the Steps tab.

5. Create a new step by selecting the New button at the bottom of the screen.

6. Enter Backup Pubs for the name and **backup database pubs to pubs_backup** for the command. Make sure Transact-SQL is selected for the Type of command.

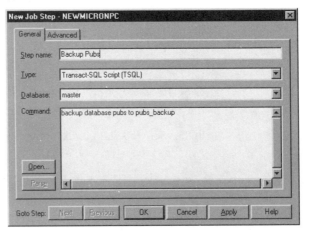

7. Select the Parse button to check the command for syntax errors. You should get an OK box. If not, fix the command until it works.

8. Select the Advanced tab.

9. Change the On Success Action to Quit the Job Reporting Success, the number of retries to 3, and the interval to 1 minute. Choose OK to save the step.

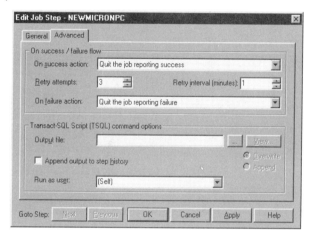

10. Go to the Schedules tab. (Note that you can assign multiple schedules to a task.)

11. Choose New Schedule.

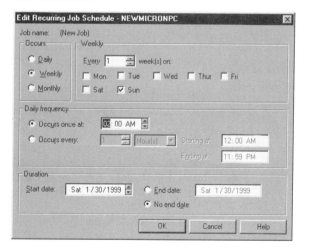

12. Enter a name for the schedule, such as automated pubs backup on Sunday morning.

13. Change the schedule for the job by selecting the Change button.

EXERCISE 8.1 (CONTINUED)

14. Change the time to 2:00 A.M. Leave it set to recur weekly on Sundays. Choose OK to save the changed schedule.

15. Make sure the schedule is enabled and choose OK to save it.

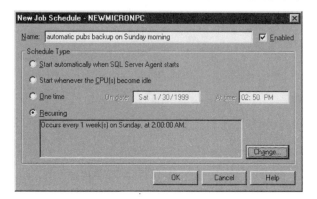

16. Choose OK to save the new job. The job should now be listed in the Jobs folder.

 Note that we cannot select any notifications until we have built operators (covered below).

Editing Jobs

You can modify a job to change its name, type, command, or schedule. In Exercise 8.2, we will edit the job we created in Exercise 8.1 to change its schedule.

EXERCISE 8.2

Editing a Job

1. In Enterprise Manager, open the Management window and open the Jobs window to see any jobs you have previously made.

2. Double-click the job we created in Exercise 8.1.

Note that we could add, edit, or rearrange steps for the job by selecting the Steps tab.

EXERCISE 8.2 (CONTINUED)

3. Go to the Schedules tab, highlight Automated Pubs Backup... and select the Edit button.

4. Click the Change button in the lower-right corner of the dialog box.

5. In the Job Schedule dialog box, change the time of execution from 2:00 AM to 1:00 AM.

6. Click OK, OK, OK to save your change.

Running Jobs Manually

Even if you have scheduled a job, you can run it manually at another time. In Exercise 8.3, we will run the job we created in Exercise 8.1.

EXERCISE 8.3

Running a Job Manually

1. In Enterprise Manager, open the Management window and open the Jobs window.

2. Highlight the job we created in Exercise 8.1.

3. Go to the Action ➤ Start Job menu to start the job, or right-click on the Job and choose Start Job.

4. If you are fast enough, you can go back to the Jobs folder and see that the status of the job has changed to Executing Job Step 0-X. After the job has finished running, the Last Run Status item should show either Succeeded or Failed, along with the date.

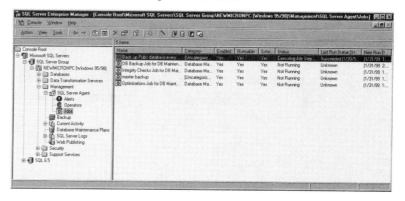

Viewing Job History

A very helpful feature of Enterprise Manager is that it keeps a record of each job's time of execution, as well as whether the job was successful or not. In Exercise 8.4, we will examine the history of the job that we ran in Exercise 8.3 to see if it was successfully completed.

EXERCISE 8.4

Examining the History of a Job

1. In Enterprise Manager, open the Management window and open the Jobs window.

2. Highlight the job we created in Exercise 8.1.

3. Go to the Action ➤ View Job History menu, or right-click the Job and choose View Job History to display the Job History screen, shown below.

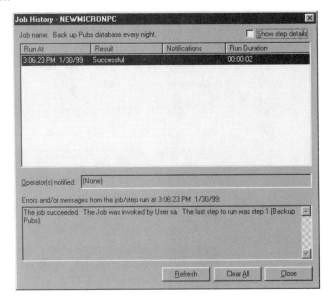

As you can see, the job is listed as Successful. Notice also you can refresh or clear the history by selecting the appropriate button at the bottom of the screen.

4. Click Close.

5. To see options for the size of the job history log, highlight the SQL Server Agent from the Management folder, right-click and go to the Properties screen and choose the Job System tab, as shown below. The default settings allow a maximum of 1000 rows of history, with a maximum of 100 rows per job. Note that you can clear the history of all jobs from here as well.

6. Click Cancel to close the dialog box.

Deleting Jobs

If you no longer need a job, you can easily delete it in Enterprise Manager. Note that if you delete a job you also delete all its steps and history.

A better choice than deleting jobs may be to disable the job temporarily. That way you can quickly enable the job if you need it back, as opposed to having to re-create the entire job. You can enable or disable the job by double-clicking a job to go to its main Properties screen.

Creating and Managing Alerts

The SQL Agent, via the alert engine, looks in the sysalerts table in order to determine which errors it should be looking for. By defining an alert, you are telling SQL Server which error codes to look for in the NT Application logs, and what action to take if an event is found.

Microsoft ✓ *Exam* *Objective*

Automate administrative tasks.

- Define alerts.

Creating an Alert

Creating alerts is somewhat intuitive. There are several basic steps:

- Define the type of alert, either an alert based on a SQL Server error message or one based on a performance monitor counter.

- If based on a SQL Server error message, define the error to look for. Alerts can be based on a generic error-message number, the error's severity, or an error happening in a specific database.

- Optionally, define the database in which the error must happen. An alert can filter error messages based on the database. For instance, an alert can be created to watch the Pubs database in case it fills up. This alert would operate only on the Pubs database; if any other database filled up, the alert wouldn't do anything.

- If based on a performance monitor counter, define which counter to monitor and the threshold that will trigger the alert.

- Define the response of the alert. Alerts can be set up to trigger jobs automatically, and/or to alert operators that the alert was activated.

- If the alert is meant to perform a job, define (or select) the job to be done. Alerts are usually created to perform a job when the alert condition is met. You can define a job that will run when the alert is triggered. Jobs can either run T-SQL statements or command-prompt programs such as `bcp.exe` or `osql.exe`.

- If the alert is meant to notify someone, define who will be notified and how this will be done. You can specify operators and whether they should receive an e-mail message and/or be paged when an alert is triggered. (See "Creating and Managing Operators" later in this chapter for details about setting up operators.)

- Activate the alert by selecting the Enabled box inside the Edit Alert dialog box (it is selected by default but can be deselected to temporarily disable an alert).

Follow the steps in Exercise 8.5 to create an alert. In this example, we will set up an alert to watch for the log of the Pubs database to get full, and to back up the transaction log (thus clearing the log) if and when the alert is triggered. In Exercise 8.6, we will create an alert that monitors the performance monitor counters for SQL Server connections.

EXERCISE 8.5

Creating an Alert Based on SQL Server Error Messages

1. In Enterprise Manager, open the Management window and open the Alerts window. You should see nine predefined alerts.

2. To add a new alert, click the New button on the toolbar, or choose Action ➤ New Alert, or right-click and choose New Alert.

3. You'll see the New Alert dialog box. In the ID: New Name field, enter **Detect Full Pubs Transaction Log**.

4. In the Alert Definition section, select the Error Number option button and enter the number 1105 in the associated box. In the Database Name drop-down list box, choose Pubs. Your dialog box should now look like the one below.

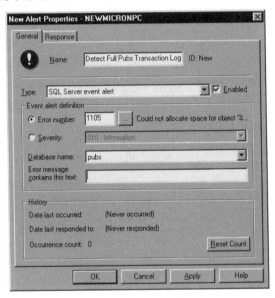

5. Go to the Response tab. Select Execute Job. In the Job to Execute drop-down list box, choose New Job. This will open the New Job dialog box.

6. In the Name box, enter **Clear the Pubs log when an alert is triggered**.

7. Go to the Steps tab and click New to add a new job step.

8. Enter **Clear the pubs log** for the name, and in the command box, enter the following T-SQL statement:

backup log pubs to pubs_log

EXERCISE 8.5 (CONTINUED)

9. Click OK, OK to save the new job, which should be listed as the job to run when the alert triggers.

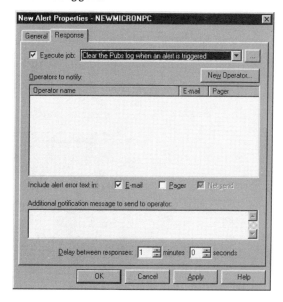

10. Click OK to save the alert. Your alert should now be listed with the default alerts.

EXERCISE 8.6

Creating an Alert Based on a Performance Monitor Counter

1. In SQL Enterprise Manager, open the Management window and open the Alerts window. You should see nine predefined alerts (as well as any you have made).

2. To add a new alert, click on the New button on the toolbar or choose Action ➤ New Alert, or right-click and choose New Alert.

3. You'll see the New Alert dialog box. In the ID: New Name field, enter **Detect when Connections go over 500**.

4. Change the Type to SQL Server performance condition alert. (Note that only SQL performance monitor counters—not all counters—are visible to the agent.)

5. Change the Object to SQL Server: General Statistics.

6. Change the Counter to User Connections.

7. Change the Alert if Counter to Rises Above.

8. Enter 500 for the value. Your alert should look like this.

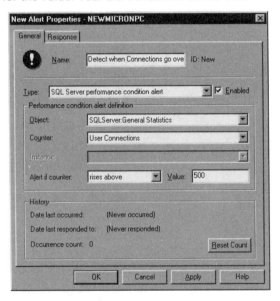

9. Choose OK to save the alert.

Editing an Alert

After you've created an alert, you can easily make changes to it. Simply return to the Manage Alerts and Operators window, highlight the alert you want to change, and click on the Edit Alert button.

Note that many of the alerts you would make based on performance monitor counters would probably be designed to send a message to someone when the appropriate counter hit a specified number. While our example in Exercise 8.6 is incomplete, we can edit the alert so that the appropriate person is notified. Defining operators and assigning them to alerts are covered below.

Editing and Creating SQL Server Error Messages

One of the great features of SQL Server is the ability to add your own error messages to the basic ones provided by SQL Server. You can call the new error message from within any T-SQL script or program by using the following command:

```
Raiserror (error_number, severity, state)
```

You can then create alerts to watch for the error messages you have defined and notify you when the error is triggered.

You edit the posting of existing error messages to the NT Application log and create and edit new messages through the Manage SQL Messages menu option of the All Tasks option when the server is highlighted. In Exercise 8.7, we will edit an existing SQL Server error message so that it won't post to the NT Application log and then create a new error message.

EXERCISE 8.7

Editing and Creating Error Messages

1. In SQL Enterprise Manager, highlight the server and select Action ➢ All Tasks ➢ Manage SQL Server Messages, or highlight the server, right-click, and choose All Tasks ➢ Manage SQL Server Messages.

2. Enter **1105** in the Error Number box and click on the Find button on the right side of the dialog box. The 1105 message appears in the dialog box.

3. Double-click the message or click once on Edit to edit the message. The Edit SQL Server Message dialog box appears, as shown below. Notice that the message itself cannot be edited, but the writing to the NT Eventlog can be disabled (or in some cases enabled).

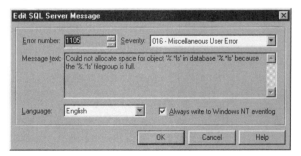

EXERCISE 8.7 (CONTINUED)

4. Click Cancel in the Edit SQL Server Message dialog box. (You should be in the Messages tab).

5. Choose New to create a new message.

6. Add a custom message to Error Number 50001 with the text **This message triggered by Custom Application. Contact the Programmers.** and check the Always Write to Windows NT Eventlog box.

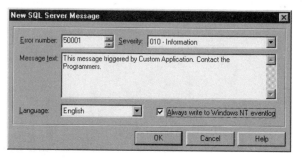

7. Click OK, then OK to close the window.

8. To test the message, start the Query Analyzer.

9. Enter and execute the following query:

```
raiserror (50001,10,1)
```

The error message that you just created should appear in the Results window.

10. Open the Windows NT event log (select Programs ➤ Administrative Tools ➤ NT Event Viewer) and select Log ➤ Application to display the Application log. The message that you entered should appear.

11. Double-click the message for more details. You should see the Event Detail dialog box with information about the error and your message.

Forwarding Events

If you have more than one server running SQL Server, you can define a central server that will receive from other servers events for which you have (or have not) defined alerts. The server that receives these events is called an *unhandled event forwarding server*.

Because SQL Server 7 also allows you to forward all events to a central server, this could cause major traffic on a large network if many SQL Servers were involved.

The server that is designated as the unhandled event forwarding server must be registered in Enterprise Manager.

Windows 95/98 cannot forward events to, or act as, an unhandled events server.

In Exercise 8.8, we will designate a server as the unhandled event forwarding server.

EXERCISE 8.8

Designating an Unhandled Event Forwarding Server

1. In Enterprise Manager, highlight the SQL Server Agent folder (found in the Management folder).

2. Go to the properties of the Agent by right-clicking and choosing Properties, or by going Action ➢ Properties.

3. Go to the Advanced tab.

4. Choose Forward Events to a Different Server and pick New Forwarding Server (or you can pick a server already registered in Enterprise Manager) from the drop-down list of servers. Enter **SERVER2** if you don't have a separate server to use.

   Enterprise Manager will warn you that it can't connect to SERVER2 and ask if you still want to register it (of course, you won't see this message if you actually do have a server called SERVER2); choose Yes. SERVER2 should now appear in the Server to Forward Events to box in the Fail-Safe tab.

5. Select Unhandled events (the default) and select Severity 15 and higher.

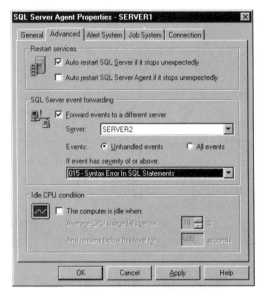

6. Because SQL Server can't connect to SERVER2, click Cancel so you don't save your changes. Of course, when you're actually designating an unhandled event forwarding server, you should click on OK to save your changes. (If you clicked on OK now, SQL Server would generate errors when it couldn't connect to SERVER2.)

Creating and Managing Operators

SQL Server is MAPI-compliant, which means that SQL Server can send and receive e-mail. This gives you the ability to define operators and their e-mail addresses in SQL Server, and have SQL Server notify those operators about the success and/or failure of scheduled or triggered jobs and alerts.

Automate administrative tasks.

- Define operators.
- Set up SQLAgentMail for job notification and alerts.

SQL Server also supports many paging services and can be configured to page operators if an alert is triggered. These paging services depend on your e-mail system's ability to decode an e-mail message in order to send a page message.

Enabling MAPI Support for E-Mail

Different versions of Windows NT implement MAPI for applications a bit differently. Windows NT 3.51 worked quite well with older versions of SQL Server, but Windows NT 4 changed the way MAPI works with services to provide better security. Because of this, Service Pack 3 or later must be used with Windows NT 4 to allow MAPI to work with SQL Server and Windows Messaging (MS Mail clients), although SQL Server and Exchange work without any service packs. Of course, since SQL Server 7 requires Service Pack 4 for Windows NT 4, installing at least Service Pack 3 is no longer an issue.

Configure SQL Server.

- Configure SQL Mail.
- Configure default American National Standards Institute (ANSI) settings.

Configuring default ANSI settings is covered in Chapter 2.

MAPI under Windows NT has the problem of not wanting to start more than one session at a time per computer. In other words, if SQL Server has a MAPI session open and you start and stop a program like Outlook, it may not connect—you must stop the MAPI session of SQL Server, start Outlook, and then restart the SQL Server MAPI session. The easiest way to do this is to stop and start SQL Agent to stop and start the MAPI session. What this means in real life is that you should not read your e-mail using the SQL Server computer if the SQL Server service is set up for e-mail operators.

There are five basic steps to installing MAPI support for Windows NT 4:

1. Create a user account for the SQL Agent and SQL Server to use

2. Create an Exchange post office box for the SQL user account

3. Log into the SQL Server computer as the SQL user account and create an Exchange profile that points to the exchange server and post office box created in step 2.

4. Log into the SQL server as someone with Administration and SA rights and assign the SQL user account (created in step 1) to the MSSQLServer and SQLServerAgent services. Stop and restart both services.

5. Assign the profile (created in step 3) to the SQL Mail portion of SQL Server. Start the SQL Mail session.

You may need to reapply the Service Pack if you add any components from the original Windows NT 4 CD. You can find Service Pack 4 for Windows NT 4 on Microsoft's Web site (http://www.microsoft.com) or on TechNet. Use the Update command from the appropriate subdirectory (x386 for Intel-compatible computers) to install the Service Pack.

In Exercise 8.9, we will install support for MAPI for Windows NT 4 and SQL Server.

EXERCISE 8.9

Installing MAPI Support in SQL Server

1. Go to User Manager and make sure you have a user account created for the SQL services. Make sure the account is set to Password Never Expires and is not set for User Must Change Password at Next Logon. Make the account a member of the domain administrators group.

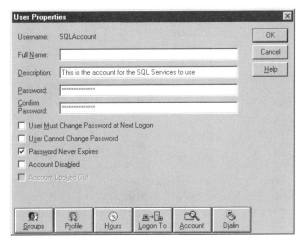

2. Start the Exchange Administrator program.

3. Create a mailbox for the SQL user account by going to the Recipients folder and choosing File ➣ New Mailbox. Enter the information for the SQL user account and assign it to the user by using the Primary Windows NT Account button. Select OK to save the mailbox.

EXERCISE 8.9 (CONTINUED)

4. Create a mailbox for your personal account if one does not already exist.

5. Log in to Windows NT as the user you created for the SQL Agent account.

6. Go to Control Panel ≻ Mail and Fax, and select Add under the profile section.

7. Leave the Microsoft Exchange Server selected and clear all the other selections. Select Next.

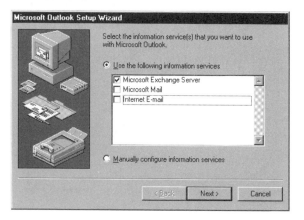

8. Enter the name of the Exchange server and the mailbox. Select Next.

9. Select No when asked if you travel with the computer. Select Next.

10. Take the default path to the Address Book. Select Next.

11. Do not choose to add Outlook to the Startup Group. Select Next.

12. Select Finish at the final screen.

13. Note the name of the profile. You will need to know this name for later steps.

14. Go to Enterprise Manager.

15. Assign the SQL account to the SQL Server service by going to the Properties screen of the server, the Security tab, and entering the domain\username and password for the account.

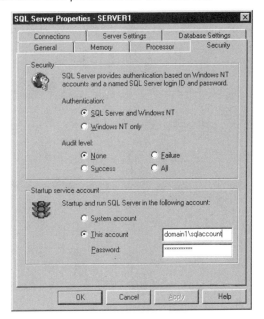

16. Assign the SQL account to the SQL Agent by going to the Properties screen.

17. On the General tab, enter the domain\username for the account, the password, and the name of the profile you created. Select OK.

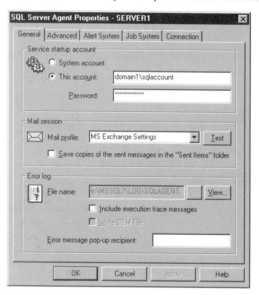

18. Start the SQL Mail session by going to the SQL Mail Configuration folder under the Support Services folder. Examine the properties of SQL Mail and make sure the profile created earlier is listed.

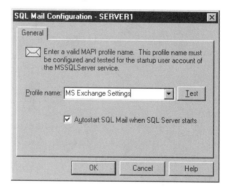

19. Select the Test button to test the profile. Select Autostart SQL Mail when SQL Starts. Select OK.

20. To start the SQL mail session right-click the SQL Mail icon and choose Start. The session should start and the arrow turn green.

Creating Operators and Testing E-Mail

To ensure that your MAPI support is configured correctly, you will want to send test messages to your operators. In Exercise 8.10, we will create an operator and test the ability of SQL Server to send messages to that operator.

EXERCISE 8.10

Creating an Operator and Testing E-Mail

1. Log in to Windows NT as your normal account (not the SQL Executive account).

2. In Enterprise Manager, go to the Operators folder under the SQL Agent and Management folders

3. Click the New button, or right-click and choose New Operator, or go to Action\New Operator.

4. In the Edit Operator dialog box, enter an operator name, such as **The NT Administrator**, and the e-mail name for the person you are logged in as, as shown below.

5. Click the Test button to send mail to the user. SQL Server should report that the message was sent successfully.

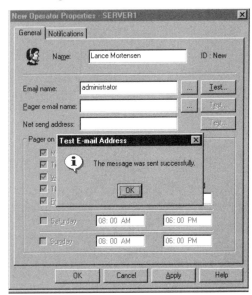

6. Click OK to save your new operator.

7. Minimize Enterprise Manager, go to your Desktop, and start your messaging client by double-clicking on the Inbox. You should have received the test message.

8. Close the Messaging Client by selecting File ➢ Exit and Log Off from the menu.

9. Go back to Enterprise Manager and go to the Notifications tab of the operator. Select all the alerts you wish to have go to this operator.

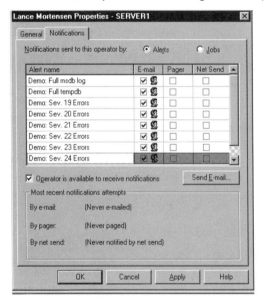

10. Select OK to save the operator.

Defining Fail-Safe Operators

After you've set up your operators (defining their working hours), you can designate a fail-safe operator in case no other operators are on duty when an alert is triggered. In Exercise 8.11, we will define a fail-safe operator.

EXERCISE 8.11

Defining a Fail-Safe Operator

1. In Enterprise Manager, highlight the SQL Server Agent folder under the Management folder.

2. Select Action ➤ Properties or right-click and choose Properties to bring up the Properties screen.

3. Go to the Alert System tab. In the Fail-Safe Operator drop-down list box, select an operator you have already set up, as shown below. Check the e-mail box as well.

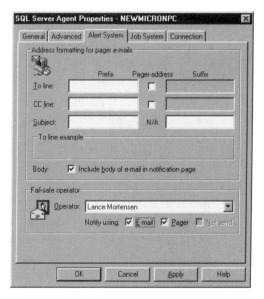

4. Click OK to save your changes.

SQL Server and the Internet

This section will introduce you to different ways of accessing data in SQL Server from Internet applications. SQL Server 7 includes a Web Assistant designed to make accessing static web pages easier than ever before.

There are also ways to access SQL data through interactive web pages. This section will cover the use of the SQL Web Assistant in detail and give you introductory information concerning other approaches to accessing data through the Internet.

Although this section may seem somewhat unrelated to the rest of the chapter, automating access to SQL data via web pages is a common reason to create and manage jobs.

Static vs. Interactive Web Pages

In the early days of the Web, most pages were static in nature. They were not really designed to give the user an interface for extensive interaction. Of course, there were stunning graphics and even some animations, but the pages were still essentially static. The presentation on a static web page consists primarily of links and text. The text and/or links might be updated periodically by the webmaster, but the page does not accept any input from the user other than to follow a link to another static page.

Static pages have their place. If the user has no need to "drill down" to specific data and can use the contents of the page as a whole, the approach can be very valid. Properly planned links and a well-organized site can give the appearance of being fairly dynamic in response to user requests when, in reality, all the work of providing that seemingly interactive experience is being performed by the webmaster or the individual responsible for maintaining current data on the site.

Interactive pages have an entirely different concept and purpose. The key participant in an interactive web page is the user. The user can provide input about the information retrieved, enter data into a data storage by filling out a web-based form, and even cause events to happen halfway around the world.

One of the most recent applications for interactive web pages is to provide merchant services. By using tools such as Microsoft Internet Information Server and Merchant Server and using SQL Server as a data store, you can build a web site to handle merchant activities ranging from taking orders in an online bookstore to transferring funds between two financial institutions. IIS handles the web traffic, Merchant Server maintains the security of the transactions, and SQL Server provides the data storage and transactional integrity. Adding Microsoft Transaction Server to the mix adds the extra element of distributed transaction processing, allowing you to coordinate the activities of multiple SQL Servers.

As you can see, with interactive web pages, the only limit is the imagination of the site architect and the developer. The goal is to provide the user with a rich interactive experience. Whether you are building your web site for internal use, as with an intranet, or planning on attracting Internet customers to your site, the reason for building your site is to provide user services.

Using the SQL Web Assistant

Although there are advantages to providing the user with an interactive experience, there is not always the need to dynamically extract information from a SQL Server. If your requirement is for static web pages that will be periodically updated by either the administrator or an automated service, then the SQL Web Assistant might be exactly the tool that you need. It doesn't make sense to pound a pin into the wall with a sledgehammer, and sometimes a static web page is completely adequate.

The web pages created by the SQL Web Assistant can be based on a stored procedure or created through a free-form query that you type as you initially run the assistant. These pages are sometimes called *push pages* because the data is pushed out of SQL Server by the queries or stored procedures that access the data. These queries or stored procedures are completely static, however. They cannot be changed by the user interacting through the browser, nor can parameters be passed to the stored procedure through the browser.

Running the Assistant

To run the SQL Web Assistant, first make sure that the SQL Server is running. If it is not running, the assistant will be unable to forward the query or stored procedure call to SQL Server for processing.

To access the SQL Web Assistant (or Wizard), go to the Web Publishing folder of the Management group in Enterprise Manager. In Exercise 8.12, we will create a new job to publish (push) web pages.

EXERCISE 8.12

Creating a Web Publishing Job

1. To create a new web publishing job start the Wizard by highlighting the Web Publishing folder and selecting Action ➢ New Web Assistant Job or by right-clicking and choosing New Web Assistant Job. This should start the introductory screen. Select Next.

2. Select the Pubs database. Click Next.

3. Notice the default name of the web publishing job. Leave the data selection on Data from the Tables and Columns that I Select. Choose Next.

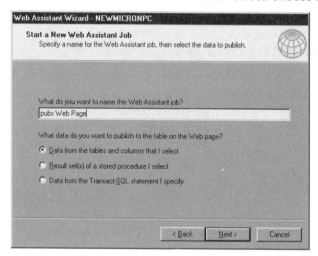

4. Select the Titles table and choose just the Title_id and Pubdate columns. Select Next.

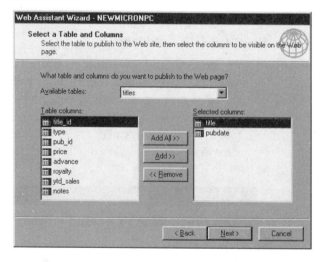

5. Leave the row selection on All of the Rows. Select Next.

6. This is one of the most important screens, as it lets you schedule when the web page will be created. To create a recurring job select At Regularly Scheduled Intervals. Choose Next.

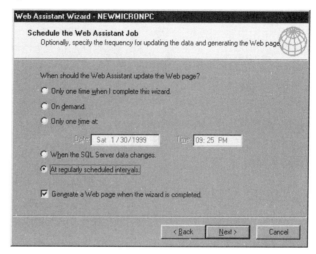

7. If you selected to update the page on a regular basis you will be prompted to select when the job will run. Leave it at the default day and time and choose Next.

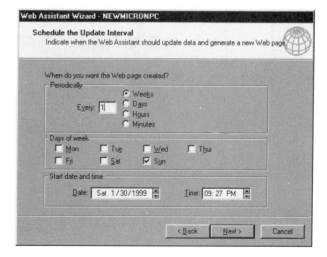

8. Enter the path to the HTML file that will be created. Note that the default path is \MSSQL7\HTML. Select Next.

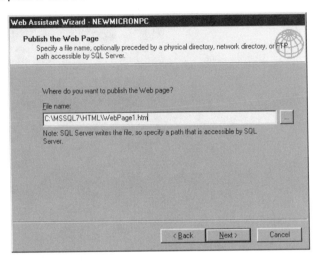

9. Leave the default settings for the formatting of the web page. (You can also specify a template for more sophisticated formatting.) Select Next.

10. Change the name of the web page and table to something more appropriate like that shown below. Select Next.

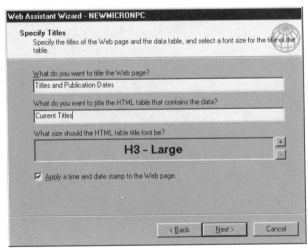

11. Leave the default settings for the Data Format. Select Next.

12. Note that you can add custom hyperlinks (such as back to your home page or to other supporting pages or companies) from this screen. Leave it set to No Additional Hyperlinks and select Next.

13. Note that you can split the results into smaller pages, or limit the row count on the next page. Leave the default settings and select Next.

14. You should now see a summary page. Note that you can back up and change any item, or generate the T-SQL code that the job will use. Select Finish to generate and run the recurring job.

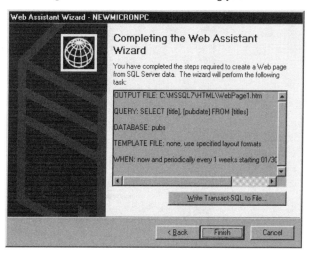

15. Select OK when the Confirmation screen comes up.

---

16. To look at your page, go to the \MSSQL7\HTML folder and open the
file you made (WebPage1.htm). It should look something like this:

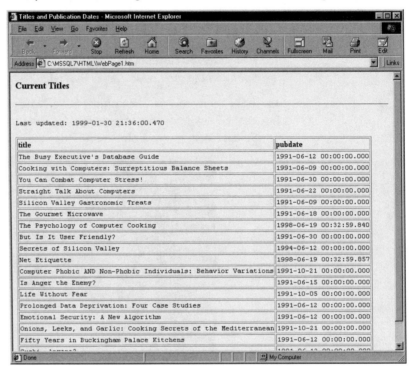

17. Go to the Jobs folder. You should see a new job entitled something
like "pubs Web Page."

18. If you examine the first step of the job it looks something like the graphic below. Note that a stored procedure is being called to read the parameters you entered when you created the web publishing job.

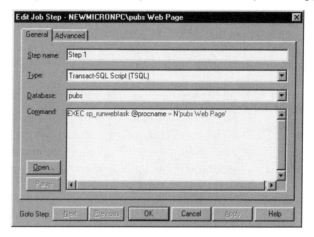

19. Close the Jobs window.

Although you can edit the web page directly after it has been generated, any changes that you make will be lost the next time the page is generated. If you wish to make permanent changes to the formatting of the page you must either change the settings inside the Web Assistant or, for a more robust approach, use an HTML template file.

You can easily edit the schedule of a recurring web job by going to the Schedule tab. You can also delete the web publishing job (in case of mistakes) from the Jobs folder.

Creating Interactive Web Pages

While static web pages are extremely simple to produce, they may not be sophisticated enough for your web site. For example, if you require that your user enter information into a database or retrieve information based on custom parameters, you may need to use interactive web pages. Interactive web pages are sometimes called *pull pages* because the user's input will pull data out of the server instead of simply accessing a static page.

WARNING Pull pages tend to place more of a strain on your server because rather than simply generating a web page at certain intervals, the browser is actually calling information directly out of the database. Significant hits to your web site can negatively affect the performance of the SQL Server.

When creating interactive web pages, there are three basic ways to get at your SQL Server data. Each of them has advantages and disadvantages. These three approaches are:

- Internet Database Connector (IDC)

- Advanced Data Connector (ADC)

- ActiveX Data Objects (ADO)

Let's look at each of these three approaches in more detail. Although they are not necessarily difficult to implement, they do require programming that is beyond the scope of this book. There are numerous resources available for additional exploration of these topics.

NOTE These three methods are not the only ways to create interactive web pages. Other approaches include CGI scripts, ISAPI applications, and others. While these other approaches are just as valid, they do require significantly more programming than the methods discussed here.

Internet Database Connector

The Internet Database Connector is an ISAPI application that retrieves live data from a database through the Internet based on a user's request through hard-coded parameters or HTML input fields. Although IDC was quite effective in its time for accessing data in an ODBC data source, it does have some restrictions.

ISAPI stands for Internet Server Application Programming Interface, the programming functions for Microsoft Internet Information Server. Unlike Common Gateway Interface (CGI) applications, ISAPI applications run in the address space of the web server and are therefore usually faster than comparable CGI applications.

The most significant restriction of IDC is that it is designed to retrieve data from a database, not to input data. This means that you would have to use additional ISAPI or CGI applications to handle the data input. For this reason, pages created using IDC are often called *dynamic* (rather than *interactive) pages*. Since they cannot accept data for input into a database, they are not truly interactive.

An easier way to solve the interactivity problem with IDC is to use stored procedures on the SQL Server and call these stored procedures from your IDC file. Parameters can be passed to the stored procedure through HTML input fields.

Another restriction lies in the fact that IDC is an ISAPI extension. This approach is therefore valid only when using IIS as your web server. Because this restriction is also present for the other two methods of interactive data access, you may not be able to do much about this one.

The last major restriction of IDC wasn't a restriction at all until about March of 1997 when Microsoft officially introduced ADO to the world. ADO is built on the OLE-DB data access model and is Microsoft's replacement for ODBC. As OLE-DB matures and OLE-DB service providers become more common, ODBC will eventually be pushed out as the primary method of accessing data through a generic API. IDC works only through ODBC and is not an OLE-DB-compatible technology.

To use IDC in your applications, you must create two text files for every query that you wish to run. One of these files will have an extension of IDC while the other will end in HTX.

The IDC file contains all the information the web server will need to connect to the data source and run the query. Among the information listed in the IDC file is the Data Source name of your database server, authentication information, the SQL statement that will be run against the server, and the name and location of the HTX file that will be used to format the output.

The HTX file is very similar in concept to the HTML template file mentioned earlier. The HTX is actually an HTML template file that will determine how the output of the database request will appear in the resulting web page. As with the HTML template used by the Web Assistant, server-side tags (<% %>) are used to indicate to the IDC application where to place the results in the HTML output.

To access the output, you can simply provide a link that points to the URL if the IDC file located in a server that has the IDC extensions installed. This IDC application can then process the query and send the results back to the calling browser by sending them through the HTX template.

Although the IDC does have some limitations in creating truly interactive pages, it is highly efficient in accessing real-time data through the Internet. Often, this can be sufficient for your requirements.

Advanced Data Connector

The Advanced Data Connector is a set of ActiveX components used to access database information through a web browser. Some ADC components run on the client inside the Browser while other components run on the web server and interact directly with the database. The ADC is without a doubt the easiest way to connect a browser to a data source and can be accessed from Microsoft at http://www.microsoft.com/adc/.

To access data through ADC, the ADC code is placed on the web page that will receive the recordset from the database server. This control is designed to interact with a server-side component called the *Advanced Data Factory*. The Factory is an ActiveX component running on the server that will accept data requests from the browser and make calls against the ADC application, an ISAPI application running on the server. The application will retrieve the results from the data source and pass the results back to the factory, which then transfers the results back to the browser.

Data updates can be made directly to the database using ADC. For maximum efficiency, however, consider isolating update transactions in temporary tables for later application to the database.

ADC Limitations

Of course, for all its ease of use and convenience, the ADC also has its limitations. First and foremost is that it is an ActiveX component running in a browser, meaning that the browser must support ActiveX and the control must be downloaded before it can be used. When providing a code source for downloading an ActiveX control created by Microsoft, always point to microsoft.com whenever possible. This way you don't have to provide resources for storing and downloading the control, and your users are guaranteed to have the most recent version of the control possible.

ActiveX Data Objects and Active Server Pages

The last approach that we will look at is the one that will require the greatest amount of programming, but will also give you the greatest level of flexibility. That is using ActiveX Data Objects with Active Server Pages. ADO is built upon the OLE-DB standard and can access databases either through ODBC or through OLE-DB service providers.

Active Server Pages are sections of HTML code that run on a web server and never in a browser. If you will remember, any time that you wish to use ActiveX components inside a web browser, the browser must first download that component and register it on the local system. If the user has their browser security set to a level that denies the download, or if your control is not properly signed, this could cause the download to fail and the process to abort. In addition, in order for a browser to have the capacity to implement ActiveX controls, the browser must support Active X and be running on a 32-bit Windows operating system. This cannot always be guaranteed, unfortunately, making some applications unavailable to such users.

Active Server Pages solve this problem by forcing all ActiveX components to run on the server; the browser will receive only pure HTML, with no controls to download and no security issues to be concerned about.

Active Server Pages are usually controlled through some scripting language such as VBScript. This server-side script gives you significant flexibility while still maintaining total client-side security. A detailed discussion of implementing active server pages is far beyond the scope of this book; however, there are abundant resources available to provide you with additional information.

Summary

In this chapter, you learned about creating and managing alerts, operators, and jobs to help you with your administrative duties.

The Msdb database holds all the information for alerts, operators, jobs, and the history of jobs. Because of this, you should schedule regular backups of this database.

The SQL Agent is a helper service that oversees the automation of jobs inside SQL Server. You must configure SQL Agent correctly before any of your alerts, operators, or jobs will work. Configuring the SQL Agent consists primarily of setting up a user account for it to use and assigning the account to the Agent.

The rest of the chapter described how to set up alerts, operators, and scheduled jobs. Alerts can watch the Windows NT eventlog, and they can cause a job to execute upon finding predefined error messages. Alerts from multiple SQL Servers can be forwarded to a central server to make management of many servers easier.

You can define operators so that SQL Server can e-mail and/or page the operator upon success and/or failure of jobs. SQL Server is MAPI-enabled, which allows it to send and receive e-mail.

Jobs can be defined that can run T-SQL statements, command-prompt commands and replication jobs. Jobs can be run on a regular basis, on demand when an alert triggers, or only once.

We finished the chapter with a look at how to automate pushing HTML web pages from SQL data and the various methods of setting up pull pages.

Review Questions

1. What rights does the SQL Agent service account need? (Choose all that apply.)

   A. Log on as a Service right

   B. Administrator group membership

   C. Backup Operators membership

   D. Server Operators membership

2. What is the API set that allows SQL Server to send and receive e-mail?

   A. TAPI

   B. EAPI

   C. OLE

   D. MAPI

3. Which database holds alert and job information?

   A. The Master database

   B. The Model database

   C. The Msdb database

   D. None—it is held in the Registry

4. How can you rebuild the Msdb database?

   A. You can't; you must reinstall SQL Server

   B. Rebuild the Master database

   C. Rebuild Msdb database

   D. Stop and restart SQL Server; the Msdb database will be rebuilt automatically

5. Where do alerts look for errors?

   A. The Windows NT Application log

   B. The SQL Server event log

   C. The Master database error log

   D. SQL Server sends errors directly to the alert engine

6. What kinds of jobs can be created? (Choose all that apply.)

   A. T-SQL (Transact-SQL)

   B. CmdExec (command prompt)

   C. Replication

   D. Active script

7. How can you create new error messages in SQL Server?

   A. You can't

   B. Run the Setup program, choose Custom, and choose Edit Messages

   C. Choose Manage SQL Server Messages when highlighting the server

   D. Go to the Messages folder and choose New Message

8. What is the best way to stop an alert for a couple of hours?

   A. Disable the alert.

   B. Set the hit counter of the alert to –1.

   C. Delete the alert.

   D. Deselect any operators that were being notified.

9. What is the operator of last resort called?

   A. Weekend operator

   B. Last-chance operator

C. Notification operator

D. Fail-safe operator

10. What is the central server that receives alerts from other SQL Server servers called?

A. Central alerter

B. Standardized alerter

C. Central control

D. Unhandled events server

11. You have four SQL Servers. Server1 is SQL 6.5 running on Windows NT Server, Server2 is SQL 7 running on Windows 98, Server3 is SQL 7 running on Windows NT Workstation, and Server4 is SQL 7 running on Windows NT Server. Which servers can be designated as a Master server in a multiserver environment?

A. Server1

B. Server2

C. Server3

D. Server4

12. You have four SQL Servers. Server1 is SQL 6.5 running on Windows NT Server, Server2 is SQL 7 running on Windows 98, Server3 is SQL 7 running on Windows NT Workstation, and Server4 is SQL 7 running on Windows NT Server. Which servers can be designated as a Target server in a multiserver environment?

A. Server1

B. Server2

C. Server3

D. Server4

13. Server1 is designated as a target server for multiserver jobs. Where will the status of the jobs it gets from the master server be recorded?

    A. Only at the master server

    B. Only at the target server

    C. At both the master and target server

    D. Nowhere

14. You want SQL Server to be able to send messages upon job completion using an Exchange operator. Which of these steps is required to create e-mail operators?

    A. Create an Exchange account for the SQL Agent service account

    B. Assign the SQL Agent service to use a service account

    C. Create an operator

    D. Assign the job to notify the appropriate operator

15. You have created a user-defined message "Please call the help desk," numbered 50001, that is configured to post to the NT Application log. Which command will display the SQL message number 50001 and post it to the Windows NT Application log?

    A. Print 50001

    B. Print (50001, 10, 1)

    C. Raiserror 50001

    D. Raiserror (50001, 10, 1)

CHAPTER

9

Creating and Implementing a
Replication Solution in SQL Server 7

Replication allows for the distribution of your SQL Server 7 data to other database engines. This includes both SQL Server 7 databases and non-SQL Server databases such as Oracle and IBM's DB2 database. This chapter covers a great deal of ground regarding replication. We will first look at the publisher/subscriber metaphor that has been implemented in SQL Server 7's replication strategy. This metaphor includes publishers, distributors and subscribers and goes a step further by including publications and articles.

Manage replication.

- Configure servers, including Distributor, Publisher, and Subscriber.
- Create publications.
- Set up and manage subscriptions.

Develop a replication strategy.

- Given a scenario, design the appropriate replication model. Replication models include single Publisher and multiple Subscribers; multiple Publishers and single Subscriber; multiple Publishers and multiple Subscribers; and remote Distributor.
- Choose the replication type. Replication types include snapshot, transactional, and merge.

This chapter discusses the factors that affect replication—transactional consistency, latency, and site autonomy influence your distribution choice, whether it be transactional, merge, or something else. It also examines the way in which replication actually works, with the various replication agents that work in concert to move your data from a publisher through the distributor and on to the subscribers.

The administrative concerns involved with replication include security issues, data definition issues, non-SQL Server 7 database issues, and other SQL Server configuration issues. Several replication scenarios can be implemented. These scenarios are important, since each scenario has specific advantages and disadvantages for a particular business situation that the replication strategy must address.

The chapter will detail how to install and run replication on your SQL Server 7 computer. We will walk through the process of setting up a distributor, a publisher, and a subscriber. We will then create a publication, subscribe to it, and check whether replication is working properly.

The chapter will also look at some optimization and troubleshooting techniques specific to our replication tasks.

Overview of Replication

We use replication to put copies of the same data at different locations throughout the enterprise. The most common of the many reasons why you might want to replicate your data include:

- Moving data closer to the user

- Reducing locking conflicts when multiple sites wish to work with the same data

- Allowing site autonomy so that each location can set up its own rules and procedures for working with its copy of the data

- Removing the impact of read-intensive operations such as report generation and ad hoc query processing from the OLTP database.

The two basic forms of replication used in SQL Server 7 are replication and distributed transactions. Whether you use one or the other type, copies of the data are current and consistent. You can also use both strategies in the same environment.

The main difference between replication and distributed transactions is in the timing. With distributed transactions, your data is 100% in synchronization, 100% of the time. When you use replication, there is some latency involved. It may be as little as a few seconds, or as long as several days or even weeks. Distributed transactions require that the replicated databases be connected at all times. If they are not, then the distributed transactions will fail. Replication does not have this requirement.

The Publisher/Subscriber Metaphor

SQL Server 7 uses a publisher/subscriber metaphor to describe and implement replication. Your database can play different roles as part of the replication scenario: it can be a publisher, subscriber, distributor, or any combination of these. When you publish data, you do it in the form of an article, which is stored in a publication. Here is a list of key terms used as part of the publisher/subscriber metaphor.

Publisher   This is the source database where replication begins. The publisher makes data available for replication.

Subscriber   The subscriber is the destination database where replication ends and either receives a snapshot of all the published data or applies transactions that have been replicated to it.

Distributor   This is the intermediary between the publisher and subscriber. The distributor receives published transactions or snapshots and then stores and forwards these publications to the subscribers.

Publication   The publication is the storage container for different articles. A subscriber can subscribe to an individual article or an entire publication.

Article   An article is the data, transactions, or stored procedures that are stored within a publication. This is the actual information that is going to be replicated.

Two-Phase Commit   Two-phase commit (sometimes referred to as *2PC*) is a form of replication in which modifications made to the publishing database are made at the subscription database at exactly the same time. This is handled through the use of distributed transactions. As with any transaction, either all statements commit successfully, or all modifications are rolled back. Two-phase commit uses the Microsoft Distributed Transaction Coordinator (MS-DTC) to accomplish its tasks. The MS-DTC implements the functionality of a portion of the Microsoft Transaction Server. In this chapter, we will focus on replication as opposed to two-phase commits.

A publisher can publish data to one or more distributors. A subscriber can subscribe through one or more distributors. A distributor can have one or more publishers and subscribers.

Articles

An article is data in a table. This data can be the entire table or just a subset of the data in the table. Your articles need to be bundled into one or more publications in order for them to be distributed to the subscribers. When you want to publish a subset of data in a table, you must specify some type of partitioning, either vertical or horizontal.

With a vertical partition, you select specific columns from your table. In a horizontal partition, you select only specific rows of data from the table. Figure 9.1 shows an example of both a vertical and a horizontal partition. Here, the horizontal partition might be useful in situations where you want to make specific rows of data available to different regions. More specifically, you could create three separate articles. One article would be horizontally partitioned based on region 1. The next article would be horizontally partitioned on region 2, and the third on region 3. Each region could then subscribe to only its regional data.

Publications

Articles must be stored in a publication, which is the basis for your subscriptions. When you create a subscription, you are actually subscribing to an entire publication; however, you can read individual articles. Referential integrity is maintained within your publication because all articles in a publication are updated at the same time.

In SQL Server 7, you can publish to non-Microsoft SQL Server computers. The replicated data does not need to be in the same sort order or data type. While it is possible to replicate to different sort orders and data types, we do not recommend it.

FIGURE 9.1

You can create articles based on subsets of your data.

Horizontal partition

ReCode	EmpID	Q1	Q2	Q3
1	5	40.1	39.8	37.7
1	7	28.7	33.5	38.2
1	8	39.9	42.2	48.1
1	13	28.8	32.8	33.7

ReCode	EmpID	Q1	Q2	Q3
2	2		44.6	
1	5		39.8	
2	3		41.7	
3	11		28.8	
1	7		33.5	
1	8		42.2	
3	22		45.5	
1	13		32.8	

Vertical partition

Replication Factors and Distribution Types

Before you can choose a distribution type, you should understand the factors that influence your decision. The three main items to consider are autonomy, latency, and transactional consistency. You must also consider the questions that must be answered in making the decision.

Autonomy   This refers to how much independence you wish to give each subscriber with regard to the replicated data. Will the replicated data be considered read-only (as in SQL Server 6.5)? How long will the data at a subscriber be valid? How often do you need to connect to the distributor to download more data?

Latency   Latency refers to how often your data will be updated. Does it need to be in synchronization at all times? Is every minute enough? What if you are a salesman on the road who dials in to the office once a day? Is this good enough?

Transactional Consistency   Although there are several types of replication, the most common method is to move transactions from the publisher through the distributor and onto the subscriber. Transactional consistency comes into play here. Do all the transactions that are stored need to be applied at the same time and in order? What happens if there is a delay in the processing?

Once you understand these factors, you need to start asking yourself other questions. Once you have answered these questions, you can decide on a distribution type.

- What am I going to publish? Will it be all the data in a table, or will I partition information?

- Who has access to my publications? Are these subscribers connected or dial-up users?

- Will subscribers be able to update my data, or is their information considered read-only?

- How often should I synchronize my publishers and subscribers?

- How fast is my network? Can subscribers be connected at all times? How much traffic is there on my network?

Distribution Types

Each of the several types of distribution you can use has different levels of autonomy, transactional consistency, and latency involved. Basically, you have snapshot replication, transactional replication, and merge replication.

Microsoft
Exam
Objective

Develop a replication strategy.

- Choose the replication type. Replication types include snapshot, transactional, and merge.

When you factor in latency, autonomy, and consistency, you end up with six different distribution types:

- Distributed transactions

- Transactional replication

- Transactional replication with updating subscribers

- Snapshot replication

- Snapshot replication with updating subscribers

- Merge replication

As shown in Figure 9.2, distributed transactions have the least amount of latency and autonomy, but they have the highest level of consistency. Merge replication has the highest amount of latency and autonomy and a lower level of consistency.

FIGURE 9.2

Distribution types

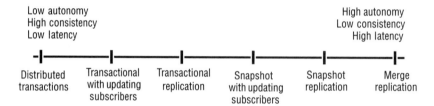

Using Distributed Transactions

When you use distributed transactions or 2PC to replicate your data, you have almost no autonomy or latency, but you do have guaranteed transactional consistency. With 2PC, either all changes are made at exactly the same time, or none of the changes are made. Remember that all the affected subscribers must be in contact with the publisher at all times.

This type of distribution is most useful in situations where subscribers must have real-time data, as in a reservation system.

For example, think of a cruise line that has only so many rooms of a particular type available. If someone in Dallas wants the Captain's suite and someone in California also wants the Captain's suite, the first one to book the room will get it. The other booking won't be allowed, because that location will immediately show that the room is already booked.

Using Transactional Replication

When you use this distribution method, transactions are gathered from the publishers and stored in the Distribution database. Subscribers then receive these transactions and must work with the data as if it were read-only. This is because any changes made to their local copy of the data might not let the new transactions being downloaded be applied properly, which would destroy the transactional consistency.

There is, however, some limited autonomy at each site. You can introduce some latency, because the subscribers don't have to be in contact at all times. Transactional consistency can be maintained as long as the subscribed data remains unchanged by the subscribers.

The advantages to this approach include the fact that transactions are relatively small items to move through the system (unlike snapshot replication, which we will look at shortly). The main disadvantage of using transactional replication is that subscribers must treat the data as read-only.

Use this distribution method when subscribers can treat their data as read-only and need the updated information with a minimal amount of latency.

This type of replication would be useful in an order processing/distribution system with several locations where orders are taken. Each of those order locations would be a publisher, and the published orders could then be replicated to a subscription database at your central warehouse. The central warehouse could then accept the orders, fill them, and ship them out.

Using Transactional Replication with Updating Subscribers

We think that this type of distribution will become the most popular form of replication in SQL Server 7. When you use transactional replication with updating subscribers, you are gaining site autonomy, minimizing latency, and keeping transactional consistency. This (in most cases) would be considered the best possible solution.

When you implement transactional replication with updating subscribers, you are essentially working with all the tenets of transactional replication. The major difference is that when you change the subscription data, 2PC changes the publishing database as well. In this fashion, your local subscriber is updated at exactly the same time as the publisher. Other subscribers will have your changes downloaded to them at their next synchronization.

This scenario can be useful for a reservation system that needs to be updated frequently, but does not need total synchronization. Let's use a library as an example here. You wish to reserve a book on SQL Server 7. You go to the computer and look up the book you wish to reserve and find that one copy is currently available. When you try to reserve the book, however, you might find that your data isn't 100% up-to-date, and the book has already been checked out. In this example, when you try to reserve your book, the subscriber automatically runs a 2PC to the publisher. At the publisher, someone has already checked out that last copy, and therefore the update fails. At the next synchronization, your subscriber will be updated with the news that the last copy has been checked out.

Using Snapshot Replication

When you use snapshot replication as your distribution method, you are actually moving an entire copy of the published items through the distributor and on to the subscribers. This type of replication allows for a high level of both site autonomy and transactional consistency because all records are going to be copied from the publisher and the local copy of the data will be overwritten at the next synchronization. Latency may be a bit higher as you probably will not move an entire snapshot every few minutes.

OLAP (Online Analytical Processing) servers are a prime candidate for this type of replication. The data at each subscriber is considered read-only and doesn't have to be 100% in synchronization all the time. This allows your MIS departments to run their reporting and ad-hoc queries on reasonably fresh data without affecting the OLTP server (which is doing all of the order-processing work).

Keep in mind that administrators and MIS ad hoc queries generally don't modify the data. They are looking for historical information such as how many widgets they sold, etc, so that data that is a few hours or even a few days old will generally not make a difference to the results returned by the queries.

Using Snapshot Replication with Updating Subscribers

The initial portion of this distribution style works just as in snapshot replication, with the added ability for the subscriber to update the publisher with new information. The updates use the 2PC protocol as described above.

This maintains a high level of site autonomy, a high level of transactional consistency, and a moderate level of latency. The data may be downloaded to the subscriber only once a day, but any updates the subscriber tries to make to data must first be approved by the publisher.

This type of distribution is useful when you have read-only data that needs to be updated infrequently. If your data needs to be updated often, we suggest that you use transactional replication with updating subscribers.

Snapshot replication might be useful when auditing your database, downloading portions of the data, and then double-checking that everything is being updated properly. The occasional mistake could then be quickly fixed and auditing could continue.

Using Merge Replication

Merge replication provides the highest amount of site autonomy, the highest latency, and the lowest level of transactional consistency. Merge replication allows each subscriber to make changes to their local copy of the data. At some point, these changes are merged with those made by other subscribers as well as changes made at the publisher. Ultimately, all sites receive the updates from all other sites. This is known as *convergence;* That is, all changes from all sites converge and are redistributed so that all sites have the same changes.

Transactional consistency is nearly nonexistent here, as different sites may all be making changes to the same data, resulting in conflicts. SQL Server 7 will automatically choose a particular change over another change and then converge that data. To simplify: Sooner or later, all sites will have the same copy of the data, but that data may not necessarily be what you wanted. For example, subscriber A makes changes to record 100. Subscriber B also makes changes to record 100. While this doesn't sound too bad, suppose the changes that subscriber A made to record 100 are due to changes that were made to record 50. If subscriber B doesn't have the same data in record 50, then subscriber B will make a different decision. Obviously, this can be incredibly complex.

You might wonder why anyone would want to use merge replication. There are, however, many reasons to use it and with some careful planning, you can make merge replication work to your advantage. There are triggers you can modify to determine which record is the correct record to use. The default rule when records are changed at multiple sites is to take the changes based on a site priority. Converge the results and then send them out. The exception to this general rule is when the main database is changed as well as all of the user databases. In this case, the user changes are applied first and then the main database changes. For example, say you have a central server that you call Main, and you have 20 sales people who are using merge replication. If one of your sales people modifies record 25 and you modify record 25 at the Main server, when the records are converged, the user changes will first be placed in the Main server and then the Main server changes will overwrite them.

If you design your publishers and subscribers to minimize conflicts, merge replication can be very advantageous. Look at the highway patrol, for example. A patrol car might pull over a car and write up a ticket for speeding. At the end of the day, that data is merged with data from other officers who have also written tickets. The data is then converged back to all of the different squad car computers. It is unlikely that the same individual will be stopped by two different police officers on the same day. If it does happen however, the situation can be remedied using either the default conflict resolution triggers, or custom triggers that the police departments can create themselves.

Replication Internals

Understanding how the transactions or snapshots are handled is essential to a full understanding of how SQL Server 7 implements replication.

When you set up your subscribers you can create either pull or push subscriptions. Push subscriptions help to centralize your administrative duties, since the subscription itself is stored on the distribution server. This allows the publisher to determine what data in the subscription and when that subscription will be synchronized. In other words, the data can be pushed to the subscribers based on the publisher's schedule. Push subscriptions are most useful if a subscriber needs to be updated whenever a change occurs at the publisher. Since the publisher knows when the modification takes place, it can immediately push those changes to the subscribers.

Pull subscriptions are configured and maintained at each subscriber. The subscribers will administer the synchronization schedules and can pull changes whenever they consider it necessary. This type of subscriber also relieves some of the overhead of processing from the distribution server. Pull subscriptions are also useful in situations where security is not a primary issue. In fact, pull subscriptions can be set up to allow anonymous connections, including pull subscribers residing on the Internet.

Non-SQL Server databases like Oracle and Access must use push subscriptions. Only SQL Server databases can use pull subscriptions.

In either a push or a pull environment, four replication agents handle the
tasks of moving data from the publisher to the distributor and then on to
the subscribers. The location of the particular agent is dependent upon the
type of replication (push or pull) you are using.

Logreader Agent   Located on the distribution server, the logreader's job
is to monitor the transaction logs of published databases that are using
this distributor. When the logreader agent finds a transaction, it moves
the transaction to the Distribution database on the distributor, transactions are stored and then forwarded to the subscribers by the distribution
agent for transactional and snapshot replication, or by the merge agent
for merge replication.

Distribution Agent   The distribution agent is responsible for moving the
stored transactions from the distributor to the subscribers.

Snapshot Agent   This agent, which is also used for snapshot replication,
is responsible for copying the schema and data from the publisher to the
subscriber. Before any type of replication can begin, a copy of the data
must reside on each subscriber. With this baseline established, transactions can then be applied at each subscriber and transactional consistency
can be maintained.

Merge Agent   The merge agent is responsible for converging records
from multiple sites and then redistributing the converged records back to
the subscribers.

We will now see how these different agents work in concert to create the
different distribution types.

 You do not have to choose a single type of distribution for all your subscribers. Each subscriber can implement a different type of data distribution.

Merge Replication

When you use merge replication, the merge agent can be centrally located on the distributor, or it can reside on every subscriber involved in the merge replication process. When you have implemented push replication, the merge agent will reside on the distributor. In a pull scenario, the merge agent is on every subscriber.

The following steps will outline the merge process and how each agent interacts with the other agents.

1. As shown in Figure 9.3, the snapshot agent that resides on the distribution server takes an initial snapshot of the data and moves it to the subscribers. This move takes place through the Distribution working folder The folder is just a holding area for the snapshot data to wait before it is moved on to the subscriber. As stated earlier, this must be done first so that later transactions can be applied.

FIGURE 9.3

How the merge replication process works

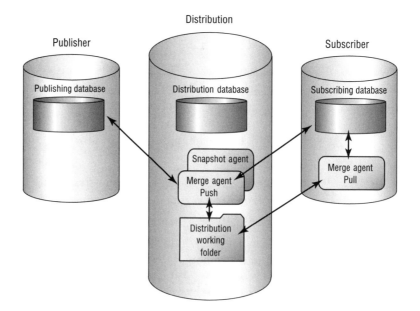

 Subscribers must have the appropriate permissions to access the Distribution working folder on the distribution server.

2. Replication can now begin.

3. The merge agent (wherever it resides) will take modifications from the publishers and apply them to the subscribers.

4. The merge agent will also take modifications from the subscribers and apply them to the publishers.

5. The merge agent will gather any merge conflicts and resolve them by using triggers. Merge information will be stored in tables at the distributor. This allows you to track data lineage.

When you use merge replication, some significant changes are made to the table schema as well as the Distribution database. These changes allow the triggers to handle conflict resolution. You should keep the following in mind when implementing merge replication:

- Several system tables will be added to the Distribution working folder.

- SQL Server creates triggers on the publishing and subscription servers used for merger replication. These triggers are automatically invoked when changes are made at either of these locations. Information about the changes is stored in the database system tables on the distribution server. With this change information your SQL Server can track the lineage or history of changes made to a particular row of data.

- The UNIQUEIDENTIFIER column is added as a new column for each table involved in the merge replication. This new column has the ROWGUID property assigned to it. A GUID is a 128-bit globally unique identifier that allows the same row of data modified in different subscribers to be uniquely identified.

Merge replication is most useful in situations where there will be few conflicts. A horizontally partitioned table based on a region code or some other ID is best suited to merge replication.

In merge replication, you cannot partition tables vertically.

Conflict Resolution in Merge Replication

Performing updates to the same records at multiple locations causes conflicts. To resolve these conflicts, SQL Server 7 adds some tables and triggers to the distribution server. The system tables on the distributor track changes made to each row. The rows are differentiated by their ROWGUID, and a history or lineage of changes is recorded for each row involved in the merge.

Using this lineage, the merge agent evaluates the current values for a record and the new values and automatically resolves conflicts using triggers. You can create your own custom conflict resolution process by customizing and prioritizing the triggers.

When you begin to customize the conflict resolution process, we would suggest that you store both the record that is converged and the conflicting records that were not converged. This allows you to manually test and optimize your triggers. Note that creating and modifying triggers are beyond the scope of this book. For more information, see the SQL Server Books Online, or *MCSD: SQL Server 7 Database Design Study Guide* by Sybex.

Snapshot Replication

When you use snapshot replication, an entire copy of the publication is moved from the publisher to the subscriber. Everything on the subscriber database is overwritten, allowing for autonomy as well as transactional consistency as all changes are made at once. Latency can be high for this type of replication if you want it to be. You can schedule your refreshes when and as often as you wish (we have found that this normally occurs once a day, either in the early morning or after the workday has been completed). Keep in mind that snapshot replication occurs on demand. This means that no data is transferred from the publisher to the distributor until a subscriber is ready to receive it. The snapshot then moves straight through. Status information is stored in the Distribution database; however, the snapshot agent and the distribution agent do all their work at the time the snapshot is initiated.

When you use snapshot replication, there is no merge agent. The distribution agent is used. If you are using a pull replication, the distribution agent is found on the subscription server. If you are doing a push replication, the agent is found on the distributor. When used in a push scenario, snapshot replication consumes a large amount of overhead on the distribution server. We suggest that most snapshot subscribers use a pull scenario at regularly scheduled intervals. The following steps (see Figure 9.4) outline the snapshot replication process.

FIGURE 9.4

The snapshot replica-
tion process

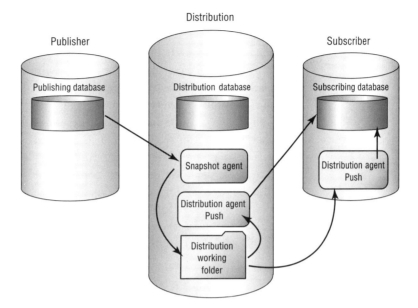

1. The snapshot agent reads the published article and then creates the table schema and data in the Distribution working folder.

2. The distribution agent creates the schema on the subscriber.

3. The distribution agent moves the data into the newly created tables on the subscriber.

4. Any indexes that were used are re-created on the newly synchronized subscription database.

This works in the same fashion when you are using snapshot replication with updating subscribers. The only difference is that the subscriber will use a two-phase commit to update both the subscription database and the publishing database at the same time. During the next refresh, all subscribers will receive a copy of the modified data.

Transactional Replication

When you use transactional replication, only the changes (transactions) made to the data are moved. Before these transactions can be applied at a subscriber however, the subscriber must have a copy of the data as a base. Because of its speed and its relatively low overhead on the distribution server, transactional replication is currently the most often used form of replication. Generally, data on the subscriber is treated as read-only, unless you are implementing transactional replication with updating subscribers. Because the transactions are so small, this type of replication is often set up to run continuously. Every time a change is made at the publisher, it is automatically applied to the subscriber, generally within one minute.

When you use transactional replication, there is no need for the merge agent. The snapshot agent must still run at least once; it uses the distribution agent to move the initial snapshot from the publisher to the subscriber. We also use the logreader agent when using transactional replication. The logreader agent looks for transactions in published databases and moves those transactions to the Distribution database. The following steps (illustrated in Figure 9.5) outline the transactional replication process.

FIGURE 9.5

The transactional replication process

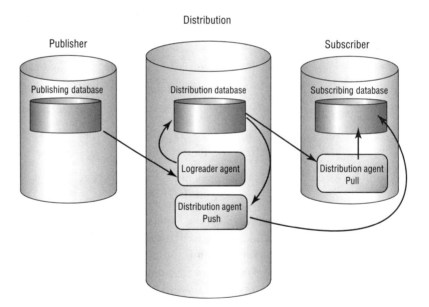

1. The snapshot agent reads the published article and then creates the schema on the subscriber and bulk-copies the snapshot over to the subscriber. (This is done only when the subscription is created or re-created.)

2. The logreader agent scans the transaction logs of databases marked for publishing. When it finds an appropriate transaction, it copies the transaction to the Distribution database. The Distribution database will store the transaction for a configurable length of time.

3. The distribution agent will then apply those transactions to the sub-scribers at the next synchronization. The subscriber then runs the sp_repldone system stored procedure on the distribution database. This marks the newly replicated transactions stored on the distributor in the Msrepl_commands table as completed.

4. When the next distribution cleanup task executes, the marked trans-actions are truncated from the distribution server.

Publication Considerations

Before you start your replication process, there are a few more things to consider. This includes data definition issues, IDENTITY column issues and some general rules that are involved when publishing. Keep the fol-lowing data definition items in mind when you are preparing to publish data:

Timestamp Datatypes A timestamp datatype is different than a date/time datatype. Timestamps are automatically updated to the current date and time whenever the record is inserted or updated. When they are rep-licated, they are changed to a binary datatype to ensure that the data from the publisher matches the data at the subscriber. If it was not altered, the timestamp will automatically update itself when the transaction is applied at the subscriber.

IDENTITY Identity values are replicated, but the IDENTITY column property is not. The identity values are copied and stored as integer datatypes—for the same reason that the timestamp is altered into a binary datatype.

UNIQUEIDENTIFIER The UNIQUEIDENTIFIER will create GUIDs that are used during merge replication. If you would like to use them your-self, you can set the default value of this column to the NEWID() function. This will automatically generate a ROWGUID. This is similar to the way that IDENTITY values are automatically generated.

User-defined Datatypes If you have created your own user-defined datatypes on the publishing server, you must also create those same datatypes on the subscriptions servers if you wish to replicate that particular column of data.

You should keep the following publishing restrictions in mind as well:

- If you are not using snapshot replication, your replicated tables must have a primary key to ensure transactional integrity.

- Publications cannot span multiple databases. All articles in a publication must be derived from a single database.

- IMAGE, TEXT, and NTEXT blobs are not replicated when you use transactional or merge replication. Because of their size, these objects must be refreshed by running a snapshot. What will be replicated is the 16-byte pointer to their storage location within the publishing database.

- You cannot replicate from the Master, Model, Msdb or Tempdb databases.

Replication Models

There are several different models you can use when you implement replication.

Microsoft ✓ Exam Objective

Develop a replication strategy.

- Given a scenario, design the appropriate replication model. Replication models include single Publisher and multiple Subscribers; multiple Publishers and single Subscriber; multiple Publishers and multiple Subscribers; and remote Distributor.

In the past, these models were referred to as:

- Central publisher
- Central publisher with a remote distributor
- Publishing subscriber
- Central subscriber
- Multiple publishers of one table

Let's look more closely at each of these and see what business situations they most accurately represent.

Central Publisher

As shown in Figure 9.6, both the Publishing database and the Distribution database are on the same SQL Server. This configuration is useful when modeling replication strategies for the following business scenarios:

- Asynchronous order processing during communication outages
- Distribution of price lists, customer lists, vendor lists, etc.
- Removal of MIS activities from the OLTP environment
- Establishment of executive information systems

Keep in mind that this model is analogous to the single publisher with multiple subscribers model. One of the most important aspects of the central publisher model is the ability to move data to a separate SQL Server. This allows the publishing server to continue to handle online transaction processing duties without having to absorb the impact of the ad hoc queries generally found in MIS departments.

You can use any type of replication here—transactional, merge, or snapshot. If you do not have to update blob objects like text, ntext, and image datatypes, we suggest that you use transactional replication here. MIS departments generally don't need to make changes to the subscribed data.

You can further reduce the impact of replication on your OLTP server by implementing pull subscriptions. This would force the distribution agent to run on each subscriber rather than on the OLTP publishing server.

F I G U R E 9.6

The central publisher
model

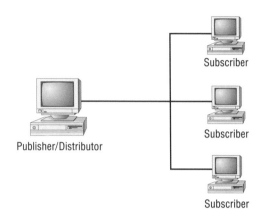

Central Publisher with a Remote Distributor

In this model, we remove the impact of the distribution process from our OLTP server, which gives us the best possible speed on the OLTP server. This model is useful in situations where you need the optimal performance out of your OLTP server. As discussed earlier, a single distribution server can work with multiple distributors and multiple subscribers. Figure 9.7 shows a representation of this strategy. The central publisher with a remote distributor is analogous to the new remote distribution model as shown in the exam objectives.

This calls for transactional replication and minimizing the impact of replication on the publishing database. By moving just transactions, rather than moving snapshots or attempting to merge data at the publisher, you can gain the most possible speed and have the lowest impact on the publisher.

F I G U R E 9.7

The central publisher
with a remote
distributor model

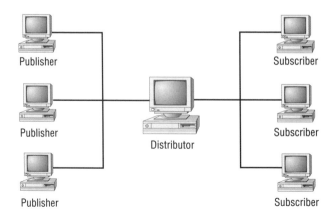

Publishing Subscriber

In the publishing subscriber model, the subscription server also acts as the distribution server. It will subscribe to the main publisher and then in turn publish the same data to other subscription servers. This is especially useful in the following business scenarios:

- Reduction of network traffic

- Reduction in communication costs over a slow or expensive link

This model can be most useful for a situation in which there is an expensive or slow communications link—transmitting data over phone lines for any length of time is not very cost-effective. With a publishing subscriber strategy, you can replicate data several times per day to a single subscriber. That subscriber can then in turn publish the same information to other SQL Servers, as shown in Figure 9.8. If you have offices in Albuquerque and London, you can reduce the long-distance communication expenses with a publishing subscriber model. The London office can then publish data to the more local Heathrow, Manchester, and Liverpool offices.

This model can be used in conjunction with any of the other models—both old models and those listed in the exam objective. It can use just about any type of replication. If the databases are small, but have frequent updates, it may be quicker to use snapshot replication and move all the data. If there are few transactions but large amounts of data, you would probably be better off using transactional replication in this scenario. You may also wish to use merge replication here, as data could be moving in both directions.

Central Subscriber

The central subscriber model shown in Figure 9.9 is very useful in the following situations:

- Roll-up reporting

- Local warehouse inventory management

- Local customer order processing

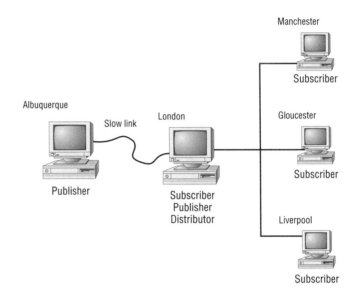

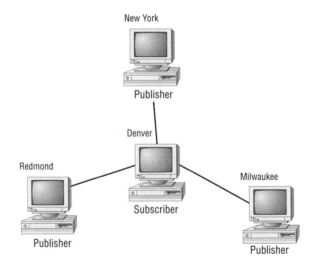

This model is analogous to the single subscriber with multiple publishers in the exam objective. You need to keep several things in mind when you attempt to use this model. Because multiple publishers are writing to a single table in the database, you must take some precautions to ensure that referential integrity is maintained. If your New York office sent an order with a key of 1000 and your Milwaukee office also sent an order with a key of 1000, you would have two records with the same primary key. You could get bad data in your database, as the primary key is designed to guarantee the uniqueness of each record. In this situation, only one of those records would post.

To make sure that this doesn't become a problem, implement a composite primary key, using the original order ID number along with a location-specific code. You could, for example, give New York a location code of NY and the Milwaukee branch a location code of MW. This way, the new composite keys would be NY1000 and MW1000. There would be no more conflicting records and both orders would be filled from the Denver offices.

This scenario is especially suited to transactional replication, as the data at the Denver site is really read-only. Snapshot replication wouldn't work here, because that would overwrite everyone else's data. You could use merge replication if the other locations needed to be able to see all the orders placed.

Multiple Publishers of One Table

This model is used when a single table needs to be maintained on multiple servers. Each server subscribes to the table and also publishes the table to other servers. This model can be particularly useful in the following business situations:

- Reservations systems

- Regional order-processing systems

- Multiple warehouse implementations

This older model is analogous to the newer multiple publishers and multiple subscribers model given in the exam objectives. Think of a regional order-processing system as shown in Figure 9.10. Suppose you place an order on Monday, and want to check on that order on Tuesday. When you call up, you may be routed to any of several regional order processing centers. Each of these centers should have a copy of your order so that you can go over the order with a salesperson.

FIGURE 9.10

Multiple publishers of
one table model

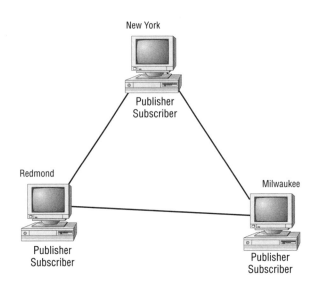

We suggest that you use transactional replication for this scenario, using some type of region code (as described in the Central Subscriber scenario). Each order processing center should publish only its own data, but it should subscribe to data being published by the other publishers. In addition, each location should update only the data it owns. This scenario is also a good candidate for the transactional replication with an updating subscriber model. In this case, each center could update data owned by another center; however, this update would take place at both servers and therefore maintain transactional consistency.

Replicating through the Internet and to Non-Microsoft SQL Server Databases

In addition to the replication scenarios already discussed, it is possible to replicate data to non-Microsoft SQL Server databases This is known as *heterogeneous database replication*. You can also replicate to databases across the Internet.

Heterogeneous Replication

Heterogeneous replication occurs when you publish to other databases through an ODBC or OLE-DB connection. In special cases, you can even use SQL Server 7 to subscribe to these ODBC and OLE-DB databases. Currently, SQL Server supports replication to Access and Oracle and IBM databases that conform to the IBM DRDA (Distributed Relational Database Architecture) data protocol. To replicate to an ODBC data source, the subscriber must meet the following ODBC driver requirements:

- Must run in 32-bit mode

- Must be thread-safe

- Must allow updates

- Must support the T-SQL DDL (Data Definition Language)

- Must fully support the ODBC Level 1 Conformance standard

When you publish to these ODBC subscribers, you need to keep the following rules in mind:

- Only push subscriptions are supported.

- ODBC does not support batched statements.

- The ODBC DSN (Data Source Name) must conform to the SQL Server naming conventions.

- Snapshot data will be sent using bulk copy's character format.

- Datatypes will be mapped as closely as possible.

Before you can subscribe to ODBC publishers, the publishers need to have an HDR (Host Data Replicator) program written. The HDR will use the SQL-DMO (SQL-Distributed Management Objects) to implement the functionality of the different replication agents necessary for SQL Server 7 to interact with the ODBC database. The SQL-DMO exposes several COM-based objects specific to replication.

Internet Replication

If you wish to enable your SQL Server to publish to the Internet, you must make some additional configuration changes to your SQL Server 7 computer. For either a push or pull style of replication, the following must be configured:

- TCP/IP must be installed on the computers where the merge agent and distribution agents are running.

- The publishing server and the distribution server should be on the same side of the firewall.

- The publishing server and the distribution server should have a direct network connection to each other (rather than a connection across the Internet). This is for both security and latency concerns.

Some additional configuration changes need to be made if you are going to allow pull subscriptions:

- Microsoft's IIS must be installed on the same server as your distribution server.

- Both the merge and distribution agents must be configured with the correct FTP address. This is done through the distribution agent or from a command prompt.

- The working folder must be available to your subscription servers.

- The FTP home folder on your IIS computer should be set to the Distribution working folder. This is normally \\ServerName\C$\MSSQL7\ ReplData.

For additional information on how to set up replication for the Internet, refer to the SQL Server Books Online.

Installing and Using Replication

In this section you will learn how to configure your servers for replication. You will then walk through the process of installing a distribution database, a publishing database, and a subscription database. You will finish this section by creating and then subscribing to an article and a publication.

Microsoft Exam Objective

Manage replication.

- Configure servers, including Distributor, Publisher, and Subscriber.
- Create publications.
- Set up and manage subscriptions.

To successfully install and enable replication, you must install a distribution server, create your publications, and then subscribe to them. Before any of this can take place, you must first configure your SQL Server.

> **NOTE** In order to install your replication scenario, you must be a member of the sysadmins fixed server role.

SQL Server Configuration

Before you can configure your SQL Server for replication, the computer itself must meet the following requirements:

- All servers involved with replication must be registered in the Enterprise Manager.

- The replication agents use the same Windows NT account that the SQL Server Agent uses. This account must have administrative rights and be a member of the Administrators group.

- The SQL Server Agent account must have the Log On As a Service advanced user right.

- If the servers are from different domains, trust relationships must be established before replication can occur.

- Any account that you use must have access rights to the Distribution working folder on the distribution server.

- The server must have a minimum of 32MB of RAM with 16MB allocated for SQL Server 7.

- You must enable access to the Distribution working folder on the distribution server. For an NT Server, this is the \\ServerName\C$\ MSSQL7\ReplData folder. On a Windows 95/98 computer, you must use the share name C$ for the defaults to operate properly. (The $ means that only accounts with administrative rights can access that particular share.)

We suggest that you use a single Windows NT Domain account for all of your SQL Server Agents. Do not use a LocalSystem account, as this account has no network capabilities and will therefore not allow replication.

Installing a Distribution Server

Because of the great amount of information that must be presented to you about the installation process, we will not be doing an exercise here. Rather, we will walk you—step-by-step—through the installation. This will be similar to an exercise, but with extra information, Please use the walkthrough as if it were an exercise.

1. Using Enterprise Manager, connect to your SQL Server.

2. Highlight your SQL Server and then choose Tools ➢ Replication ➢ Configure Publishing and Subscribers.

3. You are now presented with a Welcome screen (Figure 9.11). If you take a closer look at the Welcome screen you'll see that you can create your local computer as the distributor. Note: The SQL Server's name is Gambit. Click Next to continue.

4. You are now presented with the Choose Distributor screen (Figure 9.12). Here you will decide where the distribution server is going to be installed. Only SQL Servers that are already registered in the Enterprise Manager will be available from here.

Keep the following in mind when you choose your distributor:

- Ensure that you have enough hard-disk space for the Distribution working folder and the Distribution database.

- You must manage the Distribution database's transaction log carefully. If that log fills to capacity, replication will no longer run, which can adversely affect your publishing databases as well.

FIGURE 9.11

The Welcome screen

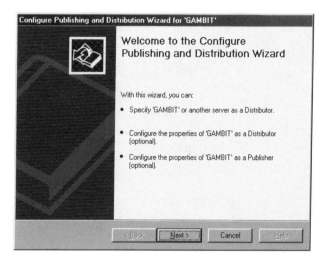

FIGURE 9.12

The Choose
Distributor screen

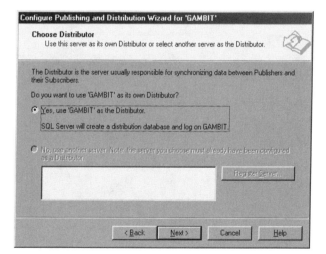

- The Distribution database will store all transactions from the publisher to the subscriber. It will also track when those transactions were applied.

- Snapshots and merge data are stored in the Distribution working folder.

- Be aware of the size and number of articles being published.

- Text, ntext, and image datatypes are replicated only when you use a snapshot.

- A higher degree of latency can significantly increase your storage space requirements

- Know how many transactions per synchronization cycle there are. For example, if you modify 8000 records between synchronizations, there will be 8000 rows of data stored on the distributor.

5. Leave the defaults and click Next to continue.

6. You can now decide whether you want to use all the default settings for your distributor. Under normal conditions, this is not a problem at all. Since we are seeing this for the first time, let's take a look at the customizable settings. Choose the Yes, Let Me… option as shown in Figure 9.13 and click Next to continue.

FIGURE 9.13

Use Default
Configuration screen

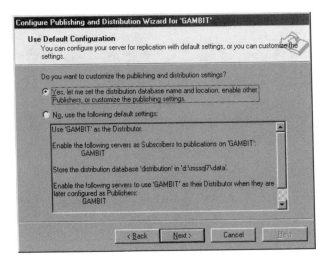

7. You are now presented with the Provide Distribution Database Information screen shown in Figure 9.14. You can supply a name for the Distribution database as well as location information for its database file and transaction log. Keep the defaults and click Next to continue.

F I G U R E   9.14

Provide Distribution
Database Information

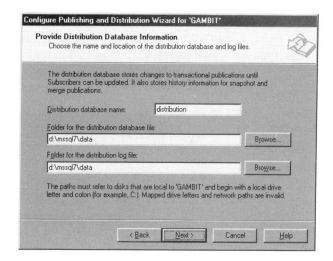

8. The Enable Publishers screen (Figure 9.15) shows all registered SQL
   Servers. You can pick and choose which servers you wish to configure
   as publishers. The ellipsis (...) allows you to specify security credentials such as login ID and password as well as the location of the
   snapshot folder. Be sure to place a checkmark next to your local SQL
   Server and then click Next to continue.

F I G U R E   9.15

Enable Publishers

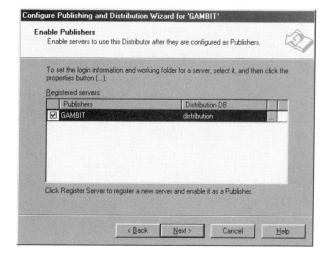

9. You are now looking at the Enable Publication Databases screen (Figure 9.16). You can select the databases on the newly enabled publisher from which you wish to allow publishing. Select the Northwind database checkbox for transactional replication (the Trans column) and then click Next to continue.

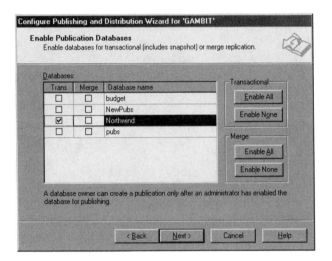

Before you can enable a publication database, you must be a member of the sysadmin fixed server role. Once you have enabled publishing, any member of that database's db_owner role can create and manage publications.

10. You are now presented with the Enable Subscribers screen shown in Figure 9.17. This is very similar to the Enable Publishers screen. For our example, we are going to use the same SQL Server for publishing, distribution, and subscribing. If you have additional SQL Servers, feel free to implement replication to them now.

If your server isn't listed here, you can click the Register button to register another Microsoft SQL Server computer. You must set up non-Microsoft SQL Servers through the Configure Publishing and Distribution screen.

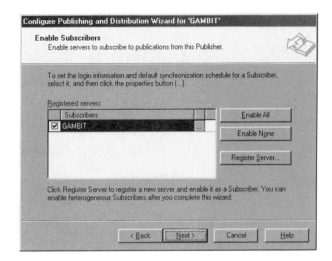

FIGURE 9.17

Enable Subscribers screen

11. Click the ellipsis to modify the security credentials of the subscription server.

12. You are now looking at the General tab of the Subscriber properties screen. Let's take a closer look at the Schedules tab shown in Figure 9.18.

13. As shown in Figure 9.18, you can specify the replication schedule for both the merge and distribution agents. The default for these values is Continuously, but you can set the schedule to anything you like (just as when creating and scheduling SQL Server jobs). Click OK to return to the Enable Subscribers screen.

14. Click Next to continue. You are now given a summary of the configuration options you have chosen. Click Finish to implement these configurations and enable the distribution server.

Now that you have successfully installed the Distribution database and distribution server you should see the Replication Monitor icon up in the Enterprise Manager console tree as shown in Figure 9.19.

FIGURE 9.18

The Schedules tab

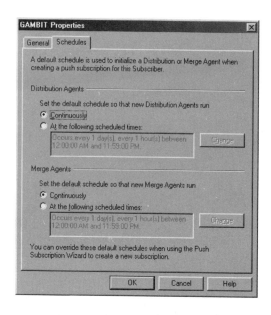

FIGURE 9.19

The Replication
Monitor icon in the
console tree

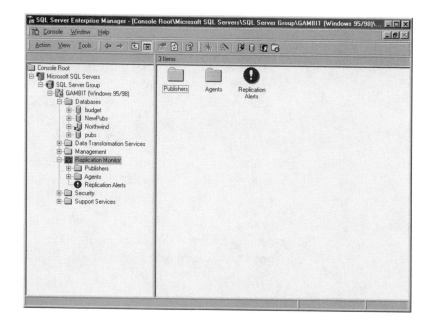

Adding a Publication

Now you can add a publication and articles to your server. When you add a new publication, you need to determine the type of replication that will be used, the snapshot requirements, and such subscriber options as updating or anonymous subscribers. You can also partition your data and decide whether you will allow push or pull subscriptions.

The Create Publication Wizard allows you to specify the following options:

- Number of articles
- Schedule for the snapshot agent
- Whether or not to maintain the snapshot on the distributor
- Tables and stored procedures you wish to publish
- Publications that will share agents
- Whether to allow updating subscribers
- Whether to allow pull subscriptions

Each publication will use a separate publishing agent by default. This option can be overridden.

In the following walkthrough, you will create a new publication based on the Categories table in the Northwind database. You will then replicate this table to the Pubs database as rtblCategories.

1. Connect to your SQL Server in the Enterprise Manager. If you expand the Databases folder (shown in Figure 9.19), you will now see a hand on the Northwind database icon. This indicates that the database has been marked for replication.

2. Highlight the Northwind database and then go to Tools ➤ Replication ➤ Create and Manage Publications. You will now be presented with the Create and Manage Publications dialog box shown in Figure 9.20.

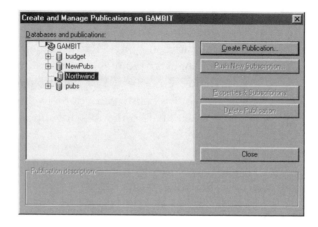

3. Highlight the Northwind database and click Create Publication.

4. The Create Publication Wizard now starts with a welcome screen. Click Next to continue.

5. You can now specify what type of publication you wish to create— Snapshot, Transactional, or Merge. For our example, select Transactional as shown in Figure 9.21 and click Next to continue.

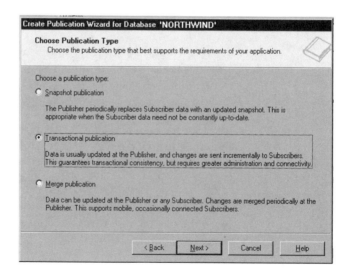

Transactional replication on the Desktop edition of SQL Server running on Windows 95/98 is supported as subscriber only. This is because the server-side network libraries for Named Pipes are required for this type of replication and are not available on Windows 95/98. Windows 95/98 Named Pipes on the client side is supported however.

6. You can now specify whether or not you wish to enable updating subscribers (Figure 9.22). As you might recall, updating a subscriber makes changes at both the subscription server and the publishing server, using a two-phase commit. Either both servers are updated or neither of them is. For this example, keep the default No, Do Not Allow... and click Next to continue.

F I G U R E   9.22

Allow Immediate-Updating Subscriptions screen

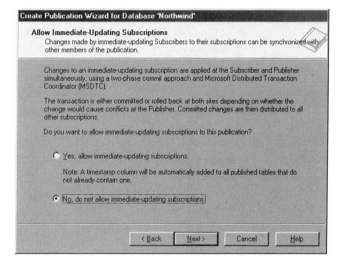

7. Figure 9.23 shows the Specify Subscriber Types screen. When we were working on the Distribution database installation, you learned that you could specify only Microsoft SQL Servers as subscribers. Although you can enable non-Microsoft SQL Servers as subscribers from here, we are not going to do that in this walkthrough. Leave the default All Subscribers Will Be... and click Next to continue.

FIGURE 9.23

Specify Subscriber
Types screen

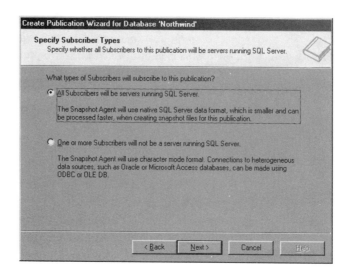

8. Here you can determine which tables you wish to publish from. In essence, you are creating your articles. Click the checkbox next to the Categories table as shown in Figure 9.24.

FIGURE 9.24

Specify Articles screen

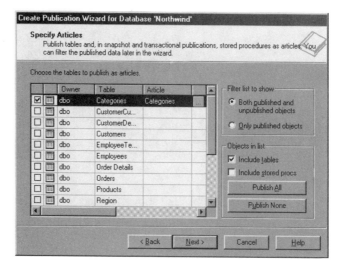

9. As you can see in Figure 9.24, selecting an article creates the ellipsis button. Click the ellipsis.

10. You are now presented with the Categories Properties pages. The General tab (Figure 9.25) allows you to specify the Article Name, a Description, the Destination Table Name and Destination Table Owner. Change the Destination Table Name to `rtblCategories` and be sure to specify the owner as dbo as shown in Figure 9.25.

F I G U R E 9.25

Categories Properties
Pages

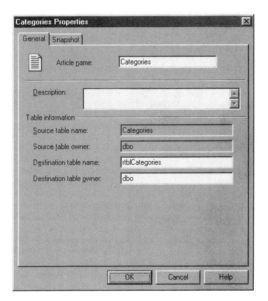

11. The Snapshot tab allows you to specify what will happen during the snapshot process. Will you drop the existing table? Will you truncate the data in it? Leave the default options and click OK to return to the Specify Articles screen. Once back at the Specify Articles screen, click Next to continue.

12. You are now presented with the Choose Publication Name and Description screen. Note that the Publication Name has been changed to Northwind_Categories. When you are finished you should have something similar to Figure 9.26. Click Next to continue.

F I G U R E 9.26

Choose Publication
Name and Description
screen

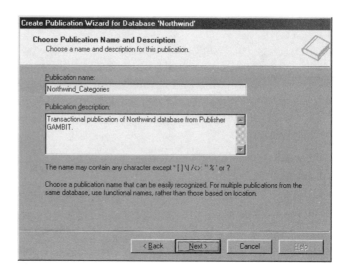

13. You now see the Use Default Properties of the Publication dialog box as shown in Figure 9.27. From here you can accept the default filtering and partitioning options, or you can customize them. Although we will not make changes to these options, let's take a look at them. Click the Yes, I Will Define… option and then click Next to continue.

F I G U R E 9.27

Use Default Properties
of the Publication
screen

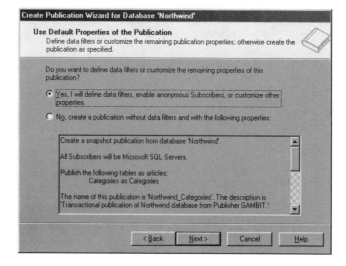

14. When you see the Filter Data screen, you can choose to filter your data or to leave it alone. Click the Yes, I Want to… option, then click Next to continue.

15. From the Filter Table Columns screen shown in Figure 9.28, you can select which columns you wish to exclude from your replication. Click Next to continue.

F I G U R E   9.28

Filter Table Columns
screen

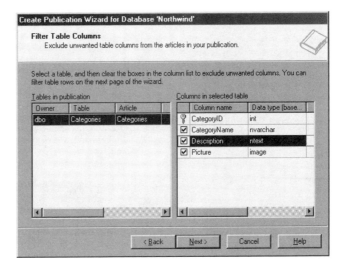

16. You can now filter the rows as shown in Figure 9.29. If you click on the ellipsis, you can create a new filter by filling in a Where clause as shown in Figure 9.30. When you are finished, click Next to continue.

17. You are now asked whether or not you wish to allow anonymous subscribers. If you have many subscribers, or you are allowing subscriptions across the Internet, you may wish to allow anonymous subscribers. Anonymous subscribers reduce some of the administration of your replication. Note, however, that this choice does not compromise security. Leave the default No, Only Known… and click Next to continue.

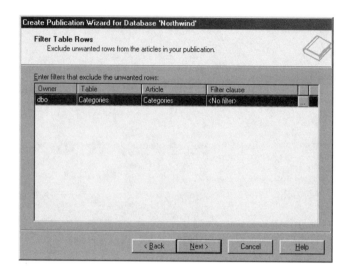

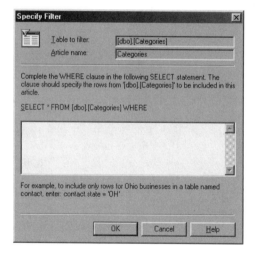

18. You are now presented with the Set Snapshot Agent Schedule screen. Remember that before replication can begin, a snapshot of your data must be moved to the subscriber to set a baseline for all future replication. Click the checkbox to indicate that you want the subscriber to create the first snapshot immediately, as shown in Figure 9.31. Click the Change button to set up your snapshot schedule. A snapshot schedule (formerly referred to as a *scheduled table refresh*) is useful when you have non-logged operations running on the publisher. If an operation is not logged, it won't be replicated. This can come in handy if you are replicating, text, ntext, or image datatypes. Click Next to continue.

F I G U R E   9.31

Set Snapshot Agent
Schedule screen

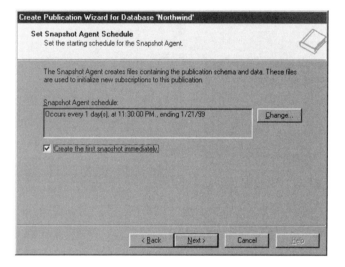

19. You are now at the Finish screen. You can review the options you have chosen and, when you are ready, click Finish to complete the creation of your publication. After some processing takes place, you will return to the Create and Manage Publications screen shown in Figure 9.20 but with changes: Your new publication—Northwind_Categories—should be listed.

20. From here, you can push this publication to subscribers or you can look over its properties and subscriptions by clicking the Properties & Subscriptions button. When you do this, you will see much of the information you entered displayed in a set of pages as shown in Figure 9.32. When you are finished, click OK to return to the Create and Manage Publications screen.

F I G U R E 9.32

Northwind_Categories
Properties screen

21. From the Create and Manage Publications screen, you can also delete your publications. Click Close to finish.

Creating a Subscription

As part of the process of creating a subscription, you will be able to specify the publishers you wish to subscribe to and a destination database to receive the published data, verify your security credentials, and set up a default schedule.

1. We are going to create a pull subscription in this example. Connect to your SQL Server and then highlight the Server and choose Tools ➤ Replication ➤ Pull Subscription to Your ServerName.

2. You are now looking at the Pull Subscription to ServerName as shown in Figure 9.33. In the rest of the examples, the ServerName is Gambit and will be reflected in the Figures and the steps.

3. Click on the Pubs database and then click Pull Subscription.

4. As always, you are presented with a welcome screen. Click Next to continue.

FIGURE 9.33

Pull Subscription to
Gambit screen

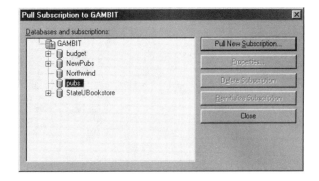

5. You can now see a list of publishers. By expanding the publishers, you can see the publications that they have made available. If you do not see your publishing server here, you can click the Register Server button to register another server. Expand your server and then click on the Northwind_Categories publication as shown in Figure 9.34. Click Next to continue.

FIGURE 9.34

Choose Publication
screen

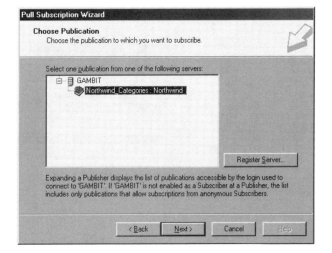

6. You must now specify the security credentials that your Synchronization agent will use for the synchronization process. Fill in **sa** and no password as shown in Figure 9.35. Click Next to continue.

FIGURE 9.35

Specify Synchroniza-
tion Agent Login
screen

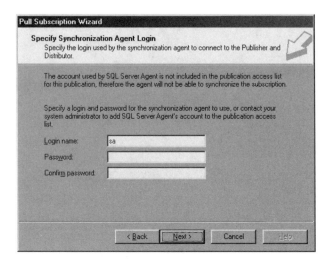

FIGURE 9.35

Specify Synchroniza-
tion Agent Login
screen

7. You must now choose your destination database. Since we clicked on the Pubs database at the beginning of this walkthrough, it should default there. If it doesn't, select it now as shown in Figure 9.36. Click Next to continue.

FIGURE 9.36

Choose Destination
Database screen

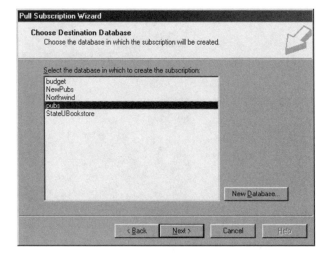

8. If the schema and tables don't already exist at the subscriber, they must be initialized there. Take the default value as shown in Figure 9.37 and click Next to continue.

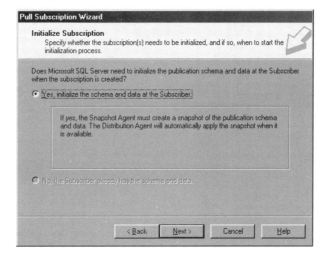

9. You can now set the synchronization schedule. For snapshots, it might be wise to set up some type of regular schedule. For merge replication, you will most likely use a manual form of synchronization called *on demand*. Since we are using transactional replication, select Continuously as shown in Figure 9.38. Click Next to continue.

10. You are now looking at the Start Required Services screen. Because all your agents use the SQLServerAgent service to interact with the various servers, the SQLServerAgent must be running. If it is not, click the checkbox to force the service to start (Figure 9.39). Once you have it running, click Next to continue.

11. You are now at the Finish screen again. As with other screens of this type, you can review your subscription. When you are satisfied, click Finish to create the subscription.

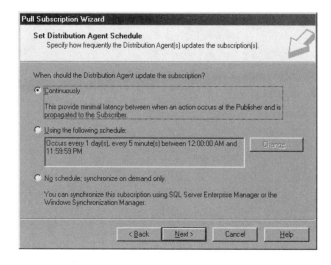

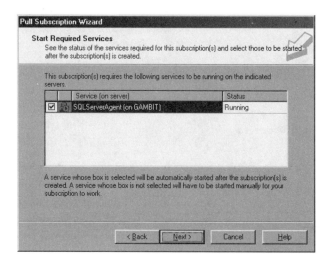

12. You should now be back at the Pull Subscription to Gambit screen, but this time your subscription should be displayed as shown in Figure 9.40. Here too, you can choose your subscription and look at its Properties pages as shown in Figure 9.41. You can also delete the subscription or reinitialize it. When you are finished, click Close.

F I G U R E   9.40

Pull Subscriptions to
Gambit screen

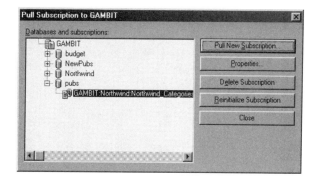

F I G U R E   9.41

Pull Subscription
Properties Pages

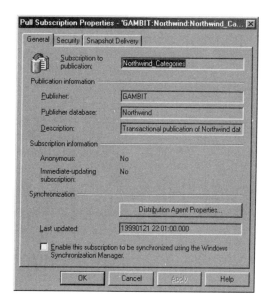

13. If you expand your Pubs database folder, you will notice that there is now a Pull Subscriptions folder in it. There is also a Publications folder under the Northwind database as shown in Figure 9.42. You can highlight these items and then double-click the publication or subscription in the right pane for additional information about them.

F I G U R E 9.42

Publications and Sub-
scriptions are shown
in their own folders
under the appropriate
database.

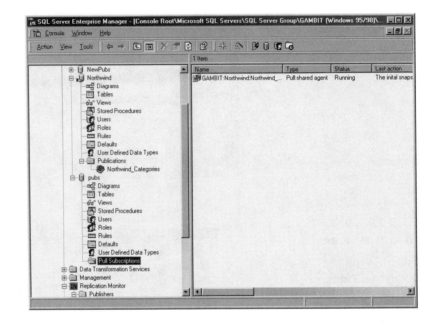

14. Although replication was supposed to begin immediately, it won't in
this case, as we created first a pull subscription and now a push subscription. Let's do a manual synchronization to get the process rolling.
In the next section, we will test our replication.

15. Expand the Pubs database and then highlight the Subscriptions folder.
You should see your subscription in the details pane.

16. Right-click the subscription and choose Synchronize Now if the text
next to the icon doesn't specify that it has been synchronized already.

Testing Replication

We can now verify that replication is running properly. In the following
steps, we will check for the initial snapshot synchronization. We will then
add some data to the Categories table and then review the data in the rtbl-
Categories table to make sure that it was replicated. Follow these steps to test
replication.

1. Connect to your database and expand the Databases folder and then the Pubs database. Click on the Tables icon. You should see the rtbl-Categories table in the details pane as shown in Figure 9.43. If you do not, you may need to refresh the tables. To do this, right-click on the Tables icon and choose Refresh from the context menu.

FIGURE 9.43

The rtblCategories table is now in the Pubs database.

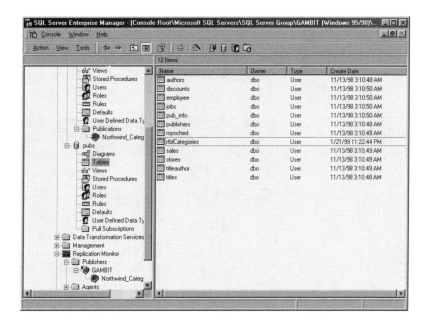

2. Now let's check our data. Open the Query Analyzer and specify the Pubs database. Run the following query to verify that there is data in the rtblCategories table.

```
SELECT * FROM rtblCategories
GO
```

3. You should have eight records returned to you. Now let's add a new record to the Categories table in the Northwind database and verify that the record has been replicated properly. Run the following code to add a new record.

```
USE Northwind
GO
INSERT INTO Categories
VALUES("Beer", "Beers of the World", "")
GO
```

4. You should get the message that one row was added. Give the server about a minute to catch up and move and apply the transaction; then run the following query:

```
USE pubs
GO
SELECT * FROM rtblCategories
GO
```

5. You should get nine records back. The last record should be the Beers of the World record as shown in Figure 9.44.

F I G U R E 9.44

Successful replication

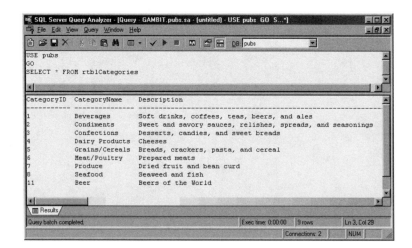

Managing Replication

Managing and maintaining replication can be very intensive work for an administrator. Microsoft SQL Server 7 has included many tools in the Replication Monitor to make this job a lot easier. Before we look at the various tools and methodologies, let's look at some of the administrative issues you should consider.

Administrative Considerations

This section provides some tips for optimizing your replication as well as some tips to minimize your administrative duties:

- Use a remote distributor to minimize the impact of replication on your publishing servers.

- Use pull subscriptions to off-load the work from the distributors to each subscriber.

- Use updating subscribers rather than merge replication if possible.

- Replicate only the data you need. Use filters to partition your data.

- Keep in mind that replication increases network traffic. Make sure your network can handle it.

- Use primary keys on replicated tables to ensure entity integrity.

- Using the same SQLServerAgent Domain account for all servers involved in replication will minimize the impact of administering security issues.

- Ensure that replication jobs and their agents are running smoothly. Check the agent histories and logs periodically.

- Create and monitor replication alerts.

- Ensure that the Distribution database and the Distribution working folder have enough space and that they have the appropriate permissions assigned to them.

- Develop a recovery and resynchronization plan. You can use replication scripts for version control as well as a huge part of the recovery process.

- When developing your replication strategy, try snapshot replication first, as it is the most straightforward form of replication. Once you have successfully installed snapshot replication, begin experimenting with transactional and then move on to merge replication.

- Keep a valid backup of the Distribution database and make sure that the database and log do not fill to capacity.

WARNING It is essential that the Distribution database and log do not fill to capacity. When this database or log fills to capacity, it can no longer receive publication information. When this occurs, the logged transactions at the publisher cannot be removed from the log (unless you disable publishing). Over time, your Publishing database's transaction log will also fill to capacity, and you will no longer be able to make data modifications.

Replication Backup Considerations

When you perform backups of your replication scenario, you can make backups of just the publisher, the publisher and distributor, the publisher and subscriber, or all three. Each of the strategies has its own advantages and disadvantages. The following list highlights these distinctions.

Publisher Only   This strategy requires the least amount of resources and computing time, since the backup of the publisher does not have to be coordinated with any other server backups to stay synchronized. The disadvantage is that restoration of a publisher or distributor is a slow and time-consuming process.

Publisher and Distributor   This strategy accurately preserves the publication as well as the errors, history, and replication agent information from the distributor. You can recover quickly as there is no need to reestablish replication. The disadvantages of this strategy are the coordination of the backups and the amount of storage and computing time necessary to perform a simultaneous backup.

Publisher and Subscriber(s)   This strategy significantly reduces the recovery time by removing the initialization process (running a snapshot). The main disadvantages of this strategy manifest themselves when you have multiple subscribers. Every subscriber will have to be backed up and restored.

Publisher, Distributor and Subscriber(s)   This strategy preserves all of the complexity of your replication model. The disadvantages are storage space and computing time. This scenario also requires the most time for recovery.

Using the Replication Monitor

You can administer your publishers, subscribers, and publications as well as the different replication agents through the Replication Monitor utility. You can look at agent properties and histories and even set replication alerts.

The replication monitor resides on the computer where the distribution server has been installed and gathers replication information about the different replication agents. This includes the agent history with information about inserts, updates, deletes, and any other transactions that were processed. Through the monitor you can also edit the various schedules and properties of the replication agents.

Follow these steps to work with the various agents:

1. Open the Enterprise Manager on the SQL Server where the distribution server was installed.

2. Expand the Replication Monitor icon, then the Agents folder and finally, highlight the Snapshot Agent as shown in Figure 9.45.

F I G U R E 9.45

The Snapshot Agent in the Replication Monitor

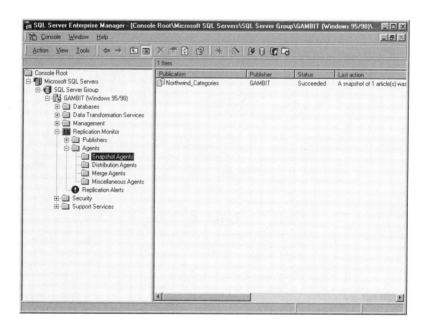

3. If you right-click Northwind_Categories in the details pane, you will see that you can view the Agent history, properties, and profile. You can also start or stop the agent. There are options to modify the refresh rate and choose the columns to view. Right-click and choose Agent History.

4. You are now presented with the Agent History as shown in Figure 9.46. You can filter the list to show information based on all sessions; sessions in the last 7 days, the last 2 days, the last 24 hours; or sessions with errors. You can also look at the Agent Profile and its settings as well as the Monitor Settings. The Monitor Settings allow you to specify how often the items in the replication monitor will be refreshed.

FIGURE 9.46

Snapshot Agent History screen

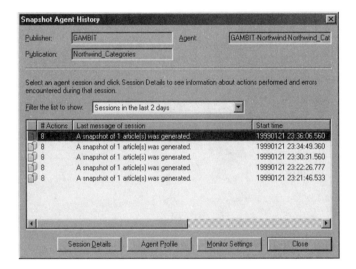

You can look at the details of a particular session, as shown in Figure 9.47. Session details include information about all the different processes that took place during the session.

5. Close the Agent History. Right-click on Northwind_Categories and choose Agent Properties. You are now looking at the Properties sheets (Figure 9.48). These operate in the same fashion as the scheduled jobs that you have already worked with. When you are finished browsing, close the Agent History.

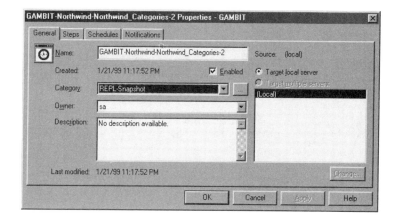

The other agents provide similar information. The history keeps track of everything that has happened during the replication. After a successful log is read and moved to the distributor and the subscriber pulls the transaction, the distribution server needs to be cleaned up. Once a transfer has been successfully completed, a cleanup job will run.

There is at least one cleanup job for every subscriber. In other words, if you have 20 subscribers to your database, you will have at least 20 cleanup jobs on the distributor. If you click on the Miscellaneous Agents folder in the console tree you will see some of the cleanup jobs that have been created (shown in Figure 9.49). These are explained below.

F I G U R E 9.49

Miscellaneous Agents'
clean up jobs

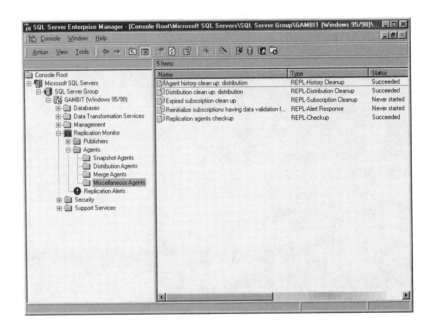

Agent History Clean up: Distribution   This job cleans up the historical information in the Distribution Agents History tables after they have aged out.

Distribution Clean up: Distribution   This job cleans up the distributor by removing transactions from the Distribution database after they have aged out.

Expired Subscription Clean up   This job removes expired subscription information from the Subscription database.

Reinitialize Subscriptions Having Data Validation Failures   This job reinitializes all subscriptions that failed because of problems with data validation.

Replication Agents Checkup This job watches for replication agents that are not actively adding information to their history logs.

Working with Replication Scripts

Now that you have replication set up and working properly, you may wish to save all your hard work in the form of a replication script. Scripting your replication scenario has the following advantages:

- You can use the scripts to track different versions of your replication implementation

- You can use the scripts with some minor tweaking to create additional subscribers and publishers with the same basic options

- You can quickly customize your environment by making modifications to the script and then rerunning it.

- Scripts can be used as part of your database recovery process

Let's do another walkthrough and create some replication scripts for our current setup.

1. Highlight your server in the console tree and then choose Tools ➤ Replication ➤ Generate Replication Scripts.

2. You are now presented with the Generate SQL Scripts pages as shown in Figure 9.50. You can script the distributor and the publications for the various replication items stored with this distribution server. The File Options tab allows you to save your script to several different file types. The default storage location for your scripts is C:\MSSQL7\Install. This particular folder holds many other scripts that are used to create and install your SQL Server and several databases.

3. The Preview button allows you to view the scripts themselves, as shown in Figure 9.51.

4. When you are finished viewing the scripts, click Close. You can now close the replication scripting property pages.

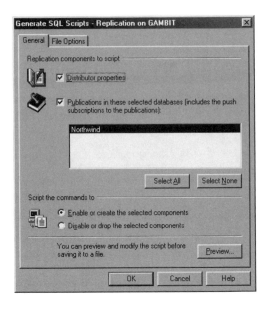

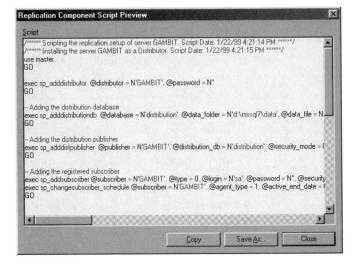

Replication of Stored Procedures

As you saw in Figure 9.51, there are many stored procedures that are used to create and install replication on your computer. Here is a short list of stored procedures that you will most likely use to gather administrative information about your SQL Server replication configuration:

sp_helpdistributor   This gathers information about the Distribution database, the distributor, the working directory and the SQLServerAgent user account.

sp_helpdistributiondb   This gathers information about the Distribution database, its files, and their location as well as information regarding the distribution history and log.

sp_helppublication   This gathers publication information and configuration options.

sp_helpsubscription   This gathers information associated with a particular article, publication, subscriber, or set of subscriptions.

sp_helpsubscriberinfo   This gathers information about the configuration setting of a subscriber, including information regarding frequency of the subscription, retry delays, and much more.

Replication and Performance Counters

Replication also exposes many new and useful performance counters that can be used in your optimization efforts. As you recall, performance counters are grouped into performance objects and are used in the SQL Server Performance Monitor With all of these new performance counters, you can track how effective your replication strategies are and then fine-tune your scenario.

Summary

Replication is used to distribute data to other database engines in your enterprise. With SQL Server 7, you can reduce the impact of OLAP operations from your OLTP environment using replication strategies. SQL Server 7 also supports replication to and from non-SQL Server databases through the Host Data Replicator.

Replication in SQL Server can be done in real-time using two-phase commit and the MS-DTC, or in real-enough time, which involves some latency between updates to a publisher and when the subscriber receives the data.

Microsoft SQL Server uses a publisher/subscriber metaphor for the distribution of data. Publishers disseminate data in the form of a publication that is further subdivided into articles. The actual transfer of data occurs through the distributor. Subscribers can subscribe and read publications and individual articles. Articles can be stored procedures, a full table, or a partitioned table. Tables can be partitioned vertically or horizontally. Vertical partitions replicate only certain columns; horizontal partitions replicate certain rows of data.

Autonomy, latency, and transactional consistency must be considered when you are developing a distribution type. These factors allow you to distribute data using distributed transactions, transactional replication with or without updating subscribers, snapshot replication with or without updating subscribers, and merge replication.

Each of these styles has certain advantages and disadvantages. You should pick the distribution type that most closely matches your business needs. Remember that when you allow updating subscribers, you must have excellent network connectivity as the subscribers use 2PC to make changes at the subscriber and the publisher simultaneously.

Merge replication allows for great autonomy and latency; however, your transactional consistency is in question until records are converged and conflicts resolved. You should attempt to minimize conflicts by partitioning your data based on a type code, such as region or salesperson ID. Conflicts are resolved using triggers located on the distribution server. You can modify these triggers to customize your conflict resolution scheme.

To do all of the moving and management of your data, Microsoft has created several agents. These include the logreader agent, the distribution agent, the snapshot agent, and the merge agent. These agents reside on different servers, depending on whether you are using a pull or a push subscription.

When you decide to publish, you should remember that replication treats user-defined datatypes, Identity and UniqueIdentifier, and timestamp columns a bit differently than you might expect. In general, these columns will be converted when they are replicated. You should also keep in mind that non-logged operations are not replicated except through a snapshot. This means that if you make changes to text, ntext, or image columns, these columns will be replicated only when you schedule a snapshot to refresh your tables.

There are several different replication models you can choose from in order to optimize and suit your business needs. These include the central publisher, the central publisher with a remote distributor, the publishing subscriber, the central subscriber and the multiple publishers of one table. You should be familiar with each of these models and which business scenarios each one satisfies.

You can replicate to heterogeneous environments; this requires the creation of an HDR (Host Data Replicator). The best way to accomplish this is to use the SQL-DMO. This exposes COM objects that allow you to programmatically create the various agents SQL Server needs to support replication. When you create your HDR, it must conform to the ODBC Level 1 conformance standard.

When you replicate to the Internet, you need to use TCP/IP, and you should keep both the publisher and the distributor directly connected on the same side of your firewall. You will also have to supply an FTP address for your Distribution working folder. By default, that name is \\ServerName\C$\MSSQL7\ReplData.

Before you can use replication, you must configure your SQL Server to handle it. This means ensuring that you have the right hardware, the right amount of RAM, and the right security credentials for your SQLServerAgent. Once that is accomplished, you install your distributor and specify the Distribution working folder. You can then the publisher and subscriber and create and manage publications and articles.

There are many administrative issues to keep in mind when you are working with replication. This includes the data definition that you will be performing, monitoring and tuning replication, scheduling synchronization, performing backups of the Distribution database, etc.

Most of your replication administration can be handled through the Replication Monitor on the distribution server. Through the monitor, you can add articles and publications, publishers, and subscribers. You can view the various agent profiles and their associated histories. You can generate replication scripts that you can use to create additional subscribers, or re-create your entire replication scenario.

While there are volumes of replication-specific stored procedures, you will most likely work with the short list provided in this chapter. Once you have replication installed and running, take a look at these stored procedures and test them out. You can gather valuable information about subscribers and publishers, a particular article and much more.

You can also tune and optimize replication by taking advantage of the various performance objects and the associated counters that replication exposes in the SQL Server Performance Monitor.

Review Questions

1. Which of the following computers stores the original data?

   A. Publisher

   B. Subscriber

   C. Distributor

   D. Replication

2. You are using transactional replication to move data from a central server to more than a dozen subscribers. Some of the subscribers are allowed to update the publisher as well as themselves. What protocol are the subscribers using through the Microsoft Distributed Transaction Coordinator to accomplish this task?

   A. TCP/IP

   B. IPX/SPX

   C. Two-phase commit

   D. Named Pipes

3. SQL Server 7 uses a publisher/subscriber metaphor to implement its replication design. As a publisher, you have made several articles available within several publications. To which of the following may authorized subscribers subscribe?

   A. The publisher

   B. The articles

   C. The publications

   D. None of the above

4. You are thinking about implementing replication at your business. As you begin to develop your replication strategy, you need to think about several different factors. Which of the following are the three most common factors that influence your decisions about the type of replication you will perform?

 A. Autonomy

 B. Geographic distance

 C. Latency

 D. Transactional consistency

5. You have set up replication from a single publisher with multiple subscribers. When changes are made at the publisher, these changes are made at exactly the same time on all of the subscribers. This type of distribution has no latency, little autonomy, and high transactional consistency. Which of the following distribution types was described?

 A. Transactional replication

 B. Snapshot replication

 C. Merge replication

 D. Distributed transactions

6. You have set up replication from a single publisher with multiple subscribers. When changes are made at the publisher, these changes are stored in a distribution database before being forwarded to the subscribers. This type of distribution has low latency, moderate autonomy, and moderate transactional consistency. Which of the following distribution types was described?

 A. Transactional replication

 B. Snapshot replication

 C. Merge replication

 D. Distributed transactions

7. You have set up replication from a single publisher with multiple subscribers. You have a number of image and text fields that are being constantly updated, along with the rest of the data. Which of the following distribution types would have the least impact on the various databases involved in the replication scenario, but still maintain moderate transactional consistency?

   A. Transactional replication throughout the day and a snapshot replication once in the evening

   B. Merge replication throughout the day and a snapshot replication once in the evening

   C. Snapshot replication the whole time

   D. Distributed transactions

8. Which type of replication will overwrite all data in the subscribed tables at the subscriber?

   A. Transactional replication

   B. Snapshot replication

   C. Merge replication

   D. Distributed transactions

9. You have many salespeople who carry laptops with them on business. You want some way for the salespeople to take orders as well as receive updates to their price lists. In order for your salespeople to keep track of what other salespeople might have quoted for a particular item, they also need to know what the other salespeople have done. In addition, a salesperson might need to add or remove items from the quote. The databases are to be updated nightly, but sometimes this is impossible and there may be a lag of as much as three days between synchronizations. Which type of replication would be best suited to this business situation?

   A. Transactional replication for the price lists and the quotes

   B. Snapshot replication for the price lists and merge replication for the quotes

  C. Merge replication for both the price lists and the quotes

  D. Transactional replication for the price lists and merge replication for the quotes

10. You are using transactional replication with a dozen subscribers. Each subscriber is using a pull subscription. Which of the following is true of the replication agents?

  A. The logreader agent and the distribution agent are on each of the subscribers

  B. The logreader agent is on the publishing server and the distribution agent is on the distribution server

  C. The logreader agent is on the distribution server and the distribution agent is on each of the subscribers

  D. The logreader agent is on each of the subscribers and the distribution agent is on the distribution server

11. Which of the following agents is responsible for converging your records?

  A. Logreader agent

  B. Snapshot agent

  C. Merge agent

  D. Distribution agent

12. You have decided to use merge replication to address your business needs. Which of the following is true?

  A. System tables will be added to the Distribution working folder and the distribution database

  B. Triggers will be created on the publishing and subscription servers

  C. Vertical partitioning will not be allowed

  D. A UNIQUEIDENTIFIER column is added for each table involved in the merge replication

13. Which of the following is true regarding replication?

   A. Other than snapshot replication, replicated tables must have a primary key to ensure referential integrity

   B. Publications can span multiple databases

   C. Blobs can be replicated using transactional replication

   D. You cannot replicate the Master, Model, Msdb, or Tempdb database

14. You have decided to use transactional replication to remove the impact of MIS on your OLTP server. Which of the following replication scenarios accomplishes this?

   A. Central publisher (single publisher with multiple subscribers)

   B. Central subscriber (single subscriber with multiple publishers)

   C. Publishing subscriber

   D. Multiple publishers of one table

15. You want to use replication to distribute data from the home office in Sacramento to your satellite offices in München, Hamburg, and Köln. What type of replication would be the most cost-effective, given the slow and expensive modem links?

   A. Central publisher (single publisher with multiple subscribers)

   B. Central subscriber (single subscriber with multiple publishers)

   C. Publishing subscriber

   D. Multiple publishers of one table

16. You have several regional offices that need to update central headquarters throughout the day. Which of the following replication models would be the most effective?

   A. A central publisher model (single publisher with multiple subscribers) that uses a RegionCode as part of the primary key

B. A central subscriber model (single subscriber with multiple publishers) that uses a RegionCode as part of the primary key

C. A publishing subscriber model that uses a LocationID as part of the primary key

D. Multiple publishers of one table using LocationIDs for the primary key

17. You have a reservation system that does not need to be running in real time. Up to 30 minutes of latency fits your business needs. You have decided to use replication with a LocationID as part of the primary key. In addition, you have stipulated that each location can only replicate its own data. Which replication strategy is best suited to your business?

A. Central publisher (single publisher with multiple subscribers)

B. Central subscriber (single subscriber with multiple publishers)

C. Publishing subscriber

D. Multiple publishers of one table

18. You currently have an Informix database that you want to be a subscriber to a Microsoft SQL Server 7 computer. In order to replicate to your Informix database, ODBC drivers will connect the database with the SQL Server. Which of the following is true when you try to replicate from SQL Server to Informix over the ODBC connection?

A. Only push subscriptions are supported

B. The connection must be made in a thread-safe 32-bit mode and support Transact-SQL's DDL

C. Data is always mapped as char or varchar

D. Only pull subscriptions are supported

19. You want to view the history of replications that have taken place at a particular subscriber. That subscriber uses a push subscription to gather its data. In addition, the data is transferred throughout the day using transactional replication. Once a week there is a scheduled snapshot replication run to refresh all the replicated data. Which of the following will allow you to view the history of snapshots applied to the subscriber?

A. Use the replication monitor on the distribution server to view the snapshot agent history

B. Use the replication monitor on the subscription server to view the snapshot agent history

C. Use the replication monitor on the distribution server to view the distribution agent history

D. Use the replication monitor on the subscriber to view the distribution agent history

20. You have a central publisher with a remote distributor set up as part of your replication scenario. You have 12 subscribers using pull subscriptions for transactional replication. You also have two additional subscribers doing merge replication. How many cleanup jobs are there on the remote distributor?

A. None; all cleanup jobs run on the publisher

B. 2

C. 12

D. 14

21. You have roughly 40 SQL Server 7 computers located throughout your enterprise. You want to set up subscription servers on about 35 of these computers. The subscriptions will all be to the same articles and publications and may have to occasionally make changes to the published data. You have decided to create the distribution server on its own stand-alone machine to reduce the impact of 35 subscribers on your publishing database. Because of the fairly light network traffic and the speed at which you need this data to be transferred to the subscribers, you have also chosen to use transactional replication with updating subscribers. In order to implement this design quickly, you have created a single subscriber and its related subscriptions. You then create a replication script. You will now tweak the replication script by changing computer names and distribute them to the other subscribers so that they can be set up in the same fashion. How would you rate this solution?

A. Excellent, and all facets will work

B. Good, but one facet won't work

C. Poor, but most facets will work

D. Horrible; none of it will work

22. You are using merge replication where a central publisher makes data available for five subscribers. A subscriber makes modifications to a record at 10:30 A.M. The publisher makes modifications to the same record at 11:02 A.M. The records are converged at 12:00 P.M. and then sent back to the clients. Which of the following is true?

A. This record will not be converged

B. Each subscriber will have its own unique version of the modified record

C. The subscriber's modification of the record will be converged to all of the other subscribers

D. The publisher's modification of the record will be converged to all of the subscribers

23. You are currently monitoring your replication model, which uses transactional replication with a remote distributor. You notice that transactions are added to the MSRepl_commands table on the Distribution database. When the transactions are applied to the subscriber, they disappear from the table a few minutes later. Which of the following is true?

A. When the transactions are applied to the subscriber the sp_repldone stored procedure is run on the distributor, and all applied transactions are marked

B. When the transactions are applied to the subscriber, the sp_repldone stored procedure is run at the subscriber and the records are marked

C. A cleanup task is run on the distributor and all marked transactions are truncated

D. A cleanup task is run on the subscriber and all marked transactions are truncated

C H A P T E R

10

Monitoring and
Optimizing SQL Server 7

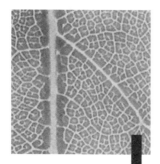

I magine for a moment that you are the Chief Operating Officer of a rather sizable company. It is your job to make sure that the company runs smoothly and that everything gets done efficiently. How will you do this? You could just guess at it, randomly assigning tasks and then just assuming that they are going to be done. Imagine the chaos that would ensue if you were to use this approach. Nothing would get done. Some departments would have too much to do, others would have nothing to do, and your company would go bankrupt.

A better approach would be to ask for reports from the various department managers and base your decisions on those reports. You might discover, for instance, that the accounting department has too much work and could use some help. Based on this report, you could hire more accountants. You might find that the production department has very little to do because the sales department has not been doing a good job, and based on this report, you could motivate sales to get to work so that production would have something to do.

Now, instead of being in charge of the entire company's operations, you are actually in charge of your SQL Server. Here too, you need to make certain that everything is getting done efficiently. Again, you could just guess at this and randomly assign tasks but that is both defeatist and an invitation to disaster. You need to get reports from your "department managers": the CPU, the disk subsystem, the database engine, etc. Once you have these reports, you can assign tasks and resources accordingly.

Most systems administrators don't perform monitoring and optimization functions because they believe they don't have the time. Most of their time is spent on firefighting, that is, troubleshooting problems that have cropped up. It's safe to say that if they had taken the time to monitor and optimize the systems, those problems might never have arisen in the first place. That makes monitoring and optimization *proactive* troubleshooting, not *reactive,* as is the norm.

In this chapter we will discuss the various methods and tools for getting the reports you need from your SQL Server. As is best with monitoring and tuning, we'll start at the bottom and work our way up; we'll discuss the tools (Performance Monitor, SQL Profiler, and Query Governor) and then move into repairs.

Using Performance Monitor

In order to get your company to function properly, you need to make certain that the very foundation of the company is doing its job. You need a management group that works well together and gets things done, a group where each will pull their own share of the load.

Microsoft ✓ Exam Objective

Monitor SQL Server performance.

With SQL Server, this management group is the computer system itself. SQL cannot function properly if it does not have available system resources such as memory, processor power, fast disks, and a reliable network subsystem. If these systems do not work together, the system will not function properly. For example, if the memory is being overused, the disk subsystem will slow down because the memory will have to write to the pagefile (which is on the disk) far too often. To keep such things from happening you will need to get reports from the subsystems; you can do this by using Performance Monitor.

Performance Monitor comes with Windows NT and is located in the Administrative Tools folder on the Start Menu. There are four views available for your use:

Chart This view displays a graph of system performance. As values change, the graph will spike or dip accordingly.

Report   The report view looks more like what you might get on a piece of paper except that the values here change with system use.

Alert   With alert view you can tell Performance Monitor to warn you when something bad is looming on the horizon, perhaps when CPU use is almost—but not quite yet—too high. This type of warning gives you time to fix potential problems before they become actual problems.

Log   This is for record-keeping. With log view, you can monitor your system over a period of time and view the information later, as opposed to viewing it real time (the default).

With each of these views, you monitor *objects* and *counters*. An *object* is a part of the system, like the processor or the physical memory. A *counter* displays the number that tells you how much that object is being used. For example, the % Processor Time counter under the Processor Object will tell you how much time your processor spends working. Table 10.1 lists common counters and their recommended values, Exercise 10.1 discusses how to use Performance Monitor for real-time data, and Exercise 10.2 describes logging data with Performance Monitor.

T A B L E   10.1:   Common Counters and Values in Performance Monitor

Object	Counter	Recommended Value	Use
Processor	% Processor Time	Less than 75%	The amount of time the processor spends working.
Memory	Pages/Sec	Fewer than 5	The number of times per second that data had to be moved from RAM to disk and vice versa.
Memory	Available Bytes	More than 4 MB	The amount of physical RAM available. This number should be low since NT uses as much RAM as it can grab for file cache.
Memory	Committed Bytes	Less than physical RAM	The amount of RAM committed to use.

T A B L E   10.1:   Common Counters and Values in Performance Monitor *(continued)*

Object	Counter	Recommended Value	Use
Disk	% Disk Time	Less than 50%	The amount of time that the disk is busy reading or writing.
Network Segment	% Network Utilization	Less than 30%	The amount of network bandwidth being used.

 In order to see the Network Segment: % Network Utilization you must install the Network Monitor Agent in Control Panel ➣ Network ➣ Services tab.

 If you don't enable the disk counters by executing diskperf –y (or –ye when using RAID), all disk counters will read zero.

EXERCISE 10.1

Monitoring with Performance Monitor

1. Log in to Windows NT as Administrator.

2. From the Start Menu, select Programs ➣ Administrative Tools ➣ Performance Monitor.

3. On the Edit menu, select Add to Chart to bring up the Add to Chart dialog box.

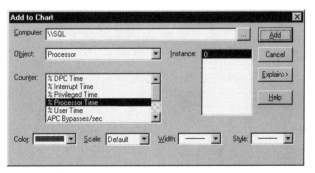

EXERCISE 10.1 (CONTINUED)

4. In the Object box, select Processor (not Process).

5. In the Counter box, select % Processor Time and click Add.

6. In the Object box, select Memory.

7. In the Counter box, select Pages/Sec and click Add.

8. Click Done and notice the graph being created on the screen.

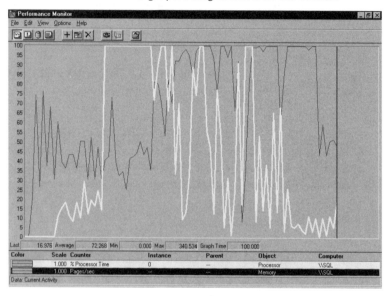

9. Press CTRL+H and notice the current counter turn white. This makes the chart easier to read.

10. On the View menu, select Report.

11. On the toolbar click the + button to bring up the Add to Report Dialog box.

EXERCISE 10.1 (CONTINUED)

12. Add the same counters and objects that you used in Chart view; then click Done. Notice the report displayed on the screen.

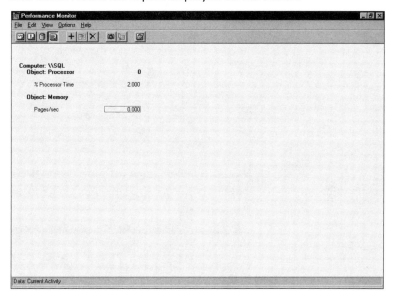

13. On the View menu, select Alert View and click the + button on the toolbar.

14. Select Processor in the Object box and % Processor Time in the Counter box.

15. Under Alert If, select Under, and in the box next to it type **100**. This will generate an alert if the processor is not busy 100% of the time. In the real world, this would be set to Over 70%, thus warning you just before it becomes a serious problem.

16. Click Add; then click Done.

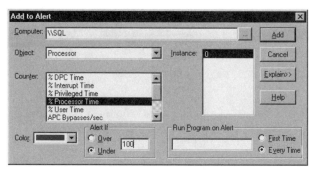

17. Watch the alerts generated for a short time then click the Alert at the bottom of the screen in the Alert Legend and press the Delete key on the keyboard.

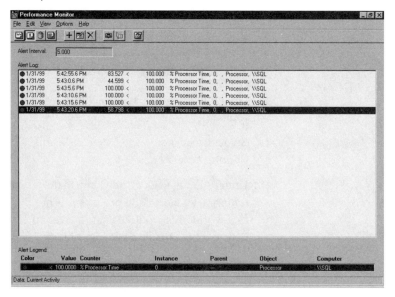

18. Exit Performance Monitor.

EXERCISE 10.2

Logging with Performance Monitor

1. Open Performance Monitor in the Administrative Tools menu.

2. On the View menu select Log.

3. On the Options menu select Log to open the Log Options dialog box.

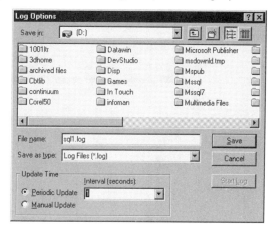

4. In the File Name box, type `c:\sql1.log`.

5. Under Update Time, set Periodic Update to 1 second.

6. Click the Save Button.

7. On the Edit menu select Add to Log and notice that you are allowed to add only objects. All counters for each selected object will be logged.

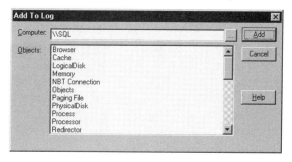

8. Under Objects, Select Processor and click Add.

EXERCISE 10.2 (CONTINUED)

9. Select Memory, click Add, and then click Done.

10. On the Options menu, select Log to open the Log Options dialog box.

11. Click Start Log to start logging.

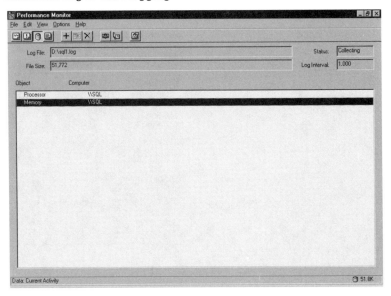

12. Wait one minute, then on the Options menu select Log and click the Stop Log button.

13. On the View menu, select Chart.

14. On the Options menu, select Data From, then select Log File and enter `c:\sql1.log` in the text box.

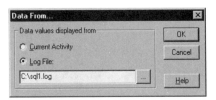

15. On the Edit menu, select Add to Chart and notice that you are allowed to add only the two objects that were logged.

EXERCISE 10.2 (CONTINUED)

16. Select the % Processor Time counter under Processor Object and click Add.

17. Select the Pages/Sec counter under the Memory object and click Add.

18. Click the Done button and notice the chart that has been created. Data is available for only the minute you logged.

19. Exit Performance Monitor.

You can monitor SQL Server as well as Windows NT using performance Monitor, since SQL provides its own objects and counters. The SQL counters you will be using most often have been preset for you and can be accessed through the Performance Monitor icon in the SQL Server 7 menu on the Start menu. Table 10.2 describes each of the counters in the preset Performance Monitor.

T A B L E 10.2: Preset SQL Performance Monitor Counters

Object	Counter	Use
SqlServer:Buffer Manager	Buffer Cache Hit Ratio	This tells you how much data is being retrieved from cache instead of disk.
SqlServer:Buffer Manager	Page Reads/sec	Number of data pages that are read from disk each second.
SqlServer:Buffer Manager	Page Writes/sec	Number of data pages that are written to disk each second.
SqlServer:General Statistics	User Connections	Number of user connections. Each of these will take some RAM.
SQLServer:Memory Manager	Total Server Memory (KB)	Total amount of memory that SQL has been dynamically assigned.
SQLServer:SQL Statistics	SQL Compilations/sec	Number of compiles per second.

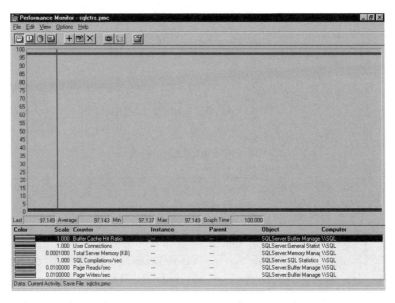

Now that you have the system resources working together, you can start creating queries. Rather than just randomly creating queries and hoping they work quickly, let's see how you can create queries and start the optimization process at the same time using Query Analyzer.

Using Query Analyzer

If you used SQL Server in its previous versions, you are probably familiar with ISQL/W, a graphic tool used for entering queries as Transact-SQL (T-SQL) code. In SQL Server 7 this has been reborn as Query Analyzer. Up to this point, you have been using this tool to enter queries and see results, but it can do more.

Microsoft ✓ *Exam* *Objective*   **Monitor SQL Server performance.**

One clue as to its enhanced capabilities comes from its name: Query *Analyzer*. It is used not only to enter queries, but also to analyze them, to see how many resources they consume, and to see how fast they run. As you will see in Exercise 10.3, it accomplishes this feat by timing each step of the execution; this includes parsing the command you typed in and checking for errors, loading the data into memory, performing the query on the data, and more. If you would like to see a graphic representation of everything SQL Server is doing with your query, you can tell it to display an execution plan (also shown in Exercise 10.3). This will display a series of icons that lead you through the execution process.

EXERCISE 10.3

Using Query Analyzer

1. On the Start Menu go to Programs, then SQL Server 7, and click on Query Analyzer.

2. When asked to log in, use Windows NT Authentication. After logging on you will see the Query window.

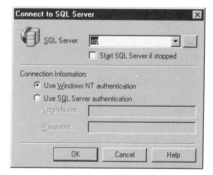

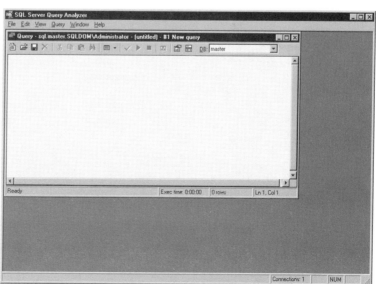

3. On the Query menu, select Current Connection Options.

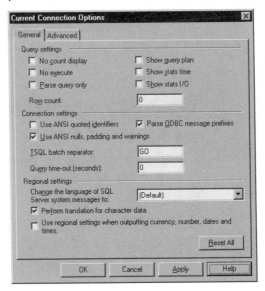

4. In the Options dialog box, check Show Stats Time and Show Stats I/O. Show Stats Time displays CPU time used, while Show Stats I/O displays disk time.

5. On the Query Menu, select Show Execution Plan to see a graphic representation of how SQL Server executes your query.

6. On the Query window toolbar, select Northwind in the DB list box to set Northwind as the default database.

7. In the Query window, type the following query:

```
select * from employees
```

8. In the Results Pane, notice the Execution and Parse and Compile times, then click on Execution Plan just below the Results pane.

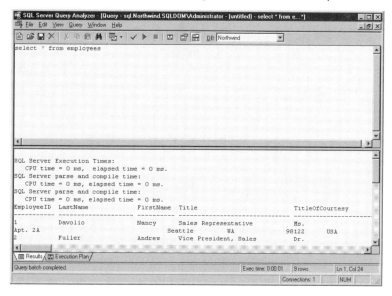

9. In the Execution Plan pane, hold your mouse pointer over each icon in turn; notice that they come with tool tips to help you better understand each step of execution.

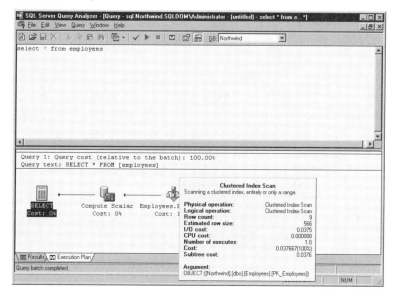

10. Close Query Analyzer.

Once the analysis is complete, you will have a better idea of how to build your queries and optimize them for speed, but you will not yet have the full picture. To get a full understanding of how your queries respond to everyday use you need to monitor them under stress—that is why we have SQL Profiler.

Monitoring with SQL Profiler

In running a company, once you have the management team working in harmony, you can focus your attention on the rest of the workforce. In this analogy, Query Analyzer would be like interviewing prospective employees; you want to be sure they have the appropriate qualifications, can fit in with the rest of the team, and will do their fair share of the work before you hire them. Like new employees, new queries need to be monitored regularly (with queries, on a day-to-day basis).

Microsoft ✓ *Exam* *Objective* | **Monitor SQL Server performance.**

Profiler allows you to monitor and record what is happening inside the database engine. This is accomplished by performing a *trace*, which is a record of data that has been captured about *events*. Stored in a table, a trace log file, or both, traces can be either shared, (viewable by everyone) or private (viewable only by the owner).

The actions you will be monitoring are called *events* and are logically grouped into *event classes*. Some of these events are useful for maintaining security, and some are useful for troubleshooting problems, but most of these events are used for monitoring and optimization (as described in Exercise 10.4).

EXERCISE 10.4

Monitoring with SQL Profiler

1. From the Start menu, go to the SQL Server menu under Programs and click Profiler.

2. If you are asked to register a server, do so using Windows NT Authentication.

3. On the File menu, select New then click on Trace to bring up the Trace Properties dialog box.

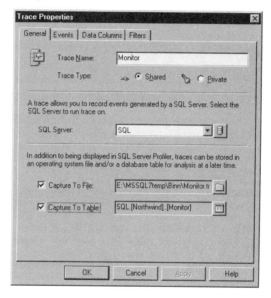

4. In the Trace Name box, type **Monitor**.

5. Select Shared as the Trace Type.

6. Check the Capture to File check box and accept the default name and location.

7. Check the Capture to Table check box and fill in the following:

   - Server: **Local**

   - Database: **Northwind**

   - Owner: **<myself>**

   - Table: **Monitor**

8. Click the Events tab.

9. Under Available Events, select Objects and click Add. This will monitor the opening and closing of objects such as tables.

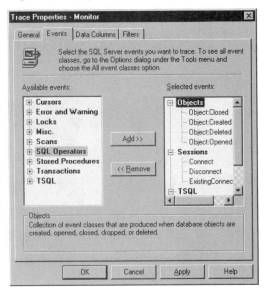

10. Click the Data Columns tab to change the data you see in the trace.

11. Under Unselected Data, select End Time and Click Add.

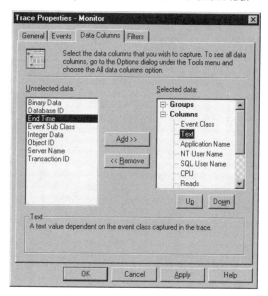

12. Click OK to start the trace.

13. Leave Profiler running and open Query Analyzer; log in using Windows NT Authentication.

14. Execute the following query:

```
use northwind
select * from products
```

15. Switch back to Profiler and click on the Pause button (double blue lines). Notice the data that was collected by the trace.

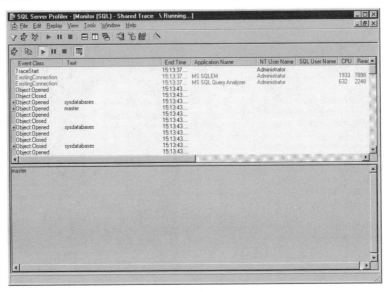

16. Close Profiler and Query Analyzer.

You may have found the amount of data collected by the trace overwhelming. That data was for only one user executing one query. Imagine trying to sort through a trace of hundreds of users with dozens of queries—a daunting task, to say the least. Fortunately, you will not be subjected to such tortures, since you can filter your trace data.

Filtering the Trace Data

Filtering is a simple process to grasp, much like making coffee. Because in most cases, you do not want the grounds saturating the finished product, you place a filter in the coffeepot to separate the grounds and the finished coffee. In this way, you get only what you want, and the rest is discarded.

The principle is the same with Profiler. When you create and execute a trace, it returns a great deal of data that you don't necessarily want or need to see. For example, a great deal of information about system objects is returned, and every application you use to access SQL (e.g., Enterprise Manager) will be recorded in the trace. To continue our coffee analogy, if you don't want the "coffee grounds" of extraneous data, you need to put a filter on the trace, as shown in Exercise 10.5.

EXERCISE 10.5

Filtering Traces

1. Open Profiler, and on the File menu, select New and then Trace to bring up the Trace Properties dialog box.

2. In the Trace Name box, type `Filter`.

3. Check the Capture to File check box and accept the default filename in the subsequent Save As dialog box.

4. Click on the Events tab.

5. Under Available Events, select Objects and Click Add.

6. Click OK to start the trace.

7. Open Query Analyzer and log in using Windows NT Authentication.

8. Execute the following query:

```
use northwind
select customerid, od.orderid, productname, quantity
from [order details] od inner join products p
on od.productid = p.productid
inner join orders o
on o.orderid = od.orderid
where customerid = 'hanar'
```

9. Switch back to Profiler and click on the Pause button. Notice the how much of the data in the trace is system data (e.g., sysdatabases).

10. On the File Menu, select Properties.

11. Click the Filters tab. You will notice that the only information filtered out is that which comes from Profiler.

12. Under Trace Event Criteria, select Object ID.

13. Check the Exclude System Objects check box and click OK.

14. Click OK on the subsequent warning that you will need to stop and restart the trace.

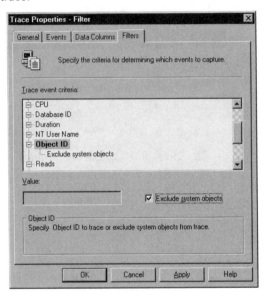

15. On the toolbar click the Stop button.

16. On the toolbar click the Start button.

17. Switch back to Query Analyzer and execute the same query as before with one change in the last line, as noted here:

```
use northwind
select customerid, od.orderid, productname, quantity
from [order details] od inner join products p
on od.productid = p.productid
inner join orders o
on o.orderid = od.orderid
where customerid = 'quick'
```

18. Switch back to Profiler and click the Pause button. Notice that no system data was captured this time.

19. Close Profiler and Query Analyzer.

The Trace Wizard is an even easier way to create traces.

Using the Trace Wizard

Unlike the wizards of fairy tales and medieval times, the Trace Wizard does not perform magic, though it may seem that way. The Trace Wizard is a very handy tool for creating a "quick and dirty" trace to get some standard information. You can create a total of six traces with this wizard (Exercise 10.6 will show you how):

Find the Worst Performing Queries   This trace will help identify which queries are the slowest by grouping the output according to the duration of each query.

Identify Scans of Large Tables   This will identify scans of large tables. If you find such scans, you may need to create some indexes.

Identify the Cause of a Deadlock   Deadlocks, caused by multiple users trying to access the same data at the same time, can slow all users down. This trace will show the chain of events leading up to the deadlock and the object that was being accessed.

Profile the Performance of a Stored Procedure   Stored procedures are T-SQL code that is stored at the server for clients to access. Improperly written stored procedures can slow the system down. This trace will help find improperly written stored procedures.

Trace Transact-SQL Activity by Application   This will show you which applications are being used the most to access SQL Server.

Trace Transact-SQL Activity by User   This trace will help you see which of your users are accessing SQL Server the most and what they are doing while logged in.

EXERCISE 10.6

Using the Create Trace Wizard

1. Open Profiler, and on the Tools menu, select Create Trace Wizard.

2. In the Create Trace Wizard Box, read through the checklist on the first screen and click Next.

3. On the next screen, select your server in the Server list.

4. In the Problem list, select Find the Worst Performing Queries, and click Next.

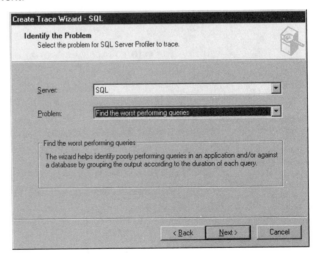

5. Select <All databases> in the Database list.

6. In the Minimum Duration box, type **1**. This will ensure that you see all queries for this exercise.

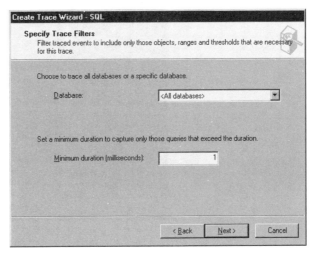

7. On the next screen, select Choose to Trace One or More Specific Applications.

8. Check the MS SQL Query Analyzer check box and click Next.

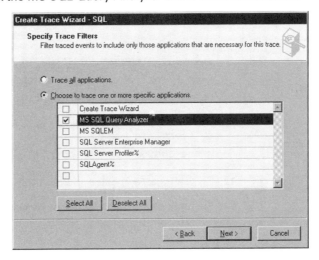

EXERCISE 10.6 (CONTINUED)

9. Leave the Trace Name set to Worst Performing Queries and click Finish. This will start the trace.

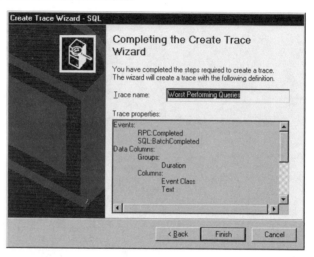

10. Open Query analyzer and execute the following query:

```
use northwind
select * from customers
```

11. On the Query menu, select New Query and execute the following query:

```
use northwind
select customerid, od.orderid, productname, quantity
from [order details] od inner join products p
on od.productid = p.productid
inner join orders o
on o.orderid = od.orderid
where customerid = 'tomsp'
```

12. Switch back to Profiler and click the Pause button.

13. Expand both Duration sections by clicking the + button next to them.

14. Expand all other sections with the + button and notice that the second query took up more CPU time than the first, making it the slower of the two.

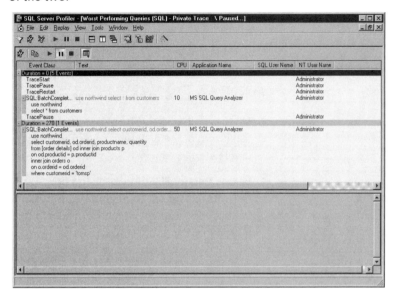

15. Close Profiler and Query Analyzer.

It is highly unlikely that you will be able—or want—to watch Profiler constantly to see whether anything important happens. This is not a problem, since you can always replay the traces.

Replaying a Trace File

When solving a problem or dealing with and untoward event, one of the first things typically done is to try to re-create the circumstances and chain of events that led up to the event. As an administrator you are going to be called in all the time to try to deal with such problems as slow response time and even server crashes.

You can re-create the problem-causing events by replaying a trace. Loading your saved traces into Profiler will allow you to replay them against the server and, in this way, to figure out exactly where the problem occurred. An especially nice touch is that you don't have to play the whole trace all at once; you can take it step-by-step to see exactly where the problem lies. Exercise 10.7 will walk you through replaying a trace.

EXERCISE 10.7

Replaying a Trace in Profiler

1. Open Profiler; on the File Menu, select Open and Trace File.

2. In the Open dialog box, select Monitor and click OK.

3. On the toolbar in the Trace window, click the Execute Single Step button (double braces {} with an arrow over the top). This will execute a single step at a time.

4. On the Replay SQL Server dialog box that appears next, select all the defaults except the Replay Rate. This should be set to Maintain Interval between Events, which will allow you to see what happens without missing any steps.

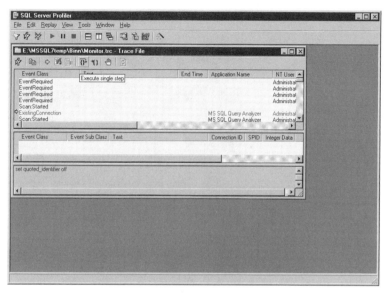

5. Scroll down and select the first line you find that contains
   SQL:BatchCompleted

6. On the toolbar, click the Run to Cursor button (an arrow pointing to
   double braces {}). This will execute all steps between the current posi-
   tion and the event you have selected.

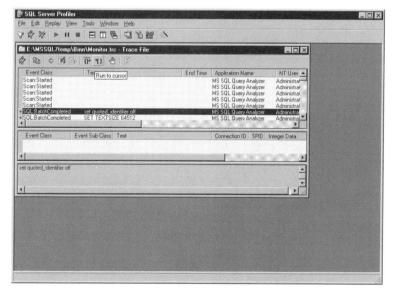

7. Click the Start Execution button (a yellow arrow) to finish replaying the trace. There is an interval between steps, since you selected the Maintain Interval check box earlier.

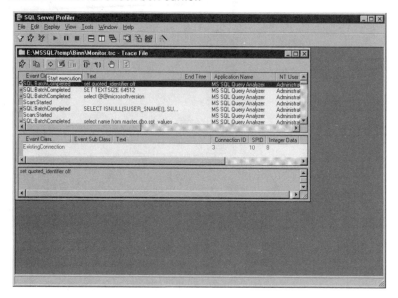

8. Close Profiler.

The Profiler is a wonderful tool for monitoring database activity and reporting problems, but that is not all it can do. Profiler comes with yet another wizard that will help you even further to improve the performance of your queries, the Index Tuning Wizard.

Using the Index Tuning Wizard

Systems, like automobiles or musical instruments, must be properly tuned to function properly. If even one SQL Server index were out of tune, it could slow down the entire system. Perhaps the wrong columns were indexed from the beginning, or maybe users have started querying different data over time, which would require the creation of new indexes. If any of this is true, your indexes need tuning.

The one thing you need before you can run the Index Tuning Wizard is a workload. You get this by running and saving a trace in Profiler. It is best to get this workload during times of peak database activity to make sure that you give the wizard an accurate load. (If you aren't sure about which events to trace, you can base your trace on the Sample 1 Trace SQL definition, which defines a standard set of events to capture.) Exercise 10.8 will show you how to use the Index Tuning Wizard.

EXERCISE 10.8

The Index Tuning Wizard

1. Open Profiler.

2. On the Tools menu select Index Tuning Wizard. This will open the Welcome screen.

3. Click Next.

4. Select the local server in the Server drop-down list.

5. Select Northwind as the database to tune.

6. Check Keep All Existing Indexes.

EXERCISE 10.8 (CONTINUED)

7. Check Perform Thorough Analysis.

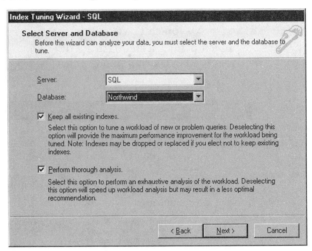

8. Click Next.

9. On the Identify Workload screen, select I Have a Saved Workload File.

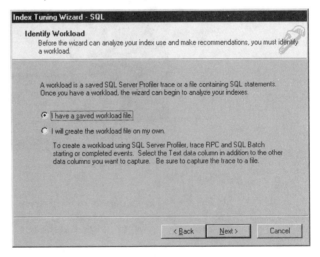

10. Click Next.

11. Click the My Workload File button.

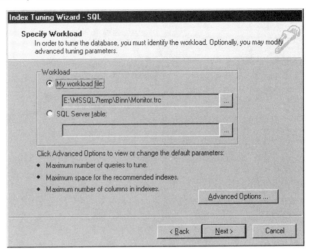

12. In the File Open dialog box select the Monitor trace (created earlier) and click OK.

13. When returned to the Specify Workload screen, click on the Advanced Options button, note the defaults, and click OK.

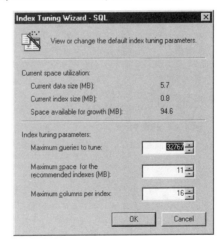

14. Click Next.

15. Under Tables to Tune, leave all available tables.

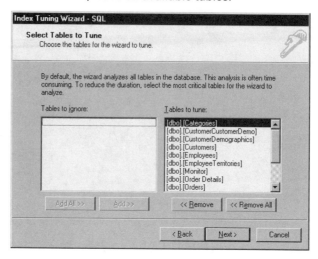

16. Click Next, and the Wizard will now start tuning your indexes.

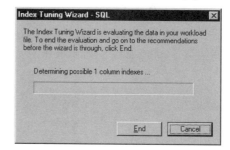

17. You will now be asked to accept the index recommendations; click Next.

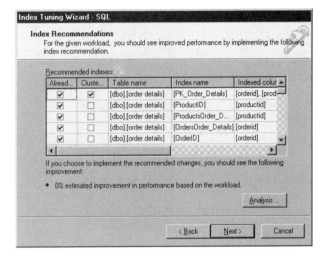

18. On the Schedule Index Update Job screen, select Apply Changes and Execute Recommendations Now.

19. Just below that, select Save Script File. In the File Name box type `E:\MSSQL7temp\Binn\tune.sql` and click Save.

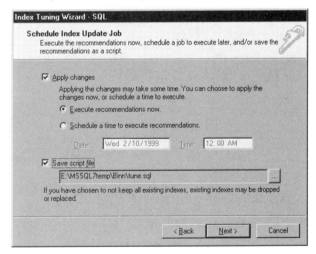

20. Click Next.

21. On the final screen, click Finish to apply the changes.

22. When you receive a message stating that the Wizard has completed, click OK.

23. Exit Profiler.

Tips and Techniques

If you want the best results from SQL Server's monitoring tools, you need to know and use the proper techniques. If you don't, the end result will not be what you are hoping for—or what you need.

Setting a Measurement Baseline

You will never know if your system is running slower than normal unless you know what normal is. That is what a measurement baseline does: it shows you the resources (memory, CPU, etc.) SQL consumes under normal circumstances. You create it before putting your system into production so that you have something to compare your readings to later on.

The first thing you need to create an accurate measurement baseline is a test network with just your SQL Server and one or two client machines. You limit the number of machines involved because all networks have broadcast traffic, which is processed by all the machines on the network. This broadcast traffic can throw your counts off, sometimes a little, sometimes quite a bit. You may instead want to consider shutting down as many machines as possible and generating your baseline off-hours.

You can then start your baseline. The Windows NT counters mentioned at the outset as well as the preset SQL counters should provide an accurate baseline with which you can compare future readings. Then you can move to the next technique.

Data Archiving and Trend Tracking

While the consequences of throwing away your SQL monitoring records are not quite as severe as facing an IRS auditor without records and receipts, you still need to save, or archive, them. One of the primary reasons to do so is to back up requests for additional equipment. For example, if you ask for funds to buy more memory for the SQL Server but don't bring any proof that the system needs the RAM, you are probably not going to get the money. If you bring a few months worth of reports, however, and say "After tracking SQL for a time we've found this…," management may be far more willing to give you the money you need. Using archived data in such fashion is known as *trend tracking*.

One of the most valuable functions of using your archived data for trend tracking is proactive troubleshooting, that is, anticipating—and avoiding—problems before they arise. Suppose you had added 50 new users to your network about three months ago and were about to do it again. If you had archived your data from that period, you would be able to recall what those 50 users had done to the performance of the SQL Server and you could compensate for it. On the other hand, if you had thrown that data away, you might be in for a nasty surprise when your system unexpectedly slowed to a crawl.

Optimizing Techniques

SQL Server has the ability to dynamically adjust most of its settings to compensate for problems. It can adjust memory use, threads spawned, and a host of other settings. In some cases, unfortunately, those dynamic adjustments may not be enough and you may need to make some manual changes.

Microsoft ✓ *Exam Objective*

Tune and optimize SQL Server.

Microsoft ✓ *Exam Objective*

Limit resources used by queries.

We'll look at a few specific areas that may require your personal attention.

Queries and Stored Procedures

The first thing to ask yourself when you are getting slow response times is whether you could be using a stored procedure here instead of a local query. Stored procedures are different from local code in two ways: They are stored on the SQL Server, so they do not need to be transmitted over the network and thus cause congestion. In addition, stored procedures are precompiled on the server; this saves on system resources, since local code must be compiled once it gets to the system.

Overall stored procedures are the way to go, but should you need to use local queries, you should consider how they are written, since poorly constructed queries can wreak havoc on your system. If, for example, you have a query that is returning every row of a table when only half of that is required, you should consider rewriting it. In addition, if your query returns only the needed rows but there are still too many, you may want to consider using *cursors*. A cursor is not the little arrow you see on your screen when you move the mouse; instead, it is used to break large result sets into smaller chunks.

Tempdb

Is your Tempdb big enough to handle the load that your queries put on it? Think of Tempdb as a scratchpad for SQL; when queries are performed, SQL uses this scratchpad to make notes about the result set. If it runs out of room to make these notes, system response time can slow down. Tempdb should be between 25 and 40 percent of the size of your largest database (e.g., if your largest database is 100MB, Tempdb should be 25 to 40MB).

Query Governor

Right out of the box, SQL will run any query you tell it to, even if that query is poorly written. You can change that by using the Query Governor. This is not a separate tool, but part of the database engine, and is controlled by the Query Governor Cost Limit. This setting tells SQL not to run queries longer than x (where x is a value higher than zero). If, for example, the Query Governor Cost Limit is set to 2, any query that is estimated to take longer than two seconds would not be allowed to run. SQL is able to estimate the running time of a query because it keeps statistics about the number and composition of records in tables and indexes The Query Governor Cost Limit can be set by using the command `sp_configure 'query governor cost limit', '1'` (the 1 in this code can be higher). It can also be set on the Server Settings tab of the Server Properties page in Enterprise manager.

NOTE If the Query Governor Cost Limit is set to zero (the default), all queries will be allowed to run.

Max Async I/O

It goes without saying that SQL needs to be able to write to disk since that's where the database files are stored, but is it writing to disk fast enough? If you have multiple hard disks connected to a single controller, multiple hard disks connected to multiple controllers, or a RAID system involving striping, the answer is probably no. The maximum number of asynchronous input/ output (Max Async I/O) threads by default in SQL is 32. That means that SQL can have 32 outstanding read and 32 outstanding write requests at a time. Thus, if SQL needs to write some data to disk it can send up to 32 small chunks of that data to disk at a time. If you have a powerful disk subsystem, you will want to increase the Max Async I/O setting.

The setting to which you increase it depends on your hardware, so if you increase the setting, you must then monitor the server. Specifically, you will need to monitor the Physical Disk: Average Disk Queue Performance Monitor counter which should be less than 2 (note that any queue should be less than 2). If you adjust Max Async I/O and the Average Disk Queue counter goes above 2, you have set it too high and will need to decrease it.

You will need to divide the Average Disk Queue counter by the number of physical drives to get an accurate count. That is, if you have 3 hard disks and a counter value of 6 you would divide 6 by 3—which tells you that the counter value for each disk is 2.

LazyWriter

LazyWriter is a SQL process that moves information from the data cache in memory to a file on disk. If LazyWriter can't keep enough free space in the data cache for new requests, performance slows down. To make sure this does not happen, monitor the SQL Server: Buffer Manager – Free Buffers Performance Monitor counter. LazyWriter tries to keep this counter level above zero; if it dips or hits zero, you have a problem, probably with your disk subsystem. To verify this, you need to check the Physical Disk: Average Disk Queue Performance Monitor Counter and verify that it is not more than 2 per physical disk (see above). If the queue is too high, LazyWriter will not be able to move data efficiently from memory to disk and the free buffers will drop.

RAID

RAID (Redundant Array of Inexpensive Disks) is used to protect your data and speed up your system. In a system without RAID, data that is written to disk is written to that one disk. In a system with RAID, that same data would be written across multiple disks, providing fault-tolerance and improved I/O. Some forms of RAID can be implemented inexpensively in Windows NT, but this uses such system resources as processor and memory. If you have the budget for it, you might consider getting a separate RAID controller that will take the processing burden off Windows NT. RAID is discussed in detail in Chapter 4, but here is a quick refresher:

RAID 0 Stripe Set This provides I/O improvement but not fault-tolerance.

RAID 1 Mirroring   This provides fault-tolerance and read time improvement. This can also be implemented as duplexing, which is a mirror that has separate controllers for each disk.

RAID 0+1 Mirrored Stripe Set   This is a stripe set without parity that is duplicated on another set of disks. This requires a third-party controller since Windows NT does not support it natively.

RAID 5 Stripe Set with Parity   This provides fault-tolerance and improved I/O.

Adding Memory

SQL Server, like most BackOffice products, needs significant amounts of RAM. The more you put in, the happier SQL will be. There is one caveat about adding RAM, however: your Level 2 cache. This is much faster (and more expensive) than standard RAM and is used by the processor for storing frequently used data. If you don't have enough Level 2 cache to support the amount of RAM in your system, your server may actually slow down rather than speed up. For the amount of memory that SQL requires, you will want to have 1MB of Level 2 cache on your system.

Manually Configuring Memory Use

While SQL is capable of dynamically assigning itself memory, it is not always best to let it do so. A good example of this is when you need to run another BackOffice program, like Exchange, on the same system as SQL Server. If SQL is not constrained, it will take so much memory that there will be none left for Exchange. This constraint is the *max server memory* setting, by adjusting it you can stop SQL Server from taking too much RAM, if for example you set it to 102,400 (100*1024[the size of a megabyte]) SQL will never use more than 100MB of RAM.

You could also set *min server memory,* which tells SQL never to use less than the set amount; this should be used in conjunction with *set working size.* Windows NT uses virtual memory, which means that data that is in memory and has not been accessed for a while can be stored on disk. The set working size option stops Windows NT from moving SQL data from RAM to disk, even if it is idle. This can improve SQL Server's performance since data will never need to be retrieved from disk (which is about 100 times slower than RAM). If you decide to use this option, you should set min server memory and max server memory to the same size and then change the set working size option to 1.

Summary

This chapter has stressed the importance of monitoring and optimization. Monitoring allows you to find potential problems before your users find them; without it, you have no way of knowing how well your system is performing.

Performance Monitor can be used to monitor both Windows NT and SQL Server. Some of the more important counters to watch are Physical Disk: Average Disk Queue (which should be less than 2) and SQLServer: Buffer Manager: Buffer Cache Hit Ratio (which should be as high as possible).

Query Analyzer allows you to see how a query will affect your system before you place it in production. The Profiler is used to monitor queries after they have been placed in general use; it is also useful for monitoring security and user activity. Once you have used Profiler to log information about query use to a trace file, you can run the Index Tuning Wizard to optimize your indexes.

Once you have created all logs and traces, you need to archive them. The various log files can be used later for budget justification and *trend tracking*. For example, suppose you added 50 users to your system six months ago and you are about to add 50 more. If you had kept records on what kind of load the last 50 users placed on your system, you would be better prepared for the next 50.

The chapter also presented some tips for repairing a slow-running system. You can change the Max Async I/O setting if your disk is not working hard enough to support rest of the system, and you may need to upgrade your disk subsystem if the SQL Server: Buffer Manager – Free Buffers Performance Monitor counter hits zero. RAID can also speed up your SQL Server. If you can afford a separate controller, you should get one to take some of the burden off Windows NT. If not, then you can use Windows NT RAID Level 1 for fault-tolerance and speed.

Review Questions

1. Your system has 64MB of RAM; you upgrade that to 512MB and find that your system has actually slowed down. What caused this?

   A. One of the SIMMs you purchased is defective

   B. You need to add more Level 2 cache to the system

   C. You need to configure SQL server to use the new RAM by adjusting the Memory setting in the Advanced Options of the Server Properties

   D. You need to make adjustments to the max server memory setting

2. You are writing a complex new query that joins columns from several tables and you are concerned about how it might affect system performance. Which tool could you use to see what this query will do to your system before implementing it?

   A. Profiler

   B. Query Governor

   C. Query Analyzer

   D. Performance Monitor

3. The problem is that you need to implement RAID on your SQL Server for fault-tolerance.

   The required objective is fault-tolerance.

   Your optional objectives are an increased disk subsystem I/O and no extra load on the processor

   The solution you choose is to implement Windows NT RAID 1.

   A. This solution produces the desired results and both optional objectives

   B. This solution produces the desired result and only one of the optional objectives

   C. This solution produces the desired result but neither of the optional objectives

   D. This solution does not produce the desired result

4. Your SQL Server is running slowly and you suspect the disk subsystem. You monitor the Physical Disk Average Disk Queue length counter in Performance Monitor and find that it is within the acceptable range. What could you do to speed up the disk subsystem?

   A. Increase the value of the LazyWriter

   B. Add another physical disk to the system

   C. Implement RAID 1

   D. Increase the Max Async I/O setting

5. You recently hired a developer to update your queries so that they would encompass some newly created tables. Your users are now complaining that the system seems slow. What can you do?

   A. Analyze the new queries with Query Analyzer

   B. Monitor the Physical Disk: Average Disk Queue counter in Performance Monitor during a period of peak activity to see if the disk subsystem can handle the new queries

   C. Create a trace with Profiler and use the trace file with the Index Tuning Wizard to improve the indexes

   D. Increase the size of Tempdb

6. True or False: It is best to generate a measurement baseline for a new server on a busy network where a load can be placed on it.

   A. True

   B. False

7. What should be the size of Tempdb?

   A. 10% of the largest database

   B. 50% of the largest database

   C. 25 to 40% of the size of the largest database

   D. 25 to 40% of the size of an average database

8. You have tuned and optimized your queries, indexes, and hardware, yet your users still complain of slow response times. What else can you do to enhance response times?

  A. Use cursors to segment the result set

  B. Split the data into multiple tables and use inner joins

  C. Use a view with your query instead of a result set

  D. Increase the size of the Windows NT pagefile

9. Which of the following RAID implementations will give the best overall performance and fault-tolerance?

  A. RAID 0 implemented with Windows NT

  B. RAID 0+1 implemented with a third-party controller.

  C. RAID 1 implemented with Windows NT

  D. RAID 5 implemented with a third-party controller

10. You need to know what kinds of queries each of your users is performing against SQL Server. What is the best way to accomplish this?

  A. Ask them via e-mail

  B. Create a trace in Profiler that gathers information on all the available events

  C. Create a trace using the Trace Wizard that will sort the data by user

  D. Use Query Analyzer to analyzer which users are using your queries

11. After using a trace in Profiler to monitor database activity, what should you do with the trace file?

  A. Delete it, as it is useless

  B. Save it on disk so you can use it later for trend tracking

  C. Archive it to tape (or another backup medium) and keep it for trend tracking

  D. Print out the trace summary, put it in a binder, and then delete the trace file

12. True or False: You should monitor SQL Server activity at peak times of the day to get accurate readings on the load placed on your server.

   A. True

   B. False

13. The problem is that you need to implement RAID on your SQL Server for fault-tolerance.

   Your solution is to implement RAID 0+1 using a third-party controller.

   A. This solution produces the desired results and both optional objectives

   B. This solution produces the desired result and only one of the optional objectives

   C. This solution produces the desired result but neither of the optional objectives

   D. This solution does not produce the desired result

14. While reading a trace performed with Profiler, you notice that it is capturing system information. How can you keep this system information out of the trace?

   A. In Enterprise Manager, go to System Properties and clear the Show Trace Information check box on the Server Settings tab

   B. In Profiler, in the Trace Properties, clear the Show System Information check box on the Server Settings tab

   C. In the Trace Properties dialog box in Profiler, on the Filters tab, select the Object ID event and check Exclude System Objects

   D. Execute `sp_showsysteminfo=0`

CHAPTER

11

Working with Remote Data and Linked Servers

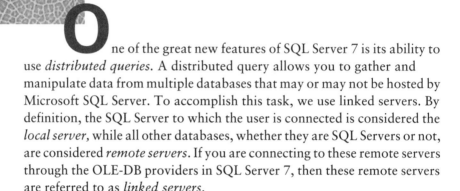

One of the great new features of SQL Server 7 is its ability to use *distributed queries*. A distributed query allows you to gather and manipulate data from multiple databases that may or may not be hosted by Microsoft SQL Server. To accomplish this task, we use linked servers. By definition, the SQL Server to which the user is connected is considered the *local server,* while all other databases, whether they are SQL Servers or not, are considered *remote servers*. If you are connecting to these remote servers through the OLE-DB providers in SQL Server 7, then these remote servers are referred to as *linked servers.*

Microsoft ✓ *Exam Objective*

Enable access to remote data.

- Set up linked servers.
- Set up security for linked databases.

This chapter introduces you to the use of linked servers. You will learn what they are, how your clients can use them, and the methods used to create them.

The first section of this chapter provides a general understanding of linked servers. You will be introduced to a few definitions and you will learn the fundamentals needed in order to create and maintain your linked servers.

The use of linked servers will be demonstrated in this section through the use of a distributed query example. Even though this section will not detail every aspect of a distributed query, it will give you a conceptual understanding of what your clients can do through a linked server.

You will learn the procedures necessary to establish a link to a variety of database systems such as Oracle and Access as well as other SQL Servers using both the Enterprise Manager and the Query Analyzer. We will also show you the procedures needed to designate your security credentials when your clients access a linked server. You will see how to set up security using both the Enterprise Manager and the Query Analyzer.

What Is a Linked Server?

Although SQL Server 6.5 could be set up to allow users to pull or manipulate data on remote servers, these remote servers were required to be SQL Servers also. Another drawback was that users could execute only stored procedures on the remote servers. Of course, these stored procedures had to be created in advance and had to reside on the remote server.

If the user wanted to pull data from a remote server, a stored procedure had to be created on the remote server to perform the SELECT statement. If the user wanted to manipulate data on the remote server, another stored procedure had to be created on the remote server to perform the INSERT, UPDATE, or DELETE statement. The user was not able to connect or JOIN tables that resided on separate physical servers.

SQL Server 7 allows the linking of remote servers that are not required to be Microsoft SQL Servers. These linked servers are accessed via an OLE-DB provider from the local SQL Server 7 computer. As a result, your users can create SELECT statements that JOIN two or more tables residing on separate servers. The fact that these tables are not on the local server is transparent to the user.

NOTE   Generically, an OLE-DB provider (from the viewpoint of SQL Server) is a registered COM (Component Object Model) object, which can establish a connection to a specific type of database. This COM object can translate statements issued from the local server into statements understood by the remote server.

For backward-compatibility, SQL Server 7 can still be configured to use remote servers that allow only for the execution of remote stored procedures.

You can upgrade a SQL Server 6.5 computer that is using remote servers to SQL Server 7 and still maintain compatibility. Once this upgrade has been performed, you can then upgrade the remote servers to linked servers.

What Is a Distributed Query?

Suppose one of your users needs information from a couple of databases that do not reside on their SQL Server 7 computer. If the other database servers have been linked, the user could create and run a distributed query. Take a look at this example:

Assume that XYZ Corporation has three databases with the following characteristics (Figure 11.1):

- A SEATTLE_MKTG database residing on the MARKETING server and hosted by SQL Server 7. The SEATTLE_MKTG database contains customer sales information.

- A WAREHOUSE database hosted by Oracle 8, which contains in-stock information.

- An INVENTORY database hosted by Microsoft Access 97, which contains parts information.

F I G U R E   11.1

Linked servers

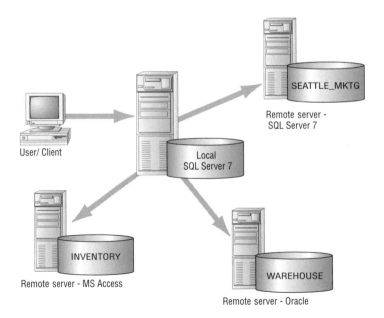

As long as the user is connected to the local SQL Server 7 computer that has been linked to the remote database servers, they could execute a query that would pull information from some or all of the databases. The user could produce a report that would list each item contained in the corporate inventory database from the INVENTORY database on the Access server. The report could include each item's total sales from the SEATTLE_MKTG database on the SQL Server 7 computer and the number of parts that were still in stock from the WAREHOUSE database running on Oracle. That report might look similar to Table 11.1.

T A B L E   11.1:   Sample Report

Part Name	Total in Stock	Total Sold
Chrome bumper, front	200	1250
Chrome bumper, rear	300	1000
Driver-side back door	15	50
Driver-side front door	15	60
Left-side mirror	1000	3000
Left-side quarter–panel	50	250
Passenger-side back door	15	50
Passenger-side front door	15	60
Rear-view mirror (3-1/2 x 5)	3000	3000
Rear-view mirror (5-1/2 x 7)	1500	500
Right-side mirror	750	2000
Right-side quarter-panel	50	250
Window: back windshield	750	3500
Window: driver-side back door	50	300

T A B L E 11.1: Sample Report *(continued)*

Part Name	Total in Stock	Total Sold
Window: driver-side front door	60	400
Window: front windshield	500	2500
Window: passenger-side back door	50	300
Window: passenger-side front door	60	400

The following SELECT statement could produce such a report:

```
SELECT part_name AS [PART NAME],
sum(part_in_stock) AS [TOTAL IN STOCK],
sum(part_quantity_sold) AS [TOTAL SOLD]

FROM INVENTORY...ITEMS ITEMS
INNER JOIN WAREHOUSE..system.INSTOCK INS
ON ITEMS.part_number = INS.part_number

INNER JOIN MARKETING.SEATTLE_MKTG.dbo.SALES SALES
ON ITEMS.part_number = SALES.part_number

GROUP BY part_name
ORDER BY part_name
```

In order to reference a table residing on a linked server, you must use a fully qualified name as in: *LinkedServerName.Database.Owner.Table.* If using a third-party OLE-DB provider, the accompanying documentation supplied by the vendor should give you a more detailed explanation on which parts of the fully qualified name are required.

Keep the following in mind when you are using fully qualified names and you are trying to link to another server:

SQL Server Use the fully qualified naming convention: (LinkedServerName.Database.Owner.Table)
Example: MARKETING.SEATTLE_MKTG.dbo.SALES

Oracle   Use the convention: (LinkedServerName...Owner.Table)
Example: WAREHOUSE...system.INSTOCK

Access   Use the convention: (LinkedServerName...Table)
Example: INVENTORY...PARTS

When executing a SQL statement in SQL Server 7, the local server is also considered the default server. If your SQL statement does not specify a server name, SQL Server 7 will default to the local default server.

In our example, the SEATTLE_MKTG database is on the MARKETING server. If your user is connected to the MARKETING server, the MARKETING server is considered the local default server. The user does not need to specify MARKETING in the SQL statement if the statement references a table in the SEATTLE_MKTG database.

Continuing with our example, the SELECT statement can be altered in the way it accesses the SALES table by removing the server name MARKETING. The example below illustrates what the SELECT statement would look like if your clients were connected to the MARKETING server.

```
SELECT part_name AS [PART NAME],
sum(part_in_stock) AS [TOTAL IN STOCK],
sum(part_quantity_sold) AS [TOTAL SOLD]

FROM INVENTORY...ITEMS ITEMS
INNER JOIN WAREHOUSE..system.INSTOCK INS
ON ITEMS.part_number = INS.part_number

INNER JOIN SEATTLE_MKTG.dbo.SALES SALES
ON ITEMS.part_number = SALES.part_number

GROUP BY part_name
ORDER BY part_name
```

Installing and Configuring Linked Servers

Creating and configuring linked servers involves two main steps:

1. Configure the link from the local server to the remote servers.

2. Configure logon security on the linked server(s) for the user(s).

Microsoft Exam Objective

Enable access to remote data.

- Set up linked servers.

Only SQL Server administrators (SA, or members of the sysadmin fixed server role) can set up linked servers, and they must be set up from the SQL Server 7 computer you wish to designate as the local server. Most of the users who will be using distributed queries will log on to this server.

When you create a link to a remote server, you have to provide several pieces of information:

Server Name   This is the mandatory name your users will use to reference the linked server.

Product Name   This is the name of the database software hosting the remote database. This parameter defaults to SQL Server if the provider name supplied is SQLOLEDB.

OLE-DB Provider Name   This is the name of the OLE-DB COM object as it is registered with the local server; it is mandatory if the product name is not SQL Server.

Data Source   This is the remote database name/alias or remote database filename, depending on which OLE-DB provider is used.

Location   This is the physical location of the remote database and depends on which OLE-DB provider is used.

Provider String   This is the setup string passed to the remote server to establish the connection or link. It can contain a remote login, remote password, remote database name, and so on, depending on which OLE-DB provider is used.

Catalog Name   This is the remote catalog or database name and also depends on which OLE-DB provider is used.

When you purchase and install a new OLE-DB provider, you should also receive documentation from the vendor specifying the required parameters and what type of information you should supply for them.

There are only two parameters that are mandatory for all providers: server name and provider name. The remaining parameters may be required, may have defaults, or may not be used at all, depending on the OLE-DB provider you choose.

As of this writing, only a few OLE-DB providers have been tested for use with SQL Server 7: SQL Server 6.5, Oracle, Access, and ODBC-compliant OLE-DB providers.

There are two ways to create a linked server: through the Enterprise Manager or by executing system stored procedures The setup procedures that follow will demonstrate both ways of creating a linked server.

When you are using the Query Analyzer, you will be using the sp_addlinkedserver and sp_addlinkedsrvlogin stored procedures. The sp_addlinkedserver system stored procedure tells your local server which OLE-DB provider to use and how to establish a connection through the provider. The sp_addlinkedsrvlogin system stored procedure tells your local server which Login ID and Password combinations to use to log onto the linked server.

Now that you have seen what parameters to use, let's see how to set up your linked servers. In the next section, you will see the procedures required to create links to SQL Server 7, SQL Server 6.5, Oracle, Access, and ODBC-compliant databases.

Linking to a Remote SQL Server 7 Database Server

Linking to a remote SQL Server 7 database is the most straightforward type of linking to configure. There are only two parameters you have to supply: the server name of the remote SQL Server 7 computer and the product name, SQL Server.

The server name should be the actual server name (the name you would use to register the remote SQL Server 7 computer in Enterprise Manager). If you decide to use a server name other than the actual name, you will have to specify the actual name of the remote server for the data source parameter.

It is better to use the actual name of the remote SQL Server 7 computer for the server name parameter, as most of the setup between the two databases will occur when you establish the link. If you specify the actual name in the data source parameter instead, the connection and setup will occur with the first distributed query run. Because of the setup time involved, this query may receive a timeout error and will have to be run again.

Follow the steps in Exercise 11.1 to use Enterprise Manager to link to a SQL Server 7 server named Marketing

---

EXERCISE 11.1

Establishing a Linked Server from within Enterprise Manager for a Remote SQL Server 7 Server Named Marketing

1. Open Enterprise Manager and connect to the computer you wish to use as the local server.

2. Right-click the Linked Servers icon and choose New Linked Server from the context menu.

3. Type in **Marketing** for the Linked Server option.

4. Select SQL Server as the Server Type. When you are finished, you should see something similar to what is shown here.

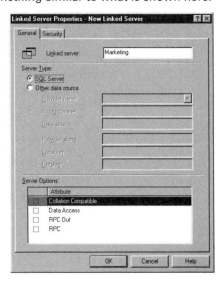

5. Click the OK button to complete the link. (You will see how to use the Security tab later in this chapter.)

You can accomplish the same thing using the Query Analyzer:

1. Open the Query Analyzer.

2. In the Login screen's SQL Server option, specify the name of the server you wish to be the local server.

3. Specify your security type by checking Use Windows NT Authentication or Use SQL Server Authentication. Type in your Login Name and Password if required and click OK (Figure 11.2).

FIGURE 11.2

The Connect to SQL Server dialog box in the Query Analyzer

4. Make sure that you are in the Master database.

5. Enter the following to add the MARKETING server as a new linked server.

```
EXEC sp_addlinkedserver 'Marketing', 'SQL Server'
```

6. If the statement ran correctly, then your results should say:

```
Server added
```

7. Close the Query Analyzer.

Linking to a Remote SQL Server 6.5 Database Server

Linking to a SQL Server 6.5 database is almost as straightforward as creating a link to a remote SQL Server 7 computer. Before you can create a link to the remote SQL Server 6.5 computer, however, you will need to prepare the remote server by executing a SQL script using the SA account or an account with SQL administrative privileges on it. You must run INSTCAT.SQL query on the SQL Server 6.5 computer. This file can be found on your SQL Server 7 installation disk under the \INSTALL directory or in the \MSSQL7\INSTALL directory on your local SQL Server 7 computer. Once you have done that, the rest of the installation is almost identical to the SQL Server 7 linked server installation.

Here are the steps needed to install and configure your SQL Server 6.5 computer for use as a linked server:

1. Copy the INSTCAT.SQL file from the \INSTALL directory on the CD or the \MSSQL7\INSTALL directory on the SQL Server 7 local server to a directory on the SQL Server 6.5 machine.

2. Start the ISQL/W utility on the SQL 6.5 computer. Select Start ➤ Programs ➤ Microsoft SQL Server 6.5 ➤ ISQL_w.

3. Supply the security credentials necessary to login to SQL Server.

4. Load the INSTCAT.SQL file by clicking on File ➤ Open… and then navigating to the INSTCAT.SQL file.

5. Click Open. The query will be loaded into the ISQL/W window.

6. Execute the script by clicking on the green triangle in the upper right corner of the query window or by pressing the Ctrl+E keys on your keyboard.

7. This script will take a couple of minutes to run and will have a great deal of output. As you scroll down the results screen, you will see several messages that instruct you to ignore the errors.

Follow these steps to create a link through the Enterprise Manager:

1. Run Enterprise Manager on your SQL Server 7 computer and connect to your local server.

2. Right-click the Linked Servers icon and choose New Linked Server from the context menu.

3. Type in **Marketing** for the Linked Server option, and choose SQL Server as the Server Type. When you are finished, you should see something similar to Figure 11.3.

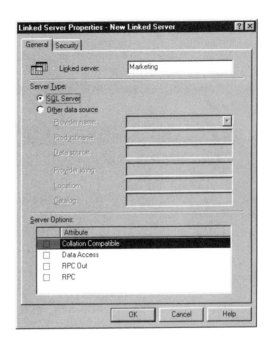

FIGURE 11.3

Linking to a SQL
Server 6.5 computer

4. Click OK when you are finished.

To use the Query Analyzer, use the same code for linking a SQL Server 6.5 computer as you did when you linked the SQL Server 7 database earlier:

```
EXEC sp_addlinkedserver 'MARKETING', 'SQL Server'
```

Linking to an Access Database

Linking to an Access database can be a bit tricky. There is a new parameter introduced called the data source that requires you to specify the complete path to the Access database. If the database is on a remote server, you may need to map a drive letter or use the UNC naming convention.

Look at this scenario:

- The Access database is on a machine named ATLANTA.

- The directory in which the Access database is located is shared as INVENTORY.

- The database file name is InvDB.MDB.

The data source parameter that you would need to specify is:

\\Atlanta\Inventory\InvDB.MDB

If you have Microsoft Access installed in the default folder, Exercise 11.2 will run normally. If you do not, you will need to locate an Access database. In the exercise, the access database (INVENTORY) is on the local computer.

EXERCISE 11.2

Establishing a Linked Server to an Access Database Named INVENTORY

1. Start Enterprise Manager and connect to your local server.

2. Right-click the Linked Servers icon and choose New Linked Server from the context menu.

3. Type in **INVENTORY** for the Linked Server option.

4. Select Other Data Source as the Server Type.

5. Select Microsoft.Jet.OLEDB.4.0 for the Provider Name.

6. For the Data Source, type in the full path of the Access database file:

   C:\INVENTORY\INVDB.MDB

7. When you are finished, you should see something similar to what is shown here.

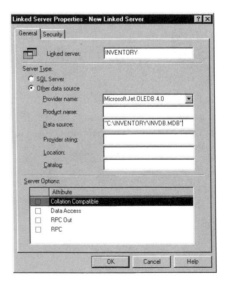

8. Click OK to complete the link.

Exercise 11.3 walks you through this same process using the Query Analyzer. If you implement SQL scripts, you can save the scripts for later use in rebuilding and reconnecting your linked server.

EXERCISE 11.3

Linking to an Access Database Using T-SQL

1. Start the Query Analyzer.

2. Log on to the local server and supply your security credentials.

3. Ensure that you are working in the Master database.

4. Run the following query to link to the Access INVENTORY database.

   ```
   EXEC sp_addlinkedserver 'IVENTORY', 'Access',
   'Microsoft.Jet.OLEDB4.0', 'C:\INVENTORY\INVDB.MDB'
   ```

5. If the statement ran correctly, then the last line in the lower half of the query window should read:

   ```
   Server added
   ```

You can use the same Microsoft.Jet.OLEDB4.0 driver to link to an Excel spreadsheet.

Linking to an Oracle Database Server

When setting up a link to an Oracle database, you will have to install two pieces of software onto your local server, Oracle client software and Oracle's SQL*Net software. The version you will need depends on your OLE-DB provider.

If you use the supplied Microsoft OLE-DB provider for Oracle, you will have to install Oracle's client software support file, Version 7.3.3.0.4 or later, and SQL*Net, Version 2.3.3.0.4 or later.

Oracle implements databases in a fundamentally different way from SQL Server. In order to access a database on Oracle from SQL Server 7, you will have to set up an *alias* to the Oracle database using Oracle's SQL*Net software. SQL*Net is the networking software used by a database system (including other Oracle servers) to talk to a remote Oracle server over a network.

The documentation accompanying the SQL*NET software details how to set up a SQL*NET alias to an Oracle database.

If you were to look at how these software packages work together, you would see that SQL Server talks to the OLE-DB layer, which talks to the Oracle client software layer, which talks to the SQL*Net layer, which in turn talks to the TCP/IP stack—which then sends the data onto the wire. Figure 11.4 illustrates this.

F I G U R E   11.4

Communicating with an Oracle Server

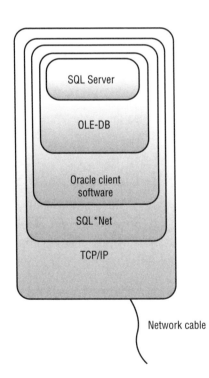

Since most of us don't have a copy of Oracle to play with, we will provide you with the steps necessary to connect to an Oracle Server, rather than give you a full-blown exercise. In the following examples, you will see how to connect using both Enterprise Manager and the Query Analyzer. The example uses the WHAlias through the SQL*Net software.

1. Open Enterprise Manager and connect to your SQL Server.

2. Right-click the Linked Servers icon and choose New Linked Server from the context menu.

3. Type in **Warehouse** for the Linked Server option.

4. Select Other Data Source as the Server Type.

5. Select MSDAORA for the Provider Name option.

6. For the Data Source, type in the name of the SQL*NET alias name for the Warehouse database: **WHAlias**. When you are finished, you should see something similar to Figure 11.5.

FIGURE 11.5

Connecting to Oracle through the SQL*Net alias

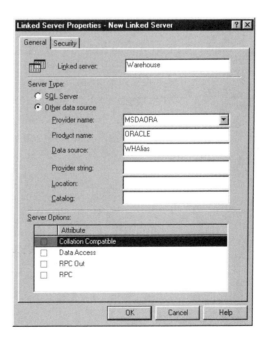

7. Click OK to complete the link.

Using Query Analyzer, you would do the following:

1. Open the Query Analyzer and connect to your local server. Be sure to provide sysadmin-level security credentials.

2. Be sure that you are using the Master database.

3. Run the following query:

```
EXEC sp_addlinkedserver 'WAREHOUSE', 'Oracle', 'MSDAORA',
'WHAlias'
```

4. If the statement ran correctly, then the last line in the lower half of the query window should read:

```
Server added
```

Linking to an ODBC Database Server

You can link to an ODBC-compliant database in one of two ways, either through a predefined ODBC data source name (DSN) or by supplying all connection information in the provider string parameter.

Whether you use a predefined ODBC DSN or the parameter string, you will still need to have the ODBC files necessary to connect to your remote database.

Generally, the ODBC files (.DLLs) necessary to connect to the remote database will be supplied by the vendor from whom you bought the ODBC connectors.

The following steps outline the process of connecting to an ODBC database that has a predefined DSN using Enterprise Manager. In this example, the DSN is ODBCINV and the database is Inventory2.

1. Open Enterprise Manager and connect to your local server.

2. Right-click the Linked Servers icon and choose New Linked Server from the context menu.

3. Type in **Inventory2** for the Linked Server option.

4. Select Other Data Source as the Server Type.

5. Select MSDASQL for the Provider Name option.

6. For the Data Source option, type in the DSN: **ODBCINV**. When you are finished, you should see something similar to Figure 11.6.

FIGURE 11.6

Linking to an
ODBC database
through a DSN

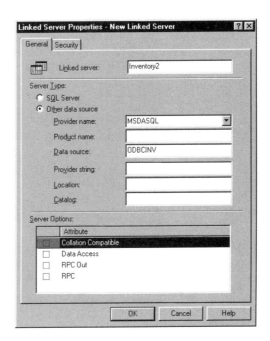

7. Click OK when you are finished. If you don't have a predefined DSN, add the following information to the provider string parameter:

```
DRIVER={Remote Server Name};SERVER=ServerName;UID=sa;PWD=;
```

You can use the following steps to link to a remote ODBC database server using Query Analyzer.

1. Open the Query Analyzer and connect to your local server.

2. From the Master database, run the following query:

```
EXEC sp_addlinkedserver 'INVENTORY2', '', 'MSDASQL',
'ODBCINV''
```

3. If the statement ran correctly, the last line in the lower half of the query window should read:

Server added

4. If you are not using a predefined DSN, run the following query:

```
EXEC sp_addlinkedserver 'Inventory2', '', 'MSDASQL', NULL,
NULL, 'DRIVER={Remote Server Name};
SERVER=Seattle;UID=sa;PWD=;'
```

 If you set up a linked server using the parameter string as mentioned above, executing the sp_addlinkedserver stored procedure is the only step you need to perform. You do not have to set up security to the remote server because the remote login ID and remote password are specified in the parameter string.

Establishing Security for Linked Servers

Once you have created a link to a remote server, you then have to set up the security to the linked server. Since security mechanisms differ from system to system, you need to specify what login ID and password you want the local SQL Server 7 computer to use on the remote system on behalf of your individual local clients or group of local clients.

Microsoft ✓ Exam Objective

Enable access to remote data.

- Set up security for linked databases.

Say that you have a client who is logging onto the local SQL Server 7 computer as JohnD. You need to tell SQL Server 7 which login ID and password to use when logging into the remote database server when JohnD tries to gain access to the remote database. If everyone on your local server is to use a different login ID and password on the remote database system, you will have to tell SQL Server 7 about each of them. To make things easier, you can designate a login ID and password on the remote database system for a group of local logins.

If you are using a Windows NT local or global group as the login account, you can map this NT group to a remote database login ID and password.

You can map a local login ID or group to a remote login ID and password through Enterprise Manager or through T-SQL using the `sp_addlinkedsrvlogin` stored procedure (in this case, you will have to know the local login ID in advance). You can save time by mapping an NT local or global group to a remote login ID. Because you are creating one mapping to one remote login ID for a group of clients you will eliminate the administrative annoyances of creating and maintaining several individual mappings.

Figure 11.7 shows the Security tab of the Linked Server property sheets. As you can see, you can use any SQL Server login ID to map to a remote database.

FIGURE 11.7

The Security tab of the Linked Server Properties sheets

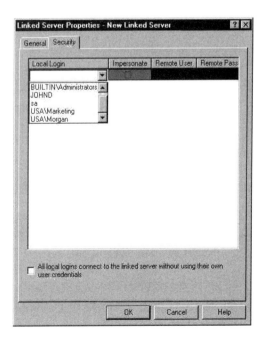

When you are setting up security to a remote database server, you will have to provide several pieces of information:

Remote Server Name   This is the mandatory name you used as the server name when linking the server.

UseSelf   This is a mandatory TRUE or FALSE parameter to specify whether or not the local SQL Server should send the local login ID's Windows NT credentials when logging onto the remote server. The default is FALSE.

Local Login ID   This is also mandatory. The login ID on the local server that you wish to map to a remote login ID, can be an NT login ID, an NT group login ID, or the login ID the client uses to log onto SQL Server.

Remote Login ID   This is the login ID to use on the remote server. Your local login ID will map to the remote login ID.

Remote Password   This is the password to use on the remote server with the remote login ID.

With security account delegation, users authenticated by Windows NT to access the local SQL server would have their NT credentials sent to the remote SQL Server to access the remote database. The UseSelf parameter specifies whether or not to send the NT credentials.

WARNING   Windows NT 4 does not support security account delegation. This type of authentication will not be implemented until Windows 2000. Until that time, the UseSelf parameter should be set to FALSE. In addition, if the remote database server is a SQL Server, that server needs to be configured to accept non-trusted connections.

Mapping Login IDs Using Enterprise Manager

This section discusses the procedures required to configure the security for different types of local logins. Here you will use Enterprise Manager to accomplish this task. In the next section, you will see the equivalent procedures using Query Analyzer.

The following steps outline the process of mapping an ID in SQL Server to a remote server using Enterprise Manager. We will be mapping the JohnD local login ID to the linked Warehouse server. The Warehouse server has an account setup as D_John with a password of passwd.

1. Open Enterprise Manager and connect to your SQL server.

2. Expand the Linked Servers icon and then right-click on the Warehouse icon. Select Properties.

3. You will now see the Properties sheet. Click on the Security tab to view the security information for this linked server.

4. In the Local Login column, click in an unused box.

5. From the drop-down list box, you can choose the local login ID that you wish to map. Choose JOHND as shown in Figure 11.8.

F I G U R E   11.8

Choosing a local login
ID to map

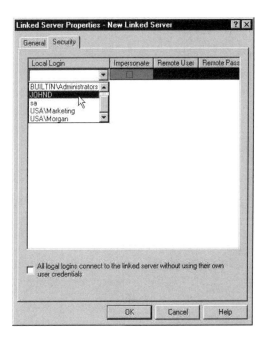

6. In the Remote Login column to the right, type in the login ID to use on the remote server: **D_JOHN**.

7. Under Remote Password, type in the password to use for the remote login just specified: **passwd**.

8. Repeat Steps 4 through 8 for each local login ID to be mapped.

9. When you are finished, click OK.

Configuring Security for an Access Database

If you are mapping to an unsecured Access database, you must use the remote login ID Admin and no password. In addition, when you set up your connections through Enterprise Manager, you need to specify the security option: All Local Logins Connect to the Linked Server without Using their own User Credentials (see below).

If you are accessing a secured Access database, you will have to make a change to your registry. Configure the registry to use the correct Workgroup Information file used by Access. You must enter the full pathname of the Workgroup Information file used by Access to this registry entry:

```
HKEY_LOCAL_
MACHINE\SOFTWARE\Microsoft\JET\4.0\Engines\SystemDB
```

Once you have made the necessary changes to the Registry, you can map your SQL Server accounts to the secured Access database.

Here are the steps necessary to connect to an unsecured Access database through Enterprise Manager. In this example, we will use the Admin ID with no password. This is the default security in an Access database.

1. Open Enterprise Manager and connect to your local server.

2. Expand the Linked Server and then right-click on the Inventory server and choose Properties.

3. Click the Security tab.

4. Specify Admin and no password. Then be sure to select All Local Logins Connect to the Linked Server without Using their own User Credentials (Figure 11.9).

5. Click OK when you are finished.

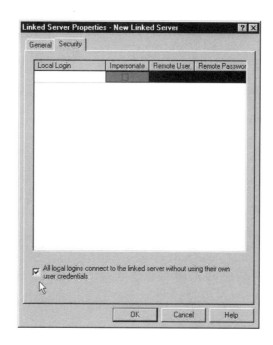

FIGURE 11.9

Connecting to an
unsecured Access
database

Mapping Login IDs Using the Query Analyzer

Follow these steps to map your login IDs using the Query Analyzer and the
sp_addlinkedsrvlogin stored procedure.

1. Open the Query Analyzer and connect to your local SQL Server 7
   database.

2. Make sure that you are in the Master database.

3. Run the following query to map the SQL Server login ID JohnD to the
   linked Warehouse server. You will be mapping in as D_JOHN with a
   password of passwd.

   ```
   sp_addlinkedsrvlogin 'WAREHOUSE', FALSE, 'JOHND', 'D_
   JOHN', 'passwd'
   ```

4. If the stored procedure was successful, you will see one of the following in the lower half of the window:

```
(0 row(s) affected)
(0 row(s) affected)
(1 row(s) affected)
```

OR

```
(1 row(s) affected)
(0 row(s) affected)
(1 row(s) affected)
```

5. Close the Query Analyzer when you are finished.

If you are mapping a SQL Server login ID that is using NT Authentication, you must specify the domain name as well as the login ID. For example: USA\Marketing would be the login ID to be mapped to D_JOHN.

Working with Access Databases

For an unsecured database, all you need to do is specify Admin for the mapped login ID and NULL for the password. Here is an example:

```
sp_addlinkedsrvlogin 'INVENTORY', FALSE, 'JOHND', 'Admin',
NULL
```

For a secured Access database, be sure that you make the necessary changes to the registry key. Once you have done that, then you can access the database using the sp_addlinkedsrvlogin stored procedure with the normal parameters. For example, if your Access database (Inventory) has a login ID of D_JOHN with a password of passwd, you would run:

```
sp_addlinkedsrvlogin 'INVENTORY', FALSE, 'JOHND', 'D_JOHN',
'passwd'
```

Summary

SQL Server 7 has an excellent new feature that can be used to run distributed queries. In the past, you could run only remote stored procedures from one SQL Server 6.5 computer to another SQL Server 6.5 computer. With linked servers, you can run both remote stored procedures and distributed queries.

To successfully create and configure your linked servers, you can use either Enterprise Manager or the Query Analyzer with the sp_addlinked-server stored procedure. When you configure your linked servers, you should keep the following in mind:

SQL Server 7   You must supply the server name and the product name (i.e., SQL Server).

SQL Server 6.5   Here you have to run the INSTCAT.SQL script on the 6.5 computer. On the local computer, supply the server name and the product name (SQL Server).

Microsoft Access   To use this, supply a fully qualified path for the data source. Add Microsoft.Jet.OLEDB.4.0 for the provider name.

Oracle   You must install the Oracle client software, the Oracle SQL*Net software, and TCP/IP. Supply MSDAORA for the provider name and the SQL*Net alias for the data source.

ODBC   You should supply MSDASQL for the provider name. Specify the DSN that you have created for the data source. If you have not created a predefined DSN, you should supply a connection string for the provider string parameter.

Once you have successfully configured your linked server, you need to specify some type of login security. If you do not specify login credentials, chances are that you will not have access to the linked server. Each type of server has its own set of security parameters. You can use the Enterprise Manager or the sp_addlinkedsrvlogin stored procedure to create your linked server login credentials. Keep the following in mind when you are configuring security for your linked servers:

- The UseSelf parameter should be set to FALSE until Windows 2000 is available.

- If connecting to a SQL Server database, the linked server must be configured to allow non-trusted connections. (This is true only until the advent of Windows 2000.)

- You must specify the remote server name and your Local Login ID. Optional parameters include the remote login ID and the remote password.

- To connect to an unsecured Access database, specify Admin for the remote login ID and NULL for the password. You should also select All Local Logins Connect to the Linked Server without Using their own User Credentials option in Enterprise Manager.

- To connect to a secured Access database, you must ensure that the following registry key is pointing at the correct Microsoft Access Workgroup Information File.

```
HKEY_LOCAL_
MACHINE\SOFTWARE\Microsoft\JET\4.0\Engines\SystemDB
```

Linked servers are an incredibly powerful new tool in the SQL Server 7 arsenal. Creating distributed queries is as simple as using the fully qualified object names in your SQL code. This new system of linked servers will be a very powerful and useful change in the way many companies do business. Linked servers and distributed queries bring about the ability to create and use distributed databases.

Review Questions

1. Which of the following database servers are supported as linked servers?

   A. SQL Server 6.5 (integrated security)

   B. SQL Server 6.5 (mixed security)

   C. Oracle

   D. Microsoft Access (unsecured)

2. Your users are complaining that their distributed query is timing out the first time they execute it. After the first time, it executes properly. The remote SQL Server 7 is physically located several hundred miles

away. Upon further investigation, you find out that there is a slow link to that location. When you check the setup of the linked server in Enterprise Manager, you see that you are using the data source parameter. Even though this is the case, the users say it works perfectly after the first run. Which of the following is a good solution?

A. Make the name in the data source parameter all uppercase

B. Make the name in the data source parameter all lowercase

C. Don't use the data source parameter; let the linked server name be the actual name, and update the query

D. Delete the linked server in Enterprise Manager and set it up again; it was incorrectly using the wrong name in the data source parameter

3. When you execute the sp_addlinkedserver stored procedure to link a remote SQL Server 6.5 computer, you receive an error message stating that there are missing system tables. Which of the following solutions should you perform?

A. Reinstall SQL Server 6.5 on the remote server

B. Apply SQL Server 6.5 Service Pack 5 on the remote server

C. Execute the INSTCAT.SQL script on the local SQL Server

D. Execute the INSTCAT.SQL script on the remote SQL Server

4. Your users are logging into your local SQL Server using non-trusted connections. You want to use one mapping for all the users to access the remote database. If the data is not sensitive and security to the data is not an issue, which of the following would accomplish your task?

A. Create a server role with public as a member and map this role to a remote login ID

B. Create a database role with public as a member and map this role to a remote login ID

C. Make the NT global group Domain Users a valid login and map it to a remote login ID

D. None of the above

5. Your users are logging into your local SQL Server using trusted connections. Your server and all your users are in the workgroup SQLDOM. You want to use one mapping for all the users to access the remote database. If the data is not sensitive and security to the data is not an issue, which of the following would accomplish your task?

   A. Create a server role with public as a member and map this role to a remote login ID

   B. Create a database role with public as a member and map this role to a remote login ID

   C. Make the NT global group SQLDOM\Domain Users a valid login and map it to a remote login ID

   D. None of the above

6. You have successfully established a link to a remote server and have mapped a few local SQL Server login IDs to their respective remote login IDs. When you run the sp_addlinkedsrvlogin stored procedure to map the local SQL Server login ID JOHND to the remote login ID JOHND, you receive the error message: "'JOHND' is not a local user. Remote login denied." When you installed the local server, you used the default settings. Which of the following will prevent you from receiving this error message?

   A. Add JOHND to the remote server

   B. Add JOHND to the local server

   C. Add JOHND as an NT login ID

   D. Use all lowercase letters (johnd) when executing the stored procedure

7. When you execute the stored procedure sp_addlinkedserver, it ends successfully, but when you click over to Enterprise Manager (which has also been open), you do not see the new linked server. Which of the following will correct the problem?

   A. Exit and reenter Enterprise Manager

   B. Reexecute the stored procedure

    C. Execute the stored procedure `sp_addlinkedsrvlogin`

    D. In Enterprise Manager, click on Linked Servers with the right mouse button and refresh the list

8. True or False: When you link to an ODBC database using a predefined user DSN, you still have to map the local login IDs to remote login IDs.

    A. True

    B. False

CHAPTER

12

Troubleshooting SQL Server 7

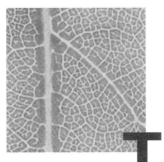

his chapter covers various troubleshooting issues you may encounter in your database administration duties. It starts with a look at some basic troubleshooting techniques, then addresses issues regarding upgrading your database from a SQL Server 6.5 database to a SQL Server 7 database. We will look at possible problems you may encounter when you perform backups and restorations in SQL Server 7 and those that may occur when you are using replication. We will examine alert management and job failures and explain how to determine which alerts and jobs are failing and how to fix these problems. The chapter will address problems you may encounter when attempting to run distributed queries. The following section discusses client connectivity issues. The inability of clients to connect to SQL Server is one of the most common problems encountered in SQL Server. We will also look at problems that may arise in trying to access databases and database objects.

Troubleshooting is not only what you know, but how you choose to implement your knowledge in a given situation. This makes the trouble-shooting process somewhat unique in the computer world. Sometimes there are hard-and-fast rules, and sometimes you have to think about the problems and take your best guess. Troubleshooting is an art, and like any artist, you need to practice it. You should take as much as possible from this book about what to do in a given situation, but there is nothing like practice. Work with the products as much as you can before you take the exams. Generally, every Microsoft Certification exam has a troubleshooting section that accounts for nearly 12% of the total number of questions offered.

The first place to look for problems with SQL Server is in the error logs in both SQL Server and the Windows NT Application Log.

SQL Server Error Log

The SQL Server Error log is a group of ASCII text files located in the \MSSQL7\Log folder. The most recent log file is called ERRORLOG. When a new log is created, the old log is renamed to ERRORLOG.1, which in turn is renamed ERRORLOG.2 and so on for up to six history logs. Note that the oldest log file, ERRORLOG.6, is not renamed but is overwritten by ERRORLOG.5.

Since the error logs are in an ASCII format, you can use any text editor to view them. This includes Notepad and MS-DOS Edit. Word processing programs that are capable of reading ASCII files (sometimes referred to as MS-DOS Text) can also be used to view the information; these include Microsoft Word and Corel's Word Perfect.

To view a log, from the Enterprise Manager, expand your SQL Server and then expand the Management folder. You can then expand the SQL Server Logs icon. You will now see the list of available SQL Server logs. If you click on a single error log in the console tree, you will see the information in that log in the right pane as shown in Figure 12.1.

FIGURE 12.1

The SQL Server logs

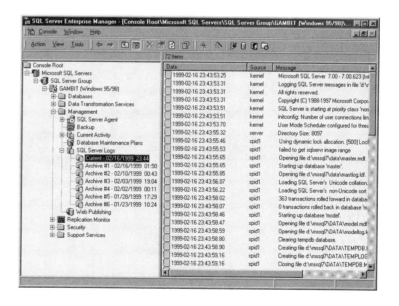

The NT Event Viewer

The NT Event Viewer can also be used to track SQL Server events and errors. The disadvantage to SQL Server administrators is that the viewer logs not only SQL Server events, but events from other applications running in Windows NT as well.

Exercise 12.1 will illustrate the differences between the same two error messages as shown in the SQL Server Error log and the NT Event Viewer.

EXERCISE 12.1

Searching for Errors

1. Open the Query Analyzer and run the following commands:

```
RAISERROR ('Chapter 12 Error, Informational Only', 1, 2)
WITH LOG
go
RAISERROR ('Chapter 12 Error, Warning', 15, 2) WITH LOG
go
RAISERROR ('Chapter 12 Error, Error', 21, 2) WITH LOG
Go
```

2. Open the SQL Server Log. Right-click the Current log and choose Refresh. In the right pane, scroll down to the bottom. You should now see the errors we just generated, as shown here.

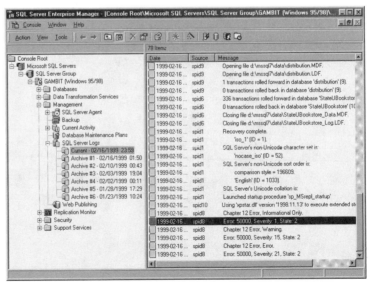

3. The log provides you with the date, the *spid* (System Process ID), and the error message.

4. Let's look at the same error messages in the NT Event Viewer. Click Start ➤ Programs ➤ Administrative Tools ➤ Event Viewer.

5. In the Event Viewer, choose Application from the Log menu.

6. Refresh the data by clicking View ➤ Refresh, or simply press the F5 key.

7. You should now see the Windows NT Application Log and the errors you just generated.

8. If you double-click the first error (the error with the stop sign) you will note that the Error is number 50,000, with a severity of 21 and a state of 2. The error message is on the following line and it reads: Chapter 12 Error, It has a severity level of Error.

9. Close the Event Viewer.

Error Message Components

Although the components of an error message are not tested, it is useful to know what the different severity levels mean to you as an administrator.

- *Error Numbers* are used to uniquely identify an error message.

- *Severity Level* tells you what type of problem has occurred in the SQL Server. Severity levels range from 0 to 25.

- *Error State* identifies the source of the error. This can be especially useful if the same error can occur in several locations.

- *Error Message* is the text associated with the error. The message tells you what the error is. Included in some error messages is a possible solution.

Severity Levels

Let's take a closer look at severity levels. Very briefly, errors from 0 to 10 are informational, 11 through 16 are user errors, 17 and 18 are resource problems, and 19 to 25 are fatal errors.

Severity 0 – 10 These are informational messages and don't generally prevent a user from working with SQL Server. User-defined errors (error numbers 50,000 and higher) will have a severity of 0 –10.

Severity 11 – 16 These are generated by users and need to be fixed by the user. These are generally errors in the syntax of their SQL statements.

Errors with a severity of 17 or 18 are system resource errors and general system errors. A user's session is not normally interrupted when one of these errors occurs.

Severity 17: Insufficient Resources This would include configurable resources such as locks and open databases allowed. The SA should handle these errors using the sp_configure stored procedures to reconfigure the system.

Severity 18: Non-Fatal Internal Error Detected When some type of internal error has been detected, you should notify the SA to handle the problem. Stopping and restarting the SQL Server will generally fix this problem.

Severity levels of 19 through 25 are fatal errors in the program code. These errors are very rare and should be investigated as quickly as possible. Errors with a severity of 20 and higher will terminate a user's connection to the SQL Server.

Severity 19: SQL Server Error in Resource This error occurs when a nonconfigurable limit has been exceeded. The SA should investigate the error and may need to call upon some type of technical support.

Severity 20: SQL Server Fatal Error in Current Process This error occurs when SQL Server code runs into a problem. Because this error affects only one process, there is a good chance that the database is still intact. The SA should KILL the process.

Severity 21: SQL Server Fatal Error in Database Process This error occurs when SQL Server finds an error in code that affects all current connections or processes running on a database. Although this error sounds disastrous, the database itself is generally still intact.

Severity 22: SQL Server Fatal Error Table Integrity Suspect This error occurs when an application damages an index or a table. You should run the DBCC CHECKTABLE, DBCC CHECKDB, and DBCC NEWALLOC commands to investigate the consistency of your database. If you find that only one object is corrupted, you might try dropping and re-creating that object. If multiple objects are corrupted, there is still a chance that the error is in cache and not on the hard disk. Try stopping and restarting the SQL Server and then run the DBCC commands again. If this did not fix the problem, then the errors have migrated to your hard disk and you should start your recovery procedures.

Severity 23: SQL Server Fatal Error Database Integrity Suspect   You should handle this error in the same manner as prescribed for Severity 22 errors.

Severity 24: Hardware Error   This error occurs when there is a hardware problem. The SA and possibly the Network Administrator should investigate the problem. In the event of media failure, you should start your recovery.

Severity 25: Internal System Error   Contact the SA immediately.

SQL Server 7 Upgrading Issues

When you upgrade from SQL Server 6.*x* to version 7, you can use the SQL Server Upgrade Wizard. As you recall, the wizard checks the syscomments tables to look for inconsistencies, and it validates permissions on users and their SQL Server logins. The database schema, objects, and data are then transformed from the 6.*x* server to the 7 server.

Microsoft ✓ *Exam Objective*	**Diagnose and resolve problems in upgrading from SQL Server 6.*x*.**

When the Upgrade Wizard finds problems with the upgrade process, an error message will be displayed that says, "One or more warnings have been logged. Please read the next screen carefully before you begin your upgrade." The Summary of Warnings screen is then displayed with the inconsistencies that the wizard found. As the administrator, you should attempt to resolve these problems. You can also find these problems stored in a log file with an "err.out" extension. The error files will be located in the following folder: \MSSQL7\Upgrade*<servername>_<date>_<time>*. The error files themselves have a naming convention of `check65-<dbid><dbname>_err.out`. For example, if the SQL Server were named Sybex, and you did the upgrade on February 27th, 1999 at 12:22:23 P.M. on the MySample database, the full path and filename for this output file would be:

```
\MSSQL7\Upgrade\Sybex_02-27-99_12:22:23\check65-019MySample_
err.out
```

You may encounter the following problems during an upgrade to SQL Server 7:

- Tempdb is too small. You should resize the Tempdb database to at least 10MB. However, we recommend that you resize the database to at least 25MB for an upgrade.

- Ensure that the database users have valid SQL Server logins in the syslogins table on the Master database.

- SQL Server stops and restarts the SQL Server during the upgrade process. To ensure that there are no problems, you should disable any stored procedures set to execute at startup.

- If you have databases with dependencies in other databases, you should upgrade all the interdependent databases at the same time.

- When SQL Server 6.5 login accounts that have a default database other than Master are upgraded to SQL Server 7, they will not be upgraded if that default database does not exist in SQL Server 7.

- If you are using two computers to perform your upgrade, you cannot use the local system account, as it has no network capabilities. The user account that you do use should have administrative capabilities on both computers.

- Disable replication and clear the associated transaction logs.

While this checklist is not complete, it does cover nearly every problem that you will encounter during an upgrade.

Troubleshooting Backup and Restore Operations

When you back up and restore databases and transaction logs you may encounter several different problems in several distinct areas. In this section, we will take a closer look at the problems you may encounter, and where the answers are not obvious, make recommendations regarding possible solutions.

Microsoft ✓ **Exam** **Objective**	**Diagnose and resolve problems in backup and restore operations.**

The backup fails with Error 3023. This means that you were attempting to do a backup during some type of database activity that is not allowed during a backup operation. You may not do any of the following during a backup:

- bcp
- CREATE INDEX
- Data file movement or resizing
- DBCC CHECKALLOC
- DBCC SHRINKDATABASE
- DBCC SHRINKFILE
- SELECT INTO

To fix this error, wait until the illegal process has completed and then reissue your BACKUP commands.

If you receive Error 3120 or 3149, you may be attempting to restore a backup with a different character set or sort order than what SQL Server is currently configured to use. SQL Server can only restore databases that have the same character set and sort order as the backup. If you encounter this error, there are several things that you can do. The best solution is to install another copy of SQL Server 7 on another computer with the proper character set and sort order and then do your recovery. Once your database has been recovered, you can use the Transfer Manager (part of Data Transformation Services) to move your schema, objects, and data from the temporarily restored database to your permanent database.

Error 3143 indicates that you are attempting to restore a non-SQL Server backup into SQL Server. This is possible in SQL Server 7 because SQL Server 7 uses the same Microsoft Tape Format that is used for NT backups. You should use the RESTORE HEADERONLY command to determine whether the backup you are looking at is in fact a SQL Server backup.

Other errors that you may encounter involve attempting to back up a transaction log when you have the Truncate Log on Checkpoint database option enabled. There is no log to back up. You may also encounter errors when restoring your transaction logs. Remember that the transaction logs must be restored in order with no gaps.

Replication Fault-Tolerance and Recovery Problems

Although replication is a fairly complex topic, replication troubleshooting is fairly straightforward. The architecture of the replication model that Microsoft implements in SQL Server 7 minimizes the areas of potential replication problems. There are three major areas and one minor area of concern. The three major areas are security, the logreader agent, and the distribution agent. A minor area is in the actual data definition you are trying to implement. Troubleshooting problems with data definition issues means you must follow the rules laid out for the different datatypes and their replication properties.

For example, while IDENTITY properties do not replicate, the value stored in the IDENTITY column will be replicated. Timestamps are replicated as binary 8 datatypes. For more information on data definition issues, please see Chapter 9, *Creating and Implementing a Replication Solution,* or refer to the SQL Server 7 Books Online.

Microsoft	**Diagnose and resolve replication problems.**
✓ Exam	
Objective	

In the following sections, we will take a closer look at security issues, the logreader agent, and the distribution agent.

Troubleshooting Security in Replication

For replication to work, the SQLServerAgent must have administrator privileges on all computers involved in the replication scenario, and the account must have network access. LocalSystem accounts cannot be used with replication.

Replication agents call the xp_loginfo stored procedure when they start up. The xp_loginfo stored procedure verifies that the SQLServerAgent has the appropriate permissions on the various servers.

This error can be a bit tricky to find. Since the agent never actually starts running, there is no error logged in the history associated with the agent. Instead, you must check the Jobs folder to find errors of this type. To fix this problem, ensure that your SQLServerAgent account is using an administrator account that has network capabilities.

You may encounter errors of this type if the various SQL Servers are not using a central domain account for the SQLServerAgent. If you must set up different accounts for the various SQL Server Agents, you might try using standard security rather than NT security for your replication needs.

Replication Will Not Run

Before replication can begin, an initial snapshot of the data must be copied to each subscriber. If the snapshot is not applied, replication cannot begin. This problem usually manifests itself in the snapshot agent or in the replication schedule.

You should make sure that the snapshot agent is running and that a snapshot has been applied to the subscribers. You can view the snapshot agent's history through the Replication Monitor in Enterprise Manager. Follow the steps outlined in Exercise 12.2 to view agent histories.

EXERCISE 12.2

Working with the Replication Monitor

1. Open the Enterprise Manager and expand the Replication Monitor folder, then the Agents folder, and finally click on the Snapshot Agent folder as shown here.

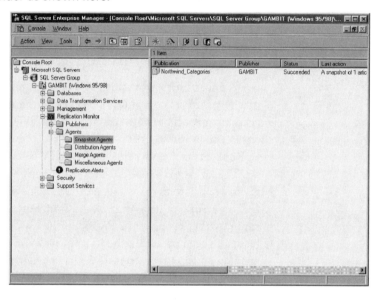

2. Right-click the Agent in the right pane of the window and choose Agent History. This will give you information regarding how often the agent has run and what the agent accomplished.

3. Verify that the jobs are running as scheduled and that errors are not occurring.

If the snapshot agent is not applying data to the subscriber, you might have problems with security between the snapshot agent and the Publishing database.

If your snapshot agent is not doing anything at all, make certain that your distribution server is online and available and that you have the appropriate permissions on the working folder at the distributor.

If the snapshot agent appears to be working properly, it's time to start looking at other possibilities.

No Subscribers Are Working

If none of your subscribers are getting replicated data, but the snapshot agent appears to be working, the problem is most likely with the logreader agent. If the logreader agent is not moving data from the transaction log of the publishing database to the distribution database, the distribution agent cannot move those records to subscribers. Since none of the subscribers is getting data, it is far more likely that the logreader, rather than the distribution agent, is not performing.

Take a look at the logreader agent in the Replication Monitor. Verify that jobs are running as scheduled and that data is moving. Verify that your distribution database is large enough to hold the replicated transactions. Verify that the all servers involved in replication have enough user connections configured for the replication tasks to work. Every publication will require a user connection from the distribution server. The distribution server in turn will require at least one user connection per subscription. Finally, you want to make sure that the Distribution database's transaction log is not full.

If all of these things check out, you might try modifying the schedule of your replication a bit. While many jobs can run in parallel, SQL Server will not allow the same job to run more than one version of itself at a time.

Several Subscribers of Many Are Not Working

When several subscribers of many are not working, it is almost definitely a problem with the distribution process. Because other subscribers are receiving replicated data, you know that the logreader process is working properly. You should check for the following problems as part of your troubleshooting duties:

- Check the distribution agent histories for the failing servers.

- Ensure that the subscription server is online and has connectivity.

- Ensure that the subscription database is available, not marked for DBO-use only, and is not set to read-only.

- Ensure that the SQLServerAgent security credentials are set properly for the subscription servers.

- Ensure that the distribution agent is not waiting to perform a manual synchronization.

Once the potential problems with the agents are out of the way, there is one other area that you need to focus on for troubleshooting replication: the recovery process. You should know what happens when various servers in the replication model are offline and the potential problems that being offline creates.

In most cases, replication will automatically recover itself and continue replicating where it left off when the server crashed.

Recovering the Publishing Server

When the publishing server goes down, the subscribers won't get replicated data. This may be an inconvenience, but SQL Server is very good about recovering from this type of problem.

The logreader agent uses pointers in the transaction logs of published databases. These pointers keep track of the transactions with which the logreader is currently working. If the publishing server is down, the logreader agent will continue from where it stopped, once the publishing server is back online.

If you have to restore the Publishing databases for some reason, then your pointers will be out of synch, as will your subscribers. You should run a snapshot to resynchronize the publisher and the affected subscribers. Replication should then proceed normally.

Recovering the Distribution Server

When your distribution server is down, replication halts. The distribution agent, however, keeps track of which transactions have been applied to which subscribers. When the distribution server is brought back online, replication should continue from where it stopped.

There are some potential problems with the replication if the distribution server has been down for an extended period of time. The distribution agent will hold transactions for a configurable amount of time (known as the *retention period)*. The default is 24 hours. After that period, these transactions will age out of the Distribution database and will not be applied to your subscribers. If this happens, resynchronize your subscribers by running a new snapshot.

If you know ahead of time that you are going to be down for an extended period of time, you can modify the time allotted for the transactions in the distribution agent.

Another potential issue with a downed distribution server is the synchronicity with the publishers. As you know, the logreader agent uses pointers in the transaction logs of published databases. If for some reason the transactions are not being applied to the distribution server, and the logreader agent is still online, the publishing server will not allow a transaction log backup. (This is why you should always maintain your Distribution database's transaction log.) If, however, the distribution server is offline, then the logreader agent does not have any pointers in the publishing database's transaction logs, and those logs can be backed up and truncated. When the distribution server comes back online, you will be forced to resynchronize your subscribers so that replication can begin again.

To avoid this problem, we suggest that you back up your distribution server at the same time that you make backups to your publishing servers. This allows the distribution database to be synchronized with the Publishing databases.

Recovering the Subscription Server

When your subscription servers go down, you simply need to bring the server back online. Replicated transactions on the distribution server will automatically be applied, and the subscriber will start running again normally.

If your subscriber is down for an extended period of time, your stored transactions on the distribution server may age out. You can change the retention period or simply resynchronize the affected subscribers.

Troubleshooting Jobs and Alerts

As an administrator, you can use jobs and alerts to proactively administrate your database. Alerts can fire off jobs that can take corrective actions. If the corrective actions fail, those jobs can then fire off additional alerts. This activity can lower your total cost of ownership by freeing you up from routine maintenance duties to work on other parts of SQL Server.

Microsoft
Exam
Objective

Diagnose and resolve job or alert failures.

When you are troubleshooting jobs, you should keep the following in mind:

- Ensure that the SQLServerAgent service is running.

- Ensure that the job is enabled.

- Ensure that the T-SQL or stored procedures in the job steps work.

- Ensure that the job owner has the appropriate permissions on all affected objects.

- Ensure that the steps operate as planned and fire in the correct order. For example, step two fires when step one completes successfully.

- If you are using e-mail or pager operators, ensure that SQL Mail is enabled and set up properly.

- Check the job history to see if the jobs are firing.

- Verify that the job is scheduled properly. SQL Server allows only one instance of a particular job to run at a time.

When you are troubleshooting alerts, many of the same cautions apply. In addition, you should verify the following:

- Ensure that the alerts are being generated in the Windows NT Application log. If the message is not sent to the Application log, then the alerts manager cannot see it.

- If you have alerts based on performance thresholds, ensure that the polling interval is set properly. SQL Server will poll the Performance Monitor every 20 seconds by default.

- If e-mail, pager, or net send notifications are not timely, check that the delay between responses is not set too high.

Troubleshooting Distributed Queries

When you are working with distributed queries, there are two main problems that you as an administrator need to worry about. These are connectivity and security.

Diagnose and resolve distributed query problems.

You should ensure that you have properly set up and configured the linked servers. For more information on how to connect to a linked server, see Chapter 11, *Working with Remote Data and Linked Servers,* or the SQL Server 7 Books Online.

Once you are connected, you may have problems running certain queries. If the query problem isn't syntactical, it is most likely a permissions problem. Ensure that you have the appropriate permissions on the various database objects on both the linked server and the local servers.

Troubleshooting Client Connectivity

SQL Server listens in on whatever protocols you have installed on the server. Clients can then communicate over any of those protocols with the SQL Server. Your clients will need to have the appropriate Net-Library installed as well as the appropriate DB-Library.

Diagnose and resolve client connectivity problems.

The default connection is over Named Pipes. In most cases, this is the fastest method of communication with SQL Server. You can also use TCP/IP or Multi-Protocol, the server-side libraries installed by default. The Multi-Protocol library has the advantage of supporting the encryption of data as it moves through the tabular data stream to and from the SQL Server.

If you wish to use a protocol other than Named Pipes at the client, you need to use the Client Network utility. With this utility, you can set the default client Net-Library as well as the DB-Library options.

Changing the Net-Library on the client affects only that client's communications with SQL Server. It does not affect any other aspect of networking for the client.

The first step to handling network problems is to determine (and isolate) where the problem is occurring. The errors could be coming from the SQL Server, the network, the front-end application, or any combination of these. Try the following to troubleshoot the problem:

Check your local connection to the SQL Server first. From the server machine, go to a command prompt and run the OSQL utility. This will verify that you do have access to SQL Server and that Named Pipes is working on the local machine.

The next step is to check your remote connection to SQL Server over Named Pipes. Exercise 12.3 shows you how to check your Named Pipes connection.

EXERCISE 12.3

Testing Named Pipes

1. To test Named Pipes, you will need a client and a server. On the server, go to a command prompt by selecting Start ➤ Programs ➤ MS-DOS.

2. At the command prompt, enter **makepipe**.

3. You should now see:

   ```
   Making PIPE:\\.\pipe\abc
   read to write delay <seconds>:0
   Waiting for Client to Connect. . .
   ```

4. The server is waiting for a client to try to use the named pipe.

5. From a client machine, enter the following:

   readpipe /S<servername> /D<string>

For example, if your server's name is Gambit and you want to send the message "testing123" to the named pipe, enter:

readpipe /Sgambit /Dtesting123

You should get something like this in response on the client machine:

```
SvrName:\\Gambit
PIPE: :\\Gambit\pipe\abc
DATA: :Testing123
Data Sent: 1 Testing123
Data Read: 1 Testing123
```

6. On the server machine, you should see something similar to this:

```
Waiting for client to send . . . 1
Data Read:
Testing123
Waiting for client to send . . . 2
Pipe closed
Waiting for Client to Connect. . .
```

7. To close the pipe, close the command-prompt window.

If this completes successfully, you know that Named Pipes is working. If it doesn't work, you will need to look for other problems. For example, you can verify that you have network connectivity by running a NET VIEW statement from a command prompt, or by double-clicking on the Entire Network icon in the Network Neighborhood. If something shows up other than your computer's name, then you know that you can see the rest of the network.

If Named Pipes comes up successfully, but you still cannot connect, you probably have a DB-Lib problem. You should verify that you have the same Network-Library and DB-Library on both the Server and the client computer. This can be done with the Setup program or with the Client Network utility as shown in Chapter 3, *SQL Server Tools and Utilities*.

Troubleshooting Database Objects and Database Access

When you cannot access the objects in your database and permissions are not the problem, you may need to verify the integrity of your database and its objects.

Diagnose and resolve problems in accessing SQL Server, databases, and database objects.

You can check the integrity of database objects by using the DBCC statements. There are several you should know for the exam—and several more to be a good administrator. This section will give you a quick overview of some of the most common DBCC statements.

- DBCC CHECKTABLE   You can run this command to verify that index and data pages are correctly linked and that your indexes are sorted properly. It will also verify that the data stored on each page is reasonable and that the page offsets are reasonable.

- DBCC CHECKDB   This command does the same thing as the CHECK-TABLE command but it does it for every table in a database.

- DBCC CHECKCATALOG   This command will check for consistency in and between system tables. For example, if there is an entry in the sysobjects table, there should be a matching entry in the syscolumns table.

- DBCC CHECKALLOC   Verifies that extents are being used properly and that there is no overlap between objects that reside in their own separate extents.

- DBCC MEMUSAGE   Provides a detailed report on the server memory allocated at startup as well as how much memory is being used by the 20 largest objects in both the procedure and data caches.

- DBCC TEXTALLOC/TEXTALL   Checks the allocation of text and image columns in a table or a database. There are two options: full and fast. Full will generate a report, whereas fast will not.

If these statements generate errors, you can try to recover data or drop and rebuild the individual database objects in question.

If other problems occur, your database may be marked as suspect. Knowing what causes a suspect database will aid in your troubleshooting efforts.

If a database file is missing or has been renamed or moved, your database will be marked suspect. To resolve this problem, find out why the file is offline or otherwise missing and bring it back online. Stop and restart the SQL Server. The automatic recovery should unmark the suspect databases.

If a database device has been moved, or if it has been renamed, or if it doesn't exist, the error log will contain Error 822. If the database files have been renamed, you should name them back to their original names and stop and restart the SQL Server. If the database is missing, you should start your recovery procedures.

The last thing that might cause a database to be suspect is a lack of permissions. This can only happen if you are using NTFS and the database files are on the NTFS partition. You can fix this problem by making the administrator the owner of the database files and make sure that the MSSQLServer service has read/write permissions on the file as well.

If for some reason the database appears to be fine, but you cannot remove the suspect status, you could run the following SQL script to manually reset the status of the database.

```
sp_configure 'allow updates', 1
GO
RECONFIGURE WITH OVERRIDE
GO
USE master
GO
BEGIN TRAN
GO
UPDATE sysdatabases
set status=0 where name=your database name'
GO
```

If more than one row is affected by the UPDATE statement, issue a ROLLBACK statement and do some further investigation; otherwise, continue with the rest of these statements.

```
COMMIT TRAN
GO
sp_configure 'allow updates', 0
GO
RECONFIGURE WITH OVERRIDE
GO
CHECKPOINT
GO
SHUTDOWN
GO
```

Summary

This chapter has covered various troubleshooting issues that you will encounter in your DBA duties as well as on the MCSE exam. We can't stress enough the importance of having real-world experience with the product. As we said earlier, troubleshooting is an art that must be practiced. The more practice you get with SQL Server 7, the easier the exam is going to be for you.

We first looked at where you can find information about how SQL Server is operating, including both informational and error messages. You can use the SQL Server Error logs as well as the Windows NT Application log. We then looked at the components of a SQL Server error message. Errors come in the form of a specific error number and a severity level. In general, errors with a severity of 0 to10 are informational, while 11 to16 are user errors and 17and 18 are resource issues. Errors with a severity of 19 to 25 should not be ignored, as these are fatal errors.

You may run into some issues during your upgrade process. Upgrade issues include a Tempdb that is too small, an invalid user login, autoexecuting stored procedures, and database dependencies.

You can run into a whole host of problems when you are attempting to back up and restore your SQL Server databases. When backing up, be sure that you are not performing any database-wide alterations, or any non-logged transactions.

Restorations can be a bit tricky if you are not using the same character set and sort order as the backed-up data. To move this type of data, use the SQL Transfer Manager.

Replication for the most part troubleshoots itself. The main problems found in replication include SQL Server security, connectivity problems, and data definition issues. To remove nearly all of the connectivity and security issues, we suggest that all SQL Servers in your organization share the same service account. If you don't wish to do this, using SQL Server security may keep security issues to a minimum.

When replication will not run, you should check the various agent histories and verify that the agents are attempting to replicate. From there, you can determine if the logreader, distribution, or snapshot agent is at fault.

Replication recovery is very simple to troubleshoot. If your servers are not down for an extended period of time, when they come back online they will resume replicating where they stopped. If the transactions have aged out of the distribution server, a simple resynchronization is generally all that is needed to recover and resume replication.

When you troubleshoot jobs and alerts, you should check the job or alert histories to verify that they are running. If they are not, you should check the schedules, T-SQL, job owner security, and the enabled properties of these items.

Distributed queries run into problems when they cannot connect to the linked servers or cannot access database objects on the linked or local server. Ensure that you have configured your linked servers properly and verify that you have the appropriate permissions on the various objects with which you are working.

Client connectivity in SQL Server can be a bit of a chore. (It seems that every time we apply a patch for a program, we no longer have access from our clients to SQL Server.) The Client Network utility can reestablish your Net-Library and DB-Library, which are necessary to connect to SQL Server over the tabular data stream.

Database objects can become unusable over time. To ensure that your database objects stay healthy and work properly, there are a variety of DBCC commands that you should run on a regular basis.

You may end up with a suspect database if you change or move data files or change the security on those files at the NTFS level. Keep these things in mind when you have a database that has been marked suspect.

Review Questions

1. SQL Server does not seem to be working properly. You can use the Enterprise Manager, but many of the jobs and alerts don't seem to be running properly. You want to find more information about the general health of your SQL Server. Which of the following logs can be used to gather information on SQL Server errors? (Select all that apply.)

   A. SQL Server error logs

   B. SQL Server Transaction log

   C. NT Application log

   D. NT Server Manager

2. You are reading through one of the error logs and notice that severity level is between 0 and 10. Which of the following types of error messages does this severity level describe?

   A. Informational

   B. Warning

   C. User

   D. Fatal

3. Your SQL Server appears to be having problems working with system resources. You look in the Windows NT Application log and find out that this is the case. What severity level would those resource errors have?

   A. 0 – 10

   B. 11 – 16

   C. 17 – 18

   D. 19 – 25

4. You have nine different SQL Server 6.5 databases in your enterprise. You are preparing to upgrade those databases to SQL Server 7 and are concerned with the upgrade process itself. Which of the following would prevent you from upgrading a SQL Server 6.5 database to SQL Server 7?

   A. Tempdb is set to 25MB

   B. Replication is enabled

   C. Character sets are different

   D. Sort orders are different

5. You are experiencing some connectivity problems with clients and SQL Server. You have checked the network cables and have found them working properly. You have used the NET VIEW command to verify that the network is working properly. You now want to check some SQL Server specific items. Which command can you use to verify that you have local access to SQL Server over a named pipe?

   A. NET OPENPIPE

   B. NET USE MSSQLServer

   C. NET VIEW /ALL

   D. osql /Usa /P

6. You are experiencing some connectivity problems with clients and SQL Server. You have checked the network cables and have found them working properly. You have used the NET VIEW command to verify that the network is working properly. You now want to check some SQL Server specific items. What command can you use to verify that you have network access to SQL Server over a named pipe?

   A. NET CHECKPIPE

   B. NET VIEW /ALL

   C. MAKEPIPE and READPIPE

   D. isql /Usa /P

7. You can run one of the following commands to verify that index and data pages are correctly linked, that your indexes are sorted properly, that the data stored on each page is reasonable, and that the page offsets are reasonable for an entire database.

A. DBCC CHECKTABLE

B. DBCC CHECKDB

C. DBCC CHECKCATALOG

D. DBCC CHECKALLOC

8. You can run one of the following commands to verify that index and data pages are correctly linked, that your indexes are sorted properly, that the data stored on each page is reasonable, and that the page offsets are reasonable for a single table in a database.

A. DBCC CHECKTABLE

B. sp_checktable

C. xp_checktable

D. DBCC CHECKALLOC

9. Which command can you use to verify that extents are being used properly and that there is no overlap between objects that reside in their own separate extents?

A. DBCC CHECKTABLE

B. DBCC CHECKDB

C. DBCC CHECKCATALOG

D. DBCC CHECKALLOC

10. To check for consistency in and between system tables you could run which command?

A. DBCC CHECKTABLE

B. DBCC CHECKDB

C. DBCC CHECKCATALOG

D. DBCC CHECKALLOC

11. You come into work on Monday and find that your Accounting database has been marked suspect. Which of the following can cause a database to be marked suspect? (Select all that apply.)

A. The database is offline

B. The database is marked for DBO use only

C. The database file is on an NTFS partition that the SQL Server does not have rights on

D. The database files have been renamed

12. You receive Error 3023 during your backup process. Which of the following activities could have generated this error? (Select all that apply.)

A. Someone ran a CREATE INDEX command

B. Someone ran a DBCC SHRINKDATABASE command

C. Someone ran a DBCC CHECKALLOC command

D. Someone ran a SELECT INTO or a bcp command

13. You have an old backup from a SQL Server 7 installation from a different branch of your company. You are attempting to restore that database on your local SQL Server 7 installation. Which of the following must be true in order to recover this database in SQL Server?

A. You must be using the same character set

B. You must be using the same sort order

C. You must use the Transfer Manager

D. You must be using the same data filenames and locations

14. You are troubleshooting your replication scenario and find that no subscribers are receiving replicated transactions. You have verified that all subscribers have network connectivity to the distribution server. You have also verified that all SQL Servers in the enterprise are using the same service account. What is most likely the problem?

   A. The logreader agent is dead

   B. The distribution process is dead

   C. The subscription process is dead

   D. The problem is internal to SQL Server and has nothing to do with replication

15. You are troubleshooting your replication scenario and find that several subscribers of many are not receiving replicated transactions. You have verified that all subscribers have network connectivity to the distribution server. You have also verified that all SQL Servers in the enterprise are using the same service account. What is most likely the problem?

   A. The logreader process

   B. The distribution process

   C. The subscription process

   D. The problem is internal to SQL Server and has nothing to do with replication

16. If you are having problems with replication, where is the easiest location to begin gathering information to troubleshoot the problem?

   A. The Alerts window

   B. The Current Activity window

   C. The Publication window

   D. The Replication Monitor window

17. You have created a Performance Monitor alert that fires when your transaction log reaches a performance threshold of 80% of capacity. The alert is generating an error to the NT Application log. You have created an alert on that error, and the alert attempts to fire a job. The job does not seem to be firing. What could be the problem? (Select all that apply.)

A. The job is not enabled

B. The job owner does not have permissions on objects that the job references

C. The SQLServerAgent service is not running

D. The T-SQL statements found in the job are not valid

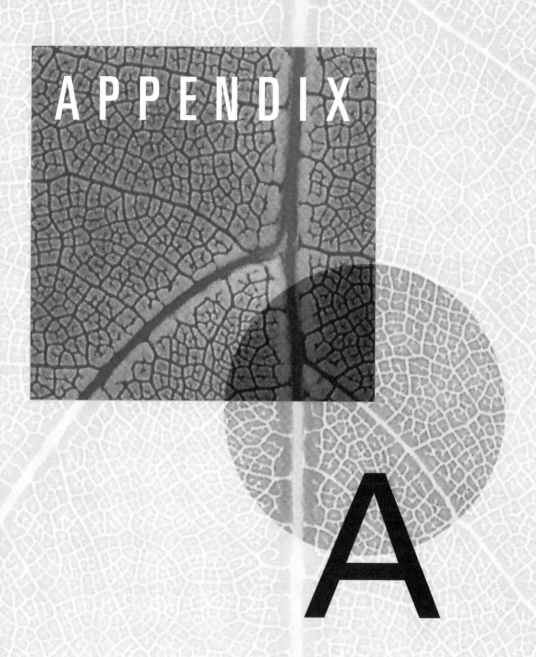

APPENDIX

A

Answers to Review Questions

Chapter 1 Answers

1. Which of the following is a database object? (Choose all that apply.)

A. Table

B. Index

C. Rule

D. Default

Answer: **A, B, C, D.** All of these are database objects.

2. Who is responsible for backing up databases?

A. The database administrator

B. The database developer

C. Database users

D. The Windows NT administrator

Answer: **A.** The database administrator is usually the one responsible for backups of the database.

3. Who is responsible for ongoing database security?

A. The database administrator

B. The database developer

C. Database users

D. The Windows NT administrator

Answer: **A.** The database administrator is usually the one responsible for ongoing database security.

4. Who is responsible for ongoing SQL Server optimization?

A. The database administrator

B. The database developer

C. Database users

D. The Windows NT administrator

Answer: A. The database administrator is usually the one responsible for optimization of the SQL Server.

5. What is the process of breaking related information into tables called?

A. Fragmentation

B. Database design

C. Normalization

D. Tabulating the data

Answer: C. To normalize the database means to design it for relational tables.

6. When a query is run in client/server computing, who actually runs the query?

A. The client

B. The server

C. Both the client and the server

D. Neither; a "middleware" application runs the query.

Answer: B. When a query is submitted to SQL Server the work is done by the server and just the results are sent back to the client.

7. SQL Server is an example of what kind of database system?

A. Flat-file

B. 3-D

C. RDBMS

D. Heirarchical

Answer: C. SQL Server is an RDBMS, or Relational Database Management System.

8. Data in relational databases is organized into:

   A. Fields

   B. Files

   C. Reports

   D. Tables

Answer: D. Data in relational databases is organized into tables, which are based on like items.

9. SQL Server 7 can run on which operating systems? (Select all that apply.)

   A. Windows for Workgroups

   B. Windows 95/98

   C. Windows NT Workstation

   D. Windows NT Server

Answer: B, C, D. SQL Server 7 can run on Windows 95/98 as well as any version of Windows NT 4 or later.

10. SQL Server 7 uses which database language?

   A. DBMS

   B. T-SQL

   C. SQL

   D. QUERY

Answer: B. Microsoft's SQL Servers have always used a version of SQL known as Transact SQL or T-SQL.

11. What is a view in SQL Server?

   A. Precompiled code

   B. A stored query

   C. A way of organizing like data

D. A way of entering default values

Answer: B. A view is like a stored query. Once created, when a view is used, the query that made the view is automatically executed.

12. Which version of SQL Server would you install if you wanted to access your SQL data running on NT Server only from a web server?

    A. The Desktop version on every client

    B. The Desktop version with Internet Connector licensing

    C. The standard version with per seat licensing

    D. The standard version with Internet Connector licensing

    Answer: D. You would probably be running the standard version if you were using NT Server as your server, and you would need Internet Connector licensing if you accessed your data via a web server.

13. The standard version of SQL Server can run on which platforms?

    A. Windows 95/98

    B. Windows NT Workstation

    C. Windows NT Server

    D. Windows NT Enterprise Server

    Answer: C, D. The standard version requires Windows NT Server, although it would usually be run on a server and not a client.

14. The Enterprise version of SQL Server can run on which platforms?

    A. Windows 95/98

    B. Windows NT Workstation

    C. Windows NT Server

    D. Windows NT Enterprise Server

    Answer: D. The Enterprise version requires Windows NT Server Enterprise Edition.

Chapter 2 Answers

1. Which batch file is used to do an unattended installation?

   A. sql70cli.bat

   B. sql70ful.bat

   C. sql70cst.bat

   D. sql70rem.bat

   Answer: C. The batch file that Microsoft has written to help automate unattended installations is sql70cst.bat.

2. If you do an unattended installation and do not specify which user account to be assigned to the SQL services, which account will be chosen?

   A. You must always specify an account to use

   B. The Administrator account

   C. The SA account

   D. The LocalSystem account

   Answer: D. Unless you specify in your .ISS file which account (and corresponding password) to use, the LocalSystem account will be used.

3. Which is the default folder for SQL 7?

   A. \MSSQL

   B. \MSSQL7

   C. \SQLServer

   D. \SQLServer7

   Answer: B. The default folder for SQL Server 7 is \MSSQL7.

4. Which is the default folder for databases in SQL 7?

   A. \DB

   B. \Devices

C. \Data

D. \Databases

Answer: C. The default folder for databases in SQL Server 7 is \Data.

5. In which Registry key will you find the majority of information on SQL Server 7 services?

A. Hkey_Local_Machine\Software\SQLServer

B. Hkey_Local_Machine\Software\Microsoft\MSSQLServer

C. Hkey_Current_Config\Software\Microsoft\SQLServer

D. Hkey_Current_User\Software\Microsoft\SQLServer

Answer: B. Information for SQL Services is held in the Hkey_Local_Machine\Software\Microsoft\MSSQLServer key.

6. What is the default folder for error logs for SQL Server 7?

A. \MSSQL\Errors

B. \MSSQL\Log

C. \MSSQL7\Errors

D. \MSSQL7\Log

Answer: D. The default folder for log files is the \MSSQL7\Log folder.

7. Which is the default login for SQL Server?

A. SQLAdmin

B. Administrator

C. Admin

D. SA

Answer: D. The SQL default login is SA (with no password) for a new installation of SQL Server.

8. How do you change the configurations for SQL Server from within Enterprise Manager? (Select all that apply.)

A. Highlight the server, right-click, and choose Settings

B. Highlight the server, right-click, and choose Properties

C. Highlight the server and choose Tools ➤ Settings

D. Highlight the server and choose Tools ➤ Properties

Answer: B, D. There is no Settings option. All settings are changed from the Properties screens.

9. What is the default port for TCP/IP and SQL Server?

A. 433

B. 520

C. 1020

D. 1433

Answer: D. The default port for TCP/IP and SQL Server is 1433.

10. How can you have two databases with different languages installed on the same server if you chose the English character set?

A. You can't

B. Choose a different sort order for each database

C. Choose the desired character set when you create the database

D. Choose the default Unicode character set, which allows different character sets in each database

Answer: D. Since Unicode uses 2 bytes to represent characters, more than 64K characters can be represented, even with the English character set.

11. How can you install SQL Server 7 so you can go back to 6.5 anytime you want? (Select all that apply.)

A. Perform an in-place upgrade

B. Install 7 in a different folder than 6.5

C. Install 7 in the same folder as 6.5 and preserve your old settings

D. Install 7 on a different server than 6.5 and upgrade the databases to SQL 7 across the wire

Answer: B, D. If you perform an in-place upgrade you essentially install SQL 7 in the same folder as 6.5, thus making it impossible to go back to 6.5.

12. What is the name of the file that contains the initialization settings for your setup of SQL Server?

A. `setup.iss`

B. `sql.iss`

C. `sqlsettings.iss`

D. `auto.iss`

Answer: A. The Setup program keeps track of all of your choices in a file called `setup.iss` in case you want to use it again later.

13. How can clients connect to SQL Server? (Select all that apply.)

A. DB-Library

B. ODBC

C. OLE-DB

D. SQL-DB

Answer: A, B, C. There is no such thing as SQL-DB.

14. What utility is used to configure ODBC connections?

A. ODBC Data Sources

B. ODBC Setup

C. ODBC Client Config utility

D. SQL Client Config utility

Answer: A. The ODBC Data Sources applet of the Control Panel is used to configure ODBC connections.

15. You have your SQL Server set to a non-standard name. Which program would you use to configure the client to use the name?

A. Enterprise Manager

B. Server Network Utility

C. Client Network Utility

D. SQL Setup at the client

Answer: C. The Client Network Utility is used to change how the client connects to SQL Server and can be used to change the default name, port, and other characteristics of the connection.

16. You have a SQL 6.5 Server with Service Pack 2 for SQL with 4GB of user databases on a Windows NT 3.51 Server with Service Pack 5. You have 2GB of free space. You wish to upgrade the computer in place into a SQL 7 Server. Which of the following will happen when you attempt to upgrade?

A. The upgrade will work correctly

B. The upgrade will not work because of a single problem

C. The upgrade will not work because of two problems

D. The upgrade will not work because of three problems

Answer: D. There are several reasons why the upgrade will not work. First, Windows NT 4 (with SP 4) is required. Second, Service Pack 3 or higher is required for SQL 6.5, and third, you should have at least 1.5 times the size of the current databases (in this case 6GB) to upgrade them.

Chapter 3 Answers

1. You have created a Full-Text index on a table with a timestamp column. What would you schedule on a regular basis to keep the index up-to-date?

A. Rebuilds of the index

B. Full repopulation of the index

C. Incremental repopulation of the index

D. Refreshes of the index

Answer: C. If there is a timestamp column in the table, you can schedule incremental repopulations; otherwise you will need to schedule full repopulations. Rebuilding the Full-Text index simply deletes and re-creates the parameters without actually populating it with data. There is no such terminology as refreshing the Full-Text index.

2. The SQL Client Network utility can be used to do which of the following? (Select all that apply.)

A. Configure network libraries

B. Add database libraries

C. Configure languages

D. Rebuild the Master database

Answer: A. As shown in Chapter 2, the Client Network utility is used to configure network library support to various clients.

3. Which of the following will start the OSQL command line utility and log you in?

A. `osql /Login sa /Pwd *****`

B. `osql /Lsa  /S`

C. `osql /Usa /P`

D. `sqlservr /Usa /P`

Answer: C. The syntax is /U<*user*> and /P<*password*> /S<*server*> (local assumed if absent).

4. You can specify the database you wish to work with in the Query Analyzer utility in which of the following ways? (Select all that apply.)

A. Use the `USE <databasename>` command in your SQL script

B. Click on the databases listbox and select your database

    C. Just run the command; it will know which database you want to use

    D. Drag and drop the database you wish to work with onto the window

Answer: A, B. You can either pick the database from the listbox or enter the USE command to switch to the desired database.

5. `SELECT Employee.FirstName, Employee.LastName, WorkInfo`
`.YearsExp FROM Employees, WorkInfo WHERE Employee.EmpID =`
`WorkInfo.EmpID`. What does this T-SQL script do?

    A. Displays all information in an employee record and all associated work information

    B. Displays first name and last name in an employee record; if they have work experience, it will display that too

    C. Displays all employees' first names and last names and their work experience where there are records that have a matching employee ID in the WorkInfo table

    D. Displays all employees' first names and last names and their work experience whether or not they have a matching employee ID in the WorkInfo table

Answer: C. The Where clause indicates that a matching record in the employee and WorkInfo tables is needed.

6. What are the benefits of stored procedures? (Select all that apply.)

    A. They are precompiled and therefore run more efficiently than normal queries

    B. They can be used in T-SQL batches

    C. They are not precompiled and therefore run more efficiently than normal queries as the optimizer can look at the current conditions and make the necessary optimizations real-time

D. They are not used in T-SQL batches

Answer: A, B. Stored procedures are precompiled and thus faster and easier to use in batch statements.

7. Who can register an extended stored procedure?

A. The SA

B. Any DBO

C. Any user

D. The sysadmin role

Answer: A, D. Both the SA account and members of the sysadmin role can create extended stored procedures.

8. How is Full-Text searching installed?

A. By default

B. By doing a Custom installation

C. By doing a global installation and then enabling it table by table

D. By doing a global installation and then enabling it database by database

Answer: B. The Full-Text Search engine is installed by doing a Custom installation and then selecting it.

9. SQL Server error messages can be viewed in the SQL Error log and which NT application?

A. NT Performance Monitor

B. NT Control Panel\Network

C. NT Network Monitor

D. NT Event Viewer

Answer: D. The Event Viewer is used to look at NT logs (including the Application log which will contain SQL events).

10. When do Full-Text Search indexes get updated?

A. Never; you have to drop and rebuild the index

B. Whenever you add or modify a row

C. Whenever you schedule it to happen

D. Whenever you trigger it manually

Answer: C, D. You can schedule the automatic updating of indexes, or you can manually trigger an index update at any time.

11. You have four SQL Servers in the same domain: Server1 is SQL 6.5 running on Windows NT Workstation, Server2 is SQL 7 running on Windows 98, Server3 is SQL 7 running on Windows NT Workstation, and Server4 is SQL 7 running on Windows NT Server. Which of these can you see in the browser window of the Query Analyzer? (Select all that apply.)

A. Server1

B. Server2

C. Server3

D. Server4

Answer: A, C, D. All the servers can be browsed from Enterprise Manager and/or Query Analyzer if they are in the same domain and are running on Windows NT. Windows 95/98 does not support Named Pipes, which is the method used to browse SQL Servers.

12. You have a database called Sales with a table called SalesTD. Which of these commands will perform a query on the table no matter which database you run it from?

A. Select all from SalesTD

B. Select * from SalesTD

C. Select * from Sales (SalesTD)

D. `Select * from Sales..SalesTD`

Answer: D. To select all columns use the *, and to specify a table and database, list it as database..table.

13. You have created a Full-Text index on a memo field that contains information about your clients. You add five clients on Tuesday, adding their occupation in the memo field. You notice that two of the new clients are dentists. On Wednesday you hurt your tooth and search for your clients that are dentists (using den*) but they don't show up. What is the probable cause?

    A. You didn't specify occupation when you built the index

    B. You built the index on the wrong column

    C. The index hasn't been updated since the new clients were added

    D. You misentered their occupation

    Answer: C. The index is probably scheduled to update once a week and hasn't been updated to reflect the new clients.

14. You register your server and want to check on some system stored procedures but the Master database does not show up in the database folder. Why is that happening?

    A. You are looking at SQL 7 running on Windows 95/98

    B. You need to edit your registration properties to display system data

    C. You need to edit your registration properties to connect with SA rights

    D. The master database is not listed with other databases—it is listed in the Configuration folder

    Answer: B. When you register servers you can specify if you want system objects (databases, tables, stored procedures, etc.) to show up. You need to edit the registration to change the configuration.

15. What is the best way to monitor the size of Full-Text catalogs?

A. Use Query Analyzer to run `sp_catalog_size` occasionally

B. Use Performance Monitor to watch the size of the catalog

C. Create a job that emails results from `sp_fulltext_catalog`

D. Create a job that emails results from `sp_catalog_size`

Answer: B. You can use Performance Monitor to monitor the size of full text catalogs.

Chapter 4 Answers

1. Which of the following system tables is used to store information about your databases?

A. Sysdatabases

B. Sysdevices

C. Sysusages

D. Sysfragments

Answer: A. The other tables listed were used in SQL Server 6.5. Every time a database is created, its information is recorded in the sysdatabases table in the master database. You should make backups of your Master database when changes to its data are made.

2. Using the Query Analyzer, you have just created a new database called Accounting with an initial size of 100MB and no Filegrowth options set and no transaction log information provided. What is the default size of the transaction log for this database?

A. 10MB

B. 15MB

C. 20MB

D. 25MB

Answer: D. The default size of a transaction log is 25% of the initial size of the data files. This can be overridden by specifying an initial size parameter when you explicitly create your transaction log.

3. What is the most granular unit of storage in SQL Server 7?

A. Record

B. Page

C. Extent

D. Allocation Unit

Answer: B. 8KB data pages are the most granular unit of storage in SQL Server 7. Eight contiguous data pages make up an extent. Extents are allocated to tables and indexes.

4. Indexes and tables can share a(n) _____ when they are first created. As these database object grow, they will be allocated their own _____. (Fill in the blanks.)

A. Page, pages

B. Extent, extents

C. Table, tables

D. Record, records

Answer: B. Indexes and tables often share the same extent when they are first created. As they fill, they will be moved to their own extents.

5. When you create or alter your database, you can specify a size parameter for the Filegrowth option. This size parameter can be expressed as which of the following? (Choose all that apply.)

A. Megabytes

B. Kilobytes

C. Bytes

D. Percentage of current database size

Answer: A, B, D. The Filegrowth parameter can be expressed in megabytes or kilobytes or as a percentage of the current size of the database. When you specify a Filegrowth, it is recommended that you also specify a Maxsize so that your database cannot fill your entire disk partition.

6. You have just taken over responsibility for an installation of SQL Server 7. The former database administrator did not keep good notes on the server. Which of the following stored procedures will give you information about the size, location, name, and type of data (data or log) of all files that a particular database is using?

   A. sp_help

   B. sp_helpfile

   C. sp_helpfilegroup

   D. sp_helpdb

   Answer: D. The sp_helpdb stored procedure is used to gather information about all the files that make up a particular database. The sp_helpfile procedure will gather information about a specific file. The sp_helpfilegroup stored procedure details information about a particular filegroup.

7. What is the maximum size of a row in SQL Server 7?

   A. 2000 bytes

   B. 4000 bytes

   C. 8060 bytes

   D. 16,000 bytes

   Answer: C. SQL Server allows row sizes of approximately 8060 bytes. Remember that an individual row cannot span more than one data page. Data pages are 8KB in size.

8. You have a database in SQL Server that stores all the transactions posted every month. The database spans three database files. Normal operation shows that this database grows from approximately 10MB at the beginning of the month to about 400MB by month end. You wish to shrink the database at the end of each month back to an initial size of 10MB. You decide to move the data to a history database on another SQL Server machine. Once this is done, you have about 398 MB of free space in your database. What command can you use to reclaim that free space and return it back to the operating system?

   A. Use the DBCC SHRINKDATABASE command with a percentage parameter and the TRUNCATEONLY parameter.

B. Use the DBCC SHRINKDATABASE command with a percentage parameter and the NOTRUNCATE parameter.

C. Use the DBCC SHRINKDATABASE command with the TRUNCA-TEONLY parameter.

D. Use the DBCC SHRINKDATABASE command with the NOTRUN-CATE parameter.

Answer: C. You must use the DBCC SHRINKDATABASE command to shrink all files in the database. To release all free memory (up to the initial size of the database) you should use the TRUNCATEONLY parameter.

9. You are estimating the storage requirements for a table defined with the following fields: Char(15), Int(4), Float(8), Char(10). How many bytes will be used to store each row, assuming no fields allow nulls? (Remember to include 2 bytes of overhead for your row.)

A. 33

B. 35

C. 37

D. 39

Answer: D. If you add up the sizes of each of the datatypes you will get 15 + 4 + 8 + 10 + 2 = 39 bytes.

10. You have a very large database and cannot make a full database backup in the time allotted. What database objects will allow you to perform a partial database backup and still ensure consistency?

A. Multiple data files

B. Multiple log files

C. Filegroups

D. There is nothing that you can do that will backup a portion of the database and ensure data integrity.

Answer: C. Filegroups allow you to make consistent database backups without having to make a backup of the entire database at one time. You should also make a backup of the transaction log. If you do not, then your filegroup backup cannot be restored.

11. You are a database developer and have been working on a database in the development environment called "devFamTree." You have finished developing and testing the database and would like to put it into production as "FamilyTree." You must first put the database into single-user mode. Which of the following commands would do this?

A. ALTER DATABASE devFamTree, 'Single User', True

B. MODIFY DATABASE devFamTree, 'Single User', True

C. EXEC sp_changedbowner, 'devFamTree', 'single user'

D. EXEC sp_dboption devFamTree, 'Single User', True

Answer: D. You use the sp_dboption stored procedure to make database option modifications.

12. You are a database developer and have been working on a database in the development environment called "devFamTree." You are finished developing and testing the database and would like to put the database into production as "FamilyTree." You have placed the database into Single-User mode and now wish to change the database name. Which of the following commands would do this?

A. ALTER DATABASE devFamTree, FamilyTree

B. MODIFY DATABASE devFamTree, FamilyTree

C. EXEC sp_renamedb devFamTree, FamilyTree

D. EXEC sp_changedb devFamTree, FamilyTree

Answer: C. You use the sp_renamedb stored procedure to rename a database. Keep in mind that in order to do this, the database must first be put into single-user mode.

13. You are evaluating hardware for your SQL Server database system. Your database must be up and running 24 hours a day, 7 days a week. You have a limited budget so new hardware is out of the question. You must ensure fault-tolerance, but you also want to optimize speed and storage. You decide to implement Windows NT's disk striping with parity, or RAID 5. How would you rate this solution?

A. This is a poor solution and does not fit the requirements

B. This is a poor solution although it appears to fit the requirements

C. This is good solution, but doesn't fit all of the requirements

D. This is an excellent solution and fits all of the requirements

Answer: D. This is an excellent solution given the scenario and requirements. You save money by using existing equipment. You gain fault-tolerance by using striping with parity. You also gain some performance as the stripe set will span at least three partitions. Striping with parity is a bit faster and uses less disk space than mirroring or duplexing.

14. You have just created several new databases on your system and are worried about recovery. You decide to make backups of each of these databases. What other database should you back up?

   A. Master

   B. Model

   C. Msdb

   D. Tempdb

   Answer: A. You should make a backup of the Master database after any modifications to your SQL Server that affect the Master database. This includes adding, altering, or dropping databases and transaction logs; new or modified SQL Server logins; and such SQL Server options as memory and user connections.

15. You are getting ready to create a new database that will be 25GB. You have 6 hard disks, each of which is 10GB in size. Which of the following data storage schemas will result in the fastest performance with the best fault-tolerance?

   A. Use RAID 5, striping with parity across all 6 hard disks, and place both the transaction log and data files on the RAID array.

   B. Use RAID 5, striping with parity across 4 of the 6 hard disks, and place your data files on them. Use RAID 1, disk mirroring on the other 2 hard disks, and place the transaction log on them.

    C. Use RAID 0, striping only across all 6 hard disks, and place both the transaction log and data files on them.

    D. Use RAID 0, striping only across 4 hard disks, and place the data files on them. Use RAID 1, mirroring on the other 2 hard disks, and place the transaction log on them.

Answer: B. Although striping with parity allows for fault-tolerance and excellent speed, using a combination of RAID 5 for your data and mirroring for the log creates a scenario in which writes to the log do not interfere with writes to the data. In addition to this, you have even better fault-tolerance for your log files.

16. You are getting ready to create a new database that will be 20GB. You have 6 hard disks, each of which is 10GB in size. Which of the following data storage schemas will result in the fastest backup performance while maintaining a high level of fault-tolerance and recoverability?

    A. Use RAID 5, striping with parity across all 6 hard disks. Create a single 20GB file for your data. Place the transaction log and data file on the RAID array.

    B. Use RAID 5, striping with parity across 4 of the 6 hard disks. Use RAID 1, disk mirroring on the other 2 hard disks, and place the transaction log on them. Create four 5GB filegroups and place them on the stripe set.

    C. Use RAID 1, mirroring for 2 of the hard disks, and place the transaction log there. Create four 5GB filegroups and place each filegroup on an individual hard disk.

    D. Create twenty 1GB data files and place them on a RAID 5 system. When you do your backups, back up a single file each day on a rotating 20-day cycle.

Answer: B. Although striping with parity allows for fault-tolerance and excellent speed, using a combination of RAID 5 for your data and mirroring for the log creates a scenario in which writes to the log do not interfere with writes to the data. In addition, you have even better fault-tolerance for your log files. By also placing your data into separate filegroups, you can now quickly back up smaller portions of your data (an individual filegroup) and still maintain integrity.

Chapter 5 Answers

1. You have several types of clients on your network: Novell, Macintosh, and Windows. What authentication method should you implement?

   A. Standard Only

   B. Windows NT Only

   C. Mixed Mode

   Answer: C. Mixed Mode. The Novell and Macintosh clients are not capable of making a trusted connection and therefore require standard mode. Your Windows clients will be able to take advantage of NT Authentication since they can make trusted connections.

2. Archie Thompson needs permission to read data from the payroll table in the Accounting database, but he should not be able to read data from any of the other tables. To which fixed database role should he be added?

   A. Db_dataselect

   B. Db_datareader

   C. Db_dataaccess

   D. None of the above

   Answer: D. Fixed database roles apply to every table in the database, not just one table.

3. Several of your users need Select, Update, and Insert permissions on a database. They should be members of which of the following database roles?

   A. Db_datareader

   B. Db_datawriter

   C. Db_datareader and db_datawriter

   D. Create a custom role

   Answer: D. Db_datareader by itself will not give enough permission and the addition of db_datawriter would grant the Delete permission. Only a custom role would work.

4. TomR is a member of the Windows NT Sales group. The Sales group has been granted access to SQL server with a Windows NT Group type account. The Sales login is a member of the db_datareader fixed database role in the Accounting database. TomR has also been given his own Windows NT User type login and has been denied Select permission on the tables in the Accounting database. Can TomR select data from the Accounting database?

A. Yes; TomR can select from the Accounting database since he is a member of the Sales group, which is a member of the db_datreader fixed database role

B. No; TomR cannot read from the Accounting database since he has been specifically denied Select permission on the database

C. TomR cannot have a separate login since he is a member of the Windows NT Sales group, which already has a login

D. Yes; but only when he connects to SQL Server as Sales instead of as himself

Answer: B. Denied access always takes precedence over any other permissions. And TomR can have a separate login even though he is a member of the Windows NT Sales group.

5. Several of your users need to be able to create objects in your database. What is the best way to avoid broken ownership chains?

A. Make all the users who need to create objects members of the db_ddladmin fixed database role

B. Make all the users who need to create objects members of the db_owner fixed database role

C. Make all the users who need to create objects members of the sysadmin fixed server role

D. Create a custom fixed server role with the proper object permissions and make those users members of this new role

Answer: A. While membership in any of these roles would have allowed users to create objects with DBO as the owner, the db_owner and sysadmin roles would grant too much administrative authority. Db_ddladmin is just the right amount of authority.

6. Some of your users need permission to create databases. What is the best way to grant this permission?

A. Make those users members of the db_ddladmin role

B. Make those users members of the sysadmin server role

C. Grant those users the Create Database permission on the master database

D. Make those users members of the diskadmin server role

Answer: C. Making the users members of the sysadmin role would work but would allow them too much administrative access on the system. Answers A and D would not work at all.

7. On your network you have the authority to administrate both Windows NT and SQL accounts. Some of your users need access to a database that will be used for a short-term project. What is the best way to grant them permissons on the database?

A. Add all the users to a Windows NT group, create a Windows NT Group login in SQL, create a user account for the login in the database, and grant permissions to the account

B. Create separate Windows NT User logins and separate database user accounts for each user; then grant permissions to each user

C. Create separate logins for each user account, create database user accounts for each role, and add those accounts to a database role

D. Assign them security equivalence to the SA account

Answer: C. A Windows NT Group is not necessary since the only reason these users are grouped together is to access this database. The best way is to give each user a separate login and make them a member of a role.

8. True or False: When you add a user to a database role using Transact-SQL (T-SQL) you do not need to create the user account first.

A. True

B. False

Answer: A. When adding a user to a database role using the `sp_addrolemember` stored procedure you do not need to create the user account first. SQL will create the user account for you.

9. What are the results of the following query: `sp_grantlogin @logi-name='domain\jordenj', @defdb='pubs'`

    A. A Windows NT login is created for JordenJ and the default database is set to Pubs

    B. A Standard login is created for JordenJ and the default database is set to Pubs

    C. A Windows NT login is created for JordenJ but the default database is not set

    D. The query fails

    Answer: D. The query will fail since the `sp_grantlogin` stored procedure on accepts the login name as an argument. A default database cannot be set with `sp_grantlogin`.

10. True or False: GaryR is a member of the sysadmin fixed server role. When GaryR creates a table in the Sales database the owner is DBO not GaryR.

    A. True

    B. False

    Answer: A. Whenever a member of the sysadmin server role creates an object in any database the owner is always DBO.

11. You are worried about default permissions in user databases in SQL Server. You propose removing everyone from the Public group and selectively adding them back in as necessary. What will the results be?

    A. Your method will work, but will not fix the problem

    B. Your method will work and will fix the problem

    C. Your method will not work, so will not fix the problem

    D. Your method will not work, but there was no problem to begin with

    Answer: D. You cannot remove users from the public role. Because the public role has no default rights to any user tables (except what you have setup in the model database) there is not a problem.

12. Security at your site is a major issue. You want SQL Server to interact with an Exchange server and you also have replication occurring. How would you configure the service accounts?

   A. Create a domain administrative account and assign it to both SQL services

   B. Create a local administrative account and assign it to both SQL services

   C. Create separate accounts for the SQL Server and SQL Agent services. Assign the domain administrative account to SQL Server and the local administrative account to the SQL Agent

   D. Create separate accounts for the SQL Server and SQL Agent services. Assign the domain administrative account to SQL Agent and the local administrative account to the SQL Server

   Answer: D. If security is an issue, you may want to create and assign different accounts to the SQL services. While the SQL Agent requires a domain account with admin rights, the SQL Server service mainly needs a user account with rights to the \MSSQL7 folder.

13. You have a database called PhoneNumbers that everyone in your company needs to be able to run queries against. You create a user called guest in the database and make it a member of db_datareader. You then assign the Windows NT group Domain Guests to SQL Server. Can all your Windows NT users access the database?

   A. Yes, it works fine as is

   B. It will work after you make Domain Guests members of the database

   C. It will work after you make the guest user a member of the public role in the database

   D. It will not work

   Answer: D. While creating the guest account is on the right track, you should have brought over the Windows NT group called Domain Users instead of Domain Guests. Domain Users automatically contains all of your NT user accounts, while Domain Guests only contains accounts that are configured as guest accounts.

14. You have a payroll database that should only be modified by the payroll application. Which of these steps should you take to ensure that users can modify data only when using the payroll application?

A. Create an application role for the database

B. Assign appropriate rights to the application role

C. Modify the application so that it triggers the application role when the application is started

D. Put the appropriate users in the application role

Answer: A, B, C. By creating an application role and having an application trigger the role you can ensure that users get their rights only when the application is run. You do not have to assign users to the role to make it work.

Chapter 6 Answers

1. What is the SQL Server 7 command to back up databases?

A. Backup database

B. Dump database

C. Backup device

D. Dump device

Answer: A. Although the dump database command is still supported, the SQL 7 command to back up databases is Backup database.

2. How do you edit a recurring (scheduled) backup?

A. You can't—you have to delete and re-create it

B. From the Database/Jobs screen

C. From SQL Agent/Jobs screen

D. From the Management/Database Maintenance Plan screen

Answer: C, D. Once you create a maintenance job, you can edit it from the Jobs windows or from the Database Maintenance Plan window.

3. What is the SQL Server 7 command to back up a transaction log?

   A. `Dump database /log`

   B. `Dump log`

   C. `Dump transaction`

   D. `Backup log`

Answer: D. Although the `dump transaction` command is still supported, the SQL Server 7 command to back up the transaction log is `backup log`.

4. What does the `no_recovery` switch do?

   A. There is no such switch

   B. It cleans out (truncates) the log without making a backup

   C. It makes a backup of the log without cleaning it

   D. It loads a backup of a database but leaves the database offline so you can continue restoring transaction logs

Answer: D. The `no_recovery` switch allows you to restore a database but not make it usable yet, so you can restore additional transaction logs.

5. When do you need to use the `replace` switch?

   A. There is no such switch

   B. When you are restoring into a database with data

   C. When you are restoring into a database that is marked read-only

   D. When the database you are restoring into has a different name than the originally backed up database

Answer: D. By using the `replace` switch you can force the backup of one database into another database.

6. What is the most efficient (as in spaced used) form of disk fault tolerance?

   A. Stripe set

   B. Mirror set

   C. Duplex set

   D. Striped-with-parity set

Answer: D. Striped with parity, also called RAID 5, is efficient, because you lose only one hard drive for the parity bit. The disadvantage is that it is not as fast as duplexing for fault-tolerance.

7. Windows NT supports which of the following?

   A. Mirroring

   B. Duplexing

   C. Stripe

   D. Striped with parity

Answer: A, B. C, D. Windows NT can create volumes with any of these formats, although you should use a hardware RAID controller if possible.

8. What program allows you to do backups graphically?

   A. Transfer Manager

   B. Backup Manager

   C. Security Manager

   D. Enterprise Manager

Answer: D. Enterprise Manager is the program you use to do your backups in SQL Server.

9. What is the command to restore a database in SQL Server 7?

   A. `Restore database`

   B. `Run database`

C. Load database

D. Undo database

Answer: A. Although the `load database` command is still supported for backwards compatibility, the `restore database` command is the SQL Server 7 command to restore databases.

10. What feature of SQL Server allows backups to run faster?

    A. SCSI support

    B. Striped backups

    C. Mirror backups

    D. Parallel striped backup

Answer: D. Parallel striped backups allow you to back up to two or more devices at the same time.

11. You have a recent full backup file of your database. Your hard drive that contained the database files (but none of the SQL system database files) crashed. After fixing the hard drive, which of these steps is redundant?

    A. Using the `sp_attach_db` command

    B. Creating the database

    C. Restoring the database

    D. Rebuilding the Master database

Answer: D. Because you lost only your user database, rebuilding the Master database is not necessary. You only use the `sp_attach_db` command when restoring databases if you had to rebuild the Master database. SQL 7 would automatically re-create the database when restoring a backup file so restoring the database is all you have to do.

12. You wish to move a database to another SQL Server. You stop the first SQL Server and move the .MDF and .LDF files to the second server. What step must you take on the second server to install the database?

   A. Restore the database from the .MDF and .LDF files

   B. Run the `sp_db_mount` command to bring the database online

   C. Create a new database and specify the path to the .MDF and .LDF files

   D. Run the `sp_attach_db` command

   Answer: D. The `sp_attach_db` command is used to take .MDF and .LDF files and attach them into SQL Server, thus bringing the database online.

13. You need to be able to restore your databases to any given time, but you have a very large database with many inserts and updates that takes three hours to do a full backup. You implement the following steps: You schedule a full backup every week, with differential backups every night. You set the Truncate Log on Checkpoint option on to keep the log small, and schedule transaction log backups every hour. Will this solution work?

   A. This solution works very well

   B. This solution will not work because you cannot combine differential backups with transaction log backups

   C. This solution will not work because you cannot schedule transaction log backups with full database backups

   D. This solution will not work because you cannot schedule transaction log backups when you have selected Truncate Log on Checkpoint

   Answer: D. If you need point in time recovery you must not set the Truncate Log on Checkpoint switch on, because you cannot back up the transaction log

14. You have three filegroups (FilesA, FilesB, FilesC). You are rotating your filegroup backups so that they get backed up every third night. You are also doing transaction log backups. The files in FilesB get corrupted. Which steps would you do, and in what order do you do the restoration?

A. Restore the transaction log files

B. Restore FilesB filegroup

C. Back up the log with the no_truncate switch

D. Restore the entire database

Answer: C, B, A. You do not need to restore the entire database if the files affected are contained only in a single filegroup (FilesB). You should always attempt to back up the log in order to capture any transactions up to the point of failure. You should then restore the filegroup, and then restore the transaction logs in order to get all of the transactions up to the point of failure.

15. You have an OLTP application that is mission-critical, but can have up to 15 minutes of unscheduled downtime. You have an adequate—but not unlimited—budget. You also run daily reports on the server that currently have to be run at night for performance reasons, but you would like to run them during the day. Which solution should you recommend?

A. RAID 5 drives for your server

B. A standby server with frequent transaction backups

C. An NT cluster server

D. Replication to another server

Answer: B. A standby server may be your best solution because it offers fault-tolerance (with a small amount of downtime), little if any performance degradation on the original server, and the ability to set the backup database to read-only status. This allows you to run reports on the standby server instead of the production server. RAID 5 drives provide disk fault-tolerance, but are slower and offer no protection from server failures. An NT cluster is a more expensive solution and would offer little or no downtime, but may not be worth it in this case. Replication can help offload reporting to another server, but it is not useful for server fault-tolerance, as publishing and subscription servers are not exact duplicates.

16. You have a 100GB database with a 25GB transaction log. You have ten 25GB drives and two hard-drive controllers. You want to minimize the time it takes to do backups and ensure fault-tolerance in case any drive fails. You also want to ensure maximum performance for your OLTP database. Which of these is the best solution?

    A. Create a 125MB RAID 5 set for the data and log. Create a single .MDF file for the data and a single .LDF file for the log. Schedule full database backups every week and transaction log backups every night.

    B. Create a 125MB RAID 0+1 set for the data and log. Create a single .MDF file for the data and a single .LDF file for the log. Schedule full database backups every week and transaction log backups every night.

    C. Create a 100MB RAID 5 set for the data and a 25MB RAID 0+1 set for the log. Create three filegroups for the data. Schedule a full backup every week, rotate filegroup backups during the week, and do a transaction log backup every night.

    D. Create a 100MB RAID 5 set for the data and a 25MB RAID 0+1 set for the log. Create a single .MDF file for the data and a single .LDF file for the log. Schedule full database backups every week and transaction log backups every night.

    Answer: C. If you need to minimize backup time you should use filegroups. RAID 5 drives will be slower than RAID 0+1 drives for an OLTP system.

17. Which of these operations can you do while performing a full database backup?

    A. Create a new index

    B. Update columns

    C. Import in a large number of rows

    D. Create a new table

    Answer: B, C. You cannot create indexes or change the database schema while a full database backup is being performed.

Chapter 7 Answers

1. Which of the following is true regarding the INSERT statement?

   A. You must have SELECT permissions in the table to which you wish to add records

   B. INSERT statements add only one record at a time

   C. An INSERT is usually logged

   D. You must have INSERT permissions in the table to which you wish to add records

   Answer: C, D. You do not need SELECT permissions to run an INSERT command. INSERTs are usually logged transactions. The INSERT statement has variations that allow multiple records to be added to a table.

2. You decide to run the following SELECT INTO statement: SELECT * INTO ##SomeTable FROM Northwind..Orders.

   Where does this new table reside?

   A. In the Northwind database as Orders

   B. In the Northwind database as ##SomeTable

   C. In the Tempdb database as Orders

   D. In the Tempdb database as ##SomeTable

   Answer: D. The ##SomeTable is a global temporary table and resides in Tempdb. Any other connections can access this temporary table. The table will be removed when the SQL Server is restarted, or if the table owner Drops the table.

3. Which of the following is true regarding the SELECT INTO statement?

   A. You must have the Select Into/Bulk Copy database option enabled

   B. You must be a member of the sysadmin database role

C. SELECT INTO statements are logged transactions

D. You must have CREATE TABLE permissions in the database

Answer: A, D. You must have the Select Into/Bulk Copy database option enabled. Because SELECT INTO statements are, by nature, non-logged transactions, you should back up your database after running them. You must have CREATE TABLE permissions in the database. This can be accomplished if you have the permission, are a member of the sysadmin server role, or are a member of the db_owner or db_ddladmin database role.

4. Your environment includes a SQL Server 7 computer and an AS-400 running DB2. Only three people in your organization have access to the AS-400, but nearly 200 need access to the data. The AS-400 currently dumps large ASCII flat files to your computer. Since you are the SQL Server administrator, it is up to you to make the data available to those 200 users. Which of the following data management techniques could be used to move the ASCII files into your SQL Server computer?

A. You can use the bcp utility

B. You can use the BULK INSERT statement

C. You can use the SELECT INTO statement

D. You can use the INSERT statement

Answer: A, B. Both the Bulk Copy utility and the BULK INSERT statement can be used to move the data into SQL Server 7. SELECT INTO and INSERT by themselves cannot gather the data from a flat file.

5. Your environment includes a SQL Server 7 computer and an AS-400 running DB2. Only three people in your organization have access to the AS-400, but nearly 200 need access to the data. The AS-400 currently dumps large ASCII flat files to your computer. Since you are the SQL Server administrator, it is up to you to make the data available to those 200 users. You decide that you want to use the Bulk Copy command-line utility. You also want the transfer to be as fast as possible. Which of the following will accomplish this task?

A. You must drop all indexes on the affected tables to avoid transaction logging

B. You must drop all data in the affected tables to avoid transaction logging

C. You must enable the Select Into/Bulk Copy database option to avoid transaction logging

D. You must enable the Truncate Log on Checkpoint database option to avoid transaction logging

Answer: A, C. To perform a fast bulk copy, you must drop indexes on affected tables and set the Select Into/Bulk Copy database option. By doing this, INSERTs are not logged.

6. Which of the following is true about the bulk copy operation?

A. Defaults and datatypes are always ignored

B. Defaults and datatypes are always enforced

C. Rules and triggers are always ignored

D. Rules and triggers are always enforced

Answer: B, C. When you perform a bulk copy operation, default and datatypes are always enforced, but rules, triggers, and constraints are always ignored. You should run some SQL statements to verify the integrity of your data.

7. You decide that you want to use the Bulk Copy command-line utility. Which permissions are required for you to perform this bulk copy operation?

A. When copying data in to SQL Server, you must have READ permissions on the file (if it is on an NTFS partition)

B. When copying data in to SQL Server you must have INSERT permissions on the table which is affected

C. When copying data out of SQL Server you must have SELECT permission on the affected tables

D. When copying data out of SQL Server you must have SELECT INTO permissions on the affected tables

Answer: A, B, C. There is no such thing as SELECT INTO permissions. You must have INSERT permissions on the affected tables when copying data in to SQL Server, and you must have SELECT permissions to copy data out of SQL Server.

8. When you bulk copy data out of SQL Server, you wish to create a flat file that uses tabs for field terminators and newline characters for the end of a row. Which of the following switches accomplish this?

A. /t \t

B. /r \n

C. /F {Tab}

D. /R {Newline}

Answer: A, B. This is a bit of a trick question. You should be familiar with the different switches available. Keep in mind that these switches are case-sensitive. The \t will specify a tab character, while \n will specify a newline character.

9. Which of the following is true about the BULK INSERT statement?

A. It is a command-line utility

B. It is a T-SQL command

C. It only reads one record at a time

D. It is reads all records in a flat file as if they are an OLE-DB recordset

Answer: B, D. The BULK INSERT statement is a T-SQL version of the bcp command. It has advantages over bcp in that it can read an entire file as if it were an OLE-DB recordset. bcp reads only one record at a time.

10. You have many users who want to work data from your SQL Server 7 computer by accessing a centrally located flat file. You decide to create a character-based flat file on a central server. Which of the following utilities can be used to create this character-based flat file?

A. bcp

B. BULK INSERT

C. The DTS Export Wizard

D. The SELECT INTO statement, with a flat file specified

Answer: A, C. You cannot use BULK INSERT or SELECT INTO statements to move data out of SQL Server.

11. You wish to use the BULK INSERT command to add a large amount of data from a flat file into SQL Server. Which of the following is true about this command?

A. You can specify a batch size to load the data in several smaller chunks, thus speeding up the transfer

B. You must be the database owner to run the BULK INSERT command

C. You must be a member of the sysadmin fixed database role to run the BULK INSERT command

D. The flat file must reside on your local hard disk to perform a BULK INSERT

Answer: A, C. If you have a large file that you are attempting to transfer, taking several small "bytes" will be faster than attempting to move all the data in a single large bite. Only members of the sysadmin fixed server role can execute the BULK INSERT command.

12. You have a large SQL Server 7 computer running a quad-processor Alpha-AXP computer. The server currently holds about 3 terabytes of data. For administrative reasons, you want to distribute portions of that data to SQL Server 7 computers running on Intel Pentium IIs throughout your organization. As part of the distribution process, you wish to include some tables, many of the views, and several of the stored procedures. You do not want to keep the security setting, however. You decide to use the DTS Import and Export engine to move the information. Which of the following is true about this solution?

A. This is a poor solution as only data will be transferred, but not the views and stored procedures

B. This is a poor solution as all data will be transferred, including the rules, defaults, triggers, constraints, and security information

C. This is a fair solution; however, all security information will be transferred

D. This is an excellent solution and fits all the required parameters

Answer: A. DTS can move only data from one OLE-DB- or ODBC-compliant data source to another OLE-DB- or ODBC-compliant data destination.

13. You have a large SQL Server 7 computer running a quad-processor Alpha-AXP computer. The server currently holds about 3 terabytes of data. For administrative reasons, you want to distribute portions of that data to SQL Server 7 computers running on Intel Pentium IIs throughout your organization. As part of the distribution process, you wish to include some tables, many of the views, and several of the stored procedures. You do not want to keep the security setting though. You decide to use the Transfer Manager to move the information. Which of the following is true about this solution?

A. This is a poor solution as only data will be transferred, but not the views and stored procedures

B. This is a poor solution as all data will be transferred including the rules, defaults, triggers, constraints, and security information

C. This is a fair solution; however, all security information will be transferred

D. This is an excellent solution and fits all the required parameters

Answer: D. The Transfer Manager is capable of moving data, schema, and database objects (like views and stored procedures) from one SQL Server 7 computer to another SQL Server 7 computer.

14. You have a large DB2 database running on an AS-400. The server currently holds about 3 terabytes of data. For administrative reasons, you want to distribute portions of that data to SQL Server 7 computers running on Intel Pentium IIs throughout your organization. Which of the following can be used to transfer the data?

A. You can use the DTS Import and Export Wizards

B. You can have the AS-400 dump an ASCII file and then you can use bcp

C. You can have the AS-400 dump an ASCII file and then you can use BULK INSERT

D. You can use the Transfer Manager to move the data

Answer: A, B, C. Since DB2 is an ODBC-compliant database, you can use DTS to move the data. If the AS-400 dumps an ASCII file, you can use bcp and the BULK INSERT command to move your data. The Transfer Manager can only work between two SQL Server 7 computers.

15. You have a DTS package object that contains a login ID, password, file name, and location as well as information about the format in which the data is stored. Which DTS package object is this?

A. Data pump object

B. Connection object

C. Step object

D. Task object

Answer: B. A data pump object is a COM-based server that is responsible for the movement of your data from source through transformation and to a destination. The connection object stores information about a connection, including login credentials, data format, and data location. The step object is tied to a task object and specifies the flow of a package. Task objects contain the actual task to be accomplished.

16. The Task object in a DTS package can perform which of the following?

A. Move data from a source to a destination

B. Run a T-SQL statement or batch

C. Execute external programs like .CMD files or .BAT files

D. Execute another DTS package

E. Execute COM-compliant scripts like VBScript

Answer: A, B, C, D, E. All answers are correct. The Task object can also gather results from another running DTS package and send e-mail using the SQLMail interface.

17. The step object in a DTS package can run in parallel when there are no precedence constraints on it. Which of the following are Step object precedence constraints?

A. On Success

B. On Failure

C. Unconditional

D. Return Codes

Answer: A, B, C, D. All answers are correct. These are the four precedence constraints. On Success will run a particular step when the previous step completes successfully. On Failure will run when the previous step failed. The Unconditional constraint will run a step when the previous step completes regardless of that prior step's success or failure. The Return Codes constraint allows a step to make return codes available to other steps.

18. You have used a third-party program in the past to move and transform your data from one location to another. The program worked well for you, but you had no method to track the lineage of your data (e.g., you wish to track the changes made to your data over time as well as changes made to the program.) You now want to use DTS within SQL Server rather than having an external program. You port most of your transformation code from the program into your DTS package. The DTS package runs perfectly for you. Where should you save your DTS package so that you can track the data lineage?

   A. Store the package in the SQL Server DTS packages area

   B. Store the package in the SQL Server repository

   C. Store the package as a COM-based object

   D. Store the package as an ASCII file

   Answer: B. When you store your package in the SQL Server repository, you can both track changes made to the package and review a history of when data was transformed. Storing the package in the SQL Server makes it available for other servers to run. A package stored as a COM-based object can easily be transferred via e-mail to other locations.

19. You want create a DTS package that can access and work with sensitive data. When you store the package, you want to give some people the ability to run the package and others the ability to edit it. For security reasons, you also want the package encrypted. Which of the following steps should you take to accomplish these goals?

A. Supply an owner password for the package

B. Supply an operator password for the package

C. Select the encrypt option for the package

D. Do nothing. Only the sysadmin can work with packages

Answer: A, B. When you set the owner password, anyone who knows the owner password can work with the internals of the package. The operator password allows users who know the password to execute the package. Any password supplied for a package automatically encrypts the package contents.

20. DTS packages can transform your data using a COM-compliant scripting language. Which of the following scripting languages is currently supported in the DTS Import/Export Wizards?

A. JScript

B. VBScript

C. PerlScript

D. None of the above

Answer: A, B, C. Other COM-compliant languages include JavaScript, Java, C++, Visual Basic, among others.

21. You are currently running SQL Server 6.5 and are thinking about upgrading to SQL Server 7. On your SQL Server 7 computer, you wish to use a different character set and sort order. You decide to upgrade the SQL Server 6.5 computer to 7 using the current 6.5 sort order and character sets. You then install another version of SQL Server 7 on the network with the new sort orders and character set. Which of the following methods of data transfer is the best choice to move your data from the recently upgraded SQL Server?

A. Re-create the objects in the destination database and use bcp to move your data

B. Re-create the objects in the destination database and use DTS to transfer your data

    C. Use the Transfer Manager to move all objects and data from the source database to the destination database

    D. You cannot transfer data with different character sets and sort orders

Answer: C. This is an excellent solution. The Transfer Manager can move data from one SQL Server 7 computer to another SQL Server 7 computer regardless of character set, sort order or platform.

Chapter 8 Answers

1. What rights does the SQL Agent service account need? (Choose all that apply.)

    A. Log on as a Service right

    B. Administrator group membership

    C. Backup Operators membership

    D. Server Operators membership

    Answer: A, B. The account needs Logon as a Service, as well as membership in the Administrators group.

2. What is the API set that allows SQL Server to send and receive e-mail?

    A. TAPI

    B. EAPI

    C. OLE

    D. MAPI

    Answer: D. MAPI (Messaging Application Programming Interface) is the set of functions that allows SQL Server to interact with Exchange and other e-mail systems.

3. Which database holds alert and job information?

    A. The Master database

    B. The Model database

C. The Msdb database

D. None—it is held in the Registry

Answer: C. The Msdb database holds alert, job, and operator information.

4. How can you rebuild the Msdb database?

   A. You can't; you must reinstall SQL Server

   B. Rebuild the Master database

   C. Rebuild Msdb database

   D. Stop and restart SQL Server; the Msdb database will be rebuilt automatically

   Answer: B. Rebuilding the Master database automatically rebuilds the Msdb database, which means that all of your previous alerts, jobs, and operators have to be restored from a backup.

5. Where do alerts look for errors?

   A. The Windows NT Application log

   B. The SQL Server event log

   C. The Master database error log

   D. SQL Server sends errors directly to the alert engine

   Answer: A. The alert engine checks the NT Application log for errors.

6. What kinds of jobs can be created? (Choose all that apply.)

   A. T-SQL (Transact-SQL)

   B. CmdExec (command prompt)

   C. Replication

   D. Active script

   Answer: A, B, C, D. T-SQL, command prompt, replication, and active script jobs can be built.

7. How can you create new error messages in SQL Server?

   A. You can't

   B. Run the Setup program, choose Custom, and choose Edit Messages

   C. Choose Manage SQL Server Messages when highlighting the server

   D. Go to the Messages folder and choose New Message

   Answer: C. You can edit the properties of system messages, or add new messages by selecting Manage SQL Server Messages when highlighting the server.

8. What is the best way to stop an alert for a couple of hours?

   A. Disable the alert.

   B. Set the hit counter of the alert to −1.

   C. Delete the alert.

   D. Deselect any operators that were being notified.

   Answer: A. You can disable alerts, which is the best way to turn them off temporarily.

9. What is the operator of last resort called?

   A. Weekend operator

   B. Last-chance operator

   C. Notification operator

   D. Fail-safe operator

   Answer: D. A fail-safe operator can be set up that gets notified if all other operators are off duty.

10. What is the central server that receives alerts from other SQL Server servers called?

   A. Central alerter

B. Standardized alerter

C. Central control

D. Unhandled events server

Answer: D. A server can be designated to receive alerts from other servers. The server receiving the alerts is called the unhandled events server.

11. You have four SQL Servers. Server1 is SQL 6.5 running on Windows NT Server, Server2 is SQL 7 running on Windows 98, Server3 is SQL 7 running on Windows NT Workstation, and Server4 is SQL 7 running on Windows NT Server. Which servers can be designated as a Master server in a multiserver environment?

A. Server1

B. Server2

C. Server3

D. Server4

Answer: C, D. To participate in a multiserver environment you must be running SQL Server 7 on Windows NT.

12. You have four SQL Servers. Server1 is SQL 6.5 running on Windows NT Server, Server2 is SQL 7 running on Windows 98, Server3 is SQL 7 running on Windows NT Workstation, and Server4 is SQL 7 running on Windows NT Server. Which servers can be designated as a Target server in a multiserver environment?

A. Server1

B. Server2

C. Server3

D. Server4

Answer: C, D. To participate in a multiserver environment you must be running SQL Server 7 on Windows NT.

13. Server1 is designated as a target server for multiserver jobs. Where will the status of the jobs it gets from the master server be recorded?

   A. Only at the master server

   B. Only at the target server

   C. At both the master and target server

   D. Nowhere

Answer: C. You can check the history and status of target jobs at the target server and at the master server.

14. You want SQL Server to be able to send messages upon job completion using an Exchange operator. Which of these steps is required to create e-mail operators?

   A. Create an Exchange account for the SQL Agent service account

   B. Assign the SQL Agent service to use a service account

   C. Create an operator

   D. Assign the job to notify the appropriate operator

Answer: A, B, C, D. To have a job notify an operator via email you must create an Exchange account for the SQL service account, make sure the SQL Agent is using the NT service account, create an operator, and assign the job to notify the operator.

15. You have created a user-defined message "Please call the help desk," numbered 50001, that is configured to post to the NT Application log. Which command will display the SQL message number 50001 and post it to the Windows NT Application log?

   A. Print 50001

   B. Print (50001, 10, 1)

   C. Raiserror 50001

   D. Raiserror (50001, 10, 1)

Answer: D. The Raiserror T-SQL command will display a SQL error message and post it to the NT Application log while the print command shows it only to the client application. The message number, its severity, and its state need to be enclosed in parentheses.

Chapter 9 Answers

1. Which of the following computers stores the original data?

   A. Publisher

   B. Subscriber

   C. Distributor

   D. Replication

   Answer: A. The publisher stores the original database values while the subscriber receives the replication. The distributor is used as a store-and-forward facility.

2. You are using transactional replication to move data from a central server to more than a dozen subscribers. Some of the subscribers are allowed to update the publisher as well as themselves. What protocol are the subscribers using through the Microsoft Distributed Transaction Coordinator to accomplish this task?

   A. TCP/IP

   B. IPX/SPX

   C. Two-phase commit

   D. Named Pipes

   Answer: C. When you use the updating subscriber distribution types, the updates made to the publisher happen simultaneously to the subscriber through the use of 2PC. The MS-DTC coordinates this effort to ensure that both databases are updated, or neither of the databases is updated.

3. SQL Server 7 uses a publisher/subscriber metaphor to implement its replication design. As a publisher, you have made several articles available within several publications. To which of the following may authorized subscribers subscribe?

   A. The publisher

   B. The articles

C. The publications

D. None of the above

Answer: B, C. Authorized subscribers can subscribe to individual articles or to an entire publication. You may not subscribe to a publisher.

4. You are thinking about implementing replication at your business. As you begin to develop your replication strategy, you need to think about several different factors. Which of the following are the three most common factors that influence your decisions about the type of replication you will perform?

A. Autonomy

B. Geographic distance

C. Latency

D. Transactional consistency

Answer: A, B, C. Autonomy refers to how much independence each subscriber will have in relation to the data they receive. Latency refers to how much time there is between synchronizations. Transactional consistency refers to how consistent your data is after a synchronization.

5. You have set up replication from a single publisher with multiple subscribers. When changes are made at the publisher, these changes are made at exactly the same time on all of the subscribers. This type of distribution has no latency, little autonomy, and high transactional consistency. Which of the following distribution types was described?

A. Transactional replication

B. Snapshot replication

C. Merge replication

D. Distributed transactions

Answer: D. This type of replication, distributed transactions, uses the 2PC protocol with the help of the MS-DTC to handle all changes in real time.

6. You have set up replication from a single publisher with multiple subscribers. When changes are made at the publisher, these changes are stored in a distribution database before being forwarded to the subscribers. This type of distribution has low latency, moderate autonomy, and moderate transactional consistency. Which of the following distribution types was described?

A. Transactional replication

B. Snapshot replication

C. Merge replication

D. Distributed transactions

Answer: A. This is transactional replication. The logreader agent scans the transaction logs of published databases and moves transactions to the distribution database. The distribution database is a store-and-forward facility. The subscribers can then have the transactions pushed to them, or they can pull the transactions down at a predetermined schedule.

7. You have set up replication from a single publisher with multiple subscribers. You have a number of image and text fields that are being constantly updated, along with the rest of the data. Which of the following distribution types would have the least impact on the various databases involved in the replication scenario, but still maintain moderate transactional consistency?

A. Transactional replication throughout the day and a snapshot replication once in the evening

B. Merge replication throughout the day and a snapshot replication once in the evening

C. Snapshot replication the whole time

D. Distributed transactions

Answer: A. In this scenario, you want to get as much data as possible to the user with the least amount of impact. This can be accomplished with transactional replication. However, non-logged operations, like changes to the text and image fields, will not be replicated. By scheduling a table refresh (snapshot) to run once every evening, you can refresh the data at the subscriber with the changes to the image and text fields.

8. Which type of replication will overwrite all data in the subscribed tables at the subscriber?

   A. Transactional replication

   B. Snapshot replication

   C. Merge replication

   D. Distributed transactions

   Answer: B. Snapshot replication generally drops the affected tables at the subscriber, re-creates them, and then uses bulk copy to move all of the data from the publisher through the Distribution working folder and on to the subscriber.

9. You have many salespeople who carry laptops with them on business. You want some way for the salespeople to take orders as well as receive updates to their price lists. In order for your salespeople to keep track of what other salespeople might have quoted for a particular item, they also need to know what the other salespeople have done. In addition, a salesperson might need to add or remove items from the quote. The databases are to be updated nightly, but sometimes this is impossible and there may be a lag of as much as three days between synchronizations. Which type of replication would be best suited to this business situation?

   A. Transactional replication for the price lists and the quotes

   B. Snapshot replication for the price lists and merge replication for the quotes

   C. Merge replication for both the price lists and the quotes

   D. Transactional replication for the price lists and merge replication for the quotes

   Answer: D. Since the price list at each salesperson's database is not being changed by the salesperson, transactional replication would be the best. Since a salesperson might look at another salesperson's quote and modify it by adding or removing specific items, merge replication is probably the best choice here.

10. You are using transactional replication with a dozen subscribers. Each subscriber is using a pull subscription. Which of the following is true of the replication agents?

    A. The logreader agent and the distribution agent are on each of the subscribers

    B. The logreader agent is on the publishing server and the distribution agent is on the distribution server

    C. The logreader agent is on the distribution server and the distribution agent is on each of the subscribers

    D. The logreader agent is on each of the subscribers and the distribution agent is on the distribution server

Answer: C. The logreader agent is always located on the distribution server. The distribution agent is on the distribution server when you are using push subscriptions. When you are using pull subscriptions, the distribution agent resides on each subscriber.

11. Which of the following agents is responsible for converging your records?

    A. Logreader agent

    B. Snapshot agent

    C. Merge agent

    D. Distribution agent

Answer: C. The merge agent is responsible for the convergence of your records.

12. You have decided to use merge replication to address your business needs. Which of the following is true?

    A. System tables will be added to the Distribution working folder and the distribution database

    B. Triggers will be created on the publishing and subscription servers

    C. Vertical partitioning will not be allowed

D. A UNIQUEIDENTIFIER column is added for each table involved in the merge replication

Answer: A, B, C, D. All these changes are implemented when you use merge replication. We suggest that, in addition to these measures, you horizontally partition your table based on a region code or some other identifying characteristic.

13. Which of the following is true regarding replication?

A. Other than snapshot replication, replicated tables must have a primary key to ensure referential integrity

B. Publications can span multiple databases

C. Blobs can be replicated using transactional replication

D. You cannot replicate the Master, Model, Msdb, or Tempdb database

Answer: A, D. Publications cannot span multiple databases. Blob objects like text, ntext, and image data can be only replicated through snapshots.

14. You have decided to use transactional replication to remove the impact of MIS on your OLTP server. Which of the following replication scenarios accomplishes this?

A. Central publisher (single publisher with multiple subscribers)

B. Central subscriber (single subscriber with multiple publishers)

C. Publishing subscriber

D. Multiple publishers of one table

Answer: A. The central publisher scenario is specifically designed to reduce the impact of MIS. It can also be useful for handling asynchronous order processing during communication outages. You can further remove the impact of publishing by using the central publisher with a remote distributor. The distribution server would be on a separate machine from the OLTP publishing server.

15. You want to use replication to distribute data from the home office in Sacramento to your satellite offices in München, Hamburg, and Köln. What type of replication would be the most cost-effective, given the slow and expensive modem links?

A. Central publisher (single publisher with multiple subscribers)

B. Central subscriber (single subscriber with multiple publishers)

C. Publishing subscriber

D. Multiple publishers of one table

Answer: C. To minimize the cost of a slow and expensive telephone line, you can use a publishing subscriber model. Essentially, the Sacramento office would publish to one of the German offices, say Köln. Köln would then take the subscribed data and republish it to its more local offices in München and Hamburg.

16. You have several regional offices that need to update central headquarters throughout the day. Which of the following replication models would be the most effective?

A. A central publisher model (single publisher with multiple subscribers) that uses a RegionCode as part of the primary key

B. A central subscriber model (single subscriber with multiple publishers) that uses a RegionCode as part of the primary key

C. A publishing subscriber model that uses a LocationID as part of the primary key

D. Multiple publishers of one table using LocationIDs for the primary key

Answer: B. The central subscriber model is fantastic for rollup reporting, local customer order processing, or local inventory management. In order to maintain transactional consistency, it is strongly recommended that you use a RegionCode or LocationID as part of the primary key in the replicated tables.

17. You have a reservation system that does not need to be running in real time. Up to 30 minutes of latency fits your business needs. You have decided to use replication with a LocationID as part of the primary key. In addition, you have stipulated that each location can only replicate its own data. Which replication strategy is best suited to your business?

A. Central publisher (single publisher with multiple subscribers)

B. Central subscriber (single subscriber with multiple publishers)

C. Publishing subscriber

D. Multiple publishers of one table

Answer: D. This business situation describes the multiple publishers of one table strategy with near perfection.

18. You currently have an Informix database that you want to be a subscriber to a Microsoft SQL Server 7 computer. In order to replicate to your Informix database, ODBC drivers will connect the database with the SQL Server. Which of the following is true when you try to replicate from SQL Server to Informix over the ODBC connection?

A. Only push subscriptions are supported

B. The connection must be made in a thread-safe 32-bit mode and support Transact-SQL's DDL

C. Data is always mapped as char or varchar

D. Only pull subscriptions are supported

Answer: A, B. Only push subscriptions to an ODBC data source are supported. These must run in a 32-bit thread-safe environment. In addition to this, ODBC does not support batched statements. When you send data, it will normally be mapped as closely as possible to the correct datatype on the subscription server.

19. You want to view the history of replications that have taken place at a particular subscriber. That subscriber uses a push subscription to gather its data. In addition, the data is transferred throughout the day using transactional replication. Once a week there is a scheduled snap-shot replication run to refresh all the replicated data. Which of the following will allow you to view the history of snapshots applied to the subscriber?

A. Use the replication monitor on the distribution server to view the snapshot agent history

B. Use the replication monitor on the subscription server to view the snapshot agent history

C. Use the replication monitor on the distribution server to view the distribution agent history

D. Use the replication monitor on the subscriber to view the distribution agent history

Answer: A. The replication monitor is only on the distribution server. You then want to look at the snapshot history. The distribution agent history is used for moving transactions, not snapshots.

20. You have a central publisher with a remote distributor set up as part of your replication scenario. You have 12 subscribers using pull subscriptions for transactional replication. You also have two additional subscribers doing merge replication. How many cleanup jobs are there on the remote distributor?

A. None; all cleanup jobs run on the publisher

B. 2

C. 12

D. 14

Answer: D. Typically there is at least one cleanup job for each subscriber and each subscription. Cleanup jobs don't run on the publisher.

21. You have roughly 40 SQL Server 7 computers located throughout your enterprise. You want to set up subscription servers on about 35 of these computers. The subscriptions will all be to the same articles and publications and may have to occasionally make changes to the published data. You have decided to create the distribution server on its own stand-alone machine to reduce the impact of 35 subscribers on your publishing database. Because of the fairly light network traffic and the speed at which you need this data to be transferred to the subscribers, you have also chosen to use transactional replication with updating subscribers. In order to implement this design quickly, you have created a single subscriber and its related subscriptions. You then create a replication script. You will now tweak the replication script by changing computer names and distribute them to the other subscribers so that they can be set up in the same fashion. How would you rate this solution?

A. Excellent, and all facets will work

B. Good, but one facet won't work

C. Poor, but most facets will work

D. Horrible; none of it will work

Answer: A. Given the business scenario, this is probably the most efficient use of your time as an administrator. In addition, this will have the least impact on the network while still maintaining a high level of transactional consistency. The scripts are a nice touch and will further speed up the installation.

22. You are using merge replication where a central publisher makes data available for five subscribers. A subscriber makes modifications to a record at 10:30 A.M. The publisher makes modifications to the same record at 11:02 A.M. The records are converged at 12:00 P.M. and then sent back to the clients. Which of the following is true?

A. This record will not be converged

B. Each subscriber will have its own unique version of the modified record

C. The subscriber's modification of the record will be converged to all of the other subscribers

D. The publisher's modification of the record will be converged to all of the subscribers

Answer: D. When publishers and subscribers make changes to a record that are then merged at the publisher, the subscribers' changes will be applied before the publishers' changes. When multiple subscribers have made changes to the same record, the converge process looks at the priorities assigned to each subscriber. The highest-priority modification will take precedence.

23. You are currently monitoring your replication model, which uses transactional replication with a remote distributor. You notice that transactions are added to the MSRepl_commands table on the Distribution database. When the transactions are applied to the subscriber, they disappear from the table a few minutes later. Which of the following is true?

A. When the transactions are applied to the subscriber the sp_ repldone stored procedure is run on the distributor, and all applied transactions are marked

B. When the transactions are applied to the subscriber, the sp_ repldone stored procedure is run at the subscriber and the records are marked

C. A cleanup task is run on the distributor and all marked transactions are truncated

D. A cleanup task is run on the subscriber and all marked transactions are truncated

Answer: A, C. Answers A and C are exactly how transactions are handled by the distributor.

Chapter 10 Answers

1. Your system has 64MB of RAM; you upgrade that to 512MB and find that your system has actually slowed down. What caused this?

   A. One of the SIMMs you purchased is defective

   B. You need to add more Level 2 cache to the system

   C. You need to configure SQL server to use the new RAM by adjusting the Memory setting in the Advanced Options of the Server Properties

   D. You need to make adjustments to the max server memory setting

   Answer: B. If your system does not have enough Level 2 cache, adding more RAM can actually slow it down. You need to have 1MB of L2 cache for a 512MB RAM system.

2. You are writing a complex new query that joins columns from several tables and you are concerned about how it might affect system performance. Which tool could you use to see what this query will do to your system before implementing it?

   A. Profiler

   B. Query Governor

   C. Query Analyzer

   D. Performance Monitor

   Answer: C. Query Analyzer is used to estimate what a query will do your system before putting that query into production.

3. The problem is that you need to implement RAID on your SQL Server for fault-tolerance.

   The required objective is fault-tolerance.

   Your optional objectives are an increased disk subsystem I/O and no extra load on the processor

   The solution you choose is to implement Windows NT RAID 1.

    A. This solution produces the desired results and both optional objectives

    B. This solution produces the desired result and only one of the optional objectives

    C. This solution produces the desired result but neither of the optional objectives

    D. This solution does not produce the desired result

    Answer: B. This solution will give fault-tolerance and increased disk I/O, but it will put a load on the processor since the operating system will be maintaining the mirror. To get both results you would use a third-party RAID controller.

4. Your SQL Server is running slowly and you suspect the disk subsystem. You monitor the Physical Disk Average Disk Queue length counter in Performance Monitor and find that it is within the acceptable range. What could you do to speed up the disk subsystem?

    A. Increase the value of the LazyWriter

    B. Add another physical disk to the system

    C. Implement RAID 1

    D. Increase the Max Async I/O setting

    Answer: D. Increasing Max Async I/O will allow SQL to handle more outstanding read and write requests, thus using the disks to their full capacity.

5. You recently hired a developer to update your queries so that they would encompass some newly created tables. Your users are now complaining that the system seems slow. What can you do?

    A. Analyze the new queries with Query Analyzer

    B. Monitor the Physical Disk: Average Disk Queue counter in Performance Monitor during a period of peak activity to see if the disk subsystem can handle the new queries

C. Create a trace with Profiler and use the trace file with the Index Tuning Wizard to improve the indexes

D. Increase the size of Tempdb

Answer: C. Since the tables and queries are new, any indexes involved have most likely not been stress tested. The Index Tuning Wizard will find and correct the problem indexes.

6. True or False: It is best to generate a measurement baseline for a new server on a busy network where a load can be placed on it.

A. True

B. False

Answer: B. You want to generate a baseline on a test network, because production networks have broadcast traffic that can throw off network and processor readings.

7. What should be the size of Tempdb?

A. 10% of the largest database

B. 50% of the largest database

C. 25 to 40% of the size of the largest database

D. 25 to 40% of the size of an average database

Answer: C. From 25 to 40% of the size of the largest database will give you the best performance. If you feel that you need more than that, consider rewriting your queries.

8. You have tuned and optimized your queries, indexes, and hardware, yet your users still complain of slow response times. What else can you do to enhance response times?

A. Use cursors to segment the result set

B. Split the data into multiple tables and use inner joins

C. Use a view with your query instead of a result set

D. Increase the size of the Windows NT pagefile

Answer: A. Using a cursor to segment the result set will get the data to the users in smaller chunks and they will see it sooner.

9. Which of the following RAID implementations will give the best overall performance and fault-tolerance?

   A. RAID 0 implemented with Windows NT

   B. RAID 0+1 implemented with a third-party controller.

   C. RAID 1 implemented with Windows NT

   D. RAID 5 implemented with a third-party controller

   Answer: B. RAID 0+1 must be implemented using a third-party controller, which will take the burden off the system processor; RAID 0+1 gives good throughput and fault-tolerance.

10. You need to know what kinds of queries each of your users is performing against SQL Server. What is the best way to accomplish this?

    A. Ask them via e-mail

    B. Create a trace in Profiler that gathers information on all the available events

    C. Create a trace using the Trace Wizard that will sort the data by user

    D. Use Query Analyzer to analyzer which users are using your queries

    Answer: C. Using the Trace Wizard to create the Trace Transact-SQL Activity by User is the easiest way.

11. After using a trace in Profiler to monitor database activity, what should you do with the trace file?

    A. Delete it, as it is useless

    B. Save it on disk so you can use it later for trend tracking

    C. Archive it to tape (or another backup medium) and keep it for trend tracking

    D. Print out the trace summary, put it in a binder, and then delete the trace file

    Answer: C. Archive the files to tape and keep them as long as you can. They will prove very valuable when you need to track trends later on. Incidentally, there is no trace summary to print out.

12. True or False: You should monitor SQL Server activity at peak times of the day to get accurate readings on the load placed on your server.

A. True

B. False

Answer: A. If you monitor SQL at peak periods, you will get a better understanding of how your system works under stress.

13. The problem is that you need to implement RAID on your SQL Server for fault-tolerance.

Your required objective is fault-tolerance.

Your optional objectives are that you want increased disk subsystem I/O, and you do not want to put any extra load on the processor

Your solution is to implement RAID 0+1 using a third-party controller.

A. This solution produces the desired results and both optional objectives

B. This solution produces the desired result and only one of the optional objectives

C. This solution produces the desired result but neither of the optional objectives

D. This solution does not produce the desired result

Answer: A. This solution will give fault-tolerance and increased disk I/O, and the load of maintaining the RAID array will be lifted off the system processor and placed on the third-party controller.

14. While reading a trace performed with Profiler, you notice that it is capturing system information. How can you keep this system information out of the trace?

A. In Enterprise Manager, go to System Properties and clear the Show Trace Information check box on the Server Settings tab

B. In Profiler, in the Trace Properties, clear the Show System Information check box on the Server Settings tab

C. In the Trace Properties dialog box in Profiler, on the Filters tab, select the Object ID event and check Exclude System Objects

D. Execute `sp_showsysteminfo=0`

Answer: C. You will need to filter out the information using the Filters tab in the Trace Properties dialog box. Note that the other options do not even exist.

Chapter 11 Answers

1. Which of the following database servers are supported as linked servers?

A. SQL Server 6.5 (integrated security)

B. SQL Server 6.5 (mixed security)

C. Oracle

D. Microsoft Access (unsecured)

Answer: B, C, D. Integrated security (analogous to NT Authentication in SQL Server 7) will not be supported until Windows 2000, when security account delegation is implemented.

2. Your users are complaining that their distributed query is timing out the first time they execute it. After the first time, it executes properly. The remote SQL Server 7 is physically located several hundred miles away. Upon further investigation, you find out that there is a slow link to that location. When you check the setup of the linked server in Enterprise Manager, you see that you are using the data source parameter. Even though this is the case, the users say it works perfectly after the first run. Which of the following is a good solution?

A. Make the name in the data source parameter all uppercase

B. Make the name in the data source parameter all lowercase

C. Don't use the data source parameter; let the linked server name be the actual name, and update the query

D. Delete the linked server in Enterprise Manager and set it up again; it was incorrectly using the wrong name in the data source parameter

Answer: C. If you are using the data source parameter, the name you chose for the server name parameter is not the actual remote server name. This means that SQL Server is having to perform much of the communication setup during the first run of the query and thus timing out over the slow link. If you use the actual name for the server name parameter, most of the communication setup is done when you configure the link.

3. When you execute the **sp_addlinkedserver** stored procedure to link a remote SQL Server 6.5 computer, you receive an error message stating that there are missing system tables. Which of the following solutions should you perform?

   A. Reinstall SQL Server 6.5 on the remote server

   B. Apply SQL Server 6.5 Service Pack 5 on the remote server

   C. Execute the INSTCAT.SQL script on the local SQL Server

   D. Execute the INSTCAT.SQL script on the remote SQL Server

   Answer: D. By default, SQL Server 6.5 does not keep the necessary system tables to become a linked server. You have to run the INSTCAT .SQL script on the remote SQL Server 6.5 computer to install the necessary system tables.

4. Your users are logging into your local SQL Server using non-trusted connections. You want to use one mapping for all the users to access the remote database. If the data is not sensitive and security to the data is not an issue, which of the following would accomplish your task?

   A. Create a server role with public as a member and map this role to a remote login ID

   B. Create a database role with public as a member and map this role to a remote login ID

   C. Make the NT global group Domain Users a valid login and map it to a remote login ID

D. None of the above

Answer: D. If your users are connecting via non-trusted connections, they are being authenticated by SQL Server and their NT credentials are ignored.

5. Your users are logging into your local SQL Server using trusted connections. Your server and all your users are in the workgroup SQLDOM. You want to use one mapping for all the users to access the remote database. If the data is not sensitive and security to the data is not an issue, which of the following would accomplish your task?

   A. Create a server role with public as a member and map this role to a remote login ID

   B. Create a database role with public as a member and map this role to a remote login ID

   C. Make the NT global group SQLDOM\Domain Users a valid login and map it to a remote login ID

   D. None of the above

   Answer: D. Answer A is invalid because you cannot create server roles. Answer B is invalid because you can only map SQL login IDs. Answer C is invalid because workgroups do not have the global group Domain Users.

6. You have successfully established a link to a remote server and have mapped a few local SQL Server login IDs to their respective remote login IDs. When you run the `sp_addlinkedsrvlogin` stored procedure to map the local SQL Server login ID JOHND to the remote login ID JOHND, you receive the error message: "'JOHND' is not a local user. Remote login denied." When you installed the local server, you used the default settings. Which of the following will prevent you from receiving this error message?

   A. Add JOHND to the remote server

   B. Add JOHND to the local server

    C. Add JOHND as an NT login ID

    D. Use all lowercase letters (johnd) when executing the stored procedure

    Answer: B. This error message indicates that you are trying to map a SQL Server login ID that does not exist on the local server.

7. When you execute the stored procedure `sp_addlinkedserver`, it ends successfully, but when you click over to Enterprise Manager (which has also been open), you do not see the new linked server. Which of the following will correct the problem?

    A. Exit and reenter Enterprise Manager

    B. Reexecute the stored procedure

    C. Execute the stored procedure `sp_addlinkedsrvlogin`

    D. In Enterprise Manager, click on Linked Servers with the right mouse button and refresh the list

    Answer: A, D. Both will read the updated system tables into memory and display them correctly.

8. True or False: When you link to an ODBC database using a predefined user DSN, you still have to map the local login IDs to remote login IDs.

    A. True

    B. False

    Answer: B. You cannot link to an ODBC database using a predefined user DSN; it has to be a system DSN.

Chapter 12 Answers

1. SQL Server does not seem to be working properly. You can use the Enterprise Manager, but many of the jobs and alerts don't seem to be running properly. You want to find more information about the general health of your SQL Server. Which of the following logs can be used to gather information on SQL Server errors? (Select all that apply.)

A. SQL Server error logs

B. SQL Server Transaction log

C. NT Application log

D. NT Server Manager

Answer: A, C. You can use the SQL Server error logs found in the SQL Server Enterprise Manager to view informational as well as error messages. These logs rotate on a six-log cycle. You can also use the Windows NT Event Viewer to read the SQL Server messages sent to the Application log.

2. You are reading through one of the error logs and notice that severity level is between 0 and 10. Which of the following types of error messages does this severity level describe?

   A. Informational

   B. Warning

   C. User

   D. Fatal

   Answer: A. Information errors have a severity level of 0 to 10. Errors between 11 and 16 are user errors, while 17 and 18 involve resource problems. Errors with a severity between 19 and 25 are fatal errors and require immediate action.

3. Your SQL Server appears to be having problems working with system resources. You look in the Windows NT Application log and find out that this is the case. What severity level would those resource errors have?

   A. 0 – 10

   B. 11 – 16

   C. 17 – 18

   D. 19 – 25

   Answer: C. Information errors have a severity level of 0 to 10. Errors between 11 and 16 are user errors, while 17 and 18 involve resource problems. Errors with a severity between 19 and 25 are fatal errors and require immediate action.

4. You have nine different SQL Server 6.5 databases in your enterprise. You are preparing to upgrade those databases to SQL Server 7 and are concerned with the upgrade process itself. Which of the following would prevent you from upgrading a SQL Server 6.5 database to SQL Server 7?

   A. Tempdb is set to 25MB

   B. Replication is enabled

   C. Character sets are different

   D. Sort orders are different

   Answer: B, C, D. When you are performing an upgrade to SQL Server 7, you cannot upgrade from one character set or sort order to another character set or sort order. To do that, you should upgrade first to a temporary SQL Server 7 computer and then use the Transfer Manager to move your data, schema, and objects. If a database is involved with replication, it cannot be upgraded. A too-small Tempdb will also cause problems during the upgrade process. It should be at least 25MB in size.

5. You are experiencing some connectivity problems with clients and SQL Server. You have checked the network cables and have found them working properly. You have used the NET VIEW command to verify that the network is working properly. You now want to check some SQL Server specific items. Which command can you use to verify that you have local access to SQL Server over a named pipe?

   A. NET OPENPIPE

   B. NET USE MSSQLServer

   C. NET VIEW /ALL

   D. osql /Usa /P

   Answer: D. You can use the OSQL command-line utility to verify that you have a local named pipe connection to SQL Server. Although MAKEPIPE and READPIPE are normally used across a network, you can open up two separate command-prompt windows on the same computer and use the MAKEPIPE and READPIPE utilities.

6. You are experiencing some connectivity problems with clients and SQL Server. You have checked the network cables and have found them working properly. You have used the `NET VIEW` command to verify that the network is working properly. You now want to check some SQL Server specific items. What command can you use to verify that you have network access to SQL Server over a named pipe?

A. `NET CHECKPIPE`

B. `NET VIEW /ALL`

C. `MAKEPIPE and READPIPE`

D. `isql /Usa /P`

Answer: C. Although MAKEPIPE and READPIPE are normally used across a network to test for Named Pipes connectivity, you can also open up two separate command-prompt windows on the same computer and use the MAKEPIPE and READPIPE utilities for testing.

7. You can run one of the following commands to verify that index and data pages are correctly linked, that your indexes are sorted properly, that the data stored on each page is reasonable, and that the page offsets are reasonable for an entire database.

A. `DBCC CHECKTABLE`

B. `DBCC CHECKDB`

C. `DBCC CHECKCATALOG`

D. `DBCC CHECKALLOC`

Answer: B. The `CHECKTABLE` command does this as well, but only for an individual table in your database. `CHECKCATALOG` and `CHECKALLOC` check for consistency between system tables and whether objects are stored properly on their extents.

8. You can run one of the following commands to verify that index and data pages are correctly linked, that your indexes are sorted properly, that the data stored on each page is reasonable, and that the page offsets are reasonable for a single table in a database.

A. `DBCC CHECKTABLE`

      B. sp_checktable

      C. xp_checktable

      D. DBCC CHECKALLOC

      Answer: A. The CHECKDB command does this as well, but for all of the tables in your database. CHECKALLOC checks that database objects are stored properly on their extents. There is no such command as sp_checktable or xp_checktable.

   9. Which command can you use to verify that extents are being used properly and that there is no overlap between objects that reside in their own separate extents?

      A. DBCC CHECKTABLE

      B. DBCC CHECKDB

      C. DBCC CHECKCATALOG

      D. DBCC CHECKALLOC

      Answer: C. The CHECKCATALOG command does this. The CHECKDB and CHECKTABLE commands verify that data on each page is reasonable and the page offsets are reasonable. CHECKALLOC verifies that objects do not overlap and reside in their own space on their extents.

  10. To check for consistency in and between system tables you could run which command?

      A. DBCC CHECKTABLE

      B. DBCC CHECKDB

      C. DBCC CHECKCATALOG

      D. DBCC CHECKALLOC

      Answer: C. The CHECKCATALOG command checks for the consistency of your database catalog, which is your database system tables. The CHECKTABLE and CHECKDB commands check the consistency of the tables in your database. CHECKALLOC checks whether objects are stored properly on their extents.

11. You come into work on Monday and find that your Accounting database has been marked suspect. Which of the following can cause a database to be marked suspect? (Select all that apply.)

A. The database is offline

B. The database is marked for DBO use only

C. The database file is on an NTFS partition that the SQL Server does not have rights on

D. The database files have been renamed

Answer: A, C, D. Any of these could make a database suspect. When a database is marked for DBO use only, it means just that. Only members of the db_owners database role, or the DBO can access the database. This does not, however, mark a database as suspect.

12. You receive Error 3023 during your backup process. Which of the following activities could have generated this error? (Select all that apply.)

A. Someone ran a `CREATE INDEX` command

B. Someone ran a `DBCC SHRINKDATABASE` command

C. Someone ran a `DBCC CHECKALLOC` command

D. Someone ran a `SELECT INTO` or a `bcp` command

Answer: A, B, C, D. All answers are correct. Any of these commands when run during the backup process will force the backup to fail with Error 3023.

13. You have an old backup from a SQL Server 7 installation from a different branch of your company. You are attempting to restore that database on your local SQL Server 7 installation. Which of the following must be true in order to recover this database in SQL Server?

A. You must be using the same character set

B. You must be using the same sort order

C. You must use the Transfer Manager

D. You must be using the same data filenames and locations

Answer: A, B. You must be using the same character set and sort order to recover a backup. You do not need to use the same data filenames and location in order to restore. If you wish to rename data files or their location, you should use the MOVE TO statement as part of your restoration.

14. You are troubleshooting your replication scenario and find that no subscribers are receiving replicated transactions. You have verified that all subscribers have network connectivity to the distribution server. You have also verified that all SQL Servers in the enterprise are using the same service account. What is most likely the problem?

A. The logreader agent is dead

B. The distribution process is dead

C. The subscription process is dead

D. The problem is internal to SQL Server and has nothing to do with replication

Answer: A. The logreader process is the most likely candidate in this situation. Since no subscribers are receiving transactions, the distribution process and snapshot agents are not likely candidates.

15. You are troubleshooting your replication scenario and find that several subscribers of many are not receiving replicated transactions. You have verified that all subscribers have network connectivity to the distribution server. You have also verified that all SQL Servers in the enterprise are using the same service account. What is most likely the problem?

A. The logreader process

B. The distribution process

C. The subscription process

D. The problem is internal to SQL Server and has nothing to do with replication

Answer: B. The distribution process is the most likely candidate in this scenario. Since some subscribers are receiving replicated transactions, we can assume that the logreader is working properly.

16. If you are having problems with replication, where is the easiest location to begin gathering information to troubleshoot the problem?

    A. The Alerts window

    B. The Current Activity window

    C. The Publication window

    D. The Replication Monitor window

    Answer: D. The Replication Monitor keeps track of all aspects of the operation of your replication scenarios. This includes the Agents folder, which tracks the performance of various replication agents and their histories.

17. You have created a Performance Monitor alert that fires when your transaction log reaches a performance threshold of 80% of capacity. The alert is generating an error to the NT Application log. You have created an alert on that error, and the alert attempts to fire a job. The job does not seem to be firing. What could be the problem? (Select all that apply.)

    A. The job is not enabled

    B. The job owner does not have permissions on objects that the job references

    C. The SQLServerAgent service is not running

    D. The T-SQL statements found in the job are not valid

    Answer: A, B, D. These choices would keep the job from running properly. Answer C would keep the job from running as well, but we know that the SQLServerAgent is running because the alert is firing.

APPENDIX

B

Glossary

ActiveX Data Objects (ADO)   A COM (Component Object Model) object set created by Microsoft intended to replace all other database access object models in future releases of Microsoft products. ADO is a very robust object model in that it defines a core set of functions and allows extensions to be built into the model to support the individual features of certain types of databases. It is specifically designed to access OLE-DB data sources.

alert   A mechanism that tells SQL Server which error codes to look for in the Windows NT Application log, and what action to take if an event is found. Alerts can be based on a severity level, an error code, and the database in which the error occurred. An alert can notify an operator and/or perform a task. Alerts are stored in the Msdb database.

alias   A mechanism that allows a login to access a database under the username assigned to another login. The alias is stored in the sysalternates system table of the database. Each login can have either a username in a database or an alias, but not both. An alias can be used to consolidate permissions under special user accounts, such as DBO. These have been kept in SQL Server 7 for backward-compatibility. SQL 7 uses the concept of roles, which replaces the need for an alias.

allocation unit   In SQL Server, a structure designed to provide a method of keeping track of which pages are allocated to which objects. When a database is created, it is divided into allocation units. When an allocation unit is created, it is built from 32 *extents*. The very first page of the first extent of the allocation unit is called the *allocation page*. The allocation page is responsible for keeping track of every extent in the allocation unit. Allocation units affect the size of the database. Databases must be created and maintained in full allocation-unit intervals, which are 8 extents, or 512KB in size.

article   The basic unit of replication. An article is one or more columns and rows of a table.

automatic recovery   A feature built into SQL Server that ensures that a database is brought up to date when the server is first started. Transactions completed since the last checkpoint process are rolled forward and put into the database, while partially completed transactions are rolled back or removed from the database. Every time SQL Server is restarted, SQL Server runs its automatic recovery feature.

B-Tree format   The format used for indexes in SQL Server. B-Tree is short for *balanced tree*. It is called this because every page of the index is exactly the same distance from the root as is every other page at the same level. A B-Tree resembles a pyramid.

BackOffice   Microsoft's line of client/server support applications that run on Windows NT Server. Some components of BackOffice are Microsoft SQL Server, Systems Management Server (SMS), Internet Information Server (IIS), Exchange Server, SNA Server, and Proxy Server.

backup device   A file or tape to which SQL Server backs up a database. Also called a *dump device*. SQL has no built-in backup devices that point to files or tapes. You will need to create all your backup devices that point to files or tapes.

backup domain controller (BDC)   A server that keeps a copy of the Authentication database from the Primary Domain Controller (PDC). Users can log on to either the PDC or any of the BDCs. Domain controllers are used for network login validation.

bcp (Bulk Copy Program)   A command-line utility used for transferring information into and out of SQL Server.

broken ownership chain   See ownership chain.

browser   See *Web browser*.

caching   A speed optimization technique that keeps a copy of the most recently used data in a fast, high-cost, low-capacity storage device rather than in the device upon which the actual data resides. Caching assumes that recently used data is likely to be used again. Fetching data from the cache is faster than fetching data from the larger, slower storage device. Most caching algorithms also copy next-most-likely-to-be-used data and perform write-caching to further increase speed gains.

character set   The set of characters that SQL Server will recognize and therefore store. Of the 256 characters contained in each character set, the first 128 are the same throughout the various code pages. The last 128 characters, also known as extended characters, differ according to the set.

checkpoint   The mechanism by which SQL Server periodically writes modified data to a hard disk. The DBO of a database may also issue a checkpoint at any time by running the Checkpoint command in the appropriate database. By default, the checkpoint process wakes up once a minute and checks every transaction log for 5 minutes' worth of changes to the data pages in cache. If 5 minutes of changes or more are found, the data pages are written to disk. This establishes a known point of consistency between the data pages on hard disk and the transactions stored on hard disk. The 5-minute period is known as the recovery interval and can be modified.

client   A computer on a network that subscribes to the services provided by a server.

Client Network utility   A utility used to configure SQL Server client Net-Libraries. It also reports on the DB-Libraries that are in use for a particular client.

client/server   A network architecture that dedicates certain computers, called *servers,* to act as service providers to computers called *clients,* on which users perform work. Servers can be dedicated to providing one or more network services, such as file storage, shared printing, communications, e-mail, and Web response.

client/server application   An application that is split into two components: computer-intensive processes that run on application servers, and user interfaces that run on clients. Client/server applications communicate over the network through interprocess communication mechanisms (IPCs).

column   The component of a table that holds individual pieces of data. In a database, a row in a table is often referred to as an entity. The column would be an attribute of the entity and describes an aspect of the row. For example, a row of data might describe an individual. A column would describe the name of the individual or the eye color, etc.

commit   The process whereby completed transactions are put into the database. SQL Server will automatically commit the data at regular intervals, or a manual commit can be initialized by the DBO or SA.

Component Object Model (COM)   COM is an object-oriented architecture for building reusable application components. COM provides a specification, or model, for what an object is and it provides services for both the creation of objects and the communication between a client and the server objects. COM replaces OLE (Object Linking and Embedding) and has other advantages. COM's most notable advances are its binary compatibility and cross-platform development capabilities, code reusability, and version control.

computer name   A 1-to-15-character NetBIOS name used to uniquely identify a computer on the network.

concurrency   The ability of SQL Server to support multiple users at the same time, even if those users want the same data.

Control Panel   A Windows software utility that controls the function of specific operating-system services by allowing users to change default settings for the service to match their preferences. The Windows Registry contains the Control Panel settings on a system and/or per-user basis.

Data Access Objects (DAO)   A set of programmable objects that Microsoft Access developers use to manipulate data through Jet, the data-access engine for Access and other Microsoft desktop products.

data cache   SQL Server does its own caching of data to speed up access to databases. The size of the data cache can be indirectly manipulated by allocating more or less RAM to SQL Server.

Data Source Name (DSN)   A user-created identifier used by ODBC to negotiate connections to any ODBC-compliant data source. A DSN consists of a server location and a driver name and can optionally contain a database name and authentication information. See also *ODBC*.

data mart   A database system concerned with live updates and new data, such as an online ordering system. See also *OLTP*, or *online transaction processing*.

data warehousing   Storage and querying of historical data, also referred to as *decision-support systems*. The main focus of data warehousing is the ability to quickly query existing data and perform complex analyses, usually looking for patterns or other relationships that are difficult to locate during the day-to-day operations of a company.

database file   In SQL Server 7, databases are stored on two types of database files. One file stores the actual data and indexes while the other file stores the transaction log. By default, the first data file has an .MDF extension. Additional data files have an .NDF extension. The transaction log files always have a default extension of .LDF.

database management system (DBMS)   An environment created specifically for the purpose of working with databases. The term *database management system* usually refers to an electronic system or a computer program designed to work with databases. Microsoft Access and FoxPro are both examples of database management systems.

Database Maintenance Plan Wizard   A wizard (step-by-step utility) provided with SQL Server 7 that helps you schedule backups and perform database optimizations and consistency checking. This wizard can also automate and schedule these routine database maintenance tasks.

database user   A SQL Server login ID that has been mapped into a particular database. Without a valid mapping, a login will not have access to a database.

datatype   A component of a SQL Server database that determines what kinds of data, such as character data, numeric data, or date/time data, can be stored in a column. A column can hold data of only a single datatype.

DB-Library   A set of functions and connectivity programs that allow clients to communicate programmatically with database engines. A database engine is responsible for processing queries, maintaining data, ensuring data consistency, and providing a mechanism for backup and restoration.

DBCC (Database Consistency Checker)   SQL Server commands used to check the consistency of databases. These commands are generally used to gather information about the status of a database rather than to make changes to it.

DBO (Database Owner)   In SQL Server, a user who has full permissions in a particular database. This includes the ability to back up and restore the database and transaction log. The SA is also considered the DBO of every database. The DBO is specified through the `sp_changedbowner` stored procedure.

DBOO (Database Object Owner) In SQL Server, a user who creates a particular database object. The DBOO has all rights on that object, including the right to allow other database users to use the object.

Default A SQL Server object assigned to a column or user-defined datatype in a table. If no data is entered, the default value will be used. This can also refer to the default database that is assigned to a SQL Server login ID. If the login attempts to run a query without specifying a database, the query will be applied to the default database.

Desktop A directory represented by the background of the Windows Explorer shell. By default, the Desktop holds objects that contain the local storage devices and available network shares. Also a key operating part of the Windows GUI.

Distributed Transaction Coordinator (DTC) The DTC helps coordinate queries that are run between two or more SQL Servers. The DTC ensures that the transaction is performed simultaneously on both servers, or not at all.

distribution server For replication in SQL Server, the server that keeps track of replication. It copies the data from the publishing server, stores it, and then forwards it to all subscribing servers. If you designate the SQL Server machine where you are installing publishing as the one that holds the Distribution database, you are installing a *local distribution server*. Designating a remote server rather than a local one as your distribution server may make better use of a WAN.

domain In Microsoft networks, an arrangement of client and server computers, referenced by a specific name, that share a single security permissions database. On the Internet, a domain is a named collection of hosts and subdomains, registered with a unique name by the InterNIC (the agency responsible for assigning IP addresses).

domain controller A server that authenticates workstation network login requests by comparing a username and password against account information stored in the user accounts database. A user cannot access a domain without authentication from a domain controller. Windows NT employs a single primary domain controller (PDC) per domain. To help off-load some of the workload, backup domain controllers (BDCs) can be created and enabled within a domain.

dump device   See *backup device*.

dynamic backup   A type of backup that allows you to back up your SQL Server databases while they are in use. Users can stay connected to the server and run most queries while a dynamic backup is in progress.

Dynamic Data Exchange (DDE)   A method of interprocess communication within the Microsoft Windows operating systems.

dynamic link library (DLL)   A set of modular functions that can be used by many programs simultaneously. There are hundreds of functions stored within DLLs.

electronic mail (e-mail)   A type of client/server application that provides a routed, stored-message service between any two user e-mail accounts. E-mail accounts are not the same as user accounts, but a one-to-one relationship usually exists between them. Because all modern computers can attach to the Internet, users can send e-mail over the Internet to any location that has telephone or wireless digital service.

Enterprise Manager   See *SQL Enterprise Manager*.

enterprise network   A complex network consisting of multiple servers and multiple domains; it can be contained within one or two buildings or encompass a wide geographic area.

Exchange   See *Microsoft Exchange*.

Explorer   The default shell for Windows 95/98 and Windows NT 4. Explorer implements the more flexible Desktop object paradigm rather than the Program Manager paradigm used in earlier versions of Windows. See also *Desktop*.

extent   In SQL Server, the unit of allocation for tables and indexes. All SQL Server objects and data are stored in tables. Tables and indexes are organized into extents. Each extent consists of eight 8KB pages. When a table or an index requires additional storage space, a new extent is allocated.

extended stored procedure   See *stored procedure*.

extranet   A network between two or more companies that takes advantage of the low-cost internet connection rather than privately held dedicated communication lines.

Fast bcp   A form of importing data with the bcp utility that takes place when there are no indexes on the table being imported to, and when the Select Into/Bulk Copy database option is set.

file allocation table (FAT)   The file system used by MS-DOS and available to other operating systems, such as Windows (all variations), OS/2, and Windows NT. FAT has become something of a mass-storage compatibility standard because of its simplicity and wide availability. FAT has few fault-tolerance features and can become corrupted through normal use over time. In the new 32-bit Windows 95/98 platforms, FAT32 is also available. FAT32 has many new features, including the ability to address more than 2GB of hard disk space.

flat-file database   A database whose information is stored in files and is accessed sequentially. Examples of flat-file database programs include dBASE, Access, FoxPro, and other personal computer databases.

group   A security entity to which users can be assigned membership for the purpose of granting a broad set of permissions. By managing permissions for groups and assigning users to groups, rather than assigning permissions to users, security administrators can more easily manage large security environments. SQL Server 6.5 differs from most network applications in that it allows a user to be a member of only one other group besides the Public group. SQL Server 7 allows users to be a member of as many groups as they please. Groups have also been renamed in SQL 7 to *database roles*.

guest user   If a specific user doesn't exist in the database permissions list, but a user called *guest* does, then users in SQL Server will have the rights of the guest user in that particular database.

horizontal partitioning   In SQL Server replication, a method by which you can publish only certain rows of a table. This is often referred to as *horizontal filtering*. See also *vertical partitioning*.

HTML   See *Hypertext Markup Language*.

HTTP   See *Hypertext Transfer Protocol*.

hyperlink   A link in text or graphics files that has a Web address embedded within it. By clicking on the link, you jump to another Web address. You can identify a hyperlink because it is a different color from the rest of the Web page.

Hypertext Markup Language (HTML)   A textual data format that identifies sections of a document as headers, lists, hypertext links, and so on. HTML is the data format used on the World Wide Web for the publication of Web pages.

Hypertext Transfer Protocol (HTTP)   An Internet protocol that transfers HTML documents over the Internet and responds to context changes that happen when a user clicks on a hyperlink.

IDE   A simple mass-storage-device interconnection bus that operates at 5Mbps and can handle no more than two attached devices. IDE devices are similar to but less expensive than SCSI devices.

IIS   See *Internet Information Server*.

index   A data structure that provides a mechanism for resolving queries more efficiently by working through a subset of the data rather than all of it. A full table scan can be avoided by using an index. In SQL Server, each table is allowed one *clustered* index. This index is the actual sort order for the data in the table. *Nonclustered* indexes consist of a list of ordered keys that contain pointers to the data in the data pages. Up to 249 nonclustered indexes can be created per table, but these occupy more space than clustered indexes do.

Indexed Sequential Access Method (ISAM)   A method of data access that uses file I/O routines with indexing and a few enhanced features. This type of data access is normally found when using flat-file databases like dBASE, FoxPro, and Access or DB2.

Industry Standard Architecture (ISA)   The design standard for 16-bit Intel-compatible motherboards and peripheral buses. The 32/64-bit PCI bus standard is replacing the ISA standard. Adapters and interface cards must conform to the bus standard(s) used by the motherboard in order to be used with a computer.

integrated security   A SQL Server security mode in which SQL Server accepts, or trusts, the Windows NT validation of a user. The Windows NT account information is used to validate the user to SQL Server. These connections are referred to as *trusted connections*.

Internet   A voluntarily interconnected global network of computers based on the TCP/IP protocol suite. TCP/IP was originally developed by the U.S. Department of Defense's Advanced Research Projects Agency to facilitate the interconnection of military networks and was provided free to universities. The obvious utility of worldwide digital network connectivity and the availability of free complex networking software developed at universities doing military research attracted other universities, research institutions, private organizations, businesses, and finally the individual home user. The Internet is now available to all current commercial computing platforms.

Internet Explorer   A World Wide Web browser produced by Microsoft and included free with Windows 95/98 and Windows NT 4.

Internet Information Server (IIS)   A server produced by Microsoft that serves Internet higher-level protocols like HTTP and FTP (file transfer protocol) to clients using Web browsers.

Internet Protocol (IP)   The network-layer protocol upon which the Internet is based. IP provides a simple, connectionless packet exchange. Other protocols such as UDP or TCP use IP to perform their connection-oriented or guaranteed delivery services.

Internet Service Provider (ISP)   A company that provides dial-up or direct connections to the Internet.

Internetwork Packet eXchange (IPX)   The network protocol developed by Novell for its NetWare product. IPX is a routable protocol similar to IP but much easier to manage and with lower communication overhead. The term IPX can also refer to the family of protocols that includes the Synchronous Packet eXchange (SPX) transport layer protocol, a connection-oriented protocol that guarantees delivery in order, similar to the service provided by TCP.

interprocess communication channel (IPC)   A generic term describing any manner of client/server communication protocols, specifically those operating in the session, presentation, and application layers. Interprocess communication mechanisms provide a method for the client and server to trade information.

intranet   A privately owned network based on the TCP/IP protocol suite.

I/O (input/output)   The process of reading and writing data back and forth from cache to disk. The smallest unit of I/O in SQL Server is the 8KB page. All I/O happens in page increments. *Logical I/O* is defined as a data read or write operation that is made to cache or disk. *Physical I/O* is subclassified as a data read or write that is made to disk only.

IP   See *Internet Protocol*.

IP address   A four-byte (32-bit) number that uniquely identifies a computer on an IP internetwork. InterNIC assigns the first bytes of Internet IP addresses and administers them in hierarchies. Huge organizations like the government or top-level ISPs have class A addresses, large organizations and most ISPs have class B addresses, and small companies have class C addresses. In a class A address, InterNIC assigns the first byte, and the owning organization assigns the remaining three bytes. In a class B address, InterNIC or the higher-level ISP assigns the first two bytes, and the organization assigns the remaining two bytes. In a class C address, InterNIC or the higher-level ISP assigns the first three bytes, and the organization assigns the remaining byte. Organizations not attached to the Internet are free to assign IP addresses as they please.

IPC   See *interprocess communication channel*.

IPX   See *Internetwork Packet eXchange*.

ISA   See *Industry Standard Architecture*.

ISP   See *Internet Service Provider*.

Jet   The data engine for Microsoft Access and other Microsoft desktop products. Microsoft Access ships with Jet. Microsoft Visual Basic also uses Jet as its native database. Jet can also be accessed by Excel, Word, Project, SQL Server 7, and PowerPoint through VBA (Visual Basic for Applications).

job   A task, such as a backup procedure, performed by a system. In SQL Server 7, you can schedule jobs to run at regular intervals or when an alert is triggered. A job can run a Transact-SQL command, a command-prompt utility, a Visual Basic or JavaScript script, or replication procedures.

kernel   The core process of a preemptive operating system, consisting of a multitasking scheduler and the basic services that provide security. Depending on the operating system, other services such as virtual memory drivers may be built into the kernel. The kernel is responsible for managing the scheduling of threads and processes.

LAN Manager   The Microsoft brand of a network product jointly developed by IBM and Microsoft that provided an early client/server environment. LAN Manager/Server was the genesis of many important protocols and IPC mechanisms used today, such as NetBIOS, Named Pipes, and Net-BEUI. Portions of this product exist today in OS/2 Warp Server and Windows NT.

LAN Server   The IBM brand of a network product jointly developed by IBM and Microsoft. See also *LAN Manager*.

LazyWriter   A system process responsible for physical I/O. The role of the LazyWriter is to flush pages from cache to disk as free buffers are needed by the system. The LazyWriter differs from the checkpoint in how it performs its work. The checkpoint process executes its work in spikes and then goes back to sleep. The LazyWriter may be continuously active, writing out pages from cache to disk as needed.

local group   A group that exists in a Windows NT computer's local security database. Local groups can reside on NT Workstation or NT Server computers and can contain users or global groups.

lock   A mechanism by which SQL Server manages concurrency. SQL Server places locks on data when it is being accessed by a client application. SQL Server locks are primarily *page* locks. This means that when a client accesses a single record on an 8-KB page, SQL Server will lock the entire page until it is appropriate to release the lock. SQL Server also supports *table* locks for times when it would make more sense to lock the entire table rather than individual pages. Row-level locking is also supported automatically with SQL Server 7.

lock escalation   The SQL Server process of increasing a lock from the page to the table level. When a transaction acquires a configured number of page locks, a table lock is set and the page locks are released. This behavior is configured through lock-escalation thresholds.

logging   The process of recording information about activities and errors in the operating system.

logical I/O   See *I/O*.

login   A name that, when combined with a password, allows access to SQL Server resources. Logins are stored in the sysxlogins system table. (For easier queries, use the syslogins view.) This table is located in the Master database only, and there is only one per server.

long filename (LFN)   A filename longer than the eight characters plus three-character extension allowed by MS-DOS. In Windows NT and Windows 95/98, filenames can contain up to 255 characters.

MAKEPIPE   A command-line utility that can be used in conjunction with the READPIPE utility to verify that the Named Pipes protocol is working properly.

MAPI   See *Messaging Application Programming Interface*.

Master database   The system database that contains all the settings for the SQL Server engine, including configurations, user accounts, and links to user databases. This information is known collectively as the system catalog.

Messaging Application Programming Interface (MAPI)   Messaging application standard developed to allow for interaction between an application and various message service providers. It is essentially a set of ANSI-standard DLLs. SQL Server 7 has the ability to generate e-mail to any MAPI-compliant message service provider (post office).

Microsoft Exchange   Microsoft's messaging application. Exchange implements MAPI as well as other messaging protocols such as POP, SNMP, and fax services to provide a flexible message composition and reception service.

Microsoft Query   A utility used to graphically create SQL statements for any ODBC-compliant data source. Microsoft Query (also called MS Query) can link to Microsoft Office applications (such as Word and Excel), and other ODBC-compliant applications and databases.

mixed security   A SQL Server security mode that combines the functionality of integrated security with the flexibility of having SQL Server manage its own login accounts. In mixed mode, Windows NT accounts can be linked into SQL Server (using trusted connections), but unique SQL Server login accounts can also be created and used if a trusted connection is not possible. This is sometimes referred to as SQL Authentication in SQL Server 7.

MMC (Microsoft Management Console)   The MMC is Microsoft's new framework utility for managing the various Windows NT services and functions. All Microsoft's new BackOffice applications use MMC, including SQL Server 7, SMS 2, and IIS 4. One of the advantages of the MMC is that different management *snap-ins* can be added to the utility at the same time, which means that management of servers is more standardized and can be done from one application.

Model database   The template database for SQL Server that is used when new databases are created. All users, groups, and security existing in this database are automatically part of any new databases, but changes made to the Model database will not affect existing databases.

MS Query   See *Microsoft Query*.

Msdb database   A SQL Server database that stores information about the alerts, tasks, events, and replication tasks created on that server by the SQLServerAgent service. The Msdb database also includes information about system operators.

multiprocessing   Using two or more processors simultaneously to perform a computing task. Depending on the operating system, processing may be done asymmetrically, wherein certain processors are assigned certain threads independent of the load they create; or symmetrically, wherein threads are dynamically assigned to processors according to an equitable scheduling scheme. The term usually describes a multiprocessing capacity built into the computer at a hardware level in that the computer itself supports more than one processor. However, *multiprocessing* can also be applied to network computing applications achieved through interprocess communication mechanisms. Client/server applications are examples of multiprocessing.

Multi-Protocol   A network library available with SQL Server 6.5 and 7. Multi-Protocol allows SQL Server to communicate over any open interprocess communication (IPC) mechanism. It also provides support for integrated security and encryption. Multi-Protocol takes advantage of remote procedure calls (RPCs) to pass information between the client and server.

multitasking   The capacity of an operating system to switch rapidly among threads of execution. Multitasking allows processor time to be divided among threads as though each thread ran on its own slower processor. Multitasking operating systems allow two or more applications to run at the same time and can provide a greater degree of service to applications than single-tasking operating systems like MS-DOS can.

multithreaded   Multithreaded programs have more than one chain of execution, thus relying on the services of a multitasking or multiprocessing operating system to operate. Multiple chains of execution allow programs to simultaneously perform more than one task. In multitasking computers, multithreading is merely a convenience used to make programs run more smoothly and to free the program from the burden of switching between tasks itself. When multithreaded applications run on a computer with multiple processors, the computing burden of the program can be spread across many processors. Programs that are not multithreaded cannot take advantage of multiple processors in a computer.

Named Pipes   An interprocess communication (IPC) mechanism that is implemented as a file system service, allowing programs to be modified to run on it without using a proprietary API. Named Pipes was developed to support more robust client/server communications than those allowed by the simpler NetBIOS. Named Pipes is the default SQL Server protocol and is required for installation.

native API   The methods of data access that are specific to a certain database management system. Also called the *proprietary interface*. (API stands for *application programming interface*.) These are generally implemented as a set of DLLs or COM-based objects.

network operating system A computer operating system specifically designed to optimize a computer's ability to respond to service requests. Servers run network operating systems. Windows NT Server is a network operating system.

New Technology File System (NTFS) A secure, transaction-oriented file system developed for Windows NT that incorporates the Windows NT security model for assigning permissions and shares. NTFS is optimized for hard drives larger than 500MB and requires too much overhead to be used on hard-disk drives smaller than 50MB.

normalization of data The process of organizing data into tables, in a consistent and complete format, in order to create a relational database.

NT Event Viewer A Windows NT utility used to view Windows NT events and errors. The Application log records SQL Server events and errors as well as events from other applications running under Windows NT.

NTFS See *New Technology File System.*

object permissions SQL Server permissions that generally allow users to manipulate data controlled by a database object. For example, to view the information in a table, you must first have the SELECT permission on that table. If you want to run a stored procedure, you must first have the Execute permission on that stored procedure. Object permissions can be granted by the SA, DBO, or DBOO.

ODBC (Open Database Connectivity) An API set that defines a method of common database access. Client applications can be written to the ODBC API. ODBC uses a Data Source Name (DSN) to make a connection to a database and to load an appropriate ODBC driver. This driver will translate client calls made to the ODBC API into calls to the native interface of the database. The goal of ODBC is to provide interoperability between client applications and data resources.

OLE-DB A method of common database access which defines an interface based on the COM (Component Object Model) rather than a traditional API interface like ODBC. The goal is similar to ODBC, which is to provide interoperability between client applications and data resources.

OLTP See *online transaction processing.*

online transaction processing (OLTP)   A type of database activity that involves frequent changes to the data stored in your database. This is the opposite of online analytical processing (OLAP) that rarely changes data, but runs frequent ad hoc-type queries to generate MIS reports.

operator   A user who is notified about certain network events. In SQL Server, operators can be defined by name, along with their e-mail and pager addresses. Operator information is stored in the Msdb database. Operators are notified about the success and/or failure of scheduled jobs and alerts.

optimization   Any effort to reduce the workload on a hardware or software component by eliminating, obviating, or reducing the amount of work required of the component through any means. For instance, file caching is an optimization that reduces the workload of a hard disk drive.

osql   A command-line utility that uses ODBC and provides a query interface to the SQL Server. You can run Transact-SQL statements as well as stored procedures and DBCC commands from osql; isql (which uses DB-Library) is also supported in SQL 7 for backward-compatibility.

ownership chain   In SQL Server, the result of a user who owns an object creating another object based on the original one, such as when a user creates a view based on a table. This ownership chain has only one object owner. If another user creates an object based on the original owner's object, this now becomes a *broken ownership chain*, because different users own objects within the permission chain. If a person who owns objects that are dependent on each other grants another person rights to the final object, then the ownership chain is unbroken. However, if the second person then grants rights to a third person, the ownership chain becomes broken, as the third person needs rights from the first person, not the second person.

page   The smallest unit of data storage in SQL Server. Every page is 8KB in size with a 96-byte header. Data rows are written to data pages, index rows to index pages, and so on.

parallel striped backup   A SQL Server backup created across two or more backup devices.

PCI   See *Peripheral Connection Interface*.

PDC   See *primary domain controller*.

per-seat license   A type of SQL Server license that allows you to pay once for each seat (person) in your company, and then use any number of connections to any number of SQL servers.

per-server license   A type of SQL Server license that allows you to pay for only a connection to a single server.

Performance Monitor   A Windows NT utility that tracks statistics on individual data items, called *counters*. You can get information about the performance of SQL Server through Performance Monitor. For example, you can monitor the log space used, the number of current connections, and memory use.

Peripheral Connection Interface (PCI)   A high-speed 32/64-bit bus interface developed by Intel and widely accepted as the successor to the 16-bit ISA interface. PCI devices support I/O throughput about 40 times faster than the ISA bus.

permissions   SQL Server security constructs that regulate access to resources by username or role affiliation. Administrators can assign permissions to allow any level of access, such as read-only, read/write, or delete, by controlling the ability of users to initiate object services. Security is implemented by checking the user's security identifier against each object's access control list.

physical I/O   See *I/O*.

preemptive multitasking   A multitasking implementation in which an interrupt routine in the kernel manages the scheduling of processor time among running threads. The threads themselves do not need to support multitasking in any way because the microprocessor will preempt the thread with an interrupt, save its state, update all thread priorities according to the operating system's scheduling algorithm, and pass control to the highest-priority thread awaiting execution. Because of the preemptive feature, a thread that crashes will not affect the operation of other executing threads.

primary domain controller (PDC)   In a Microsoft network, the domain server that contains the master copy of the security, computer, and user accounts databases (often referred to as the SAM database) and can authenticate workstations or users. The PDC can replicate its databases to one or more backup domain controllers (BDCs). The PDC is usually also the master browser for the domain.

procedure cache   After SQL Server fulfills its requirements for RAM from the RAM assigned to it, the rest is assigned to cache. The cache is divided into a data cache and a procedure cache. The procedure cache contains stored procedures that have been run by users or the system. The ratio of procedure cache to data cache is now set automatically by SQL Server 7.

process   A running program containing one or more threads. A process encapsulates the protected memory and environment for its threads.

Program Developers' Kit (PDK)   Extra SQL Server documentation and programming examples useful to developers who wish to know which DLL (dynamic link library) functions are available and how they work in SQL Server.

Public group   See *Public role*.

Public role   A role that exists in every SQL Server database. Any rights granted to the Public role automatically apply to all users in the database, including the guest user (if present).

publication   In SQL Server replication, a collection of *articles*. Subscribing servers can subscribe to an entire publication only. In earlier versions of SQL Server, it was possible to subscribe to an individual article in a publication.

publishing server   In SQL Server replication, the server that has the original data and is making that data available to other replication servers.

pull page   A model of Web-page creation in which a server-side process requests data dynamically from the database when the Web browser makes the request. No static page is created. The HTML response to the request is created dynamically by the server-side process.

push page   A model of Web-page creation in which static Web pages are created by executing queries on a SQL Server and formatting the output in HTML. This HTML page is placed on a Web server and can be accessed by a Web browser. Although the pages can be updated frequently, they are still static pages.

query   A request sent to SQL Server to manipulate or retrieve data. Queries can have many formats, but the most common are known as SELECT queries.

Query Analyzer   An interactive SQL interface for Windows, this utility allows you to run all the same commands that the OSQL command-line utility does. It has an added advantage of being a Windows interface. This allows you to run multiple queries and view the results of such queries in their own separate windows.

query optimizer   In SQL Server, a mechanism that determines which index (or no index) will result in the lowest amount of logical I/O. This is done by evaluating the data and the restrictions that the query is requesting. With this information, the query optimizer estimates how many pages will be read for each possible scenario and chooses the scenario with the lowest estimated page I/O.

RAID 0   RAID 0 writes data across multiple hard-disk partitions in what is called a *stripe set*. This can greatly improve speed as multiple hard disks are working at the same time. RAID 0 can be implemented through the use of Windows NT software or on third-party hardware.

RAID 1   RAID 1 uses disk mirroring, which writes information to disk twice—once to the primary file, and once to the mirror.

RAID 5   RAID 5 (*striped with parity*) writes data to hard disk in stripe sets. Parity checksums will be written across all disks in the stripe set; they can be used to recreate information lost if a single disk in the stripe set fails.

RAID 10   RAID 10 (sometimes referred to as RAID 1 + 0) implements striping as in RAID 1and then mirrors the stripe sets.

Remote Data Objects (RDO)   A COM (Component Object Model) encapsulation of the ODBC API. RDO is a very thin layer of software that provides an object model for calling the ODBC API.

read-ahead   A SQL Server mechanism for retrieving data from disk into cache before the data is actually needed. Separate read-ahead threads pull the data into cache, thus freeing the query thread to process the data that it finds in cache.

READPIPE   A command-line utility that can be used in conjunction with the MAKEPIPE utility to verify that the Named Pipes protocol is working properly.

Registry   A database of settings required and maintained by Windows NT and its components. The Registry contains all the configuration information used by the computer. It is stored as a hierarchical structure and is made up of keys, hives, and value entries. You can use the Registry Editor (REGEDT32 or REGEDIT) to change these settings.

relational database   A database composed of tables that contain related data and other objects, such as views, stored procedures, rules, and defaults. Also, a database of related information that supports the SQL query language. SQL Server databases are stored on database devices.

relational database management system (RDBMS)   A database management system that supports true data, transactional integrity, and a server-side relational database engine. SQL Server is an RDBMS.

Remote Procedure Calls (RPC)   A network interprocess communication mechanism that allows an application to be distributed among many computers on the same network.

removable media database   A SQL Server 7 database created on a removable medium, such as a CD-ROM or floppy disk. Removable media databases can be sent to another location and used from that location.

replication   For SQL Server systems, the ability to automatically copy data and changes made to data from one server to another server. The data may not be copied immediately, so replication is used when "real-enough-time" data replication is needed. In replication, the change is made to one server and then sent out to one or more servers. There is another type of replication called two-phase commit, which is used in conjunction with the MS-DTC to provide 100% synchronization 100% of the time.

roll back   To cancel an entire transaction if any part of the transaction fails and undo any changes made to data.

row   In a SQL Server database, a complete set of columns within a single table; it represents a single entity in a table.

RPC   See *Remote Procedure Calls.*

rule   In a SQL Server database, an object that is assigned to a column so that data being entered must conform to standards you set. Rules can enforce domain integrity (a valid range of values). You can create rules to enable pattern matching, enable a range of values, or force a selection from a list of values.

SA, sa (System Administrator)   The default login ID for SQL Server; the global administrator of the SQL Server system. This ID has no restrictions on what it can do within the SQL Server environment. By default, anyone who has logged in to SQL Server will be able to use the SA account unless you change this.

SAM   See *Security Accounts Manager.*

scheduling   The automation of tasks in SQL Server. Tasks that can be automated include backups, transfers, index creation and reorganization, and other maintenance procedures.

script   A saved query that has an .SQL extension by default. Scripts can be loaded, edited, and run from Query Analyzer or osql. Scripts can also be created by Enterprise Manager for existing databases and objects. Scripts are saved as ASCII text and generally have an .SQL extension.

SCSI   See *Small Computer Systems Interface.*

security   Measures taken to secure a system against accidental or intentional loss of data, usually in the form of accountability procedures and use restriction. SQL Server security is based on the server, database, and database objects.

Security Accounts Manager (SAM)   The module of the Windows NT Executive that authenticates a username and password against a database of accounts, generating an access token that includes the user's permissions. Also known as the *Directory database.*

security identifier (SID)   A unique code that identifies a specific user or group to the Windows NT security system. Security identifiers contain a complete set of permissions for that user or group.

server   A computer dedicated to servicing requests for resources from other computers on a network. Servers typically run network operating systems such as Windows NT Server. The basic functionality of a server can be added to by installed programs such as SQL Server.

service   A process dedicated to implementing a specific function for other processes. Most Windows NT components are services. SQL Server is composed of two main services, MSSQLServer, which is the main database engine; and SQLServerAgent, which is the helper service. Additional services that make up the SQL Server include the MS-DTC (Microsoft Distributed Transaction Coordinator), used for two-phase commits; and the Index server, which can allow SQL Server to run queries that use Web page indexes.

Service Pack   A group of bug fixes and enhancements offered by Microsoft on a (semi) regular basis. There are various Service Packs for different applications. As of this writing, the current Service Packs include Windows NT 3.51 Service Pack 5 and NT 4 Service Pack 4.

severity level   For a system error, a component of the error message that provides information about the error. Levels from 0 to 10 are informational, 11 to 16 are user errors, 17 and 18 are resource problems, and 19 to 25 are fatal errors.

SID   See *security identifier*.

Small Computer Systems Interface (SCSI)   A high-speed, parallel-bus interface that connects hard disk drives, CD-ROM drives, tape drives, and many other peripherals to a computer.

sort order   In SQL Server, an option that determines how the system will collate, store, and present data. The sort-order options available depend on the character set chosen. The most important sort-order descriptions include dictionary order, binary order, case-sensitive, and case-insensitive.

spid (server process ID)   In SQL Server, the number that identifies a connection currently accessing the SQL Server machine. It is most often found in the Enterprise Manager in the Activity window, or by running the sp_who stored procedure.

SQLServerAgent   A SQL Server service that can take care of automating tasks on your server. The service includes managers that can handle alert processing, tasking, event processing, and replication. It works for local automation with the local system account, but for many activities that occur over the network, it will need to be assigned a separate logon account that has administrative rights to the computer, as well as the *Log on as a Service* right.

SQL-DMO (SQL Server Distributed Management Objects)   An interface that exposes COM-based objects that other programs can take advantage of to manipulate the SQL Server Engine and the SQLServerAgent utilities.

SQL Enterprise Manager   The main SQL Server administration program provided with SQL Server 7. Multiple servers can be monitored and maintained by SQL Enterprise Manager. The Enterprise Manager works with SQL Server through the SQL-DMO.

SQL login   See *login*.

SQL Server administrator   The individual usually responsible for the day-to-day administration of SQL Server databases. The administrator takes over where the programmer stops.

SQL Server Books Online   All the books that normally ship with Microsoft SQL Server, in an electronic format.

SQL Server developer   The individual responsible for designing, programming, and populating SQL Server databases.

SQL Server Engine   The core service (MSSQLServer) that performs all query-related activities of SQL Server as well as the data storage and management.

SQL Server Web Assistant   A SQL Server 7 utility that facilitates the creation of push Web pages. It can use the SQL Executive service to schedule the creation of the static Web pages in order to keep them more current.

SQL Trace   A SQL Server file created by the SQL Profiler utility used to monitor who is running what on a SQL Server machine. It is used primarily to audit security in SQL Server and for optimization purposes.

SQLMaint   A SQL Server utility that can be used to create tasks that will take care of day-to-day administration of SQL Server. This includes automating backups, updating statistics, and rebuilding indexes. SQLMaint is configured by the Database Maintenance Plan Wizard.

SQL Profiler   A SQL Server utility that can be used to create trace files. Trace files can track all connections to SQL Server and what those connections are doing. These are often used for security and for optimization.

statement permissions   SQL Server permissions that allow database users and groups to perform tasks that are not specific to objects. These permissions are generally related to the creation of certain database objects.

stored procedure   In SQL Server, a set of Transact-SQL statements combined together to perform a single task or set of tasks. This object is like a macro, in that SQL code can be written and stored under a name. Invoking the name actually runs the code. Because stored procedures are precompiled, they run much more quickly and efficiently than regular queries do. There are three types of stored procedures: *system, user-defined,* and *extended. System stored procedures* are shipped with SQL Server and are denoted with an sp_ prefix. These are typically found in the Master database. *User-defined stored procedures* can be registered with the system by the SA. *Extended stored procedures* work outside the context of SQL Server and generally have an xp_ prefix. These are actually calls to DLLs.

system stored procedure   See *stored procedure.*

system table   Tables in relational databases that are used for administrative purposes by SQL Server. For example, in the Master database, the sysxlogins table, which holds SQL logins and passwords, is a system table. The Master database has two sets of system tables. The first set, known as the system catalog, tracks information about the configuration of SQL Server as a whole. Every database also has a database catalog made up of system tables that track configuration information about that particular database. This would include the objects in the database as well as the permissions granted on those objects. System tables generally begin with the "sys" prefix.

subscribing server   In SQL Server replication, the server that gets data originating on the publishing server and updates one or more tables with both new and changed data.

suspect database   A database that SQL Server believes to be corrupt or otherwise unavailable. A database can be marked suspect for a number of reasons, such as when a database device is offline or has been removed or renamed.

table   In a SQL Server database, the object that contains rows and columns of data.

Taskbar   The gray bar at the bottom of the screen; it replaces the Task Manager in previous versions of Windows. The Taskbar holds the Start menu button and buttons that represent running programs It is used to switch between running programs and to choose the Start menu.

Task Manager   An application that manually views and can close running processes in Windows NT. In Windows 95/98, the Task Manager is called the Close Program window. Task Manager can also be used to view CPU and memory statistics. Press Ctrl+Alt+Del to launch the Task Manager.

TCP   See *Transmission Control Protocol*.

TCP/IP   See *Transmission Control Protocol/Internet Protocol*.

TechNet   Microsoft's monthly CD-ROM set that contains patches to existing programs, technical notes about issues (bugs), and white papers describing technologies in more detail. Most of the information in TechNet can also be found on Microsoft's Web site.

Tempdb database   A SQL Server database reserved for storing temporary objects. These may be tables or stored procedures and can be created implicitly by SQL Server or explicitly by the user. The Tempdb database is also used to store server-side cursors.

thread   A list of instructions running on a computer to perform a certain task. Each thread runs in the context of a process, which embodies the protected memory space and the environment of the threads. Multithreaded processes can perform more than one task at the same time.

T-SQL   See *Transact-SQL*.

Transact-SQL (T-SQL) SQL is a database language, originally designed by IBM, that can be used not only for queries but also to build databases and manage security of the database engine. Microsoft SQL Server uses Transact-SQL (T-SQL), an enhanced version of the SQL language, as its native database language.

transaction A logical set of one or more commands that need to be processed as a whole in order to make a complete unit of work.

Transaction SQL See *Transact-SQL*.

transaction log In SQL Server, a reserved area in the database that stores all changes made to the database. All modifications are written to the transaction log before writing to the database. The transaction log provides a durable record of database activity and can be used for recovery purposes.

Transmission Control Protocol (TCP) A transport layer protocol that implements guaranteed packet delivery using the Internet Protocol (IP). See also *TCP/IP, Internet Protocol*.

Transmission Control Protocol/Internet Protocol (TCP/IP) A suite of network protocols upon which the global Internet is based. TCP/IP is a general term that can refer either to the TCP and IP protocols used together or to the complete set of Internet protocols. TCP/IP is the default protocol for Windows NT.

trigger A SQL Server object that is a stored procedure. A trigger activates when data is added, updated, or deleted from a table. Triggers are used to ensure that tables linked by keys stay internally consistent with each other.

trusted connection See *integrated security*.

two-phase commit A type of data replication for SQL Server. With two-phase commit, two or more SQL Server computers either complete a transaction simultaneously or not at all. The Distributed Transaction Coordinator (MS-DTC service) is designed to help manage these types of transactions.

UNC See *Universal Naming Convention*.

Uniform Resource Locator (URL)   An Internet standard naming convention for identifying resources available via various TCP/IP application protocols. For example, `http://www.microsoft.com` is the URL for Microsoft's World Wide Web server site, while `ftp://ftp.microsoft.com` is a popular FTP site. A URL allows easy hypertext references to a particular resource from within a document or mail message.

Universal Naming Convention (UNC)   A multivendor, multiplatform convention for identifying shared resources on a network.

user   In SQL Server, a database-specific identifier that maps to a login and allows access to database resources. If a user is mapped to a login entry in the sysxlogins system table of the server, that login is allowed access to the database and database objects. Users are stored in the sysusers system table of each database.

username   A user's account name in a login-authenticated system (such as Windows NT and SQL Server).

VBSQL   One of the interfaces provided with the native API of SQL Server. VBSQL is designed for use from Visual Basic and Visual Basic for Applications (VBA) applications.

vertical partitioning   In SQL Server replication, a method by which you can publish only certain columns of a table. This is often referred to as a vertical filter. See also *horizontal partitioning*.

view   In SQL Server, an object that is usually created to exclude certain columns from a table or to link two or more tables together. A view appears very much like a table to most users.

Web browser   An application that makes HTTP requests and formats the resultant HTML documents for the users.

Web page   Any HTML document on an HTTP server.

Win16   The set of application services provided by the 16-bit versions of Microsoft Windows: Windows 3.1 and Windows for Workgroups 3.11.

Win32   The set of application services provided by the 32-bit versions of Microsoft Windows: Windows 95/98 and Windows NT.

Windows 3.11 for Workgroups   The current 16-bit version of Windows for less-powerful, Intel-based personal computers; this system includes peer-networking services.

Windows 95/98   The current 32-bit version of Microsoft Windows for medium-range, Intel-based personal computers; this system includes peer-networking services, Internet support, and strong support for older DOS applications and peripherals. SQL Server 7 (Desktop version) can run on Windows 95/98.

Windows NT   The current 32-bit version of Microsoft Windows for powerful Intel, Alpha, PowerPC, or MIPS-based computers. The system includes peer-networking services, server-networking services, Internet client and server services, and a broad range of utilities. Windows NT Workstation is a version of Windows NT that is primarily used on desktop and laptop computers, but can act as a server for up to 10 simultaneous connections.

Windows NT Server is a version of Windows NT that is primarily used as a file/application server that can theoretically have thousands of simultaneous users connected to it. Windows NT Server Enterprise Edition is designed for large corporations and supports more powerful hardware.

SQL Server 7 (Desktop or regular version) runs on either version of Windows NT. SQL Server 7 Enterprise Edition requires Windows NT Enterprise Edition.

Workgroup   In Microsoft networks, a collection of related computers, such as a department, that don't require the uniform security and coordination of a domain. Workgroups are characterized by decentralized management as opposed to the centralized management that domains use. See also *domain*.

World Wide Web (WWW)   A collection of Internet servers providing hypertext-formatted documents for Internet clients running Web browsers. The World Wide Web provided the first easy-to-use graphical interface for the Internet and is largely responsible for the Internet's explosive growth.

WWW   See *World Wide Web*.

Index

Note to the Reader: Throughout this index *italics* page numbers refer to figures; bold page numbers refer to primary discussions of the topic.

SQL Server 7 Administration

Exam 70-028: Objectives

OBJECTIVE	PAGE NUMBER
Planning	
Develop a security strategy. Assess whether to use Microsoft Windows NT accounts or Microsoft SQL Server logins; Assess whether to leverage the Windows NT group structure; Plan the use and structure of SQL Server roles. Server roles include fixed server, fixed database, and user-defined database; Assess whether to map Windows NT groups directly into a database or to map them to a role; Assess which Windows NT accounts will be used to run SQL Server services; Plan an *n*-tier application security strategy, and decide whether to use application roles or other mid-tier security mechanisms such as Microsoft Transaction Server; Plan the security requirements for linked databases.	157, 161, 173, 205, 212
Develop a SQL Server capacity plan. Plan the physical placement of files, including data files and transaction log files; Plan the use of filegroups; Plan for growth over time; Plan the physical hardware system; Assess communication requirements.	106, 107, 116, 141
Develop a data availability solution. Choose the appropriate backup and restore strategy. Strategies include full database backup; full database backup and transaction log backup; differential database backup with full database backup and transaction log backup; and database files backup and transaction log backup. Assess whether to use a standby server. Assess whether to use clustering.	225
Develop a migration plan. Plan an upgrade from a previous version of SQL Server; Plan the migration of data from other data sources.	40, 288
Develop a replication strategy. Given a scenario, design the appropriate replication model. Replication models include single Publisher and multiple Subscribers; multiple Publishers and single Subscriber; multiple Publishers and multiple Subscribers; and remote Distributor. Choose the replication type. Replication types include snapshot, transactional, and merge.	384, 389, 402
Installation and Configuration	
Install SQL Server 7.0. Choose the character set; Choose the Unicode collation; Choose the appropriate sort order; Install Net-Libraries and protocols; Install services; Install and configure a SQL Server client; Perform an unattended installation; Upgrade from a SQL Server 6.*x* database.	23, 24, 26, 27, 35, 38, 43, 53
Configure SQL Server. Configure SQL Mail; Configure default American National Standards Institute (ANSI) settings.	44, 52, 357
Implement full-text searching.	95
Configuring and Managing Security	
Assign SQL Server access through Windows NT accounts, SQL Server logins, and built-in administrator logins.	161
Assign database access to Windows NT accounts, SQL Server logins, the guest user account, and the dbo user account.	177